Employment Relations

E. Kevin Kelloway, Ph.D
Professor
Department of Management
Saint Mary's University
Halifax, NS B3H 3C3

Employment Relations

The Psychology of Influence and Control at Work

Edited by
Jean F. Hartley and Geoffrey M. Stephenson

BLACKWELL
Oxford UK & Cambridge USA

First published 1992
Reprinted 1995

Blackwell Publishers, the publishing imprint of Basil Blackwell Ltd
108 Cowley Road
Oxford OX4 1JF, UK

Basil Blackwell Inc.
238 Main Street
Cambridge, Massachusetts 02142
USA

Library of Congress Cataloging in Publication Data

Employment relations: the psychology of influence and control at work / edited by Jean F. Hartley and Geoffrey M. Stephenson
p.   cm.
Includes bibliographical references and index.
ISBN 0–631–18354–X (pbk.: alk paper)
1. Personnel management—Psychological aspects.
2. Interpersonal relations.   3. Industrial relations.
I. Hartley, Jean, 1953–   .
II. Stephenson, G. M. (Geoffrey Michael)
HF5549.E713   1992
658.3′001′9—dc20   91–27042
                                                                 CIP

British Library Cataloguing in Publication Data

A CIP catalogue record for this book is available from the British Library.

Typeset in 9½ on 11 pt Garamond
by Times Graphics, Singapore
Printed and bound by Athenæum Press Ltd.,
Gateshead, Tyne & Wear.
This book is printed on acid-free paper

Contents

Contents

List of Contributors

Marilyn Aitkenhead, 68 Dulverton Rd, Leicester.

Peter J. Carnevale, Department of Psychology, University of Illinois, Urbana-Champaign 603 East Daniel St, Champaign, IL 61820

Julie Dickinson, Department of Occupational Psychology, Birkbeck College, University of London, Malet St, London WC1E 7HX

Nicholas Emler, Department of Psychology, University of Dundee, Dundee DD1 4HN

David E. Guest, Department of Occupational Psychology, Birkbeck College, University of London, Malet St, London WC1E 7HX

Jean F. Hartley, Department of Occupational Psychology, Birkbeck College, University of London, Malet St, London WC1E 7HX

Patricia A. Keenan, Department of Psychology, University of Illinois, Urbana-Champaign 603 East Daniel St, Champaign, IL 61820

Tom Keenoy, Cardiff Business School, University of Wales, Colum Drive, Cardiff CF1 3EU

Caroline Kelly, Department of Psychology, Birkbeck College, University of London, Malet St, London WC1E 7HX

John Kelly, Department of Industrial Relations, London School of Economics, University of London, Houghton St, London WC1A 2AE

Paul S. Kirkbride, Ashridge Management College, Berkhamsted, Herts HP4 1NS

Bert Klandermans, Department of Social Psychology, Free University, Amsterdam, de Boelelaan 1081, Amsterdam

Sonia Liff, Warwick Business School, University of Warwick, Coventry CV4 7AL

Ian E. Morley, Department of Psychology, University of Warwick, Coventry CV4 7AL

Wally S. Mueller, School of Psychology, Curtin University of Technology, GPO Box U 1987, Perth 6001, Western Australia

Gordon E. O'Brien, School of Social Sciences, Flinders University, Bedford Park, South Australia 5042

Geoffrey M. Stephenson, Institute of Social and Applied Psychology, Beverley Farm, University of Kent, Canterbury CT2 7LZ

George Strauss, Institute of Industrial Relations, University of California, Berkeley, California 94720

Henk Thierry, Faculty of Psychology, Work and Organization Psychology, University of Amsterdam, Roeterstraat 15, 1018 WB Amsterdam

Introduction: the Psychology of Employment Relations

Jean F. Hartley and Geoffrey M. Stephenson

The Background to Contemporary Issues

The 1980s were a time of change and sharp debate in the study and practice of employment relations. The 1990s are also challenging and changing our assumptions about the basis and conduct of relations between employees and management: so this is an interesting period in which to be concerned with the theory and practice of employment relations. Old certainties, assumptions and values are open for re-examination; new forms of employment contract, styles of management, and styles of worker representation are being tested; there are changing views and values about the rights and responsibilities of being a manager, and being an employee. This chapter is concerned with mapping some of this changing ground and with showing how psychology can contribute to the multi-disciplinary debates about employment relations theory and practice.

There are differing views on the degree to which employment relations have changed in the last decade (see, for example, Bassett, 1986; MacInnes, 1987; Edwards and Sisson, 1989. Kochan et al., 1986; Kelly and Kelly, 1991) and various opinions about the reasons for and stability of any changes. Nevertheless, a consideration of employment relations over the last decade will be useful in highlighting some significant threats and opportunities for academics, managers, employees and employee representatives. It will also help to illustrate the specific role which psychology can contribute. Furthermore, this consideration of past and present is valuable in showing what we understand by the term 'employment relations'. Employment relations we take to be the processes of motivation of and control over the ways in which employment is carried out and rewarded in industrialized societies. Traditionally, this field has been known as industrial relations but we prefer the term employment relations because of its broader connotations, including non-industrial employment settings and also individual as well as collective aspects of employment. However, in many respects, the two terms (as well as that of employee relations) can be used interchangeably and this will happen here.

Psychology contributes to the understanding of employment relations by focusing on the behaviour of individuals, groups and organizations in employ-

1

ment. Employment relations is a mutli-disciplinary area which also includes sociological, political, economic, legal and historical perspectives. The challenge for psychologists is to make a distinctive but integrative contribution to the theory and practice of employment relations. Our analysis of change in the 1980s focuses on psychological issues but in their wider context.

A survey of changes in the 1980s is important because it indicates a movement away from the narrower concerns of the post-war period when industrial relations was principally concerned with the development of stable, formalized collective institutions and procedures. This was as true for the USA (Kochan et al., 1986) as it was for Britain (e.g. Flanders 1965; Donovan Commission, 1968) and some other parts of the industrialized world. At that time, unions were growing in Britain, and union decline in the USA was not as evident or severe as it later became. Employment relations was a growth industry, both for academics and practitioners. Collective bargaining, in its different institutional and legal frameworks in various countries, seemed to be accepted by academics, public sector management and trade unions as the essence of employment relations. Events of the 1980s challenged much of this.

Changes in the 1980s

In the 1980s (some would argue earlier), developments in industrial and employment structures led to major changes in employment relations. Several factors deserve mention. Many industrial countries faced both recession and industrial restructuring in the 1980s, and this is apparently a continuing prospect. Capital has relocated on a global scale, and markets and production have internationalized in many sectors. This has increased competitive pressures between firms and between regions. Restructuring has included the closure of firms in traditional industries and new developments in the service sector. Firms have increased in employment size, although workplaces have become smaller. In countries such as Britain, de-industrialization has gathered pace. The effects of recession, of redundancy and of pressures to increase productivity, quality and flexibility have had considerable impact on employment relations. In Europe, restructuring will continue both as a consequence of the Single European Act of the European Community and as eastern Europe changes politically and economically. Restructuring is also changing the basic forms of employment, as illustrated by the decline of skilled industrial full-time employment (traditionally undertaken by males) and by a move towards more insecure, part-time service sector work (where jobs are increasingly being held by women with childcare responsibilities). In addition, the introduction of new technology, especially information technology, continues to reduce the number of jobs, transform job requirements and change work relations.

In many countries, though especially in Britain and the USA, governments have encouraged the greater mobility of capital and labour by legislation and by means of their behaviour as employers. Job protection through individual or collective rights has declined and, in Britain trade union immunities have been eroded by the law. Furthermore, the 1980s saw changes in the demographic structure of the workforce. In the late 1980s the number of school-leavers declined, forcing many employers to consider alternative sources of labour, such as women with childcare responsibilities, members of ethnic minorities and older workers. Employees in these categories have distinctive needs, expectations and power bases in the workplace which impinge on employment relations.

Unions, managements and employees have been forced to come to terms with many of these industrial and employment changes. Some have changed their strategies, values, attitudes and behaviours to cope with change. Others have been less affected, either directly or in terms of their responses. Some changes have been more prototypical than extensive (see Bassett, 1986) and some may not last. For example, the early 1980s saw much debate about strike-free deals and pendulum arbitration but these developments have already declined in perceived significance. As the 1980s recede into history, it is easier to take a longer term perspective and to observe continuities rather than change (e.g. MacInnes, 1987). Some changes have occurred more in the rhetoric of employment relations than in the substance and therefore need to be treated with caution. Nevertheless, we shall now list some changes in employment relations, which are mooted to have occurred over the last decade, in order to elucidate perspectives on the relevance of psychology to employment relations.

Decline in trade union membership　　In Britain, union membership fell between 1979 and 1987 by more than 3 million or 25 per cent (Towers, 1989). In the USA, decline had started in the mid-1950s but had gained pace in the 1970s so that, by 1985, only 19 per cent of the non-agricultural workforce was unionized (Kochan et al., 1986). In Western Europe, union membership declined in all but three Scandinavian countries, with especially heavy losses for Britain, France, Italy and the Netherlands (Visser, 1988). Traditional industries had long been a bastion of union membership, but the economic strength of these industries was being severely eroded. Employment growth is taking place in part-time work, in the services sector, and in small workplaces. Can the unions recruit in these new sectors? To do so effectively will require a detailed understanding of the needs and expectations of employees in these areas and their motivation for joining. Do employees value trade unions in the workplace and, if so, in what ways? Does the decline in membership represent a decline in employees' preparedness to act collectively or is that determined by other factors? Employers are also crucial in influencing union membership. How do they perceive the role and functions of trade unions? And how are employees affected by their employer's expectations?

Unions' narrowing sphere of influence　　In addition to membership loss, there has been a reduced role for trade unions especially in Britain and the USA. This is notable in the workplace and also at national level. In Britain, a number of surveys suggest that the *machinery* of union–management negotiations remains intact at workplace and organizational level but that unions are less influential than previously (Terry, 1986; Legge, 1988; Marginson et al., 1988). Legge calls this the 'empty shell' hypothesis of change in industrial relations. The evidence seems to be that the recession of the early 1980s did not trigger 'macho management' (Edwards, 1985). There was little dismantling of procedures (with some exceptions; Claydon, 1989) but increasingly management bypassed trade unions as a channel for communication. Quality circles, team briefings, newsletters, videos and non-union based joint consultation were all reported to be on the increase, though doubts were raised about the performance of these new techniques. These developments none the less have raised questions for managers and employees about the role and functions of trade unions in the workplace. Are trade unions still perceived as necessary by employees and managers? Why do managements support the proactive involvement of unions in managing change in some European countries (such as the former West Germany), whilst acquiescing in their marginalization in some other countries?

New union strategies Some trade unions have responded proactively to the decline in their membership and influence by developing new strategies. Trade union mergers were very much in evidence in Britain in the 1980s (Waddington, 1988). Union federations in Britain and the USA (the TUC and AFL-CIO) co-ordinated procedures and campaigns for union recruitment. Individual unions placed increased emphasis on recruitment (e.g. Kelly and Heery, 1989; Beaumont and Harris, 1990). There was a shift in emphasis in some unions towards a stronger interest in the gains to be achieved through employment legislation rather than solely through collective bargaining. And there was an increased concern with promoting recruitment through the provision of services of individuals and through bargaining over issues of importance to women. All of these strategies require individual and organizational adjustment to change and raise some interesting questions for the psychology of employment relations. How far are these strategies explicitly recognized as such by union activists and officials? What are the criteria for perceived success? What will be the consequences for employees' evaluations of union roles and relationships with management? How will these changes affect management attitudes and behaviour? How can these changes be evaluated?

Human resource management Managerial attempts to adapt to the increasing competitive pressures of the market and to the pressures for productivity and flexibility have been varied. Several initiatives attracted attention in the 1980s. One of the most important in rhetorical if not practical terms was the advent of 'human resource management' (Guest, 1987; Kochan et al., 1986; Keenoy, 1990). Human resource management can be characterized as emphasising a concern with the development and utilization of employees, based on their being seen as a strategic component of competitiveness. Human resource management purports to be an integral part of the business strategy (supposedly in contrast to many personnel policies). Guest (1987) doubts that it is being implemented effectively in Britain, though it has undoubtedly raised a new debate in employment relations about appropriate ways to manage employees while pursuing high quality and high productivity (Storey, 1989).

Indeed, it has perhaps been one of the liveliest areas of debate in employment relations in the 1980s. Whatever its empirical base, HRM generated new ideas – and new values – concerning motivating and controlling employees. Significantly, it is predominantly non-union, having arisen as a personnel strategy in the non-union sector (Foulkes, 1980; Kochan et al., 1986). Perhaps part of the reason for its prominence also is that it addresses an issue which is familiar enough in the psychology of organizational behaviour but which has been somewhat neglected within traditional industrial relations: how to *motivate* rather than simply control employees. This involves examining a range of ways of influencing employees in order to engender commitment, genuine flexibility and adaptability and employee concern about quality. The rise of interest in HRM has raised new questions about 'old-style' industrial relations. What are the alternatives to managing employees within a collective bargaining framework? Would employees, trade unions and management agree or disagree that old-style industrial relations involved consistency and fairness but neglected initiative, motivation and flexibility?

Non-union firms   These became more evident in the 1980s in both the UK and the USA. In the 1970s they were regarded by many academics as an aberrant form which would disappear with a public policy promotion of collective bargaining. By the 1980s the picture had changed. The majority of new start-ups tended to be non-union. In addition, when established firms moved to green-field sites, there was a trend towards non-unionism (Bassett, 1986; Edwards and Sisson, 1989). In the USA, too, the trend was markedly non-union (Kochan, 1988). Not only were such firms growing numerically but also many of them were highly successful, in both personnel and economic terms. There was clearly something to be learnt from such firms. What can they tell us about the successful management of staff? Are employees content not to have union representation? Can employment relations be successfully managed without collective representation for employees? From whose perspective, if any, is this a desirable trend?

Japanese management and production techniques   In Western industrialized countries there has been an interest in the 'Japanization' of industry (Turnbull, 1986; Oliver and Wilkinson, 1988). Methods of production used in large Japanese companies have been imported along with the foreign investment brought by the Japanese. In addition, some non-Japanese companies have tried to emulate the production and personnel policies which appear to have contributed significantly to Japanese economic success. Japanese-style production methods (including just-in-time manufacturing) and personnel policies (including no unions or weak company-based unions, and the engendering of high levels of employee flexibility and commitment) have been assiduously studied and in some cases adopted. Here again, whatever one's beliefs about the efficacy or desirability of such policies, they embody an alternative to the view that collective bargaining is the central feature of employment relations. What are the psychological processes occurring within the workplace which have contributed to a low level of apparent conflict, to high productivity and to high commitment to quality? Can this be consistently produced in a different culture and a different economic context? How far can employees who are used to more traditional industrial relations adapt to these changed managerial and employment relations practices?

Flexibility in organizations   From the early 1980s, there has been a growing interest in the more flexible deployment of labour in organizations. Newer technologies, global markets and short product life-spans might require great adaptation and change in the work required of employees. There are also other pressures for employee flexibility as a result of recession and restructuring. Handy (1984) suggested that organizations in the future would be less likely to offer employees stable jobs and secure employment. Atkinson and Meager (1986) proposed that organizations would wish to increase both numerical and functional flexibility by offering insecure contract-based employment ('numerical flexibility') and by encouraging broader job categories and multiskilling ('functional flexibility') (see also Pollert, 1988). These changes will affect the character of the 'psychological contract' of employees with their organization. Former certainties based on stable and enduring job categories, grades and pay rates may be eroded, and employees' perceptions of pay and effort equity and possibly of job insecurity may change, affecting morale, performance and employment relations.

Numerical flexibility, with its different types of contract, suggests a differential strategy for the management of labour, with the careful selection, retention and reward of core employees, while peripheral employees are treated as substitutable. The implications from an employee perspective are profound: collective organization and the pursuit of claims and interests are considerably more difficult for temporary staff employed on an insecure basis. Both their temporariness and their substitutability provide them with little by way of a power base. Can trade unions be perceived as useful by a peripheral workforce? Will a core workforce wish not to 'rock the boat' by engaging in union membership or activity themselves? And if functional flexibility is about developing new skills, tasks and responsibilities for employees, how easily does this sit with traditional collective bargaining which has often, on the part of both management and unions, focused on issues of equity, based on job comparability, and emphasized the elaboration of clear jobs, tasks and procedures? The development of flexibility flies in the face of efforts to formalize, stabilize and bureaucratize employment relations. Flexibility also raises questions about the effectiveness of collective bargaining as a vehicle for change (Marsden and Thompson, 1990; Daniel, 1990).

Decline in industrial action   Statistical data suggest that the 1980s witnessed changes in the patterns of strike frequency and type. Strikes are often taken to be an indicator of industrial conflict more generally. In Britain, the unusually high level of strike action of the 1970s gave way in the 1980s to a sharp reduction in the number of strikes, the number of strikers involved, and the number of working days lost (except in the public sector where strike levels increased). Decline in union militancy has also been observed in Europe and the USA. Both the recession and legislative change to reduce trade union immunities have contributed to the reduction but further exploration is needed to understand the meaning of the 1980s pattern. It has been suggested that employees, as a consequence of the savage economic climate of the 1980s, now have a changed attitude to work, to management and to employment relations. This has been termed 'new realism'; a burying of the 'them and us' attitudes of conflict and class. But is this true? The evidence is far from compelling (see Kelly and Kelly, 1991 for a detailed review) and needs further investigation. This is a critical area in the psychology of employment relations because if attitudes and values have changed then the behavioural changes ought to be relatively permanent, while if low levels of conflict result from expedient compliance following an erosion of the power base, then a changed context may herald a return to conflictual employment relations.

A matter of related interest has been the promotion, in some circumstances, of the 'no-strike deal' (Basset, 1986; Towers, 1989). Such deals may include a provision for pendulum arbitration of disputes without recourse to strike action. Although evidence is growing that arbitration of this sort works less well in Britain then in its country of origin, the USA, it raises interesting psychological questions about how disputes are conceptualized, promoted and prosecuted. Will attempts to circumvent or pre-empt conflict in this way succeed?

Decline of collectivism   It has been suggested that the 1980s witnessed a decline in collectivism and the promotion of more individualistic frameworks of employment (e.g. Edwards and Sisson, 1989; Kochan et al., 1986; Terry, 1991). The evidence for this is various: the trend towards non-unionism; the bypassing of existing unions through direct communications; the increase in merit-based and performance-related pay; the increased use of performance appraisal; individual (non-union based) grievance procedures; careful attention to selection and induction; the introduction of profit-sharing and share-ownership schemes and the attempts to foster organizational commitment and loyalty. In Britain, legislative changes have profoundly weakened the rights of the collectivity and strengthened those of the individual (Dickens, 1990). Union leaders, too, have suggested that employment relations in the future will be more fragmented and individualized (e.g. Edmonds, 1984). Again, these developments raise questions for the future, for both the theory and the practice of employment relations. Was the prominence of collectivism, and collective bargaining in particular, an historically located phenomenon? Do employees still perceive a need for collective organization? How far do some of the personnel practices outlined above promote a sense of individualism? And do they promote a sense of identification with the organization or not?

We have spent quite a considerable time outlining some of the changes which have occurred – or which are believed to have occurred – during the 1980s and which make the outlook for the rest of the 1990s vitally different from the employment relations of the 1970s. There are very different views about the extent and the stability of the changes which have taken place, and an even greater variety of interpretations. For example, conventional wisdom suggests that industrial relations are no longer an issue: the combination of legislation and recession had led to the eradication of conflictual industrial relations because the combination of fear and new realism on the part of workers has elicited radically new behaviours. Therefore, there is little point in studying employment relations: the subject is effectively obsolete. More plausibly, a second view suggests that employment relations still exist and are significant for economic performance, but that they have been transformed in character. Writers such as Bassett (1986) and Kochan et al. (1986) have argued that important and significant changes are taking place, especially the developments on green-field, non-unionized sites. They point to these as providing some prototypes for future employment relations although also noting the continuing role for aspects of traditional employment relations. Third, sceptics argue that employment relations has simply been 'business as usual' (e.g. MacInnes, 1987; Batstone, 1984). Such commentators pointed to the continuities with the past and the *lack* of change. While change was talked up in both academic and practitioner circles, the evidence on the ground was harder to find. Research in specific areas fitted this view to some extent: for example, human resource management (Guest, 1990); training (Rainbird, 1990); the limited use of new employment legislation by employers (Evans, 1987); and evidence of 'new realism' attitudes (Kelly and Kelly, 1991).

The debate will no doubt continue for some while yet as to whether the 1980s have effected significant changes in employment relations. However, our analysis has indicated that, regardless of the extent and permanence of the new prototypes and new developments, they have raised important psychological questions about the understanding of employment relations.

The Study of Employment Relations Today

Even without the developments we have outlined, it was possible to criticize industrial relations for having had a narrow concern with the institutions of job regulation, such as had been promoted by influential writers including Dunlop (1958), Flanders (1965) and Bain and Clegg (1974). An institutional perspective continues to be an important component of the field. However, its dominance, until recently, of the field left little scope for a psychological perspective on employment relations (Hartley and Kelly, 1986). Also, the emphasis in the industrial relations literature on institutions in unionized settings left significant areas of employment out of the picture. For example, it did not include a consideration of employment in which trade unions are prohibited (for example, in the armed forces and now in a part of the Civil Service); or where trade unions or staff associations are weakly organized (for example, in police forces, and in many low paid industries) or where they are largely seen to be irrelevant (for example, in many small businesses). In addition, a feminist critique of 'old-style' industrial relations would be that it focused on male full-time workers in large organizations, thereby ignoring to a large extent the experiences of women in employment relations. If employment relations really is about 'the conditions under which work is done' (Walker, 1979, p. 11), then any analysis needs to be applicable to non-unionized as well as unionized workplaces. It should apply to the employment conditions of the jobbing builder, the family running the corner shop, the surgeon who would never dream of joining a trade union (even though she/he belongs to the BMA!), the new army recruit, the student working part-time in a pub, the woman working as a home worker, the au pair, and so on as well as those employees working in large organizations such as multinationals, and central and local government. The analysis should in principle be capable of including such variety, even though much of the research is taking place in large organizations. Keenoy (1985) makes this point with humour: the answer to the question, 'who's got an industrial relation?', is anyone who is involved in employment.

Our central argument is that the study of employment relations today must be concerned with the full range of employment experiences. This is not to endorse nor favour a particular form of employment relations – there is much to be alarmed about for employees in some of the newer style employment relations – but rather to say that theoretically we need to be clear about what we understand by employment relations and what models we use, in a way that allows for the existence of a diversity of employment practices.

Hyman's (1975) definition of industrial relations as 'the processes of control over work relations' invites a psychological analysis of employment relations, and can also be used comfortably with the diversity of employment relations which have emerged in the 1980s. The concept of control includes rules but can be seen as embracing also coercion, persuasion, normative influence, culture and ideology. Keenoy's (1985, p. 39) definition adapts that of Hyman: 'the administration and control of the employment relationship in industrialized societies'. This is quite a broad definition and it allows for a range of employment relations, be it a small corner shop or a large multinational.

The definition of Walker (1979) also encompasses a diversity of employment contexts: 'Industrial relations are essentially concerned with the accommodation between the various interests that are involved in the process of getting work done' (p 11). Walker's definition is much broader since it does not focus exclusively on control. Definitions based on control derive from the 1960s and 1970s when academics were trying to explain the 'industrial unrest' of that period. Control is an important process for both managers and employees: managers wanting to co-ordinate and direct labour towards organizational goals, and employees wanting to retain some degree of autonomy and power over their effort and rewards. Walker's definition allows for a range of other ways in which influence can be exerted. It recognizes the inherent mixture of co-operation and conflict which exists in any employment relationship. It recognizes that the interplay of the needs, motivations and skills of the main protagonists will influence the goals that are pursued, and that the struggle for control is but one factor in a complex equation which determines the conditions under which work is done.

The 1980s showed us that control was only half of the equation. The phenomenal development of the non-union sector in the USA and its significant increase in the UK suggests that the imposition of control alone does not solve organizations' problems of productivity and quality. A regime of compliance is unlikely to lead to flexibility, high quality products and high output, such as is demanded by the environments of many contemporary organizations. For example, quality has been a critical concept in the 1980s for both the private and the public sectors. The developments in employment relations of the 1980s have partly been experiments about how to improve quality. We do not mean to suggest that quality cannot be achieved in institutionalized settings; far from it. Trade unions can be centrally involved in change and development, as in the former West Germany, and as in some organizations (Kochan and Dyer, 1976; Flanders, 1964). Some pressures for management to think creatively about quality, flexibility and performance have come from employees themselves, who have rising expectations about the quality of working life.

All of these developments convey a renewed emphasis on a variety of means of motivation as well as control. We argue that motivation and control are inextricably bound up together because of the nature of employment relations. The new initiatives from non-union companies, and from human resource management, are interesting partly because they are based on attempts to increase employee motivation. Motivation has been a neglected part of the employment relations literature (except, of course, as financial remuneration but that is only part of the issue). However, it is also important that motivation is not examined in isolation from issues of management and worker control.

The Contribution of Psychology

Employment relations have an irreducibly psychological component. Because employment relations are one form of social relations, the beliefs, perceptions, attitudes, values, expectations and behaviour of individuals and groups are an integral component in their analysis. Providing analysis at that level is an important contribution which psychology can make to the understanding of the theory and practice of employment relations. In addition, organizational psychology contributes theories, concepts and research which are concerned with behaviour in organizational settings, and with the organizations themselves as the unit of analysis. Indeed, it is at such a level that some interesting developments have been taking place (Brett, 1980; Hartley, 1988), both in psychology and in employment relations.

However, while psychology can contribute to the understanding of employment relations at the level of the individual, group and organization, its role is not to achieve disciplinary hegemony. Employment relations is a multi-disciplinary field and so the academic or practitioner must be prepared to draw on a range of disciplines and levels of analysis. If one wants to understand what motivates employees to become involved in workers' participation in management, then the issue must be examined in an institutional context. Similarly, it is invalid to attribute differences in union joining to gender or personality if the explanation of the correlations observed lies with the industry or occupation in which the employees are working. Therefore, any analysis of psychological issues needs to be placed in an environmental and institutional context. This is a considerable challenge for social scientists and, in our view, provides much of the excitement and reward of working in this field.

That said, what *is* the contribution of psychology to employment relations? There has been a strand of psychological interest in employment relations for many years (e.g. Myers, 1933; Stagner and Rosen, 1965; Kornhauser et al.,

1954). There are valuable accounts of the history of psychology's concern with this area by Strauss (1979), Gordon and Nurick (1981), Gordon and Burt (1981), and Huszczo et al. (1984). Several commentators have also written of the problems and possibilities for psychologists in becoming involved with the study of employment relations (e.g. Hartley and Kelly, 1986; Hartley, 1988; Hartley, 1984; Brotherton and Stephenson, 1975; Stephenson and Brotherton, 1979; Gordon and Nurick, 1981; Brett, 1980; Brett and Hammer, 1982).

Psychology's emphasis is on explaining individual, social and organizational behaviour and processes. Developmental perspectives help us to understand how employees are socialized before they enter the workplace. Theories of cognition, causal attribution, perception, decision-making, attitude formation and motivation help us to understand the bases of individual and social behaviour. Theories of group membership and group identity, persuasion, communication, compliance, inter-party bargaining, social norms, leadership and power contribute to understanding the complexities of how groups come not only to influence each other but also to resist such attempts at influence. At the organizational level, the role of formal and informal structures, systems of power, culture and ideology, participation and strategy development can be analysed. These are the areas to which psychology can, and has, made contributions which may be utilized in the field of employment relations. Crucially, psychology's role is to throw light on the social processes underlying the creation of different forms of employment relations and the means whereby the varieties are sustained and changed (see also Hartley and Kelly, 1986; Hartley, 1992). In addition, psychology can assist greatly our understanding of relevant individual, social and organizational outcomes, such as absenteeism and turnover, militancy, industrial relations climate, morale, effort, productivity and attitudes to change.

So much for the protestations of opportunity: the test lies in how psychologists can employ their particular skills and to what effect. Thus, it is to the question of psychology and employment relations in this book that we now turn.

The Structure of the Book

The book is divided into five parts. We start with a focus on the experience of employment relations from a developmental perspective (Part 1), moving to a consideration of the strategic issues faced by the respective parties in employment relations (Parts 2 and 3), before considering some core problems of interparty relations (Part 4), and issues arising in the broader organizational and sociopolitical area of employment relations (Part 5). Within this broad framework, there is ample scope for illustrating the contribution of psychology to traditional concerns of 'industrial relations' and to the understanding of some, but not all, of the recent development noted above.

Not all of the contributors are psychologists, but in all cases the authors adopt a psychological perspective or raise psychological questions to a greater or lesser extent in their examinations of the issues. For example, in Part 1 there are three chapters concerned with understanding the attitudes, values and perceptions that employees bring to the workplace. Before we analyse how employees and managers interact over the employment contract, we need to examine their expectations and preconceptions. Julie Dickinson and Nicholas Emler (chapter 1) examine the processes of 'economic socialization' whereby 80 per cent of children end up with a level of literacy and focused ambitions which ensures that they enter occupations differing little in status from those of their parents. The psychological determinants of these processes are examined in some detail. Their chapter, by imaginatively drawing upon studies across a wide range of topics in child development, indicates how poorly the occupational dimensions of socialization has been served. Gordon O'Brien (chapter 2) examines more directly the impact of work itself upon individual development but demonstrates also that the centrality of work in individuals lives varies from one culture to another, and from one employment condition to another. In this chapter we come to appreciate the complexity of the interaction between the developmental (psychological), economic and socio-political domains, in understanding individuals' understanding of the employment relationship.

Finally in this section Paul Kirkbride (chapter 3) provides an analysis of power in social relationships. Although, in the abstract, relative power is determined by respective control over resources and outcomes, it is the exploitation of resources in everyday argument and rhetoric that affects who is influential in the employment relationship. The effective use of rhetoric, it is observed, is not the prerogative of any one party to the relationship, and our understanding of power in employment relations is greatly enhanced when we look in detail at the linguistic and ideological processes that are invoked.

Part 2 concerns the management of employment relations. Until recently, it has been habitual to focus the study of industrial relations on the activities and influence of trade unions. However, research has shown that it is management, with its superior economic and cultural power resources which sets the pace in employment relations (e.g. Brown, 1981; Marginson et al., 1988; Kochan et al. 1986), both in shaping trade union organization (Terry, 1983) and, indeed, in influencing aggregate union membership levels (Bain, 1970; Bain and Price, 1983). So we start our consideration of the *parties* in employment relations by examining management. Tom Keenoy (chapter 4) examines how managers use their advantages to gain effective control: 'manufacturing consent' (of the workforce) is a key issue. This chapter introduces us to the paradoxes and tensions that are inherent in trying both to motivate and to control employees, and to the inevitable complexities of managing people in organizations. He indicates the varieties of ways in which managements have tried to do this, and develops the concept of control 'syndromes' or strategies. He discusses the problems arising from having continuously to construct control anew if employees are to pursue managerial objectives willingly. David Guest (chapter 5) explores the psychological justifications and evidence for the recent trend among managements to try to influence employee behaviour by enhancing employee commitment. He places this in the broader context of the debate on human resource management, and the difficulties faced by organizations when attempting to introduce coherent policies in that area. Henk Thierry (chapter 6) concludes Part 2 by examining how managers use pay to motivate and control their workforces and some of the difficulties inherent in reward structures from a psychological point of view. It is apparent from the variety of objectives that may be pursued by a rational pay policy that pay is a vastly under-exploited resource, all too frequently an occasion for disappointing rather than motivating employees.

Part 3 examines the other principal party in employment relations: workers and their representatives. In this section we look particularly at trade unions, though workers also organize themselves in staff or professional associations or else do not organize collectively at all. Jean Hartley (chapter 7) explores the social psychological underpinnings of theories of trade union joining and develops and accounts which integrates structural and psychological factors. Existing accounts of the social processes involved are critically examined. Bert Klandermans (chapter 8) explores activism once employees have joined, and examines trade unions as organizations rather than simply as social movements. He demonstrates how it is that participation by the membership in union decision-making is not a prerequisite of influence over the leadership: threat of withdrawal of (financial) support is a key factor.

Part 4 explores some core social processes of employment relations. Ian Morley (chapter 9) views intra-organizational bargaining as a key, pervasive and continuing process in negotiation. Negotiation is viewed as a relationship by and through which participants manage changes in their environment. The relationship passes through intra-organizational and inter-organizational phases, and this is illustrated with a number of case studies which show that the respective processes of 'internal' and 'external' adjustment cannot readily be separated. In a complementary contribution (chapter 10) Peter Carnevale and Patricia Keenan review the now considerable experimental and other literature on the processes of inter-organizational bargaining (and third-party intervention), emphasizing those results which have direct implications for the organization of bargaining structures in employment relations. A model emphasizing the respective parties' concerns for own and other outcomes is used to explain the character of their strategic relationship, for example 'problem solving' or 'contending'. The development of this 'dual-concern' model and the complementary 'strategic choice' model of mediator behaviour illustrates the value of integrating results from both laboratory and field research. John Kelly and Caroline Kelly (chapter 11) turn their attention to the consequences of the failure to reach an agreement through negotiation. They evaluate the evidence that exists in support of psychological theories of strike action, strikes being the most visible and most researched form of industrial action. They propose a contingency model of employee decision-making; indicating that the psychological basis of the decision to strike is dependent on factors of situation and identity.

In Part 5, we adopt a broader, organizational perspective and we turn to examine some key political issues in employment relations. Sonia Liff and Marilyn Aitkenhead (chapter 12) argue that the problems of implementing equal opportunities comprise an increasingly important issue in employment relations, requiring for their solution an understanding of the social psychological dynamics that are involved. George Strauss (chapter 13) outlines the variety of forms which worker participation in management can take, and draws attention to some of the inherent tensions and problems associated with different forms. This review is especially important in the context of new developments to involve employees (such as share ownership schemes), and has policy implications for employee relations in Europe after '1992'. The final chapter by Wally Mueller (chapter 14) contributes to debates about the development of flexibility, new technology and new forms of employment contract and about their implications for the relationships, especially that of power, between managers and employees.

For reasons of space, a number of possible chapters have had to be discounted. We had anticipated initially including a chapter which would bring together the disparate literatures of organizational change and collective bargaining; we might have had more on Japanese companies, or some of the developments in Europe, or an examination of stress at work from an employment relations perspective, or a look at issues of recruitment and retention, such as selection, appraisal, training. There are clearly many areas where psychology can contribute to the debate about employment relations. However, by focusing on parties and processes, we hope that we have provided a broad basis for analysing and understanding not only contemporary employment relations but also future patterns, including those developments that we can see foreshadowed and those that we cannot yet imagine.

References

Atkinson J. and Meager N. (1986) Is flexibility just a flash in the pan? *Personnel Management,* September, 26–9.

Bain G. S. (1970) *The Growth of White-Collar Unionism.* Oxford: Clarendon Press.

Bain G. S. and Clegg H. A. (1974) A strategy for industrial relations research in Britain. *British Journal of Industrial Relations,* 12, 91–113.

Bain, G. S. and Price, R (1983) Union growth: Dimensions, determinants and destiny. In G. S. Bain (ed), *Industrial Relations in Britain,* Oxford: Blackwell. 3–33.

Bassett, P (1986) *Strike Free: New Industrial Relations in Britain.* London: Macmillan.

Batstone E. (1984) *Working Order.* Oxford: Blackwell.

Beaumont, P. B. and Harris R. I. (1990) Union recruitment and organizing attempts in Britain in the 1980s. *Industrial Relations Journal,* 21, 274–286.

Brett J. M. (1980) Behavioral research on unions and union-management systems. In B. Staw and L. Cummings (eds), *Research in Organizational Behavior,* 2, Greenwich, Conn: JAI Press. 177–213.

Brett, J. M. and Hammer, T. H. (1982) Organizational behavior and industrial relations. In T. A. Kochan, D. J. Mitchell and L. Dyer (eds), *Industrial Relations Research in the 1970s: Review and Appraisal.* Madison, WI: Industrial Relations Research Association. 221–281.

Brotherton C. J. and Stephenson, G. M. (1975) Psychology in the study of industrial relations. *Industrial Relations Journal,* 6, 42–50.

Brown, W. (1981) *The Changing Contours of British Industrial Relations.* Oxford: Blackwell.

Claydon, T. (1989) Union derecognition in the 1980s. *British Journal of Industrial Relations,* 28, 214–24.

Daniel, W. W. (1990) Needed: A policy for industrial relations. *Policy Studies,* 11, 1, 20–8.

Dickens, L. (1990) Learning to live with the law? The legislative attack on British trade unions since 1979. *New Zealand Journal of Industrial Relations*, 14, 37–52.

Donovan Commission (1968) *Royal Commission on Trade Unions and Employers' Associations Report* Cmnd 3623 London: HMSO

Dunlop J. T. (1958) *Industrial Relations Systems*. New York: Holt, Rhinehart and Winston Press.

Edmonds, J. (1984) Decline of the big battalions. *Personnel Management*, March, 18–21.

Edwards P. K. (1985) The myth of the macho manager, *Personnel Management*, 17, 32–5.

Edwards, P. K. and Sisson, K. (1989) Industrial relations in the UK: Change in the 1980s. Swindon: Economic and Social Research Council.

Evans, S. (1987) The use of injunctions in industrial disputes. *British Journal of Industrial Relations*, 23, 419–35.

Flanders A. (1964) *The Fawley Productivity Agreements: A Case Study of Management and Collective Bargaining*. London: Faber.

Flanders A. (1965) *Industrial Relations: What is wrong with the system?* London: Faber.

Foulkes, F. (1980) *Personnel Practices in Large Non-Union Companies*. Englewood Cliffs, NJ: Prentice-Hall.

Gordon, M. E. and Burt, R. E. (1981) A history of industrial psychology's relationship with American unions: Lessons from the past and directions for the future. *International Review of Applied Psychology*, 30, 137–56.

Gordon, M. E. and Nurcik, A. J. (1981) Psychological approaches to the study of unions and union-management relations. *Psychological Bulletin*, 90, 293–306.

Guest, D. E. (1987) Human resource management and industrial relations. *Journal of Management Studies*, 24, 503–21.

Guest, D. E. (1990) Human resource management and the American dream. *Journal of Management Studies*, 27, 377–97.

Handy C. (1984) *The Future of Work*. Harmondsworth: Penguin.

Hartley J. F. (1984) Industrial relations psychology. In Gruneberg M. and Wall T. (eds.) *Social Psychology and Organizational Behaviour*. Chichester: Wiley. 149–81.

Hartley J. F. (1988) Psychology and industrial relations: social processes in organizations. *International Journal of Comparative Labour Law and Industrial Relations*, 4, 53–60.

Hartley, J. F. (1992) The psychology of industrial relations. In Cooper, C. L. and Robertson, I. (eds) *International Review of Industrial and Organizational Psychology*, Chichester: Wiley.

Hartley J. F. and Kelly J. E. (1986) Psychology and industrial relations: from conflict to cooperation? *Journal of Occupational Psychology*, 59, 161–76.

Huszczo, G. E., Wiggins, J. G. and Currie J. S. (1984) The relationship between psychology and organized labor: Past, present and future. *American Psychologist*, 39, 432–40.

Hyman, R. (1975) *Industrial Relations: A Marxist Introduction*. London: Macmillan.

Keenoy, T. (1985) *Invitation to Industrial Relations*. Oxford: Blackwell.

Keenoy T. (1990) Human resource management: The case of the wolf in sheep's clothing? *Personnel Review*, 19, 3–9.

Kelly, J. E. and Heery, E. (1989) Full-time officers and trade union recruitment. *British Journal of Industrial Relations*, 27, 196–213.

Kelly J. E. and Kelly C. (1991) Them and us: a social psychological analysis of the "new industrial relations". *British Journal of Industrial Relations*, 29, 25–48

Kochan, T. A. (1988) The future of worker representation: An American perspective. *Labour and Society*, 13, 183–201.

Kochan T. A. and Dyer, L. (1976) A model of organizational change in the context of union-management relations. *Journal of Applied Behavioral Science*, 12, 59–78.

Kochen T. A., Katz H. C. and McKersie R. B. (1986) *The Transformation of American Industrial Relations.* New York: Basic Books.

Kornhauser, A., Dublin, R. and Ross, A. (eds) (1954) *Industrial Conflict.* New York: McGraw-Hill.

Legge, K. (1988) Personnel management in recession and recovery: A comparative analysis of what the surveys say. *Personnel Review*, 17, 1–72.

MacInnes J. (1987) *Thatcherism at Work.* Milton Keynes: Open University Press.

Marginson, P., Edwards, P. K., Martin, R., Purcell, J. and Sisson, K. (1988) *Beyond the Workplace: Managing Industrial Relations in the Multi-Establishment Enterprise.* Oxford: Blackwell.

Marsden, D. and Thompson, M (1990) Flexibility agreements and their significance in the increase in productivity in British manufacturing since 1980. *Work, Employment and Society*, 4, 83–104

Myers, C. S. (1933) *Industrial Psychology in Great Britain* (2nd ed.) London: Cape.

Oliver N. and Wilkinson B. (1988) *The Japanization of British Industry.* Oxford: Blackwell.

Pollert, A. (1988) The 'flexible firm': Fixation or fact? *Work, Employment and Society*, 2, 281–316.

Rainbird, H. (1990) *Training Matters: Union Perspectives on Industrial Restructuring and Training.* Oxford: Blackwell.

Stagner, R. and Rosen H. (1965) *The Psychology of Union-Management Relations.* London: Tavistock.

Stephenson G. and Brotherton C. (1979) *Industrial Relations: A Social Psychological Approach.* Chichester: Wiley.

Storey, J. (1989) *New Perspectives on Human Resource Management.* London: Routledge.

Strauss G. (1979) Can social psychology contribute to industrial relations? In Stephenson G. and Brotherton C. (eds.) *Industrial Relations: A Social Psychological Approach.* Chichester: Wiley, 365–97.

Terry, M. (1983) Shop steward development and managerial strategies. In G. S. Bain (ed) *Industrial Relations in Britain.* Oxford: Blackwell, 67–91.

Terry, M. (1986) How do we know if shop stewards are getting weaker? *British Journal of Industrial Relations*, 24, 169–79.

Terry, M. (1991) Annual review article 1990. *British Journal of Industrial Relations*, 29, 97–112.

Towers B. (1989) Running the gauntlet: British trade unions under Thatcher, 1979–1988. *Industrial and Labor Relations Review*, 42, 174–5.

Turnbull, P. (1986) The 'Japanization' of production and industrial relations at Lucas Electrical. *Industrial Relations Journal*, 17, 193–206.

Visser, J. (1988) Trade unionism in Western Europe: Present situation and prospects. *Labour and Society*, 13, 125–82.

Waddington, J. (1988) Trade union mergers: A study of trade union structural dynamics. *British Journal of Industrial Relations*, 26, 409–30.

Walker K. F. (1979) Psychology and industrial relations: a general perspective. In Stephenson G. and Brotherton C. (eds.) *Industrial Relations: A Social Psychological Approach.* Chichester: Wiley, 5–31.

Part I

Socialization into Employment

1

Developing Conceptions of Work

Julie Dickinson and Nicholas Emler

Introduction

Working for a wage is a relatively recent innovation in the history of the human species. When first introduced on a large scale only 200 years ago, as part of the factory system of production, it was considered so unnatural that only criminals and paupers could be induced to accept it (Hearn, 1978). It has become by far the most predominant means of making a living in Western or Western style industrialized societies. Perhaps 85 per cent of those who earn their living do so by selling their labour for a wage. And though there is nothing in the least bit natural in this economic arrangement, (LeClair Jr & Schneider, 1968) young people now arrive at the verge of adulthood apparently accepting it as normal and, in varying degrees, prepared for its peculiar qualities and requirements.

The wage relation is only one of the peculiarities of modern ways of organizing work. Another is the degree to which work is specialized. To take an extreme comparison, the hunting economy of Eskimos historically involved most of the community doing the same basic tasks; there was little division of labour. In the UK today more than 20,000 distinct kinds of job are recognized in official statistics. Work roles and relationships in the employment sector tend to be formalized and impersonal (cf. Weber, 1947). Work is not merely highly specialized but also highly integrated and one consequence of this is the central role of timetabled routines, and the transition from a task to a time emphasis in work (Thompson, 1967).

A third peculiarity of work is the operation of power and control. The organization of large-scale production involves chains of command in which position determines the amount of control over both the task and other members of the workforce. The problem of control in large and complex organizations has given rise to both professional management and trade unions. Changes in the means of production may involve negotiation as well as co-ordination between groups. Thus the world of work is a political as well as a technological creation.

The relevant preparation for this world is both intellectual and moral. It is intellectual in the sense that children are equipped to varying degrees with special

19

cognitive skills. Perhaps most notable among these is literacy. However, intellectual preparation shades into the moral by equipping children with an understanding of aspects of employment relations. Thus children may learn that pay varies as a function of job characteristics such as skill or responsibility, but also that these contingencies are in some degree right and just. The moral preparation also involves an understanding of the kinds of authority relations that prevail in the workplace. Finally, there is something to be learned about the rights and responsibilities of being an employee; about the relationships with supervisors, subordinates and fellow workers and, beyond these, with customers, the state and the legal system; and about groups concerned with employees, such as professional associations and trade unions.

These various processes and their individual results may be called collectively 'economic socialization', though of course they represent only part of children's economic socialization, since children are also prepared for other kinds of economic role, such as purchasers of goods and services (see Berti and Bombi, 1988). We shall consider in more detail some of the outcomes of childhood preparation for employment relations. First, though, we must say something about the processes by which this preparation is accomplished, the processes of development and socialization.

The nature of development and socialization

Psychology has now all but abandoned the idea that the child is a passive *tabula rasa* fashioned by culture to fit comfortably and compliantly into predetermined roles. Instead, we recognize that children actively think about and try to make sense of their experience. The theory of development most closely associated with this view of the child, which may be called 'constructivism', we owe largely to the work of Jean Piaget. Unfortunately, however, many influential proponents of constructivism have ruled out the play of particular social or cultural influences upon the child's intellect and consciousness (Gibbs and Schnell, 1985; Turiel, 1983). Consequently, constructivists have little to say about the influence of socializing agents, such as family, peer group, school or mass media. But let us look at what they do say about the process of development.

The Piagetian Interpretation of Development

The story begins with Alfred Binet (1908), whose work was based on two assumptions: that the environment presents us with problems, and that the capacity to solve these problems extends progressively over at least the first fifteen years of life. He recognized, in other words, that young children simply do not have the same problem solving capacities as adults, and that one can chart their intellectual growth in terms of the problems that they are able to solve.

Piaget built on these insights with a crucial one of his own: the repeated activity of problem solving is itself the engine which drives intellectual growth.

Piaget then spelt out in great detail both the mechanics of growth and the structure of the problems that children are able to solve at each step in their development. Most of the problems that he described are concerned with logical or physical relations, with concepts such as space, time, mass, number and causality. The principal mechanism of change is 'equilibration' which is the process of balancing elements of knowledge (Piaget, 1970). When they do not balance, when for example a child applies two different sets of ideas to the same problem and notices that they contradict one another, then there is a potential for cognitive growth.

Piaget did briefly show that the analysis he had made of the developing child's relations with the material world could also be applied to relations with the social world (e.g. Piaget, 1932). This world too, he supposed, would constantly present the child with problems and puzzles; the child, in trying to solve these, would gradually transform the capacities that he or she had available for their solution. But developmental psychology had to wait for more than thirty years before there were serious attempts to take a constructivist approach to explain understanding of the social world.

As we shall see later, much of our current knowledge of economic socialization has come out of later work within a Piagetian framework. Before examining this later work, we need to look a little further at the assumptions of constructivism. The fundamental ideas are that knowledge is self-generated and that the basic cognitive structures or systems involved are universal. In other words, wherever and whenever children are born and whatever the circumstances of their lives, they will always ultimately come to the same conclusions about the way the universe works, having proceeded through the same sequence of intellectual changes. This is because the universe is presumed to be independent of culture, while the cognitive structures through which these workings are comprehended are presumed to be built up in a certain, logical order.

The Socialization of Constructivism

We have criticized this view in detail elsewhere (Emler, 1987; Emler et al., 1990) and will make only the following two points here. One is that both Binet and Piaget took a biological view of intellect; they regarded intelligence as part of the individual human organism's adaptation to the world around it. This tends to obscure the extent to which adaptation to the environment occurs at the level of groups and cultures. We are not denying that children actively think about their experience, nor that their powers of intellectual analysis evolve slowly, through stages, nor even that their inbuilt inclination to try to make sense of their experiences contributes to this evolution. The issue is rather *why* they think what they think. Culture, we believe, plays a significant part in this in two ways. First, each new generation does not have to rediscover from scratch how the world works. A culture presents children not just with problems but with solutions to problems and arguments for different solutions; and different cultures have accumulated different stocks of wisdom.

Second, the particular organization of a culture and its economy ensures that certain problems arise more frequently and insistently than others. Thus, Dasen (1974) has shown that the children of Australian aborigines, whose hunter-gatherer economy involves journeying long distances in relatively featureless environments, develop spatial concepts more rapidly than concepts of quantity, weight and volume. The reverse was true for children from an urban industrial environment. Berry (1971) states the argument in more general terms: children acquire cognitive skills that are 'ecologically functional', that is, they are relevant to the economy of the culture.

Our other major criticism of Binet and Piaget, therefore, is that much of the intellectual contents they present as universal are in fact the intellectual priorities of a particular economy and culture. Intelligence tests following Binet are heavily biased towards sampling logical and numerical skills and the comprehension of written materials. We have become accustomed to regard these as the essence of human intelligence, yet they are probably specializations of human intellect, skills particularly prioritized in an industrial culture and no more indigenous to humans than the skills of riding bicycles or playing pianos.

Our point is that the intellectual capacities that children develop and the speed and completeness with which these are acquired are powerfully shaped by culture and indeed by the position that children and their families occupy in the economic structure of society. Certain skills, certain representations of reality and interpretations of social arrangements are cognitively complex and will take many years for the average child to assimilate. But the gradual and systematic nature of their acquisition should in no way obscure their social origins.

The Instruments and Agents of Economic Socialization

If the basic process of socialization is social influence, it none the less has many contributing sources. These include language, the family, the media, peers, and the school. Though these are in reality inseparable from one another in their operation, we consider them here briefly and separately.

1   *Language.* All children normally grow up learning at least one language. As Brown (1965) has pointed out, one illustration of the economic role of languages is that they contain category systems which divide up the world in particular ways. Some of these are relevant to the economy of the society using the language. Thus, a Hanunoo child, in learning the names for 92 different kinds of rice, learns also to distinguish the entities to which these names apply and so learns something of economic significance.

2   *The family.* The family and particularly parents influence the intellectual development of children; they shape their educational attitudes and aspirations, their personality, and their occupational values; they provide models or exemplars of economic roles, and may directly provide access to particular occupations. A most important factor in whether or not young people join a trade union is

parental influence (De Witte, 1989; see also chapter 7).

3   *Mass media.* The mass media are sources of much incidental information both about occupations, through the depiction of real and fictional examples, and about the kinds of people – in terms of social background, ethnicity, sex and age, for example – who hold them. How many young, black, female bank managers have been seen in TV dramas? Television transmits information about the income, lifestyle and prestige associated with different occupations. Since British children spend the equivalent of almost 100 school days per year watching TV (Giddens, 1989), it would be odd if television did not shape expectations and aspirations. Indeed, a very early study of the effects of television on children (Himmelweit et al., 1958), when viewing hours were much shorter, showed that perceptions of high status jobs had shifted from what was locally prestigious, such as foreman in a local factory, to professional jobs, such as lawyer or journalist.

The news media are a particularly important source of information about industrial disputes and conflict. It is very likely that children gain most of their knowledge about strikes, lock-outs and other forms of industrial action from news coverage and that consequently their ideas are influenced by the political stance of the media towards the dispute. Since most adolescents are profoundly uninterested in current affairs as discussed on the television and radio, their ideas are shaped in broad, affective terms, such as feeling that strikes are damaging and bound to fail, rather than developed in terms of understanding the nature of the employment contract or negotiating bodies (Dickinson, 1990b).

Mass media are peculiarly modern and, as such, may play some special part in children's preparation for the modern arrangement of employment relations. Lerner (1958) certainly regarded mass media as intimately associated with the emergence of modern economic systems. As McLuhan (1967) saw, the medium itself is a form of message; it conveys something about the appropriate forms in the industrial economy, namely, formalized, separated from personal relationships, controlled by an elite of technical experts, and involving little feedback.

4   *Peers.* Sadly there has been little research on the role of peers in economic socialization, yet it seems likely that they play an important socializing role, particularly in adolescence. Given that patterns of peer association are among the best predictors of drinking, smoking and delinquency, it would be surprising if they were unrelated to some of the other consequential things that adolescents choose to do, such as stay on or leave school at 16. We do know that peer relationships (Emler and Reicher, 1987) are likely to be related to attitudes to institutional authority and we suspect that they are connected with career choices and with training and work-related attitudes.

5   *School.* Formal and compulsory state schooling to the mid teens is another modern institution. There is little doubt that its role in economic socialization is central. It is less obvious precisely what this role is. Some scholars have argued that school is more significant as an agent of selection for economic roles than of training. For them, in Danziger's (1971) view, for example, school is an extended

test of the child's capacity and willingness to accommodate to the demands of the employment system. Others argue that, rather than an attempt to train to fulfil these demands, school is also an important introduction to the principal features of this system: reward for effort and skill, co-ordination of activities through formal authority, emphasis on technical criteria for positions within the organization, and stress on timetables.

The Products of Economic Socialization

What does a modern economy, and particularly one based extensively on employment, require of economic socialization? The answer is probably 'rather a lot' and more than can be fully covered in this chapter, so we have focused on five areas: cognitive skills, distributive justice, authority, selection for work roles and employment relations in the workplace.

Cognitive skills

The most conspicuous cognitive skill among adults in an employment culture is literacy. When Max Weber argued that the dominant organizational form would be the bureaucracy, he meant that it would be organization centred on structured roles and relationships where a major instrument of organizational control is the written word. This kind of organization depends on staff capable of making and referring to written records.

Industrialization, mass urbanization and the bureaucratization of economic institutions have developed together. In a survey of 73 countries, Lerner (1958) showed that these processes are also closely related to levels of literacy within a population. Thus, once urbanization has reached about 10 per cent, literacy becomes closely correlated with urbanization. It is as if such forms of social organization cannot function unless a large proportion of the population can read and write. It takes many years to become proficient in reading and writing skills; reading level norms are specified in education systems at least up to twelve years. Presumably literacy skills are sufficiently vital to a modern economy to defer eligibility for employment relations until they are acquired by most children.

There is also evidence that schooling may be a necessary condition for the acquisition of those higher level intellectual skills that Piaget called 'formal operations' (e.g. Inhelder and Piaget, 1958). Formal operations include capacities of hypothesis testing and the formulation of abstract if–then propositions. These abilities do not emerge until adolescence and seldom emerge without formal education. Even then, most adults fail to develop these skills completely. It thus seems likely that if an employment economy requires individuals with the capacity for formal operations, it does not require this of every adult member. Precisely who needs such skills and why remains for the moment unanswered.

Distributive justice

Remuneration for employment varies enormously (see Marsden, 1983). In the UK there is no legal minimum wage and it is not uncommon for people to be paid less than £2.00 per hour. At the other end of the scale, the chief executives of some corporations receive salaries in excess of half a million pounds a year. Of course, there are disagreements about the justice of these differentials; most people would like more, whatever their current income, and most probably think that they deserve more. What is far more remarkable is that there is not a great deal more dissatisfaction and discord about income differentials. In effect, people's estimates of what is fair are not indexed to absolute standards. Again, it seems that most adults have been prepared in childhood to accept some very detailed and differentiated standards of just desserts for work. How does this happen?

Partly, it is a matter of intellectual development. The study of children's understanding of the means of production and the relationship between work and money has revealed a fairly stable developmental sequence between 4 and 11 years (e.g. Danziger, 1958; Furth, 1980; Jahoda, 1979; Berti and Bombi, 1988). The youngest children usually fail to draw a connection between employment and wages. They may realize that many adults go to work and that money is required to buy food and other goods but think that work is a voluntary activity and that money comes from change in shops or banks or even God. By 6 or 7 years, they recognize that money is obtained by working and often make a stark distinction between the working 'rich' and unemployed 'poor'.

These children's understanding of the processes of production and employment, however, is still very naïve. For example, they do not connect the sale of goods with income for the producers. They may think that factory owners are given money by the government or banks to pay the workers or even that the factory owner has to earn money elsewhere, in another job. They may imagine that teacher's wages come directly from pupils' parents, that bus drivers' wages are the fares that they receive or that bosses earn less than workers because 'nobody pays them' (Berti and Bombi, 1988; Dickinson, 1986).

At 8–9 years, children begin to understand that there is an exchange relationship between the employer and the worker and to assume a simple relationship between the amount of money earned and the amount of work done. The next two or three years see a growing awareness that the relationship between the amount of work and the amount of money is less straightforward and that different types of jobs receive different pay.

Insight into the relationship between employment and money entails some degree of co-ordination between knowledge of three different aspects of work: production of goods, selling of goods and exchange of labour for wages. Jahoda (1984), Berti and Bombi (1988) and Furth (1980) have all argued that the development of insight into economic relations is dependent upon cognitive growth and that the ability to make connections between different aspects of production is restricted by the child's ability to make inferences and to integrate pieces of knowledge.

This makes for universal similarities in the sequence of development but the rate of progress can be affected by experience and the availability of information. For example, children whose fathers run small businesses show accelerated development of the understanding of the exchange of goods for money (Jahoda, 1983; Berti and Bombi, 1988) whilst children further removed from work often entertain early misconceptions. Jahoda (1979) found that the children of unemployed parents were likely to think that everyone's income came from social security. Berti and Bombi (1988) found that Italian middle class children thought that all money was handed out by the bank or council whereas working class children, whose fathers worked in the local Fiat factory, attributed a similar omnipotent role to Fiat. The rate of development can also vary between economic spheres. Berti et al. (1982) found that the children of factory workers understood much more about factory production than agricultural production.

To understand wage relations, children need to develop conceptions of the principles which underlie payment. Piaget's (1932) work on distributive justice suggested that early beliefs about the desirability of parity in the distribution of rewards are displaced in development by the principle of equity. That is, children begin to believe that people should be rewarded in accordance with their relative contributions. More recent research on children's allocation decisions has confirmed this trend (Hook and Cook, 1979). Beyond 6–7 years, children are increasingly likely to allocate rewards between others on the basis of relative effort, time worked or amount of work done.

A similar developmental change has been observed in children's beliefs about the desirability of wage differentials. Connell (1977) asked children aged 5 to 16 years whether it was fair that some people were rich and some poor. The youngest children thought it unfair, but with increasing age more children thought that the differences were fair and justified by the effort people expended to acquire wealth. Siegal (1981) also found an increase between 6 and 13 years in the attitude that inequality in wages was fair. Emler and Dickinson (1985) found a similar age pattern in the rejection of equality as an appropriate basis for payment. Dickinson (1990a) found that most adolescents also gave qualified support to inequalities in wages as they perceived them. They tended to support differentials between high and average wages but to think that low paid jobs should earn a 'bit more'. Class differences were uncovered by Emler and Dickinson (1985) and Dickinson (1990a); middle class children and adolescents expressed greater support for wage differentials than did their working class peers.

It is worth noting that, although children rapidly come to support inequality in wages, their perceptions of the degree of inequality are far from accurate. Studies in which children are asked to estimate wages have revealed that young children perceive very little inequality between jobs and systematically underestimate incomes (Emler and Dickinson, 1985; Siegal, 1981). The estimates and the perceived differentials increase with age but still fall short of accuracy. Even adults lack accurate knowledge of how much is paid for most jobs (Dickinson, 1986). In other words, people will say wage differentials are fair even when they are ignorant of the size of these differentials.

Emler and Dickinson (1985) found that both working class and middle class Scottish children believed that income differences were fair, but that the middle class children perceived significantly larger differences than the working class children. This finding has been replicated in both the USA and France, though somewhat less clearly in the latter case (Emler et al., 1990).

One implication of this class difference is that middle and working class children at the age of 10–12 years, when they are embarking on a critical stage of their educational careers, have quite different assumptions about the economic consequences of their efforts. If working class children believe that there is very little difference between the pay of a professional and that of a manual worker, they may feel that there is little reason to invest in educational credentials. Middle class children, recognizing that there are substantial differentials, might be expected to feel rather differently.

Although children and most adults are poorly informed of the *amount* of income inequality between occupations, they rapidly acquire an understanding of the *rank order* of jobs in terms of wages and social status (Dickinson, 1986). It is likely that concepts of broad occupational strata (e.g. white collar versus blue collar) are gained first, then further differentiated in terms of the social standing of jobs, and that income is then inferred from social standing. An early study by Jahoda (1959) revealed that Scottish children as young as 6 years were sensitive to some visual cues to socio-economic status, such as clothing and housing. They frequently described pictures of working class and middle class stereotypes in occupational terms: 'workman', 'painter', 'plumber', 'gentleman', 'business-man', 'doctor', etc. By early adolescence, rankings of occupational prestige and income are very similar to those of official measures of socio-economic status (Himmelweit et al., 1952; Dickinson, 1990a). Perceptions of occupational prestige are widely shared; class differences exist only in so far as working class adolescents tend to overestimate the prestige of skilled manual jobs (Himmelweit et al., 1952; Weinstein, 1958; Dickinson, 1990a) and middle class children are more conscious of occupational status (Simmons and Rosenberg, 1971; Dickinson, 1990a).

It appears that children, as soon as they become aware of wage differentials, begin to acquire a stock of justifications for them. It seems likely that children are confronted with a particular pattern of distribution which they learn is extensively defended by 'equity-like' arguments, rather than that they apply equity principles to decide what relative incomes should be.

The child's capacity to understand and reproduce these arguments will undoubtedly be limited by cognitive capacity. There is even the intriguing possibility that an understanding of strict proportional equity is beyond the capacity of many adults, its logical structure requiring formal operations (Hook and Cook, 1979).

However, the precise nature and application of arguments for equity, and indeed the priority accorded to such arguments, will all derive from their currency in the individual's social environment. Certainly, children in more collectivist cultures, such as that of Japan, will give less weight to equity than to parity (Mann et al., 1985). Similarly, middle class children in fee paying schools where there is strong encouragement to gain academic qualifications are more likely than their working class, state educated peers to relate income to qualifications and training (Dickinson, 1990a).

It seems likely that justifications for wage differentials are acquired, at least initially, by imitating the language used to refer to jobs in the media or in adult conversation. Clichés abound. For instance, justifications for the wages of a doctor tend to refer to 'dedication' and 'importance to the community' whereas those for a factory manager refer to 'responsibility' and 'decision making' (Dickinson, 1987). Clearly both professions could be said to be important to the community and to involve dedication, responsibility and decision-making but mention of the jobs seems to trigger different connotations. However, thinking about jobs is not constrained to a crude stimulus-response reaction, as even primary school children can debate the criteria on which jobs are rated, and argue that the quality attributed to one job is equally applicable to another. Dickinson (1986) found that children who attributed high wages to a quality such as 'skill' often went on to argue that other jobs were equally skilled and should consequently be better rewarded.

It has already been noted that children employ equity as the main principle underlying wage differentials. Indeed, both children and adults tend to explain and justify wage differentials in terms of individual contributions: education, responsibility, hours worked, effort, uncomfortable or dangerous working conditions, importance to the community, and so on (Dickinson, 1990a; Dornstein, 1985) and references to most of these criteria are found in all age groups. Up to 25 per cent of adults and smaller percentages of children and teenagers sometimes relate wages to sociological and economic factors such as market forces, bargaining power in the labour market and the prestige attached to certain roles or skills (Dickinson, 1986). Greater numbers acknowledge the importance of such factors when presented with statements based on sociological and economic arguments (Dickinson, 1990c) but individualistic arguments are predominant. This tendency to relate wages to relative individual contributions rather than factors beyond individual control probably reflects the moral tones in which wage differentials are debated, particularly during wage disputes.

To conclude this section, by the time young people enter the labour market they are equipped with the argumentative terms of employment relations. They are already discussing the cash value of jobs in terms of skill, responsibility, effort, and qualifications, and therefore prepared for a particular framework for debating and negotiating a definition of a fair day's pay.

Legal–rational authority

Weber argued that a defining characteristic of bureaucracy was the nature of the authority exercised within it. He referred to it as legal–rational authority. Katz and Kahn (1978) note that obedience to authority in bureaucracies depends substantially on employee's willingness to obey someone because he or she is formally entitled to exercise authority and is doing so within legitimate limits. This willingness, Katz and Kahn conclude, must be in part a consequence of socialization.

Respect for authority certainly has its origins in the family, but legal–rational authority is rather different from the kind commonly exercised by parents. To the extent that parents successfully wield authority over their children, this is likely to be embedded in the personal relationship between these individuals, at least to begin with. However, legal–rational authority does not depend on personal ties, whether of affection, respect, fear or anything else, between people. Instead, it is based on recognition that 'obedience is owed to the legally established impersonal order. It extends to the persons exercising the authority of office under it only by virtue of the formal legality of their commands and only within the scope of authority of the office' (Weber, 1947, p. 328). Bureaucracy in effect formalizes roles and role relationships. The rights and obligations of office holders, to whom they are answerable, for what they are responsible, and over whom and what they have authority, are formally set down, at least in theory; in theory because, as Weber exphasized, this is an idealization of employment relations. In practice much is left unspecified and there remains considerable scope for negotiation, interpretation, and discretion (see also chapters 3 and 4). But the basic point remains: employment relations are in principle governed by formalized and impersonal requirements.

Research by Adelson (1971), Kohlberg (1976) and Furth (1980) suggests that children do not recognize the formal and impersonal elements in role relations until they reach adolescence. They are not initially able to recognize that relations between people can be regulated by anything beyond personal inclinations or preferences. 'Societal decisions are thought to emanate from the free will of a particular person' (Furth, 1978, p. 251). In other words, the distinction between the formal and the personal is a cognitively complex notion which appears relatively late in development.

Several studies have revealed, however, that even quite young children, 7- and sometimes even 5-year olds, perceive authority to have limits (Damon, 1977; Turiel, 1983; Tisak and Turiel, 1984; Piaget, 1932). These studies show that children believe that a person's authority is limited to what is also morally justifiable, though there is some evidence of childhood insights closer to Weber's concept of bureaucratic or legal–rational authority. Laupa and Turiel (1986), for instance, found that children distinguished between orders given by someone authorized to do so and orders given by people lacking such authority.

The setting for Laupa and Turiel's (1986) example was the school, and there are grounds for thinking that experience of school is the single most important socializing experience here. Formal schooling is the child's first extended introduction to a bureaucracy, and one which bears marked similarities to employing organizations. The school is clearly separated off from domestic life. Activities within it are organized according to a timetable. Within the institution, and between the hours formally laid down, individuals relate to one another in terms of their respective formally defined roles. Performances are appraised according to universalistic criteria and authority is exercised impersonally.

It seems sensible therefore to ask how children represent social relations in this context. Emler et al. (1987) examined Scottish and French children's representations of the teacher as an organizational role. They found that almost all children by the age of 11 recognized that there is a hierarchy of authority in the school and that teachers are in their turn subject to the authority of persons, such as head teachers, above them in this hierarchy. By this age almost all children recognized that teachers did not have the power to alter or ignore any rule, and most also believed that it was wrong for teachers to allow their personal preferences to influence decisions about which pupils they would and would not help. In these cases the middle class children were more likely to show these insights than the working class, and the French children were more sophisticated about these bureaucratic features than the Scottish.

Scottish and French children, however, did also have some rather different views about the obligations of office holders. The Scottish children believed that teachers were bound to enforce regulations whatever their personal feelings about the fairness of these regulations. This belief was more widespread among the middle class children and among the older children, and it is tempting therefore to see this as a growing awareness of the objective constraints on officials. However, almost all of the French children believed that the teacher should do what was fair, whatever the regulation required. Likewise, while Scottish children believed that it was appropriate for teachers to justify their actions by invoking the regulations which required them, the French children rejected this idea. This suggests that children progressively assimilate culturally dominant interpretations rather than developing a single objective understanding of a factual reality. Generally, French children seemed more 'sophisticated' about bureaucracy, i.e., recognizing its features earlier, but they were also more critical of its requirements.

We know from a large body of research that children develop increasingly sophisticated capacities for the analysis of moral issues as they grow older (Piaget, 1932, Kohlberg, 1984), and we have already seen that these include capacities for judging the justice of allocation decisions. These capacities also relate to understanding the purpose and origins of rules, and the nature of duties and responsibilities.

Lawrence Kohlberg and his colleagues have amassed extensive evidence for the view that there are distinctive styles or types of moral reasoning, perhaps as many as five or six; that the majority of individuals tend to employ just one or at most two of these; and that they will apply them to a range of situations. However, this evidence also indicates that preferred styles change over the life-span. For this reason Kohlberg also referred to the distinct styles as development stages.

Of particular interest to us are what Kohlberg called the 'conventional' stages, 3 and 4. Both types of reasoning, as the name suggests, appeal to shared standards of morality or obligation, which flow from membership in a particular society, to resolve moral problems. However, the third type considers what is fair or right only in terms of relations between individuals. A person using this style of reasoning will argue that conflicts of interest should be resolved by taking the perspective of persons with whom one has personal ties or persons who conform to in-group stereotypes of virtue or decency.

The fourth type defines justice in terms of a formal set of rules and regulations. Kohlberg (1976) referred to this as a 'social system' perspective. All parties to disputes are formally equal as members of the social system; in deciding what is fair or right, one takes the perspective not of any particular individual but of a member of the social system. Justice at this stage is a function not of relationships between individuals but of the relation between each individual and the community or system. Disputes are resolved by considering what is necessary to maintain the social order. In positive terms, justice is a function of appropriate rewards by society for merit; rewards are earned by complying with system requirements.

The obligation to comply with legal authority is distinguished from the obligation to comply with standards of decent, considerate interpersonal behaviour. The personal requirement to act virtuously or with good intentions is subordinated to the impersonal requirements of an office to discharge specified duties. The parallels with bureaucratic administration, as defined by Weber, are obvious; these distinctions are fundamental to the idea of legal–rational authority.

It is also of interest, therefore, that this 'stage 4' style of reasoning is seldom used by anyone below 16–18 years, though stage 4 or a mixture of 3 and 4 is the most commonly used form by adults in Western society (Colby and Kohlberg, 1987). And it is of interest that stage 4 reasoning is rarely found amongst members of rural, preliterate, pre-industrial societies (Snarey, 1985). This suggests two conclusions. The first is that an economy based on employment relations does require a distinctive moral orientation. The second is that childhood socialization will bring most individuals to the brink of this orientation only by the time that they are eligible for employment relations. One might suppose that direct experience of employment relations is necessary to establish this orientation. However, the first to achieve it will normally be the educational high achievers who stay on in full-time education when their peers are leaving for jobs. Amount of formal education is in fact one of the strongest correlates of style of moral reasoning preferred in adulthood.

Kohlberg's is of course a constructivist theory and as such represents different types of moral reasoning as forming stages in a universal and natural developmental progression. We prefer the view that certain types are cognitively more complex than others and require differing degrees of intellectual capacity to assimilate but that preference among adults for one type rather than another owes much to a social system which requires and sustains that moral orientation.

Sophistication in moral outlook is not everything, however. People also differ in their attitude to formal authority, independently of the insights into its principles that they can articulate. Differences in these attitudes become particularly apparent in adolescence (Emler and Reicher, 1987; Reicher and Emler, 1985). Attitudes as a whole become less uniformly positive at least between 12 and 16 years, though it should be said that they are still positive rather than negative; most 16-year olds do express belief in the impartiality of institutional authority and do assert that those exercising such authority should be obeyed. Girls are on average even more positive than boys (Emler and Reicher, 1987) though there is some disagreement about the cross-national generality of this difference (Rigby, 1989).

Finally this research provides further evidence of the central role of formal schooling in the development of attitudes to institutional authority. Attitudes to such authority as encountered in the school are highly correlated with attitudes to institutional authority more generally (Reicher and Emler, 1985; Rigby and Rump, 1979).

Selection for work roles

The matching of people to occupations is a little like the matching of people to marriage partners. Both processes are steeped in a language of choice markedly at variance with reality. In both cases the matches that occur are highly predictable from factors over which the individuals involved exercise little or no choice at all. In the case of occupations these include their sex, social background, area of residence, parents' occupations, ability and personality. Moreover in both processes the matching is seldom ideal but it does have some advantages over random allocation. Given the tenacity of this illusion of choice, one is inclined to suppose that it has some advantages even if the scope for genuine choice is in practice very narrow. Cognitive dissonance theory tells us that one benefit lies in the illusion of choice of occupation. Things that one believes oneself to have chosen rather than having been constrained to accept are more appreciated in any sphere of life.

Jencks (1972) points out that one reason why this myth of choice is easy to maintain is that most young people have very little idea of what job they want to do and change their aspirations easily and frequently. Thus they may not notice when early ambitions are thwarted, at least not their own personal ambitions. Simmons and Rosenberg (1971) found that American adolescents were aware of socio-economic and racial disadvantage and were cynical about equal opportunities, but that they were still optimistic about their own chances; 97 per cent believed that they had 'as good or better a chance to rise in the world than most'.

Durkheim (1964) saw that the problem of occupational choice for Western society was in persuading its members to accept limited, finite and specific aspirations in a context of almost limitless options. The problem is solved principally in two ways, by self-selection and social selection. The first ensures that individuals put themselves forward only for certain opportunities. As Bourdieu and Passeron (1977) have observed, more people eliminate themselves before exams, by never seeking to embark upon the relevant course of study or to present themselves for the examination, than are ever eliminated by the exams themselves. The second entails more overt and direct constraints on decisions. Though in practice these two processes are interdependent, the distinction has the advantage of directing our attention to the internal and psychological as well as the immediate external forces operating on choice.

Gottfredson (1981) argued that the interaction of cognitive development, social knowledge and occupational perceptions led to four stages in the development of occupational preference. In the first stage, corresponding to 3–5 years, children are aware of occupations only as adult roles but, by the next stage, at 6–8 years, gender stereotypes of adult roles and developing gender identity begin to affect occupational preferences. Sex-typed choices appear. The third stage, at 9–13 years, sees a growing awareness of social class and educational differences in relation to the prestige level of jobs and children start to orientate themselves to jobs considered suitable to their class background. Finally, personal interests, values and competencies direct occupational choices within the boundaries laid down by gender, class and ability. At each stage in this process, changes in occupational aspirations match changes in social and personal identity: instead of perceiving social structural limitations on their future careers, children see the circumscription as natural and desirable.

If we examine the factors of gender, class background and personality in more detail we can see the manner in which selection and choice interact.

1   *Gender.* Within the first eighteen months of life, most children have learned to label themselves as their parents and other adults do, namely as a boy or a girl (Money and Erhardt, 1972). They then set about learning what this label means; in effect learning a script for the role of male or female. These scripts outline among other things not only the virtues and talents that are peculiar to each sex but also and centrally the economic and occupational roles that each plays. What children understand of the script, their progress in learning it, and the qualities displayed in rehearsal are all limited by intellectual development, as are their perceptions of the degree of optionality involved. Thus, 6-year olds may play at doctors and nurses, not only casting themselves in these parts strictly by sex but also believing that it could not be any other way. The idea that occupations may be matters of taste and preference will emerge only later (Kohlberg and Ullman, 1974).

By then, however, tastes and preferences will have been strongly shaped. Girls do not flock to jobs in engineering, though they are theoretically free to do so, since they apparently regard an interest in heavy machinery as unfeminine (and probably have seen no examples of female engineers). Nor will they study technical subjects or computing in school in numbers similar to boys. Stein (1971), for example, has shown that by the age of 11–12 years children have internalized a sex-typing of areas of achievement which has repercussions for effort, achievement standards and expectations of success. Boys in their turn will rule out all kinds of careers which they have learned to regard as either unmasculine or too low in status or both. These acquired inclinations are then reinforced by strong biases in the perception and evaluation of male and female performances.

2   *Social class and schooling.* The single most important determinant of occupational status is amount of education (e.g. Jencks, 1972) and working class children, since they usually end up with less education than middle class children, mainly end up in working class jobs. There are certainly economic obstacles to educational achievement (in the USA, for example, middle class students are less likely to have to work their way through college) but Jencks argued that the most important factor in educational success was attitude to education. Middle class children have more positive attitudes because they have higher occupational aspirations and are under pressure from home to do well at school.

For instance, Dickinson (1986) found significant differences in the occupational aspirations of middle and working class adolescent boys. The middle class boys specified professional jobs such as 'doctor' and 'engineer'. The working class boys chose jobs from a much wider socio-economic range and frequently named skilled manual jobs such as 'electrician' or 'lorry driver' as their first choice.

However, despite the differences in the status of the occupational choice, both middle and working class adolescents tended to give the same reason for their choice: it was simply an 'interesting job'. Few subjects referred to wages, responsibility, training or skill and none mentioned the sex or class appropriateness of the job.

Aspirations also interact with perceptions of what is realistic. Rosen (1964), in an experimental study of occupational choice, found that subjects who were asked to rate jobs in order of preference, before and after having been given (false) information about their chances of getting the jobs, raised their rating of jobs for which they thought they stood a good chance and lowered their rating of those for which they stood little chance. This must raise some doubt as to whether social class has a direct affect on career aspirations or whether these are the outcome of other variables associated with social class.

3 *Personality and attitudes.* Personality factors probably do help to determine the particular kind of occupation entered but the relationship between personality and occupation probably lies in the process of selection itself rather than in the process of selecting 'the right kind of personality for the job'. Hogan et al. (1988) have argued that personality influences selection and promotion, but not necessarily in ways that maximize the matching of personality to job requirements.

One obvious personality characteristic is intellectual ability, though, as Jencks (1972) points out, cognitive differences account for only part of the variation in eventual occupational status; he estimates the correlation for white, non-agricultural males in the USA at 0.50 (and this is largely owing to the influence of cognitive skills on educational credentials). Cognitive skills have much less impact on job success or income. It may be sensible for employers to give more weight to educational credentials than to intelligence test scores, especially if the former reflects other kinds of personality differences relevant to employment.

One such is attitude to authority. For some jobs employers are as likely to be interested in whether their employees will arrive at work on time, will behave properly, will accept authority, and will do what they are told, as they are in the employees' powers of intellect. Indeed, these points may be more important than relative skill or ability since, in many cases, more skill is involved in driving to work than in many of the jobs performed once one has arrived (Blackburn and Mann, 1979). We have already seen that marked differences in attitudes to authority are apparent in adolescence. Moreover, educational attainment is very sensitive to these differences. In a recent study of British 16–20 year olds, it was found that attitudes to authority more powerfully predicted educational achievement than any other variable measured, including social class background (Emler and St James, 1990). This therefore offers some support for Danziger's (1971) view that formal education is largely an extended test of the child's willingness and ability to accommodate to the requirements of a bureaucratic system.

There are two structural factors worth mentioning which have an important effect on selection for work roles. The first is kinship networks and their role in creating specific job opportunities. In the East London docks during the 1970s, no more than 10 per cent of those employed there were unable to name at least one relative working in the docks; direct father to son inheritance, what is called in industrial relations the 'dads and lads' system of recruitment, accounted for two thirds of the jobs (Hill, 1976).

The second is the area of residence. Locales differ in the number as well as the kind of employment opportunities available. A young person may leave school with few formal qualifications in one part of the country and immediately be taken on by a local employer. In a more depressed area, another young person leaving school with the same lack of qualifications may find her or himself almost indefinitely unemployed.

Employment relations in the workplace

One of the defining aspects of embarking upon employment is that employees enter into a contract with the employer which specifies the roles, rights and responsibilities of each partner in the agreement. There are formal and informal aspects of this contract. The formal aspects tend to be written down and might include state legislated practices, such as the right to maternity leave, as well as conventions particular to the organization, such as the number of weeks of paid holiday leave. The informal parts of the contract are not written and are often discovered only after the employee has entered into the formal contract (see chapter 4). What kind of preparation do children have for the formal and informal aspects of the employment contract? What expectations do they have before they start work? To what extent do they realize that this contract may be negotiated and have they any idea how this may be done? Entrance into an employment contract is also entrance into the world of trade unions, wage bargaining, negotiation and confrontation, employment legislation, colleagues and workmates, perks and fiddles. Little is known about this aspect of economic socialization and it is probable that young people begin work still largely ignorant of the means of challenging and changing the employment contract and of the nature of the relationships between various groups involved in the contract.

It is certainly the case that young children have a rather different perception of management and ownership from adults. It is not until around the age of 6–7 years, when children have grasped the idea that people receive wages, that they begin to conceive of a 'boss'; even then, a boss is just the person who pays the workers (Berti and Bombi, 1988; Danziger, 1958; Strauss, 1952). At this age, children do not see employers as having authority and they are not very sure where employers obtain the money to pay the workers, so the boss may be seen as simply a rich person who pays people out of savings! Children's awareness of a hierarchy of authority emerges in the next two or three years, although owners and managers are poorly distinguished and 'bosses' are believed to become so either by being elected or by buying or building the factory. By 10–11 years, children are beginning to realize that the boss sells the products or services in order to pay the workers and that owners may delegate supervision to managers.

We have already discussed the importance of the school in providing a preparation for authority relations at work. It seems likely that just as children perceive limits to the power and responsibility of teachers they also perceive limits to that of managers, foremen, shop stewards, and so on. However, little research touches directly on this area. Some research on 10–16 year olds' understanding of industrial conflict (Dickinson, 1990b), in which the children were asked to explain in their own words the causes of strikes and the role of trade unions, found that 25 per cent attributed strikes to disputes about working conditions. The likelihood of this response increased with age from 17 per cent amongst the 10–13 year olds to 46 per cent amongst the 14–16 year olds. Fifty per cent felt that strikes were a bad idea compared with 20 per cent who thought that they were a good idea and 22 per cent who thought that it depended on the circumstances. This disapproval appears not to be related to the idea that employment disagreements rarely arise, since very few subjects accused strikers of being greedy or of striking over trivia, nor was it the case that strikes were seen as an unnecessary means of pressure, since only 5 per cent suggested negotiation as an alternative. Instead, disapproval focused on the harm that strikes did to both the company and the workers in terms of cutting production, producing unemployment, and the loss of wages during the strike. Many also believed that strikes were a waste of time as they were rarely successful.

This cynicism was also reflected in Furnham's (1987) investigation of British 16–18 year olds' beliefs about the economy. More than half believed that companies do not give employees a fair share of company earnings; conversely, however, a similar percentage believed that workers, if they want higher wages, should work harder and produce more. In general it seems that young people, at least from 10–11 years onwards, are aware that the workplace is not an entirely amicable place where power and control is uncontested and where everyone is happy with the outcome. On the other hand, there is still some suggestion that children are quite naïve about the kinds of disputes that arise and their means of solution. For instance, one 15-year old boy (Dickinson, 1990b) argued that employees should not strike for more money as their wages were 'bound to go up anyway with inflation'.

Perhaps some of the vagueness which characterizes adolescent conceptions of authority and conflict within employment is related to children's ignorance of the nature of many work roles. Dickinson found that only 26 per cent of 10–12 year olds were able to explain the purpose or role of trade unions in any way. Indeed, most of this group had never heard of trade unions. By 14–16 years, 85 per cent of adolescents can provide a reasonably accurate account of the role of trade unions. There was a very significant class difference in knowledge about trade unions: 74 per cent of middle class, privately educated adolescents compared with 42 per cent of working class, state educated adolescents could explain the role of trade unions. This is an ironic finding given that middle class adolescents are less likely to go on to join trade unions (cf. De Witte, 1989). The ignorance of adolescents about trade unions is perhaps all the more surprising considering the amount of media attention paid to certain prominent union disputes in the 1980s (e.g. the 1984 'Miners' strike'). Naïvety about industrial relations is reflected in the finding that almost all adolescents could account for strikes but few could describe trade unions.

However, the majority of adolescents who were aware of the role of trade unions had a positive view of them. Most saw them as helping or protecting workers, especially in organizing strikes or wage claims. About 15 per cent mentioned their importance as a means of mediation between workers and management, or as a means of group organization to put pressure on management. Most reservations concerned the 'closed shop' or unions having 'too much power'. Furnham (1987) found that 65 per cent of 16–18 year olds agreed with the statement 'unions are too powerful' and it is possible that these sentiments reflected public opinion generally in the mid 1980s (Marsh, 1990). Given the media coverage, it is not clear from where adolescents gain their positive attitudes towards unions but it is possible that the teenage years bring a greater awareness of workplace conflict and of the experiences of employees and that adolescents then begin to realize that workers' rights may need the protection of a trade union. Consequently trade unions are accepted as a necessary and important part of employment for some people in some circumstances but this does not mean that adolescents are personally predisposed towards joining trade unions. Cregan and Johnston's (1990) study of the intentions of 16-year old school-leavers in London towards trade union joining suggested that these young people were largely indifferent towards trade unions. Only 20.7 per cent of those who had a choice wanted to join a trade union. The remaining 79.3 per cent were negative or unsure. Of those who later joined a trade union, the highest percentages of the reason given referred to values and norms ('to support it', 49%; 'expected to', 14%; 'everyone else is in it', 11%) and not to the material benefits of trade union membership. The majority of reasons given by those who did not join a trade union referred to lack of interest and lack of opportunity ('not asked', 40%; 'had not thought', 9%; 'not interested', 16%, 'not decided', 7%; 'don't know', 9%). Trade unions in the first few months of employment for this young worker group were perceived as having little bearing on their lives.

It is highly likely that much of the preparation for industrial relations occurs once young people have commenced full-time work. De Witte (1989) found that 18–30 year old Flemish men and women were most likely to give the reason for joining a union as the provision of individual help, advice or protection, whether or not they were members of a trade union. However, the factors which best predicted membership were firstly the extent to which a person's friends belong to a union, secondly the extent to which parents encouraged joining a union and only thirdly the extent to which the person experienced difficulties with the employer. British research also shows that provision for joining a recognized trade union within the workplace is a very important factor in the decision to join a trade union (cf. Cregan and Johnston, 1990; Spilsbury et al., 1987; see also chapter 7 on trade union joining) in this area but there seems to be very little preparation for ways of influencing the employment relationship prior to entering work. Yet we discussed just how early and how thorough is the process of selection for work roles. The absence of preparation for influencing or controlling the contract and the wealth of preparation for specific, limited roles would seem to be complementary ways of ensuring the continuation of the current system of

employment relations. Perhaps the often criticized rigidity of industrial organizations owes much to socialization which prepares young people to fit into
employment slots rather than to meet the challenge of production co-operatively.

Conclusion

Many of the qualities that typify the dominant character structure in an
employment culture are already strongly established before individuals actually
enter employment relations: notions of fairness; the vocabulary of equity; the
cognitive orientations of literacy, numeracy and formal operations; appropriate
attitudes to time; an understanding of the nature of bureaucracy and
legal–rational authority. Much of the task of sorting individuals into the
thousands of different employee roles has also occurred, and perhaps the greater
priority is that this extensive pre-sorting should occur rather than achieve
perfect matches.

If a broad principle can be discerned in all of this it is that the system selects
in terms of the degrees to which prototypical socialization is accomplished. The
more an individual matches the prototype of the perfectly socialized member of
an industrial culture – a positive attitude to institutional authority, strong
commitment to the principle of equity, highly developed literacy skills, capacity
for abstract thought, a social system perspective on moral obligations – the
greater his or her chances (but probably his, since merely being male puts one
closer to the prototype) of being selected into higher status occupations. The same
considerations concerning socialization also help to clarify the difficulties that may
face the creation of employment economies in cultures without employment
traditions.

In this chapter we have been unable to explore many other aspects of
socialization and its results, such as preparation for the role of employer, or that
of entrepreneur. Nor have we attempted to assess the relevance of socializing
experiences given that the emphases on equity and the formality of role
relationships seem to reflect a somewhat idealized view of employment
relations. We can only signal to the reader that these additional issues exist. We
hope that we have shown that developmental psychology has a contribution to
make to understanding contemporary employment relations. In order to
understand such things as authority relations, support for pay differentials and
attitudes towards strikes it is necessary to understand the forces that have
shaped people and the perceptions, attributions and values that people bring to
the workplace.

As we noted at the start of this chapter, our system of employment relations is
a peculiar and complex state of affairs and in many ways idiosyncratic. Yet
everyone, or nearly everyone, learns to accept this system as normal. The
developmental processes described in this chapter help to explain some of the
stability in employment relations, such as why industrial disputes are rare and
often limited in scope. For instance, pay, whilst it is often a focus for disputes, is
contested within limited points of reference, such as seeking parity with similar

workers in more affluent branches of the same industry, rather than seeking smaller differentials between workers and management. It is just as important in employment relations to understand why strikes *do not* occur as to understand why they do: i.e. why a conflict of interest does not turn into an expressed conflict (see Hartley, 1984), as the Marxist theory (cf. Bottomore and Rubel, 1963) of class struggle would predict. Perhaps part of the answer lies in the very gradual and incremental manner in which children are introduced to differences in work roles, wages and authority and to the values, theories and explanations that rationalize these differences. In the process, they come to see these differences as inevitable, logical and perhaps even desirable and, as such, do not perceive any conflict of interests nor any alternative to the situation.

Clearly what happens in life up to the age of 16–18 has profound consequences for what happens in the world of employment beyond that age. However, many research questions remain to be answered. Some of these have been noted above; for instance, the effects of peer influences on career expectations and the effects of media coverage of industrial disputes on developing conceptions of conflict in employment. One very important question that needs to be answered is the extent to which young people are prepared not for fitting into existing employment roles but for changing conditions and patterns of employment. The structure of work in Western countries has changed dramatically in the last two decades. Many manual jobs have disappeared as computer-aided machines have been developed to fulfil the tasks previously undertaken by machine operators. There is an increasing demand for skilled labour, particularly for the control and development of new technology. Demographic changes are affecting the composition of the workforce and those supported by the workforce. There has been a decline in the proportion of the population under 20 years but people are living longer and enjoying more years of retirement. Finally there is increasing concern about the effects of industrial pollution and the rapid consumption of scarce resources which may soon present a threat to many traditional forms of production. There are new problems of production to be met and consequent changes in work roles, working life and lifestyles. The challenge for the future is that young people must develop conceptions of work when the concept of work itself is changing.

References

Adelson, J. (1971) The political imagination of the young adolescent. *Daedalus*, 100, 1013–50.

Berry, J. W. (1971) Ecological and cultural factors in spatial perceptual development. *Canadian Journal of Behavioral Science*, 3, 4, 324–36

Berti, A. E. and Bombi, A. S. (1988) *The Child's Construction of Economics*. Cambridge: Cambridge University Press.

Berti, A. E., Bombi, A. S. and Lis, A. (1982) The child's conceptions about means of production and their owners. *European Journal of Social Psychology*, 12, 221–39.

Binet, A. (1908) Le développement de l'intelligence chez les enfants. *Année psychologique*, 14, 1–94.

Blackburn, R. M. and Mann, M. (1979) *The Working Class in the Labour Market.* London: Macmillan.

Bottomore, T. B. and Rubel, M. (eds) (1963) Karl Marx. *Selected Writings in Sociology and Social Philosophy.* London: Penguin.

Bourdieu, P. and Passeron, J. C. (1977) *Reproduction: In Education, Society and Culture* (tr. R. Nice). London: Sage

Brown, R. (1965) *Social Psychology.* New York: Free Press.

Colby, A. and Kohlberg, L. (1987) *The Measurement of Moral Judgement.* Cambridge: Cambridge University Press.

Connell, R. W. (1977) *Ruling Class, Ruling Culture.* Cambridge: Cambridge University Press.

Cregan, C. and Johnston, S. (1990) An industrial relations approach to the free rider problem: Young People and trade union membership in the UK. *British Journal of Industrial Relations,* 28, 84–104.

Damon, W. (1977) *The Social World of the Child.* San Francisco: Jossey-Bass.

Danziger, K. (1958) Children's earliest conceptions of economic relationships (Australia). *Journal of Social Psychology,* 47, 231–40.

Danziger, K. (1971) *Socialization.* Harmondsworth: Penguin.

Dasen, P. R. (1974) The influence of ecology, culture and European contact on cognitive development in Australian Aborigines. In J. W. Berry and P. R. Dasen (eds), *Culture and Cognition: Readings in Cross-Cultural Psychology,* London: Methuen, pp 381–408.

De Witte, H. (1989) Why do youngsters join trade unions? Paper given at the Fourth West European Congress on the Psychology of Work and Organization. April.

Dickinson, J. (1986) The development of representations of social inequality. Unpublished Ph.D. thesis. Dundee University.

Dickinson, J. (1987) The development of beliefs about socio-economic structure. Paper given at the British Psychological Society Section Conference, Oxford. September.

Dickinson, J. (1990a) Adolescent representations of socio-economic status. *British Journal of Developmental Psychology,* 8, 4, 351–71.

Dickinson, J. (1990b) Children's understanding of industrial disputes. Unpublished paper.

Dickinson, J. (1990c) Business students' and social science students' explanations for wage differentials: moral versus political and economic rhetoric. In S. E. G. Lea et al. (eds), *Applied Economic Psychology in the 1990s* (Proceedings of the 15th Annual Colloquium of the International Association for Economic Psychology), Exeter: Washington Singer Press. 788–99.

Dornstein, M. (1985) Perceptions regarding standards for evaluating pay equity and their determinants. *Journal of Occupational Psychology,* 58, 321–30.

Durkheim, E. (1964) *The Division of Labor in Society.* New York: Free Press.

Emler, N. (1987) Moral development from the perspective of social representations. *Journal for Theory of Social Behaviour,* 17, 371–88.

Emler, N. and Dickinson, J. (1985) Children's representation of economic inequalities: the effects of social class. *British Journal of Developmental Psychology,* 3, 191–8.

Emler, N. and Reicher, S. (1987) Orientations to institutional authority in adolescence. *Journal of Moral Education,* 16, 108–16.

Emler, N. and St James, A. (1990) Staying on at school after sixteen: Social and psychological correlates. *British Journal of Education and Work,* 3, 61–70.

Emler, N., Ohana, J. and Dickinson, J. (1990) Children's representations of social relations. In B. Lloyd and G. Duveen (eds), *Social Representations and the Development of Knowledge,* Oxford: Blackwell.

Emler, N., Ohana, J. and Moscovici, S. (1987) Children's beliefs about institutional roles:

A cross-national study of representations of the teacher's role. *British Journal of Educational Psychology*, 57, 26–37.

Furnham, A. (1987) The determinants and structure of adolescents' beliefs about the economy. *Journal of Adolescence*, 10, 353–71.

Furth, H. G. (1980) *The World of Grown-Ups*. New York: Elsevier.

Gibbs, J. and Schnell, S. V. (1985) Moral development 'versus' socialization: A critique. *American Psychologist*, 40, 1071–80.

Giddens, A. (1989) *Sociology*. Cambridge: Polity Press.

Gottfredson, L. S. (1981) Circumscription and compromise: a developmental theory of occupational aspirations. *Journal of Counselling Psychology*, 28, 545–79.

Hartley, J. F. (1984) Industrial relations psychology. In M. Gruneberg and T. Wall (eds), *Social Psychology and Organizational Behaviour*, Chichester: Wiley 149–81

Hearn, F. (1978) *Domination, Legitimation and Resistance: The Incorporation of the Nineteenth Century English Working Class*. Westport, Conn: Greenwood Press.

Hill, S. (1976) *The dockers: Class and tradition in London*. London: Heinemann.

Himmelweit, H., Halsey, A. H. and Oppenheim, A. N. (1952) The views of adolescents on some aspects of the social class structure. *British Journal of Sociology*, 3, 148–72.

Himmelweit, H. T., Oppenheim, A. N. and Vince, P. (1958) *Television and the Child: an Empirical Study of the Effects of Television on the Young*. Oxford: Oxford University Press.

Hogan, R. Raskin, R. and Fazzini, D. (1988) *The Dark Side of Charisma*. Unpublished manuscript. Tulsa Institute of Behavioral Sciences.

Hook, J. and Cook. T. (1979) Equity theory and the cognitive ability of children. *Psychological Bulletin*, 86, 429–45.

Inhelder, B. and Piaget, J. (1958) *The Growth of Logical Thinking from Childhood to Adolescence*. New York: Basic Books.

Jahoda, G. (1959) Development of the perception of social differences in children from 6–10. *British Journal of Psychology*, 50, 159–75.

Jahoda, G. (1979) The construction of economic reality by some Glaswegian children. *European Journal of Social Psychology*, 9, 115–27.

Jahoda, G. (1983) European 'lag' in the development of an economic concept: a study in Zimbabwe. *British Journal of Developmental Psychology*, 1, 113–20.

Jahoda, G. (1984) The development of thinking about socio-economic systems. In H. Tajfel (ed.), *The Social Dimension: European Developments in Social Psychology* (vol. 1), Cambridge: Cambridge University Press, 69–88.

Jencks, C. (1972) *Inequality*. Harmondsworth: Penguin.

Katz, D. and Kahn, R. L. (1978) *The Social Psychology of Organizations*. (2nd ed.) New York: Wiley.

Kohlberg, L. (1976) Moral stages and moralization: The cognitive–developmental approach. In T. Lickona (ed.), *Moral Development and Behavior: Theory, Research and Social Issues*, New York: Holt, Rinehart & Winston, 31–53.

Kohlberg, L. (1984) *Essays on Moral Development* (vol. 2), *The Psychology of Moral Development*. San Francisco: Harper & Row.

Kohlberg, L. and Ullman, D. (1974) Stages in the development of psychosexual concepts and attitudes. In R. C. Friedman, R. M. Richart and R. L. Vande Wiele (eds), *Sex Differences in Behavior*, New York: Wiley, 209–22.

Laupa, M. and Turiel, E. (1986) Children's conceptions of adult and peer authority. *Child Development*, 57, 405–12.

LeClair Jr, E. E. and Schneider, H. K. (1968) *Economic Anthropology*. New York: Holt, Rinehart and Winston.

Lerner, D. (1958) *The Passing of Traditional Society*. New York: Free Press.

McLuhan, M. (1967) *The Medium is the Massage*. New York: Random House.

Mann, L., Radford, M. and Kanagawa, C. (1985) Cross-cultural differences in children's use of decision rules: A comparison between Japan and Australia. *Journal of Personality and Social Psychology*, 49, 1557–64.

Marsden D. (1983) Wage structure. In G. Bain (ed.), *Industrial Relations in Britain*, Oxford: Blackwell, 263–90.

Marsh, D. (1990) Public opinion, trade unions and Mrs Thatcher. *British Journal of Industrial Relations*, 1, 57–65.

Money, J. W. and Erhardt, A. (1972) *Man and Women, Boy and Girl*. Baltimore: Johns Hopkins University Press.

Piaget, J. (1932) *The Moral Judgement of the Child*. Harmondsworth: Penguin.

Piaget, J. (1970) Piaget's Theory. In P. H. Mussen (ed.), *Carmichael's Manual of Child Psychology* (vol. 1), New York: Wiley, 703–32.

Reicher, S. and Emler, N. (1985) Delinquent behaviour and attitudes to formal authority. *British Journal of Social Psychology*, 3, 161–8.

Rigby, K. (1989) Gender, orientation to authority and delinquency among adolescents: a cross-cultural perspective. *Journal of Moral Education*, 18, 2, 112–7.

Rigby, K. and Rump, E. E. (1979) The generality of attitude to authority. *Human Relations*, 32, 469–87.

Rosen, M. (1964) Valence, expectancy and dissonance reduction in the prediction of goal striving. In V. H. Vroom (ed.), *Work and Motivation*, New York: Wiley.

Siegal, M. (1981) Children's perceptions of adult economic needs. *Child Development*, 52, 379–82.

Simmons, R. G. and Rosenberg, M. (1971) Functions of children's perceptions of the stratification system. *American Sociological Review*, 36, 235–49.

Snarey, J. (1985) Cross-cultural universality of socio-moral development: A critical review of Kohlberg's research. *Psychological Bulletin*, 97, 202–32.

Spilsbury M., Hoskins, M., Ashton, D. J. and Maguire, M. J. (1987) A note on the trade union patterns of young adults. *British Journal of Industrial Relations*, 25, 267–74.

Stein, A. H. (1971) The effects of sex-role standards for achievement and sex-role preference on three determinants of achievement. *Developmental Psychology*, 4, 219–31.

Strauss, A. L. (1952) The development and transformation of monetary meanings in the child. *American Sociological Review*, 17, 275–86.

Thompson, E. P. (1967) Time, work discipline and industrial capitalism. *Past and Present*, 38, 56–97.

Tisak, M. and Turiel, E. (1984) Children's conceptions of moral and prudential rules. *Child Development*, 55, 1030–39.

Turiel, E. (1983) *The Development of Social Knowledge*. Cambridge: Cambridge University Press.

Weber, M. (1947) *The Theory of Social and Economic Organisations*. New York: Free Press.

Weinstein, E. A. (1958) Children's conceptions of occupational stratification. *Sociology and Social Research*, 42, 278–84.

Further Reading

There are no texts which cover the whole area of this chapter. Those listed over provide deeper coverage of specific areas.

Childhood social and economic development

Berti, A. E. and Bombi, A. S. (1988) *The Child's Construction of Economics.* Cambridge: Cambridge University Press. This is an interesting and informative account of the development of economic concepts in childhood. Chapters cover children's concepts of the means of production, money, profit, banks and interest and work roles. A cognitive developmental perspective is adopted to explain developmental changes.

Cole, M. and Cole, S. R. (1989) *The Development of Children.* New York: Scientific American Books. A good introduction to developmental psychology which covers social development.

Education and selection

Bourdieu, P. and Passeron, J. C. (1977) *Reproduction: In Education, Society and Culture* (tr. R. Nice). London: Sage.

Jencks, C. (1972) *Inequality.* Harmondsworth: Penguin. Both these texts deal with the issue of how education can contribute to the reproduction of class structure in society. Bourdieu and Passeron develop theories of the processes by which children are led to select similar occupational roles to those of their parents. Jencks utilises a great deal of research and statistics to back his thesis that working class children are systematically disadvantaged.

2

Changing Meanings of Work

Gordon E. O'Brien

Introduction

Reasons for studying work meanings

Modern psychologists have studied the meaning of work from a subjective viewpoint in that their focus has been the employees' estimation of work and its functions. There have been at least three reasons for this approach. The first reason is the wish to monitor possible changes in work commitment and the work ethic. Some writers have raised the possibility that work expectations over the past fifty years have changed owing to increased education and affluence. Workers now want more than pay, security and good physical working conditions. They also want jobs that allow them to express their natural and acquired skills. Consequently, work has acquired expressive meanings that assume equal, if not more, importance than traditional material or instrumental meanings. Others have argued that the importance of expressive meanings has been overrated and that a considerable proportion of the workforce in industrialized societies still see their jobs in instrumental terms. Hence, a large number of studies have sought to resolve these alternative views by examining the prevalence of instrumental and expressive work meanings.

A second reason for research into work meanings is the wish to predict employee reactions to technological change. Jobs are rapidly changing as a result of the introduction of computers, microprocessors and information-based technology. Low skill jobs are being eliminated and people are being replaced by machines while new, skilled jobs are being created which require skilled, committed workers who will be responsive to such jobs requiring flexibility, initiative and involvement. There are differences in opinion about the effects of new technologies on job content, however. Some argue that many new jobs are being de-skilled by designers with an instrumental orientation. These jobs offer little opportunities for the exertion of personal capabilities and therefore provide mainly material rewards. Do employees have work orientations that will fit the new jobs? Another important question that is sometimes addressed is the ability of some workers to adjust to a life without jobs. If work is a central life interest that serves economic and non-economic functions, how can present and future unemployed people find work outside of paid employment?

A final reason for studying work meanings is the wish to assess their implications for employee–union–management relations. If workers really want jobs that provide personal fulfilment as well as pay and security, how will management provide such jobs? Will unions expand their traditional demands for good pay and working conditions to include demands for jobs which satisfy employees' desire for work that utilizes their skills and satisfies their needs for autonomy and participation? Will issues of job quality become a source of industrial conflict and, if so, how can conflict be resolved?

These are some of the reasons for examining work meanings. This review will briefly survey the available research during the past thirty years. Most of this research has described work meanings on the basis of employee responses to interview and survey questions. Four different types of studies will be described. In turn, we shall consider economic and non-economic work functions, work as a central life interest, instrumental and expressive work orientations, and work values. The review will assess these studies and the associated explanations of these findings. Finally, the implications for job design and industrial relations will be discussed.

Research on the Meaning of Work

The lottery question

Some researchers have tried to ascertain the meaning of work for employees by asking them if they would continue to work if they received enough money to live comfortably for the rest of their working age. The first such study was conducted by Morse and Weiss (1955). In their interviews they asked employed males the following question: 'If by some chance you inherited enough money to live comfortably without working, do you think that you would work anyway or not?' Eighty per cent of their respondents said that they would still continue to work. The researchers interpreted this result as showing that work meant more to employees than simply an activity that earned them money. In order to find out the non-economic functions of work, they also asked for the reasons why respondents would continue working. The reply format was open-ended and the answers were coded into eleven categories. The four major responses (given by 10 per cent or more) were 'to keep occupied', 'feel lost without work', 'without work I would not know what to do with time' and 'keeps you healthy'. Thus, it appears that most employees thought that work had a principal function of structuring their time. Relatively few saw work as an interesting activity or a social obligation. Another main finding of this study was that answers differed somewhat according to social class. Whereas working class employees largely saw work as an activity that could occupy their time, middle class employees tended to emphasize the potential of work as a source of enjoyment and accomplishment.

Subsequent studies using the same or a similar question have since been published. Some studies asked respondents to consider what they would do if they won a lottery; hence the general question is frequently referred to as the 'lottery question'. Such studies confirm the major finding that the majority of employed people would work even if they were guaranteed financial security (see table 2.1). The results have been extended to show that young workers tend to be more committed to working than older workers. Also, in most studies males are more likely to report an intention to keep on working than females. There is also evidence that the intention to work, even if economic security is assured, varies across cultures. The strongest evidence is provided by Harpaz (1989), who reported a large survey using random samples in seven different countries. The Japanese sample showed that 93 per cent of employees would continue working and this was the highest percentage reported. The lowest percentages were 69 per cent for the UK and 70 per cent for West Germany. Between these extremes were the USA, Israel, the Netherlands, and Belgium with percentages in the middle to high eighties.

The results do not necessarily show that employees would want to continue working at their same jobs, however. In the original study by Morse and Weiss (1955), 61 per cent of middle class employees would continue in the same job but only 34 per cent of working class employees said that they would remain in their present job. Warr (1982) also found that a considerable proportion of employees who report that they would work in the absence of financial need would seek different jobs. Thirty-five per cent of males and 29 per cent of females said that they would try to change jobs. The intention to change jobs was greater for young workers than older workers and also for workers in unskilled jobs than for those in managerial or professional jobs.

All researchers assume that the answers to the lottery or inheritance question measure the degree to which employees are committed to work. Work commitment has been defined in different ways but generally refers to the degree to which individuals see work as a central life role and wish to expend effort in work activities. However, the relationship between the hypothetical lottery question and work commitment is unclear. Only one study could be found which provides support for the assumed relationship. Mannheim and Rein (1981) found a negative relationship between their measure of work centrality and the wish to stop work. For Israeli employees they found that those willing to stop work had lower work centrality than those who wished to continue in employment. Obviously more research is needed; for example, to examine whether responses to the hypothetical lottery question predict actual work behaviour. The best kind of study would be to examine what happens to employees who actually receive a large amount of money through either inheritance or some form of gambling. Do these people choose work or leisure activities that are consistent with their reported intentions? If they choose to continue working as predicted, do they choose different jobs and do they expend effort that is reflected in high intrinsic motivation and performance? Another type of study that is needed would examine the work commitment, motivation and job performance of those who want to continue working even where they had guaranteed financial security and would compare them with employees who indicate that they would prefer to leave working when they were financially secure.

Table 2.1 Percentage of people who would work even if there were no economic necessity to work

Author(s)	Sample	Country	Percentage who would continue working		
Morse and Weiss (1955)	Representative, male employed (N = 401)	USA	80		
Tausky (1969)	Representative, male, blue collar employed (N = 267)	USA	82		
Kaplan and Tausky 1974	Unemployed male and female (N = 275)	USA	80		
Campbell, Converse and Rodgers (1976)	Representative, male and female employed (N = 1114)	USA	Male 74 Female 59		
Quinn and Staines (1979)	Representative samples of employed males and females (N = 1522, 2083, 2273)	USA	1969 67 1973 67		
Vecchio (1980)	Representative sample of employed males (N = 1099)	USA	72		
Mannheim and Rein (1981)	Random sample of employed males (N = 755)	Israel	85		
Warr (1982)	Random sample of employed males and females (N = 3355)	UK	Male 69 Female 65		
Williams (1983)	Telecommunication employees, 98% male (N = 944)	Australia	72		
Harpaz (1989)	Random sample of employed males and females (N = 8763)	7 countries:	*Total*	*Male*	*Female*
		Japan	93	95	91
		USA	88	90	86
		Israel	87	89	86
		Netherlands	86	87	86
		Belgium	84	87	79
		West Germany	70	75	62
		UK	69	66	71

Without evidence of this kind, it is not possible to be confident that the lottery question studies measure work meanings, commitment to work or adherence to a work ethic. It is still plausible to interpret the findings in other ways. One explanation is that responses simply reflect socially desirable norms. Most respondents might answer as they do because they think that this is what is expected of them in the context of societies that socialize members to train for and value work as a source of identity and a major form of social obligation. A somewhat related explanation is that socialization to work in industrial societies has shaped people to depend on social institutions, especially work organizations, for purpose and meaning in their lives (De Grazia, 1962). They have as a result no inner resources to find their own life meanings and would not seek a self-directed life without imposed structures that provide direction and a socially conferred identity.

Hence, to argue that the lottery question studies demonstrate that the majority of employees in industrialized societies demonstrate a high commitment to work because work satisfies many non-economic functions is not a satisfactory interpretation. The continuation of such studies will not substantiate this interpretation unless alternative explanations are tested. It is bad science not to evaluate competing hypotheses and the mechanical repetition of studies on the lottery question in the future would not appear to serve any good purpose. It is necessary to understand why employees respond as they do and the explanation must be complex enough to explain individual differences in responses owing to age, occupation, gender and culture.

Work as a central life interest

In an early article, Dubin (1956) maintained that work was not a central life interest for most industrial workers. He devised a scale to measure the relative meaning of work and non-work activities: the central life interest scale. Central life interest was operationally defined as an expressed preference for a given locale or situation in carrying out an activity. Each of the forty questions asked the respondents to indicate their preference for either a work activity or a non-work activity or a 'neutral' response. Neutral responses indicated indifference to the type of activity or no definite preference for work or non-work locations. The format is illustrated by the following question:

> I would most hate
> . . . . . missing a day's work
> . . . . . missing a meeting of an organization I belong to
> . . . . . missing almost anything I usually do.

The items sampled activities dealing with formal aspects of behaviour in organizations, the technological aspects of the environment, informal or inter-personal group activities and general everyday activities. Respondents as a rule were labelled job-oriented if they preferred the job-related option for a majority of items.

In 1956 Dubin reported that 24 per cent of North American workers were not job-oriented and inferred that these workers gained most of their life meaning in non-work roles. 'Industrial man seems to perceive his life history as having its center outside of work for his intimate human relationships and for his feelings of enjoyment, happiness, and worth' (Dubin, 1956, p. 140). However, in a subsequent review of central life interest studies it is clear that there is wide variability in the proportion of employees who are job-oriented. The proportions range between 12 and 85 per cent (Dubin, et al., 1976). Dubin and his co-workers concluded that work orientations were affected to a considerable extent by the nature of jobs and organizations. They did not, however, try to specify what dimensions of jobs or occupations induced either job or non-job orientations.

Dubin has made an original contribution in attempting to define and measure the relative importance of work and non-work roles to individuals. In addition, his work has led to studies that seemed to establish the meanings assigned to work by individuals with different life interests. However, it has not been established that work centrality is a stable disposition, nor has it been shown that the majority of employees in Western industrialized societies are not job-oriented. Results are inconsistent and suggest, as Dubin himself agrees, that job-orientation is a function of job, occupation, and work experience. The most reasonable interpretation is that work rather than non-work activities are preferred to the extent that the job allows personal choice, skill-use and the opportunity for self-expression. Furthermore, work orientations are not clearly related to attachments to the work environment. Non-job oriented employees are just as likely to appreciate autonomy and self-expression as job-oriented employees.

From the definition of job orientation it would be predicted that job-oriented employees would invest more effort in their work, be better qualified, and consequently achieve higher levels of job performance than non-job oriented employees. This hypothesis was not supported by Dubin and Champoux (1974). Job orientation did not predict the quality of performance of blue collar males or clerical females. Supervisors rated the job-oriented males as relatively high on initiative, application and co-operation, but relatively low on adaptability. If anything, this suggests that job-oriented employees are perceived as busy, friendly but rigid. This public façade, however, does not translate into high performance. Could not this façade be consistent with their questionnaire responses in that job-oriented employees, so designated, are those who say that they prefer work activities without meaning that work outcomes are really important to them?

The general problem of the relative importance of socialization or job experiences as determinants of work importance was addressed by Mannheim and Dubin (1986). They distinguished three related measures of work importance. First is the central life index which measures work importance of employees by examining their behavioural preferences. Second is job involvement (Lodahl and Kejner, 1965) which taps employee work motivation. The third measure is work role centrality which is designed to measure salience of work to personal identity. Mannheim and Dubin, in a study of Israeli employees, posed a key question by asking whether these three types of work importance were determined by family and educational socialization or whether they are affected by job experiences. Unfortunately, their design did not enable strong inferences to be made as it was a cross-sectional study. Ideally, work values should be measured repeatedly over time as individuals experience the changing influences of family, education and training. Then, as these individuals become employees and experience different kinds of task and organizational structures, further measures should be taken. The study also did not examine the association between the three measures of work importance, since only the work centrality measure (Mannheim, 1975) was used. Work centrality was higher for males than females, and higher for those with greater amounts of educational and technical education. Employees with high job satisfaction and in jobs with high task autonomy had higher work centrality scores than those with low autonomy jobs and low job satisfaction. The relationship between job satisfaction and work centrality was the same as that found in a previous cross-sectional study (Mannheim and Rein, 1981).

These results suggest that work importance is a response to both educational and job experience. More research of a longitudinal kind is necessary to strengthen causal generalizations. The only longitudinal study that appears to be available at present indicated that both job involvement and central life interest scores are sensitive to task experience (Lounsbury and Hoopes, 1986).

Meaning of work project

The largest study on the meaning of work was conducted by an international team of researchers who surveyed over 14,000 employees in eight countries from 1978–84 (MOW, 1987). The countries included Belgium, Israel, Japan, the Netherlands, the UK, USA, W. Germany and Yugoslavia. Apart from theoretical interest, the researchers saw the study of work meanings as a way of understanding applied problems of job mobility, turnover, productivity, and organizational design. They expected work meanings to be partly determined by individual factors, such as gender, age, education and personality. Work meanings were also expected to be a function of structural factors, such as technology, unemployment rates and culture.

The research is complex and difficult to summarize. The major results are presented in the 1987 volume but sub-analyses have also appeared elsewhere (England, 1988a, b; England and Quintanilla, 1989; de Keyser et al., 1988; Harpaz, 1985, 1986) and apparently will continue to be published. Information was obtained using cross-sectional interview surveys of target groups and national representative samples of employees. The target groups compared samples of unemployed, retired, chemical engineers, teachers, self-employed businesspeople, tool and die makers, white collar workers, textile workers, temporary workers, and students. All of the work meaning variables were measured through a variety of questions which were factor-analysed in order to describe the main components of work meanings.

Three main core concepts were defined: work centrality, work goals, and societal norms about working. These concepts were emphasized in the writings of England (1988a, b; England and Quintanilla, 1989) but other concepts were

Table 2.2 Work centrality scores across countries and
occupations: Range 2–10

Country (National samples N = 8749)		Occupations (Target samples N = 5895)	
Japan	7.78	Chemical engineers	7.54
Yugoslavia	7.30	Self-employed	7.45
Israel	7.10	Teachers	7.26
USA	6.94	Textile workers	7.07
Belgium	6.81	Tool/die makers	6.89
Netherlands	6.69	Unemployed	6.85
W. Germany	6.67	White collar	6.66
UK	6.36	Retired	6.63
		Students	6.48
		Temporary workers	6.22

Source: Adapted from MOW, 1987

measured and discussed in the major report (MOW, 1987). Work centrality was defined as the degree of importance that working has in the life of an individual. Operationally, it was measured by two items. One was a single item that simply asked the respondent to rate the importance of working in his or her total life on a Likert scale. The other item required the respondent to allocate 100 points between five life areas (leisure, community, work, religion, family) to indicate the relative importance in his or her life. The mean scores on work centrality across countries and occupations are shown in table 2.2. Work centrality correlated 'about' 0.20 with work involvement (measured by hours worked) and work commitment (measured by the lottery question).

Work goals were defined as the relative importance of eleven job attributes which individuals prefer or look for in their work life. The attributes ranked were: opportunity to learn, good interpersonal relations, opportunity for promotion, convenient work hours, variety, interesting work, job security, match between job requirements and ability, pay, good physical conditions, and autonomy. From factor analysis, two components were obtained. One was labelled *economic* goals, loading on extrinsic or instrumental items such as pay and job security. The other was labelled *expressive* goals and loaded highly on autonomy, interesting work, and good job–ability match. Each respondent was allocated two scores on work goals that reflected the extent to which they considered economic and expressive goals as important in their work. The third measure used to define meaning of work patterns was endorsement of societal norms about working. Two norms reflected both duties and rights. Agreement with the obligation norm was measured by answers to questions about whether people should contribute to society by working, should save money for the future, and should value working regardless of its nature. By contrast, agreement with an entitlement norm was assessed by responses to questions about whether individuals have the right to meaningful work, retraining when needed, and participation in work decisions.

Using a randomly selected sample from each country, eight clusters or patterns of work meaning were obtained (England, 1988a; England and Quintanilla, 1989). These eight patterns are depicted in table 2.3.

Each pattern is defined by the three dominant or extreme scores on the five variables. The first four patterns (A–D) describe employees with relatively low work centrality who neither see work as being important in their lives nor as being a source of personal fulfilment. The employees, especially for patterns C and D, have an instrumental orientation to work. The fifth pattern (E) seems to describe workers who are withdrawn. They are described as valuing neither economic nor expressive goals. The last three patterns (F–H) comprise workers who have high work centrality. They also tend to have relatively high expressive goals, seeing work as an important activity for self-expression, autonomy and skill-use.

None of these patterns is country-specific but there are considerable national differences in the distribution of patterns. Japan, for example, has a relatively high proportion of work-centred, expressive patterns while the USA and W. Germany have higher proportions of non-work centred instrumental patterns. Age, gender, education and occupation are also related to meaning of work patterns. Less educated males and females are more likely to endorse an instrumental, low work-centred pattern than are the more educated. Males tend to have higher centrality for work than females. Finally, expressive patterns are over-represented in occupations with high skill and status. Unfortunately, the relative importance of these variables as predictors of work meaning patterns is hard to ascertain because no multivariate analyses have yet appeared.

The implications of various work patterns for work and leisure behaviour is speculative, since no data were collected on objective work outcomes. England (1988a) does provide some evidence on the relation between desired work outcomes and work patterns. He considers that instrumental patterns (A, B and C) induce low outlays of work effort and this explains why employees reporting these patterns desire less in terms of job satisfaction and work quality. The high work centrality, expressive patterns (F, G and H), by contrast, invest more work effort and desire high levels of work quality and job satisfaction.

The meaning of work studies are impressive in their magnitude. Using large samples in different countries, they show that there is considerable complexity in employees' responses to questions about work importance, preference for economic or expressive work goals and sensitivity to societal norms about work as a duty and a right. The stability of the responses, however, has yet to be demonstrated because the studies are cross-sectional. Many of the co-authors do assume that the responses are stable and have implications for job design and acceptance by employees of new computer based systems of working. Admittedly, it is generally agreed that the meaning of work, as measured, is a function of a developmental process that is determined by education, personality, life-stage, and job experience (Quintanilla and Wilpert, 1988), but does this logically justify the view that work meanings are relatively stable and can be

Table 2.3 Patterns of work meanings

Meaning of work pattern	Work centrality	Components of work meanings				% of total sample
		Work goals		Societal norms		
		Economic	Expressive	Obligation	Entitlement	
A Non-work centred, non-economic, non-duty oriented.	Low	Low	—	Low	—	12.4
B Non-work centred, duty oriented.	Low	—	Low	High	—	19.4
C Economic.	—	High	Low	Low	—	13.0
D High rights and duty, economic.	—	High	—	High	High	8.4
E Low rights and duty, non-economic.	—	Low	—	Low	Low	5.4
F Moderate work-centred, non-economic, duty oriented.	High	Low	—	High	—	12.3
G Work centred, expressive.	High	Low	High	—	—	10.8
H Work centred, balanced work values.	High	High	High	—	—	18.4

Source: Adapted from England, 1988a; England and Quintanilla, 1989

considered components of 'work personality' (England and Quintanilla, 1989)? As argued in the review of studies on the lottery question, it is likely that work meanings reflect job experience. Employees with relatively empty, low quality jobs are not socialized towards expecting personal fulfilment in work and do not expect that work can be much more than a duty and a means of income. This does not necessarily mean that they would be unappreciative of jobs which allowed and required self-expression. Even the economic and instrumental employees want good quality jobs that provide skill-use and autonomy. Quintanilla (1988) reports that over 92 per cent of employees in the meaning of work studies would prefer jobs high on intrinsic aspects (autonomy, interesting work, skill-use). Fifty eight per cent would still prefer a job high on intrinsic attributes even if they were offered 50 per cent more pay to do a low quality job. Hence it would be a mistake to assume that work meanings have anything to do with work behaviour and work preferences. Further research might clarify these issues but, until it appears, the use of MOW data to allocate and select workers for different managerial and technological systems is not warranted and is potentially discriminatory. If economic, instrumental workers had the opportunity to experience intrinsic satisfactions as well as economic ones, they could, in a short period of time, experience their work as meaningful, important and valued because of its intrinsic attributes.

Work values

Apart from the meaning of work studies, there is a body of research that has endeavoured to use self-report scales to ascertain what employees want from their jobs, i.e., their work values. Work values refer to desired attributes of an employee's job system and range from general to specific. General values include Protestant work ethic (Hulin and Blood, 1968; Stone, 1975, 1976; Wanous, 1974), need strength (Hackman and Oldham, 1980; Porter, 1961, 1962) and instrumental or expressive work orientation (Goldthorpe et al., 1968; O'Reilly, 1977). Specific values are measured by asking employees the extent to which they want certain attributes, such as autonomy or skill-use, in their jobs (Baker and Hansen, 1975; Humphrys and O'Brien, 1986; O'Brien and Dowling, 1980; O'Brien and Humphrys, 1982; Wall and Lischeron, 1977; Wall and Payne, 1973).

Work values are generally considered as potential predictors of job satisfaction and performance. A simple congruency hypothesis is explicitly or implicitly espoused. If the job is meaningful, in the sense that it allows expression of values, then it is predicted that employees will be satisfied and productive. Conversely, jobs that are perceived as not being meaningful produce dissatisfaction and low productivity. Thus, job satisfaction and performance are considered to be negatively related to the degree of discrepancy between work values and the extent to which these values can be expressed in a given job. There is no evidence that work values affect performance either directly or through their interaction with job attributes. There is some evidence that job satisfaction is moderated by the need to express growth needs on the job as well as by the interaction between desired and actual job attributes. However, the magnitude of the effects are very small and by far the most important determinants of job satisfaction are actual job attributes: skill-utilization, influence and variety (O'Brien, 1986). As far as performance is concerned, work values may be considered indirect indices of work motivation, but performance of individuals and groups is only partly a matter of motivation. Performance is largely determined by ability and the situational structure which may or may not facilitate the use of abilities (O'Brien, 1984b). The weak result on the relation between work values and satisfaction has not been properly explained but it is possibly because of the employees not having insight into what really determines their satisfaction. Some support for this view comes from a study by Humphrys (1981) who asked employees to rate the value or importance that they placed on various intrinsic and extrinsic job attributes. He measured employees' job satisfaction and found that the actual predictors of job satisfaction did not resemble the valued factors. For example, skill-utilization was the major determinant of job satisfaction but most employees ranked this as relatively low in importance compared to pay, security and friendly co-workers. In summary, the work value studies show that there are considerable differences in general and specific work values among employees. Work values appear to be a product of both education (Dowling and O'Brien, 1981; Lindsay and Knox, 1984) and job experiences. High levels of education and of job skill induce intrinsic or expressive work values whereas poorly educated people and those in low skill jobs value extrinsic or instrumental values such as pay and security. However, there is practically no evidence to show that these value differences affect performance and satisfaction.

Explanations for Variation in Work Meanings

Research on the meaning of work has produced many studies which report that the large majority of employees view work as an important activity even if not a central life interest. There is consistent evidence that most would work even if there were no economic necessity. However, a significant number would prefer to continue working only if their jobs offered interesting work. This finding is sometimes interpreted as a reflection of individual differences in what employees want from work. Not all seem to want work that allows expression of personal needs for skill-use and autonomy. Many want work because it relieves boredom, structures time, and maintains social contacts. The most detailed exploration of individual differences in work meanings was made by the MOW researchers who identified patterns of work meanings on the basis of differences in work centrality, preference for economic or expressive goals, and variations in individual endorsement of social obligation norms. All of the work meaning studies combined show that people want to work but display considerable differences in the reasons that they report for the meaningfulness of their work. Unfortunately, the studies were not designed to explain these differences in work meaning. Certainly determinants of work meanings were suggested, such as education, personality, culture, age, gender and job history but the relative importance of these determinants was not examined. The research agenda was confined to showing the prevalence of work commitment and the varieties of work meanings that presumably need to be taken into account in understanding employee reactions to changing work environments. One explanation of differences in work meanings which appears central is in terms of job experience.

The central role of job experience

A considerable amount of evidence has shown that job content can affect work attitudes, cognitive functioning, work values and personality (Kohn and Schooler, 1983; O'Brien, 1986). Even taking a vacation from work can affect work values such as job involvement and work centrality (Lounsbury and Hoopes, 1986). Employees obviously vary in the type of jobs that they obtain. Professional and skilled workers experience jobs that are relatively high in skill-use, autonomy, variety and status. These factors lead to high job satisfaction, personal autonomy and relative freedom from psychological distress (stress, anxiety, depression). Thus, professional and skilled work, apart from its economic value, is likely to induce a positive valence for work in the future. In terms of learning theory, activities associated with positive reinforcements acquire positive valence. Hence employees in highly skilled jobs will report a desire for working because of its potential intrinsic satisfactions, even if economic rewards are not salient. By contrast, employees in relatively low skilled jobs have not experienced intrinsic satisfaction. Work has offered little more than income and a means of occupying time. Satisfaction may come from some non-economic factors such as friendship with co-workers or a feeling of social worth in being able to be a provider in the face of unpleasant tasks and lack of opportunities for craftsmanship. Hence work tasks, compared to work outcomes, have fairly low attractiveness and could be relinquished if economic security were guaranteed. Thus, the proportion of unskilled workers answering 'yes' to the lottery or inheritance question is lower than those from skilled jobs. Certainly a majority of unskilled workers say that they would keep working but this could be attributable to at least three reasons. First, they indicate that they would work at more interesting work. Second, having experienced relatively low incomes, they find it difficult to imagine a life where a comfortable income is guaranteed. Third, they had experienced a work life that did not induce a degree of self-directness which promoted confidence in their ability to use their free time in a way that could lead to a structured and meaningful life (Kohn and Schooler, 1983; O'Brien, 1986).

An explanation in terms of the effect of task structure on attitudes and intentions is not new. Among psychologists there is a peculiar reluctance to take it seriously. An exception is Lafitte (1958), in his little known but pioneering study of social structure and personality in the factory. He showed that factory workers found work satisfactory and meaningful to the extent that it provided adequate wages, good physical conditions and friendly co-workers and managers. The idea that work was meaningful because it provided opportunities for personal development through the provision of activities for learning, responsibility and personal control was entirely foreign. Work had never provided such opportunities, so their cognitive representation of work never included these intrinsic factors as potential dimensions which defined the meaning of work. That work could offer more than they had experienced was not countenanced because they believed that it was unrealistic to expect that they would have the power to change the nature of their jobs. To put it another way, they not only experienced personal deprivations in their work but also suffered as a consequence the 'deprivation of awareness' (Touraine, 1967).

Task experience can also explain why women employees are less likely than men to want to continue working when provided with financial security. The quality of women's work is generally lower than that of men's work and hence intrinsic satisfactions are lower and lead to relatively low work valence. Furthermore, although change may be taking place, most women employees have had two major work activities: paid employment and home-making. During the period of most studies in this area, the 1950s to the 1980s it is possible that most women worked to supplement family income and so work was not seen as a major source of personal fulfilment.

Jobs and psychological functioning

Another type of study which can support the thesis that work meanings reflect job experience comes from the research on the effects of jobs on personality functioning. Generally, these studies show that jobs which are low in complexity or which fail to use employee's skills not only produce dissatisfaction and stress but also induce intellectual inflexibility and a low sense of personal control. Consequently, employees so affected would not seek or desire work that requires challenge and self-direction.

The studies on direct and reciprocal effects between job content and personality have been reviewed elsewhere (O'Brien, 1986; Warr, 1987). They show that job content can significantly determine:

1 Intellectual style (Kohn and Schooler, 1973, 1978, 1981, 1982, 1983).
2 Depression (Brousseau, 1978; Brousseau and Prince, 1981).
3 Self-competence (Mortimer and Lorence, 1979).
4 Beliefs in internal and external control (Andrisani and Nestel, 1976; O'Brien, 1984a, 1984b).
5 Desires or needs for self-direction, learning and personal accomplishment (Kohn and Schooler, 1983; Orpen, 1979; Wall and Clegg, 1981).

Most of these studies were longitudinal rather than cross-sectional and thus provide strong support for causal inferences. Typically, the designs controlled for selection effects and also were able to show that job content rather than organizational structure was the major determinant of personal outcomes. The most extensive set of studies has been conducted by Kohn and his associates. Briefly, they found that bureaucratic, hierarchical work organizations produced a large proportion of jobs that were low on what they termed occupational self-direction. Occupational self-direction refers to the amount of personal direction that a job provides and is a function of substantive complexity, the closeness of supervision, and routinization. Jobs low on occupational direction produced job alienation as measured by distress (dissatisfaction, anxiety, depression), low personal self-direction and low intellectual flexibility. A summary of Kohn and Schooler's model is shown in figure 2.1.

Employees in jobs with high occupational self-direction maintained relatively high levels of personal self-direction and intellectual flexibility together with low levels of distress. The results are interpreted by a simple generalization explanation. Kohn and Schooler argue that employees are shaped by what they have to do. Thus, if jobs do not provide opportunities for self-direction and skill-use, then incumbents eventually do not seek complexity in either their work or non-work activities. They also come to prefer conformity to self-direction. Lacking personal autonomy, they also are prone to psychological distress without necessarily being aware of the relationship between their personal orientation and their degree of distress.

These processes are supposed to be similar across cultures. Kohn and Schooler would probably acknowledge that there are differences in work meanings and expectations across cultures, as shown by many studies (e.g. Hofstede, 1980; MOW, 1987). However, they would argue that such differences do not moderate the relationship between job experiences, cognitions and personality. There is considerable support for their argument, since their theory has been supported by replications in many cultures including the USA, Italy, Japan and Poland.

The general implication of such research is that job experiences shape employees' self-images and consequently their views of what they can do in their work and non-work environments. If they lack occupational self-direction, they may not see themselves as self-directed and they do not seek or desire work that requires self-direction, autonomy and skill-use. Such consequences also have implications, it seems, for job performance. Considerable research has shown that employees who do not believe in the efficacy of personal or internal control perform worse than those who believe that life, including work, affords them considerable opportunities for exercising initiative and effort in their pursuit of desired rewards (O'Brien, 1984a; Spector, 1982).

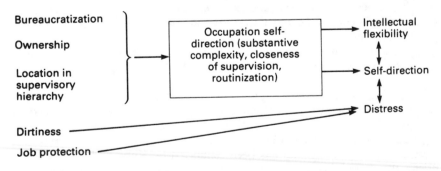

Figure 2.1 A schematic representation of Kohn and Schooler's theory about the effects of work on personality.

Conclusion

This brief review on the meaning of work has surveyed recent literature in the social sciences which is pertinent to an understanding of contemporary work meanings and how they may have changed during the last forty or fifty years. Despite limitations in quantity and methodology, there is increasing evidence that jobs are meaningful, in the sense that they shape job attitudes and relatively stable personality variables such as intellectual flexibility, self-direction, personal control, anxiety, and depression. There is reasonable evidence to support Kohn and Schooler's (1983) view that people become what they do. If a job is empty, it produces an 'unemployed self' (Gouldner, 1969). Personal identity is largely defined by an individual's capabilities and if these capabilities are thwarted by a job that does not foster or allow expression of such capabilities, then there are strong pressures on the employee to adapt to structural imperatives by altering his or her attitudes, values, and even personality. A fortunate few may alter or change their job but most have to adapt to jobs that were designed on principles not of personal fulfilment but rather of efficiency (Davis and Taylor, 1972). Work motivation theories which assume that job fulfilment is largely a matter of effort, ability and persistence also assume not only that life meaningfulness is what the individual makes of his or her opportunities but also that work organizations are flexible enough to allow 'the cream to rise to the top'. There is a value bias to this orientation which could reflect the cultural and occupational standing of North American academics but is hardly substantiated by evidence about the constraining pressures of class socialization and work structures.

Evidence based on self-report measures of the meaning of work showed that employees generally recognized that work was meaningful, not only in terms of its economic functions but also because it was capable of structuring time and of providing, for some, opportunities for social interaction, identity and challenge. The large majority of employees, consequently, would work even if their economic security were guaranteed. In the thirty or so years during which studies of this kind have been conducted, there have been no substantial changes in the proportion who would continue working even if wealth were assured. This finding, at first sight, seems inconsistent with the central life interest research which initially showed that work, for the majority of life employees, was not a central life interest. Even if this were so, it does not preclude the possibility that work is important to employees, although family and leisure might be more important. The meaning of work project identified many different meanings ascribed to work, which were defined by questions about work centrality, expressive and instrumental functions, and agreement with social norms about work. Similarly, there are wide differences in employee ascriptions of work values, either general or specific. It is difficult to interpret these differences in work meanings and values. Some writers (e.g. de Keyser et al., 1988) believe that they are important for understanding how various employees will adapt to new information technologies. Presumably jobs that are high in skill and autonomy are assumed to be suitable for employees with high work centrality and a high desire for expressive or intrinsic job attributes. A related assumption is that low skill, routine jobs are best suited to workers with low work centrality and instrumental values.

There are a number of difficulties with this. One is that there is little evidence that work meanings and values are related to work attitudes, such as job satisfaction and job performance. There is some evidence that work centrality is negatively related to organizational commitment (Dubin et al., 1975; Mowday et al., 1982), but organizational commitment, which is defined as the strength of an individual's identification with and involvement in an organization, has a very weak relationship to job performance. Of all of the work meanings and work outcomes mentioned in this chapter, the only concept to predict job performance is internal–external control or self-direction. Internally controlled employees perform better than those who are externally controlled.

If work meanings and values do not predict job behaviour, what do they really measure? The self-report measures do describe employees' views about their jobs in response to specific questions. These views are clearly related to their education, culture and job experiences. On the basis of the evidence, the most important determinant of work meanings is the nature of the job or jobs that employees have to do. If the job is of low quality, offering little more than tedious work and income, then this is what an occupant will see in the job. On the other hand, job incumbents will see work as an important source of intrinsic satisfaction as well as money if the job provides skill-utilization and autonomy. This is not a novel conclusion, although it is not endorsed strongly by most writers on the meaning of work. An exception already noted is Lafitte (1958), who was one of the first writers in industrial psychology to argue that work meanings should not be interpreted as personality variables but rather as cognitive adaptations to an imposed job structure.

Implications for job design and employment relations

These alternative explanations imply different underlying values. If one regards work meanings and work-determined personality as relatively fixed, then a conservative approach to job design is likely to be adopted. The problem of matching people to jobs will be largely a matter of selection for given jobs that are produced by current technologies. This is often associated with a recommendation that leisure be enriched for those with poor jobs or no jobs. A typical viewpoint is expressed by Strauss (1963). Noting that many employees do not seek self-expression in their work, he thinks that this may be fortunate, since there are relatively few jobs that allow self-expression.

> Should we say, 'Thank God for the number of people who have made an apparent adjustment to routine jobs. Would that there were more.'? Perhaps . . . it would be best to devote our resources to ever-shortening the work week and helping people to enjoy their leisure more fully.
>
> (Strauss, 1963, pp. 55–6)

An alternative strategy is to design jobs so that employees can enjoy their work, perform well and grow psychologically. In discussions of the new information technology, many writers sound a hopeful note that new job design practices will be used which accommodate human as well as efficiency needs (Gill, 1985; Joyce, 1987; Shepherdson, 1984; Wall and Martin, 1987; Wilson and Rutherford, 1987). Unfortunately, there is little evidence that humane methods of job design are being used. Information technology appears to provide enriched jobs for some but it is also apparent that many jobs are being de-skilled. The prospects for an enlightened approach to the problem of person–job match seems to be depressing. Radical applications of job enrichment are not likely to be made by managerial psychologists who accept work meanings and values as given and who seek to fit people into existing job slots. In a sense, to talk about cultural and societal work ethics and meanings is misleading. There is little evidence that there is, or has been, a work ethic (Rose, 1985). Instead, there is a set of expressed meanings which are largely determined by existing job experiences and which are mostly instrumental because current methods of job design are instrumental. As Fox maintains:

the existing design of work and work organizations rests on a given distribution of power in society, and that power superiority has lain, and still lies, with those whose interests or objectives led them to impose a wholly instrumental criterion.

(Fox, 1980, p. 191)

The obvious solution is that efforts should be made to correct the instrumental approach to job design. Collaboration between unions and management in this problem is essential but so far is not forthcoming, though there have been some attempts to include quality of worklife issues in union–management negotiation and consultation (Gill, 1985). Unions, for understandable reasons, have been somewhat tardy in endorsing job design interventions. First, there is their need to concentrate on basic questions of pay, security and physical working conditions. Second, there is a general suspicion that job redesign interventions, which are initiated by management with the help of industrial psychologists, are designed to manipulate employees without really changing jobs or the distribution of power (Greenberg and Glaser, 1981). This applies to employee participation schemes and semi-autonomous groups, as well as to job enrichment. The management bias of most social science interventions is well documented (Carey, 1977, 1980). A classic example is the use of research on employee–management consultation to justify worker participation schemes that inculcate management goals without providing better jobs or real power to employees over job procedures. The so-called classic paper by Coch and French (1948) is still the basis of many attempts to improve job quality, productivity, and employee/union–management relationships. This study has been criticized on many grounds but basically it describes a technique for management to change workers' attitudes without giving them influence or changing their jobs. Unions and employees are unlikely to drop their suspicion of such research until industrial psychologists take account of both union and management goals.

A third reason why unions have been reluctant to make job quality a major issue of negotiation with management is a lack of information about the effects of job experiences on work meanings, stress, personality and job performance. Social scientists have a responsibility to make this information available in an even-handed way. Good jobs – those that match employee capabilities to job requirements – benefit employee well-being as well as individual and group productivity. A final reason for union officials not being vocal about the need for job quality is the lack of employee demands for it. In terms of the explanation of work meanings, the quietude of many employees is understandable. Those who have meaningful jobs do not need to ask for job design. Those who have meaningless jobs do not expect change. Either they have no insight into the effects of jobs on them or their jobs have shaped them towards conformity and lack of self-direction. Thus, level of consciousness could be raised by information about the potential power of jobs to thwart their personal development but this is unlikely to be sufficient. Real change in their job conditions, which is initiated by informed unions and management, is the best way of changing instrumentally oriented workers towards an appreciation of the personal value of work that is both well paid and interesting.

In conclusion, this chapter has argued that there is no evidence to show that there have been changes during the last fifty years in the meaning of work. Certainly, from an historical viewpoint, work meanings have changed (Tilgher, 1930) but within modern industrial society there is no evidence of change. The available research has shown differences in work meanings that appear to be a product of job experiences. Just as educational experiences can shape job expectations (chapter 1), so can job experiences shape work meanings.

References

Andrisani, P. J. and Nestel, G. (1976) Internal–external control as a contributor and outcome of work experience. *Journal of Applied Psychology*, 76, 156–65.

Baker, S. H. and Hansen, R. (1975) Job design and worker satisfaction: A challenge to assumptions. *Journal of Occupational Psychology*, 48, 79–81.

Brousseau, K. R. (1978) Personality and job experience. *Organizational Behavior and Human Performance*, 22, 235–52.

Brousseau, K. R. and Prince, J. B. (1981) Job–person dynamics: An extension of longitudinal research. *Journal of Applied Psychology*, 66, 59–62.

Campbell, A., Converse, P. E. and Rodgers, W. L. (1976) *The Quality of American Life*. New York: Sage.

Carey, A. (1977) The Lysenko syndrome in Western social science. *Australian Psychologist*, 12, 27–38.

Carey, A. (1980) Social science, propaganda and democracy. In P. Boreham and G. Dow (eds), *Work and Inequality* (vol. 2), Melbourne: Macmillan, ch. 3, pp. 60–93.

Coch, L. and French, J. (1948) Overcoming resistance to change. *Human Relations*, 1, 512–32.

Davis, L. E. and Taylor, J. C. (1972) *Design of Jobs*. Harmondsworth: Penguin.

De Grazia, S. (1962) *Of Time, Work and Leisure*. New York: Doubleday.

de Keyser, V., Qvale, T., Wilpert, B. and Quintanilla, S. (1988) *The Meaning of Work and Technological Options*. Chichester: Wiley.

Dowling, P. and O'Brien, G. E. (1981) The effects of employment, unemployment and further education upon the work values of school leavers. *Australian Journal of Psychology*, 33, 185–95.

Dubin, R. (1956) Industrial workers' worlds: A study in the central life interests of industrial workers. *Social Problems*, 4, 131–42.

Dubin, R. and Champoux, J. E. (1974) Workers' central life interests and job performance. *Sociology of Work and Occupations*, 1, 313–26.

Dubin, R., Champoux, J. E. and Porter, L. W. (1975) Central life interests and organizational commitment of blue-collar and clerical workers. *Administrative Science Quarterly*, 20, 411–21.

Dubin, R., Hedley, R. A. and Taveggia, T. C. (1976) Attachment to work. In R. Dubin (ed.), *Handbook of Work, Organization, and Society*, Chicago: Rand McNally, ch. 7, 281–341.

England, G. W. (1988a) Patterning of work meanings in Japan, Germany and the USA. Paper prepared for the 1988 International Congress of Psychology, Sydney, Australia. September.

England, G. W. (1988b) The variety of work meanings: USA, Germany and Japan. In V. de Keyser et al. (eds), *The Meaning of Work and Technological Options*, Chichester: Wiley, ch. 4.

England, G. W. and Quintanilla, S. (1989) Effects on work meaning patterns in six countries. In B. J. Fallon, H. Pfister and J. Brebner (eds), *Advances in industrial organizational psychology*, Amsterdam: North Holland, 177–87.

Fox, A. (1980) The meaning of work. In G. Esland and G. Salamen (eds), *The Politics of Work and Occupations*, Milton Keynes: Open University Press, ch. 5, 139–91.

Gill, C. (1985) *Work, Unemployment and the New Technology*. Cambridge: Polity Press.

Goldthorpe, J. H., Lockwood, D., Beckhofer, F. and Platt, J. (1968) *The affluent worker: Industrial Attitudes and Behaviour*. Cambridge: Cambridge University Press.

Gouldner, A. (1969) The unemployed self. In R. Fraser (ed.), *Work: Twenty Personal Accounts*, vol. 2, Harmondsworth: Penguin, 346–65.

Greenberg, P. and Glaser, E. (1981) Viewpoints of labor leaders regarding quality of worklife improvement programs. *International Review of Applied Psychology*, 30, 157–75.

Hackman, J. R. and Oldham, G. R. (1980) *Work Redesign*. Reading, Mass: Addison-Wesley.

Harpaz, I. (1985) Meaning of working profiles of various occupational groups. *Journal of Vocational Behavior*, 26, 25–40.

Harpaz, I. (1986) The factorial structure of the meaning of work. *Human Relations*, 39, 595–614.

Harpaz, I. (1989) Non-financial employment commitment; a cross-national comparison. *Journal of Occupational Psychology*, 62, 147–50.

Hofstede, G. (1980) *Culture's Consequences: International Differences in Work-related Values*. Beverly Hills: Sage.

Hulin, C. L. and Blood, M. R. (1968) Job enlargement, individual differences, and worker responses. *Psychological Bulletin*, 69, 44–55.

Humphrys, P. (1981) The effect of importance upon the relation between perceived job attributes, desired job attributes and job satisfaction. *Australian Journal of Psychology*, 33, 121–33.

Humphrys, P. and O'Brien, G. E. (1986) The relationship between skill-utilization, professional orientation and job satisfaction for pharmacists. *Journal of Occupational Psychology*, 59, 315–26.

Joyce, P. (ed.) (1987) *The Historical Meanings of Work*. Cambridge: Cambridge University Press.

Kaplan, H. R. and Tausky, C. (1974) The meaning of work among the hard-core unemployed. *Pacific Sociological Review*, 17, 185–98.

Kohn, M. L. and Schooler, C. (1973) Occupational experience and psychological functioning: An assessment of reciprocal effects. *American Sociological Review*, 28, 97–118.

Kohn, M.L. and Schooler, C. (1978) The reciprocal effects of the substantive complexity of work and intellectual flexibility: A longitudinal assessment. *American Journal of Sociology*, 84, 24–52.

Kohn, M. L. and Schooler, C. (1981) Job conditions and intellectual flexibility: A longitudinal assessment of their reciprocal effects. In D. J. Jackson and E. F. Borgatta (eds), *Factor Analysis and Measurement in Sociological Research*, Beverly Hills: Sage, 281–313.

Kohn, M. L. and Schooler, C. (1982) Job conditions and personality: A longitudinal assessment of their reciprocal effects. *American Journal of Sociology*, 87, 1257–85.

Kohn, M. L. and Schooler, C. (1983) *Work and Personality: An Inquiry into the Effects of Social Stratification*. Norwood, NJ: Ablex.

Lafitte, P. (1958) *Social Structure and Personality in the Factory*. London: Routledge & Kegan Paul.

Lindsay, P. and Knox, W. E. (1984) Continuity and change in work values among young adults: A longitudinal study. *American Journal of Sociology*, 89, 918–31.

Lodahl, T. M. and Kejner, M. (1965) The definition and measurement of job involvement. *Journal of Applied Psychology*, 49, 24–33.

Lounsbury, J. W. and Hoopes, L. L. (1986) A vacation from work: Changes in work and nonwork outcomes. *Journal of Applied Psychology*, 71, 392–401.

Mannheim, B. (1975) A comparative study of work centrality, job rewards and satisfaction. *Sociology of Work and Occupations*, 2, 99–101.

Mannheim, B. and Dubin, R. (1986) Work role centrality of industrial workers as related to organizational conditions, task autonomy, managerial orientations and personal characteristics. *Journal of Occupational Behaviour*, 7, 107–24.

Mannheim, B. and Rein, J. (1981) Work centrality of different age groups and the wish to discontinue work. *International Journal of Aging and Human Development*, 13, 221–32.

Morse, N.C. and Weiss, R. (1955) The function and meaning of work and the job. *American Sociological Review*, 20, 191–8.

Mortimer, J. T. and Lorence, J. (1979) Work experience and occupational value socialization: A longitudinal study. *American Journal of Sociology*, 894, 1361–85.

MOW International Research Team (1987) *The Meaning of Working*. London: Academic Press.

Mowday, R. T., Porter, L. W. and Steers, R. M. (1982) *Employee–Organization Linkages: The Psychology of Commitment, Absenteeism and Turnover*. New York: Academic Press.

O'Brien, G. E. (1984a) Locus of control, work and retirement. In H. Lefcourt (ed.), *Research with the Locus of Control Construct* (vol. 3). New York: Academic Press.

O'Brien, G. E. (1984b) Group productivity. In M. Gruneberg and T. Wall (eds), *Social Psychology and Organizational Behaviour*, Chichester: Wiley, ch. 3, 37–70.

O'Brien, G. E. (1986) *Psychology of Work and Unemployment*. Chichester: Wiley.

O'Brien, G. E. and Dowling, P. (1980) The effects of congruency between perceived and desired job attributes upon job satisfaction. *Journal of Occupational Psychology*, 53, 121–30.

O'Brien, G. E. and Humphrys, P. (1982) The effects of congruency between work values and perceived job attributes upon the job satisfaction of pharmacists. *Australian Journal of Psychology*, 34, 91–101.

O'Reilly, C. A. (1977) Personality–job fit: Implications for individual attitudes and performance. *Organizational Behavior and Human Performance*, 18, 36–46.

Orpen, C. (1979) The effects of job enrichment on employee satisfaction, motivation, involvement, and performances: A field experiment. *Human Relations*, 32, 189–217.

Porter, L. W. (1961) A study of perceived need satisfaction in bottom and middle management jobs. *Journal of Applied Psychology*, 45, 1–10. Porter, L. W. (1962) Job attitudes in management: Perceived deficiencies in need fulfilment as a function of job level. *Journal of Applied Psychology*, 46, 375–84.

Quinn, R. P. and Staines, G. L. (1979) *The 1977 Quality of Employment Survey*. Ann Arbor: University of Michigan.

Quintanilla, S. (1988) Work values and new technologies. In V. de Keyser et al. (eds), *The Meaning of Work and Technological Options*, Chichester: Wiley, ch. 5.

Quintanilla, S. and Wilpert, B. (1988) The meaning of working: scientific status of a concept. In V. de Keyser et al. (eds), *The Meaning of Work and Technological Options*, Chichester: Wiley, ch. 1.

Rose, M. (1985) *Reworking the Work Ethic*. London: Batsford Academic.

Shepherdson, K. V. (1984) The meaning of work and employment: Psychological research and psychologist's values. *Australian Psychologist*, 19, 311–20.

Spector, P. (1982) Behavior in organizations as a function of employees' locus of control. *Psychological Bulletin* 91, 482–97.

Stone, E. F. (1975) Job scope, job satisfaction and the Protestant ethic. *Journal of Vocational Behavior*, 7, 215–24.

Stone, E. F. (1976) The moderating effect of work-related values on the job scope–job satisfaction relationships. *Organizational Behavior and Human Performance*, 15, 147–67.

Strauss, G. (1963) Some notes on power equalization. In H. J. Leavitt (ed.), *The Social Science of Organizations*. Englewood Cliffs, NJ: Prentice-Hall.

Tausky, C. (1969) Meanings of work among blue collar men. *Pacific Sociological Review*, 12, 49–55.

Tilgher, A. (1930) *Work: What it has Meant to Men through the Ages*. New York: Harcourt Brace.

Touraine, A. (1967) L'Aliénation de l'idéologie à l'analyse. *Sociologie du Travail*, 9, 192–201.

Vecchio, R. P. (1980) The function and meaning of work and the job: Morse and Weiss (1955) revisited. *Academy of Management Journal*, 23, 361–7.

Wall, T. D. and Clegg, C. W. (1981) A longitudinal field study of group work redesign. *Journal of Occupational Behavior*, 2, 31–49.

Wall, T. D. and Lischeron, T. A. (1977) *Worker Participation*. Maidenhead: McGraw-Hill.

Wall, T. D. and Martin, R. (1987) Job and work design. In C. Cooper and I. Robertson (eds), *International Review of Industrial and Organizational Psychology*, Chichester: Wiley, ch. 3, 61–91.

Wall, T. D. and Payne, R. (1973) Are deficiency scores deficient? *Journal of Applied Psychology*, 58, 322–26.

Wanous, J. P. (1974) Individual differences and reactions to job characteristics. *Journal of Applied Psychology*, 59, 616–22.

Warr, P. B. (1982) A national study of non-financial employment commitment. *Journal of Occupational Psychology*, 55, 297–312.

Warr, P. B. (1987) *Work, Unemployment, and Mental Health*. Oxford: Clarendon Press.
Williams, C. (1983) The 'work ethic', non-work and leisure in an age of automation. *Australian and New Zealand Journal of Sociology*, 19, 216–37.
Wilson, J. and Rutherford, A. (1987) Human interfaces with advanced manufacturing processes. In C. Cooper and I. Robertson (eds), *International Review of Industrial and Organizational Psychology*, Chichester: Wiley, ch. 4, 93–115.

Further reading

de Keyser, V., Qvale, T., Wilpert, B. and Quintanilla, S. (1988) *The Meaning of Work and Technological Options*. Chichester: Wiley. Various authors discuss work meanings and their implications for work design.
Fox, A. (1980) The meaning of work. In G. Esland and G. Salamen (eds), *The politics of work and occupations*. Milton Keynes: Open University Press, ch. 5, 139–91. An excellent and provocative review from a sociological perspective.
Morse, N. C. and Weiss, R. (1955) The function and meaning of work and the job. *American Sociological Review*, 20, 191–8. The original classic study that inspired most empirical research on the meaning of work.
MOW International Research Team (1987) *The meaning of working*. London: Academic Press. An account of the largest cross-cultural study on work meanings and their implications for job and organizational design.
Tilgher, A. (1930) *Work: What it has meant to men through the ages*. New York: Harcourt Brace. Somewhat dated but a thoughtful and readable discussion of the function of work from an historical perspective.
Warr, P. B. (1982) A national study of non-financial employment commitment. *Journal of Occupational Psychology*, 55, 297–312. A large study on work meanings in the UK.

3

Power

Paul S. Kirkbride

The Neglect of Power in Industrial Relations Theory

The importance of power in social life generally, and in the more discrete arena of employment relations, is difficult to over-emphasize. Power is inherently entwined in the very fabric of social interaction. As Giddens has argued, the 'study of power cannot be regarded as a second-order consideration in the social sciences. Power cannot be tacked on, as it were, after the more basic concepts of social science have been formulated. *There is no more elemental concept than that of power*' (1984, p. 283; emphasis added). The concept is also central to the field of employment relations. If, following Hartley and Stephenson (this volume, Introduction) and Hyman (1975), employment relations is seen as focusing on the processes of influence and control over work, then it can be easily observed that power is centrally implicated in these phenomena.

The notion of power is commonly used, almost unconsciously and in a 'taken-for-granted' fashion, by lay observers in order to elucidate episodes and events in employment relations. Indeed, for most lay observers, employment relations is characterized by conflict, in the form of collective industrial action by employees and resistance by employers, and by the utilization of power resources by both parties in order to 'win' such confrontations. This 'taken-for-granted' utilization of power as an explanatory variable is mirrored in the theoretical literature of employment relations, where even a cursory examination reveals the importance of power as a conceptual support to theoretical development and explanation. In the systems theory of Dunlop (1958), power is seen as a major component of the environmental context faced by the actors in the employment relations system. He notes that the 'actors . . . are regarded as confronting an environmental context at any one time. The environment is comprised of three interrelated contexts: the technology, the market or budgetary constraints and the *power relations and status of the actors*' (pp. vii–ix; emphasis added).

The author would like to thank Jim Durcan, Sara Tang, Steve Walters, and the Editors for their respective contributions to this chapter while retaining sole responsibility for the final version.

Allan Flanders, from the related theoretical perspective of Oxford liberal-pluralism, has argued that employment relations is essentially a rule-making process in which the driving forces and outcome determinants are both economic and political. Thus, the process of joint regulation is seen as 'primarily a political institution' in which 'the parties have many other considerations in mind apart from the conflicting interests of their constituents as buyers and sellers of labour' (Flanders, 1970, p. 226). In more general and less institutional terms, the pluralist framework regards organizations as comprising a variety of stakeholders drawing their differential power from a variety of sources and thus conceptualizing power as the medium through which divergences of objectives and interests are mediated and resolved (Mintzberg, 1983).

Similarly, the 'action theory' of employment relations (Schienstock, 1981) also adopts power as a fundamental element. The interests of such theorists in the processes of exchange and interaction inevitably lead to a consideration of bargaining and bargaining power and to the suggestion that employment relations should be viewed as an exchange conditioned by relative bargaining power (Somers, 1969). Finally, it can be clearly seen that the concept of power is intrinsically embedded in Marxist theories of the employment relationship. Employment relations from this perspective is viewed as an antagonistic market or exchange relationship characterized by an asymmetry of power resources (Hyman, 1975).

Yet, despite this almost unanimous acceptance of power as a fundamental underpinning element, it is possible to argue that the concept remains relatively undeveloped in the employment relations field. For example, Dunlop makes no attempt to define power, merely noting that the 'relative distribution of power among the actors in the larger society tends to a degree to be reflected within the industrial-relations system' and arguing that his concern 'is not with the distribution of power within the industrial-relations system, the relative bargaining powers among the actors, or their controls over the processes of interaction or rule setting. Rather the reference is to the distribution of power outside the industrial-relations system which is given to that system' (1958, pp. 11–12). Thus, a major explanatory variable is perfunctorily neglected and a detailed exposition of the processes of power in employment relations is rejected in favour of a form of environmental determinism. Flanders, despite his focus on the political nature of the joint regulation process, fails to explain the nature of power or to address it directly, preferring, it seems, to use it as an unarticulated common-sense term. The nature of power is perhaps most fully developed in the Marxist perspective (Hyman, 1975), although even here the concept remains relatively neglected and only partially explained.

Hyman sees an increasing power struggle over control as a central feature of industrial relations and defines power as the 'ability of an individual or group to control his (their) physical and social environment' and, as a sub-process, the 'ability to influence the decisions which are and are not taken by others' (1975, p. 26). Hyman also acknowledges that the control of ideological as well as material resources can be a form of power, arguing that the 'ability to overcome opposition is one sign of power; but a more subtle yet perhaps even more significant form of power is the ability to preclude opposition from even arising simply because, for example, those subject to a particular form of control do not question its legitimacy or can see no alternative' (1975, p. 26). While Hyman identifies the importance of both material and linguistic resources and the key question of ideological hegemony, he is unable to explore them in any detail or to demonstrate how such resources are utilized at a micro level.

Given the relative neglect of power by industrial relations theorists and yet the centrality of the concept to our understanding of employment relations, we need to look outside the narrow confines of the employment relations literature in order to obtain greater knowledge of power and power processes. In particular we shall draw upon the disciplines of sociology and psychology for illumination.

The Nature of Power: Central Issues

The one-dimensional view of power

Power is often simply regarded as the ability to attain one's objectives by forcing others to accede and/or the ability to get someone to do something that they would not otherwise have done. Thus, the seminal sociological definition by Weber suggests that power is 'the probability that one actor in a social relationship will be in a position to carry out his own will despite resistance, regardless of the basis on which this probability rests' (1947, p. 139). In a similar vein, but from a different perspective, Dahl has suggested that 'A has power over B to the extent that he can get B to do something that B would not otherwise do' (1947, pp. 202–3). In this view it is assumed that a conflict, in terms of objectives and preferences, exists between the parties and the stress is clearly upon concrete, observable behaviour. The parties will attempt to achieve their objectives and to affect outcomes in the decision-making arena by the use of power strategies based upon the resources that they possess. Thus, the relative power of the parties can be measured by the extent to which they can 'win' issues and influence decisions. This view has been termed the 'one-dimensional' view of power (Lukes, 1974).

Employment relations contains a set of identifiable actors (employers, managers, employees, unions/associations, and the state) who seek to influence a set of decisions or issues. We also have a situation where conflicts of interest are likely between these 'stakeholders'. Each actor will thus attempt to mobilize resources to affect decisions in her/his favour. A review of outcomes will then provide a picture of the relative power balance and dynamics in the employment relationship.

For example, economists often seek to observe power indirectly in the employment relationship via the effect that it has on the outcome of the bargaining process. These effects are usually measured objectively in terms of wage rate differentials which are seen to reflect, at least in part, differences in bargaining power between workgroups, unions, or industries (Mishel, 1986). On the macro level, the overall power of trade unions (*vis-à-vis* employers) is often measured in terms of changes in relative wages between unionized and non-unionized labour and changes in labour's share of the national income (Lewis, 1963). In all of these approaches, power is inferred from changes in related phenomena rather than being directly observed. Thus, power is often replaced by 'proxy' variables, such as rate of change of union density, trade union 'pushfulness', and strike activity.

An excellent example of detailed industrial relations research into power from this perspective is provided by Edwards (1978, 1983) in her work on relative union power in the coal mining industry in the UK. In her first study she decided to adopt the one-dimensional 'objective of measuring power in respect to particular decision outcomes' (1978, p. 1) via two power measures. The first, *bargaining power*, was 'measured by reference to the ability of the colliery manager or NUM representatives to get their own way in cases of decisions where the objectives of the two sides are in conflict' (p. 3). The second, *control*, was 'based upon the manager's and NUM representatives' ability to get their own way in the decision process regardless of whether the decisions were the subject of conflict' (p. 3). These measures were then used to analyse data from two collieries. The bargaining power measure revealed that management had greater bargaining power than the union at both collieries, notwithstanding the fact that in one colliery the union was more powerful than in the other. The control measure revealed the ability of management to decide or control most issues in both collieries.

In a later study, Edwards (1983) re-focused on the concept of control which was again measured in two ways: first, by the parties' records of the outcomes of actual cases of decision-making (an 'issue' approach) and, second, by the respective parties' perceptions of their levels of control (a modified 'reputational' approach). These measures were then operationalized in eight collieries and the results compared. The first outcome measure revealed that management held the prerogative to make almost all decisions and that the greatest union incursions occurred in the cases of issues where national agreements gave a right of consultation. The second perceptual measure also revealed extensive managerial control, with union control 'largely confined to the relatively minor areas of colliery activity' (1983, p. 60).

Whilst the one-dimensional approach is easy to operationalize, it is not without its problems. To the extent that it identifies the 'winners' of contested decisions, it enables observers to determine the 'most powerful' actor in a situation. However, this perspective ignores the fact that the 'losing' party may actually possess a substantial amount of power and thus does not discriminate between an issue where one party only just manages to 'win' and an issue where one party 'wins' easily. Our argument is analogous to the result of a football match where a scoreline of 2–1 could equally reflect a lucky victory or flatter the defeated team. In order to address this deficiency we should have to focus more directly on the resource possession which facilitated the 'winning' of decisions and on the processes by which the 'win' was achieved. The one-dimensional focus on identifiable decisions and visible decision-makers also ignores the fact that some decisions may be withheld from the bargaining and decision-making arena and that the 'real' decision-makers may be concealed from public view.

The two-dimensional view of power

This critique has become known as the 'two-dimensional' view of power (Lukes, 1974). Power is, of course, exercised in the making of decisions but it is also exercised when one social actor is able to control the decision agenda and thus prevent other actors from raising potentially threatening issues (Bachrach and Baratz, 1962). This result is achieved via the 'mobilization of bias' which refers to the set of values, beliefs, and institutional procedures and practices which operate to the benefit of certain individuals or groups and to the detriment of others. Thus, power is also present in the processes of 'nondecision-making' where demands for change to the *status quo* are suffocated before they can be voiced; or suppressed before they can reach the decision-making arena; or, in the last resort, distorted or destroyed in the process of implementation. For example, if the management of a company are able to keep issues such as new product development, introduction of new technology, and manufacturing deployment out of the joint decision-making arena, and thus non-negotiable, then employees and their representatives are left responding only when and where the employment effects become clearly visible.

In employment relations, management are able to 'mobilize bias' as a result of their superior economic resources and ability to control unilaterally procedures and channels of communication. It is therefore not surprising that the one-dimensional focus on observable decisions often 'presents a biased picture of workplace industrial relations by over-estimating the power of employees and their representatives and by under-estimating that of management' (Edwards, 1983, p. 68). Hence the use by Edwards in her later work (1983, 1987) of perceptual measures which 'provide a much more accurate description of workplace power . . . because they cover at least some of the unobservable processes through which outcomes are determined in the workplace' (1983, p. 66). In the case of her own empirical work, Edwards is arguing that the observable one-dimensional methods revealed managerial superiority in bargaining power but that the 'real' situation, as revealed by perceptual measures, was one of even greater managerial dominance.

The three-dimensional view of power

The two-dimensional perspective, although a distinct improvement over the one-dimensional view, still assumes the existence of an observable conflict in that non-decisions are, in effect, decisions. This focus ignores the fact that power might involve the obfuscation of 'real' conflicts by the propagation of a 'false' consensus. As Lukes has argued, A may exercise power over B 'by influencing, shaping, or determining his very wants' (1974, p. 23) and, as we have already seen, this conception of power has been adopted by Hyman (1975) in his exposition of Marxist industrial relations. The three-dimensional approach draws attention to the possibility that one actor (probably management) may exercise ideological, as well as economic, control. One can thus envisage a situation of hegemony where workers unwittingly accept managerial definitions of reality and thus obviate the need for more visible means of control and naked power utilization. How is this hegemony created? Some see management pursuing strategies of 'responsible autonomy' whereby managerial authority is maintained and increased by inculcating certain managerial values (such as competitiveness, efficiency, or other organizational goals) into the workforce, so that employees begin to act 'responsibly' in an internalized manner without the need for external 'direct control' (Friedman, 1977; see also Chapter 4). Hardy (1985) identifies a variety of means of 'unobtrusive power', including the manipulation by management of symbols, language, myths, rituals and ceremonies. One can therefore easily see the current managerial interest in the engineering of corporate cultures as the result of a desire for more subtle, and yet penetrating, control mechanisms.

One micro-level example of a managerial attempt to create such hegemony can be taken from the author's own empirical research in an engineering company (Kirkbride, 1986a, 1986b). During negotiations with worker representatives and during consultative committee meetings, the Personnel Director continually repeated that there could be 'no negotiation under duress'. He thus constantly argued that his management team (or indeed any management) would never continue negotiations while the workforce were engaged in any form of sanctions or industrial action. Over time he managed to convince worker representatives of the 'truth' of this assertion, to the extent that his statements were never challenged. In addition, the use of such sanctions was considered and rejected by worker representatives based on his principle, despite the obvious falsity of his argument which could easily be contradicted by reference to the use of sanctions by employees in other organizations, which cases are reported widely in the media.

Sources of power

Implicit in the views of power presented above is the notion of resource possession and utilization. Outcomes are determined by the mobilization of resources controlled by the respective parties. Thus, the actor with the most resources is potentially the most powerful and so actors can attempt to increase their power by acquiring resources. The classic approach to sources of power, and thus a resource approach, is that of French and Raven (1968) who identify five common bases of power: reward power (based on the ability to confer or withhold rewards); coercive power (based on the ability to use physical sanctions); legitimate power (based upon the right to issue orders and be obeyed as a result of organizational rank); referent power (based on force of individual personality or charisma); and expert power (based on possession of knowledge and skills).[1] In the employment relations context, management can be seen to rely principally on legitimate power, via their 'managerial prerogative', and on reward power, via pecuniary incentives for desired behaviour. On occasion, employees may defer to management owing to their perceived superior knowledge and skills or because of the reference power of individual 'excellent' managers. Employee power, from this framework, can be seen to stem largely from the ability to coerce management via collective organization and, in certain cases, from the possession of key production or technological skills.

One can distinguish two variants of the resources perspective (Bacharach and Lawler, 1981). The first is the 'sanction' or 'costs' approach which argues that power resides in the ability to 'punish' or 'sanction' the other party. For example, it may be suggested that the basis of trade union power lies largely in the ability to inflict costs on employers, via strikes, slowdowns, or boycotts, or to threaten to do so (Rees, 1977). In order to be able to do this, certain conditions must exist and thus unions are likely to be more powerful in situations of high union density, efficient union organization, low union fragmentation, and high bargaining centralization (Craypo, 1986; Mishel, 1986). Levinson (1966) has developed a model of relative bargaining power which weighs the relative costs of agreeing or disagreeing with the opponent's position and terms for settlement. Thus, the bargaining power of A is high if the costs to B of disagreement with A's terms greatly outweigh the costs to B of agreement. Similarly, the power of B is a function of the relative costs to A of disagreeing or agreeing with B's terms. An obvious difficulty with the operationalization of this perspective is the fact that perceptions of costs are subjective.

This focus on the relative power of the parties naturally leads us towards the second major variant of the resource perspective; the 'dependence' or 'exchange' approach (Emerson, 1962). Here power is viewed as the property of a social relationship and the focus is thus on the mutual dependence of the parties. Absolute power is seen to reside in the dependence of the other and relative power in the relative dependency of each party. This basic approach was developed in the case of organizational sub-unit power by the 'strategic contingencies' perspective (Hickson et al., 1971). Here power is seen as a function of the ability of a sub-unit to increase dependence by coping with organizational uncertainty; by decreasing one's substitutability in the organization; by increasing one's centrality in the workflow and organizational structure (pervasiveness); and by increasing the immediacy or speed with which organizational processes can be halted or affected. In a similar vein, Astley and Sachdeva (1984) have highlighted the importance of network centrality in the generation of intra-organizational power by noting that actors located at tightly coupled, interconnected nodes in the organizational network have greater power because their immersion in multiple interdependencies makes them functionally indispensable. Of course one can separate network location from associated resource control. As Cook has noted, 'power derives not only from resource dependencies within specific exchange relations, but also has a structural component, namely the position or location of an actor within the exchange network' (1977, p. 72).

The strategic contingencies model has been usefully applied to the employment relations arena by Marchington (1975), who suggests that two crucial factors determine relative workgroup power. The first, *disruption* (workflow pervasiveness and immediacy), refers to the ability of a workgroup to halt production and is a measure of short-term power capacity. The second, *replaceability* (substitutability and coping with uncertainty), refers to the ability of a workgroup to increase indispensability and is a measure of long-term power capacity. This model can be applied, via the use of simple operational indices, to generate a

league table where workgroups are ranked according to the dependence on them of other parties. While this approach succeeds in mapping out structural relationships and positions, it tends to ignore the origins of such structures. Workgroups have power because of their structural position but how they come to occupy this position is not explained. This deficiency is particularly serious if we apply the analysis to management. Obviously management gain power from their resource possession and structural position but their ability to acquire resources and to maintain this structure, via their power to set the 'rules of the game', also needs to be explored.

It may be argued, however, that the key variable in a power relationship is not the possession of resources by one party but the perception of these resources by the other. Thus, an essential part of the negotiation process involves attempting to inflate artificially in the minds of one's opponents the resources under one's control and the costs of disagreement. Taking this argument further, one could replace the focus on resource bases with a focus on 'motive bases' or the reasons for compliance (Etzioni, 1961). As Astley and Sachdeva argue, 'subordinates obey superiors not so much because they are dependent on the latter, but because they believe that the latter have a right to exercise power by virtue of their position' (1984, pp. 105–6). These concerns would, as we shall see later, naturally lead towards an examination of the use of ideological resources by management in order to secure employee compliance.

Levels of power

A central dichotomy which emerges from the vast power literature, mirroring a more general divergence in psychological and sociological theory, is that between action and structure. Some theorists see power as the capacity or potentiality of an actor to achieve desired goals and outcomes, while others see power as in some way embedded in social structures and institutions. The employment relations literature also reflects this duality with the outcome approach operating on the action level and the resource perspective located at the structural level. Recently, however, attempts have been made to achieve a theoretical synthesis between these seemingly contradictory perspectives (Giddens, 1976, 1979).

Giddens' 'structuration' theory argues that social life exists on a series of three analytically separate levels; namely, action, mediation, and structure. On the surface level of action are the physical and verbal 'acts' of individuals while at the deeper level of structure are the patterns of social activity and regularities of elements in social life. These are not seen as mutually exclusive domains but as linked via the level of mediation. This represents the ways in which action draws upon and reproduces structures and the ways in which structure constrains action and, yet, is modified by it.

Power, as an 'elemental concept', is present on all levels but exists in different forms. On the surface level one can refer to 'transformative capacity' or the 'capability of an actor to intervene in a series of events so as to alter their course' (Giddens, 1976, p. 111). Such transformative capacity obviously draws upon resources for its accomplishment. Yet such resources are not freely available and their distribution is instead determined by structures of economic and political domination. This structural imperative obviously places limits on the transformational 'acts' that can occur, while at the same time such 'acts' reinforce and reproduce that very structure. Transformational 'acts' are facilitated by resource possession while, simultaneously, differential resource access reproduces the structure of domination. Resources are the mechanism which mediates between the levels of action and structure and are thus the means through which power is exercised and by which structures of domination are reproduced. In employment relations we can suggest, for example, that the transformative capacity of management is a function of access to resource bases, such as authority, expert power, and remunerative power, and that access to such resources is a reflection of the general economic domination of management. This asymmetry of resources places limits on the ability of the employees to exercise power and to achieve desired outcomes.

Power is also related to another 'elemental concept', that of meaning. Power resides in the ability to impose one's own definitions of the situation or meanings and this is usually achieved via the communication process. Also, in order to exercise power, one may have to communicate one's objectives, demands and intentions to the other party. Thus, transformative capacity can be accomplished via rhetoric, which can be defined as 'the use of a "form of word-delivery" which is lavish in symbolism and, as such, involves several layers of meaning' (Gowler and Legge, 1983, p. 198). Rhetoric can be seen as drawing upon deeper 'legitimizing principles' or 'acceptable motives for action' (Armstrong et al., 1981, p. 36), which are held by the actor (or actors) and which, in turn, are drawn from a particular world view or ideology. Thus, management may unilaterally issue certain edicts which reflect certain acceptable motives or principles (such as 'the right to manage' or 'efficiency') which are themselves drawn from a wider 'managerial ideology'.

Power in the Employment Relationship

After this brief and inevitably partial review of the central features of the power literature, we can now proceed to sketch an outline model of power in the employment relationship (figure 3.1) which will explicitly address two of the central weaknesses that arise from the existing theoretical focuses on resource and outcome power. These are the processes of resource mobilization on the one hand and the origins and prior distribution of such resources on the other. The first concerns the level of action while the latter concerns questions of domination.

Action and rhetoric

How are resources mobilized in order to influence decisions and thus the creation of rules? If resources are to be used to persuade the other party, then they have to be revealed and displayed. One's opponent needs to be aware of the potential

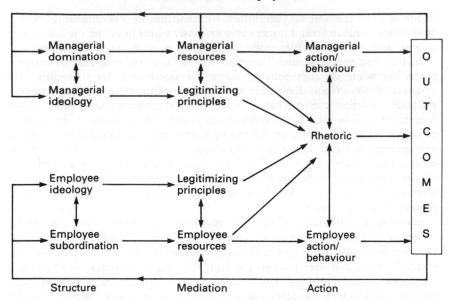

Figure 3.1 Power in the employment relationship

costs of resisting one's demands. In situations of large resource disparity, the communication of this fact is often sufficient to ensure compliance by the weaker party. However, in situations of greater resource equality, or situations where there is a lack of accurate knowledge about relative resource possession, resources may have to be mobilized in order to affect outcomes via the ability to inflict costs.

For example, a major resource to a trade union during a wage negotiation may be the density of union membership in the organization or plant. During the negotiations, union representatives may take the opportunity to remind management of this fact, with the clear implication that the union would be able to count on overwhelming support in the case of strike action. This may be ignored by the management side who believe that, union density notwithstanding, the overall resource balance is still in its favour. At this stage, the union may have to resort to action of some sort to reinforce its demands.

Outcomes can be affected by either 'industrial action' or by the use of rhetoric and argument. Industrial action can be taken by either side, employers or employees, and would typically include such phenomena as strikes, slowdowns, restriction of output, and sabotage by employees, or suspensions, dismissals, and lockouts by employers. At a less extreme level it could also refer to unilateral managerial decision-making (drawing upon managerial authority) or the ignoring of a managerial rule by a workgroup (drawing upon their powerful central position in the workflow).

Action here also refers to 'inaction' and thus encompasses the processes of nondecision-making. It should also be noted that such action is often directed at improving resource possession rather than at affecting outcomes. Thus, a workgroup may take action to decrease its substitutability in order to increase its power position prior to an attempt to affect the outcome of a crucial 'issue'.

In the majority of instances in employment relations, however, no action is taken by the parties and instead rhetoric, or the 'tactical action' dimension of power (Bacharach and Lawler, 1981), is employed. Rhetoric serves several purposes. It represents both the articulation of 'legitimizing principles' or 'vocabularies of motive' and the signalling of the possession and threatened use of resources. It is also used to exaggerate or inflate one's own resource position and thus to change the opponent's perception of the power balance. In addition, it may be suggested that rhetoric can be used as a form of power, in and for itself, divorced from the structural asymmetry of resources. During the 1990 ambulance workers' dispute, many commentators recognized the rhetorical skills of Roger Poole, the chief union negotiator, and his calm and reasoned presentation of the case, as a key resource and power factor for the union side.

Several writers have noted the importance of organizational 'talk' as a form of power. Gronn (1983, 1984) discusses the 'administrative power' of committee talk while Czarniawska-Joerges and Joerges identify the importance of 'organizational talk' which is seen as 'both the use of verbal symbols in an attempt to structure meaning and . . . actions based on this meaning' (1988, p. 171). They demonstrate how different linguistic devices (such as labels, metaphors, and platitudes) are used as unobtrusive forms of organizational control, via a labelling process, and suggest that these 'linguistic artifacts enable [management] to manage meaning by explaining, coloring, and familiarizing, as opposed to the traditional control methods of commanding, fighting, and punishing' (1988, p. 188). This view is echoed by Gowler and Legge (1983) who argue that management often seek to create and legitimize managerial prerogative by use of a symbolic and expressive language in a process which they term the 'rhetoric of bureaucratic control'. This process, via the management of meaning, 'contributes to management as a political activity concerned with the creation, maintenance, and manipulation of power and exchange relations in formal work organizations' (p. 198). As an example of the manipulation of meaning in employment relations, one could perhaps cite the 'respect for the individual' themes contained in many corporate mission and culture statements (e.g. Hewlett-Packard, IBM) which often serve to reinforce, and yet cloak, an 'anti-union' philosophy and policy.

Of course, the use of rhetoric is open to both parties in the employment relationship. Even in situations of resource imbalance, the weaker party possesses a certain amount of power, and one of the forms that this can take is the skilled use of rhetoric and argument. In order to illustrate this point we can consider a further example from the author's own empirical research work (Kirkbride, 1988a, 1988b). Bettavalve Placid Limited (pseudonym) is the fluid engineering division of a wider engineering group. At the time of the research study, Bettavalve Placid did not recognize any trade unions and operated a managerially structured Works Committee system of joint consultation. In addition to regular meetings of this Committee, 'negotiations' also took place separately between management and senior employee representatives over major issues regarding terms and conditions of employment. Despite the deliberate attempts to create the illusions of 'power parity' and 'joint regulation', it was clear that management were the stronger party. In such a situation it is therefore unsurprising that the management side succeeded in 'winning' virtually all of the important issues which arose during the two years of the study. Yet, despite the workers' resource power disadvantage, there were occasions when their side could have utilized powerful legitimizing arguments and skilled rhetoric to achieve favourable outcomes.

One such case involved the rescinding, at the orders of Group Headquarters, of a traditionally enjoyed extra day's holiday above the national engineering agreement entitlement. Bettavalve Placid management were generally against the Headquarters decision but felt forced to attempt to implement it. During the negotiations, management felt unable to construct any valid legitimizing arguments and quickly fell back on the simple assertion of managerial prerogative and the fact that, even with the loss of the 'extra day', they were still complying with the terms of the national agreement. In contrast, the workers' side tentatively developed a full repertoire of arguments and principles, including 'consistency', 'precedent', 'fairness', and 'equity'. Yet, despite their 'superiority' in terms of arguments, the workers' side failed to retain the extra day of holiday even though management were actually willing to concede and to refer the issue back to Group Headquarters if faced with sufficient opposition.

One could simply explain this result by reference to the structure of domination and resource inequality within Bettavalve Placid but this would ignore the subtle dynamics of micro-level power processes, as domination has to be continually reinforced and reproduced. In fact, on the level of discourse, there were several factors which prevented the workers' side from pressing home their potential advantage in terms of legitimizing principles. First, lack of negotiating discipline and confusion on the workers' side led to a dissipation of the arguments and so their full force was reduced. Second, management were able to take advantage of these negotiating weaknesses by deliberately compounding confusions and slanting the discussions away from the central issue. Third, the workers' side failed to use all of the potential power available to them. For example, no reference was made to the fact that the erosion of a positive differential, which originally was probably intended to discourage unionization, might now lead to increased union recruitment and penetration into the company. Finally, the actual language used by the union negotiators may be said to have continually signalled their subconscious acceptance of the managerial prerogative. Instead of referring to the *taking away* of a *right* or *entitlement*, they constantly referred to the fact that management had *not granted* the *privilege* of an *extra* day of holiday which was a *benefit* which workers had traditionally *enjoyed*. Thus, the fact that the workers' side were unable to achieve even this minor victory can be partly explained by their lower levels of formal education and comparative lack of sophisticated negotiation training. As access to such training and general education can be said to be differential, then one can argue that structural societal resource inequities are reproduced at the level of language.

Material and linguistic resources

The mediation level of the model deals with resources. In rather an artificial fashion, we can separate resources into two forms: physical or material, and linguistic. As we have already considered the material sources of power in an earlier section, we can now turn our attention to the latter. Armstrong et al. (1981) have suggested that in 'any cultural setting there are certain acceptable motives for action [what we will call 'legitimising principles'] which are, in turn, embedded in the characteristic world view (ideology) of that culture' (1981, p. 36). Thus, in order to affect outcomes, the representatives of the parties (management and employees) must identify, and then articulate, acceptable motives which are drawn from a wider ideology. The ideologies of each group provide a bounded repertoire of such principles which can be articulated in appropriate situations. Management can rely on a series of such legitimizing arguments, including their 'legal right' to manage and their right to issue 'reasonable orders', and more general principles such as 'competitive pressures' and the need for 'efficiency' and 'profitability'.

Because managerial ideology is generally dominant, workers are usually reduced to using management's own principles and arguments against them (Kirkbride, 1988b) or appealing to what Armstrong et al. have termed 'consensual principles of justification' (1981, p. 95). These include appeals to consistency of treatment or rule application, earlier precedents, fairness of treatment, natural justice, and ethical standards of behaviour. In addition there are, on occasions, 'accepted principles of justification which do not derive from the dominant ideology nor are centered on relatively independent norms and expectations of general application' (1981, p. 112). These 'resistance principles' actually seek to confront and challenge directly managerial authority and are drawn from the more radical elements of worker ideology. Examples would include craft autonomy, property rights in jobs, and the right to participate in key managerial decisions.

Domination, hegemony, and disciplinary power

The second major weakness of existing conceptualizations of power in employment relations concerns the origins and prior distribution of resources. In order to address this question we have to move to the structural level of the model, which is represented by domination or 'asymmetries of resources employed in the sustaining of power relations' (Giddens, 1979, p. 93). Thus, in a manner reminiscent of Dunlop, the distribution of resources in employment relations is seen as a reflection of the prevailing distribution in the wider society. While the dominance of management is usually ensured by their possession of greater economic resources in the long term, such domination has to be constantly reinforced and reproduced within the workplace. And, as we have already seen, it is useful to be able to exert more subtle methods of control via ideological means rather than having to resort to the coercive power of economic resources. This is effected by the creation of a managerial ideology which serves to legitimate managerial authority and to manage meanings in such a way as to preserve the *status quo* by attempting to assert the 'naturalness' and 'efficiency' of managerial dominance. In this way, a situation of hegemony is created whereby workers are prevented from challenging the basis of their domination. Hegemony at the workplace therefore takes the forms of such commonplace notions as the 'managerial prerogative', the 'sovereignty of management', and the 'right to manage'.

Employees thus face an additional asymmetry of resources in ideological terms. 'Whereas managerial ideology comprises a relatively coherent body of thought, comprehensively expressive of management interests, this is far from the case with the fragmentary counter-ideology available to workers' (Armstrong et al., 1981, p. 43). Thus Beynon (1973) has referred to the limited 'factory consciousness' of car workers in Halewood, while Nichols and Armstrong (1976) described the value systems of workers at 'Chem Co' as inchoate, inconsistent and incomplete. More recently, the confusion evident in the National Union of Mineworkers' presentation of their case during the 1984–5 dispute can be said to have contributed to their failure to gain industry-wide support.

Also pervasive at the structural level is the process of 'disciplinary power' which operates by organizing human bodies in time and space in order to achieve maximum utility coupled with maximum obedience (Foucault, 1979). This is achieved in organizations in several ways: by physical constraints on movement and freedom (such as provided by the assembly line) or on association and interaction (via individual offices or workstations); by surveillance (by means of open plan offices and information technology); or by the control of employee activity via timetables, rules, and other forms of regimentation, such as the application of Taylorist work measurement systems (Taylor, 1911). Of course, this conception of power does not necessarily imply intentionality but instead stems from the logic and rationality of both modernism and capitalist organization (Clegg, 1989).

Yet the control by management of resources at the structural level does enable them to exercise power and control as a deliberate strategy via apparently neutral mechanisms. Thus, the managerially imposed division of labour can be seen not as a simple technical and economic expedient but as a mechanism of control. Similarly, organizational hierarchies and hierarchical distinctions can be seen as control mechanisms in both actual and symbolic ways. Thus, hierarchies serve to isolate employees into controllable units (as does the division of labour) while hierarchical distinctions are the structural manifestations of the labelling process (Czarniawska-Joerges and Joerges, 1988). It may be argued that the rules, regulations and procedures which comprise the modern corporation are not only neutral and technical attempts to rationalize but also control processes which operate via the 'hegemony of bureaucratic procedure' (Goldman and Van Houton, 1977). For example, while the increasing formalization of disciplinary policies and procedures within organizations over the last twenty years has offered workers certain 'rights' and protection against cavalier managerial action, at the same time such procedures have codified disciplinary practice around a set of key managerial principles (now enshrined in Tribunal precedent) and have thus legitimated and depersonalized managerial discipline.

Culture and Power Relations

Kluckhohn and Strodtbeck (1961) have argued that all human societies face certain basic human issues and dilemmas and it has been suggested that power (or relation to authority) is one of these 'core' dimensions of culture (Hofstede, 1980; Inkeles and Levinson, 1969). We may hypothesize that responses and attitudes towards power within organizations might vary cross-culturally in at least three respects. First, one may suggest that the willingness to exercise power and the manner or 'directness' of such exercising may vary between cultures. Second, echoing Etzioni's (1961) notion of compliance, one could hypothesize that the willing acceptance of domination and subjugation to authority will vary cross-culturally. Finally, it may be argued that reactions to overt conflict situations will also be culture specific. In order briefly to illustrate these points, we can consider differences in power orientation between Western countries, represented by the UK, Canada and the USA, and Chinese societies, including the People's Republic of China (PRC) and other 'Nanyang' or overseas Chinese societies, such as Hong Kong, Singapore, and Taiwan. This contrast is deliberately chosen in order to illustrate very different approaches to power relations, conflict resolution, and negotiating behaviour.

Power distance

According to Hofstede, power distance refers to the relative power of superior and subordinate. The 'power distance between a boss B and a subordinate S in a hierarchy is the difference between the extent to which B can determine the behavior of S and the extent to which S can determine the behavior of B' (1980, p. 99). More generally, power distance refers to the existence of large power disparities between individuals, groups, and social strata and the acceptance of this state of affairs as right and natural. The Power Distance Index (PDI) values for selected Western and Chinese countries, based on questionnaire responses to Hofstede's Values Survey Module, are shown in table 3.1.

From this we can see that the three Western countries are all relatively low in terms of power distance whereas all of the Chinese countries are high. The high Chinese position on power distance has several implications for employee relations in Chinese societies. High power distance involves the greater use of autocratic and paternalist managerial styles, greater centralization of decision-making, and 'taller' organizational pyramids (Hofstede, 1980). Employees are more likely to evaluate positively close supervision and less likely to disagree openly with the boss or to trust other employees. The implications for the dynamics of the employment relationship in such cultures are clear.

Conflict preferences

Perhaps the most well known and widely accepted model of conflict handling preferences is that of Thomas (1976), which identifies five different conflict handling styles (competing, collaborating, compromising, avoiding, and accom-

Table 3.1 Power Distance Index (PDI) scores for
selected Western and Chinese countries: range 94–11

Country	Score
Singapore	74
Hong Kong	68
Taiwan	58
USA	40
Canada	39
UK	35
Mean	51

Source Hofstede, 1980, p. 104

modating) which result from different levels and mixtures of assertiveness and
co-operativeness (figure 3.2).

Competing is a power-oriented mode in which one pursues one's own concerns,
at the other person's expense, in a manner which is both assertive and

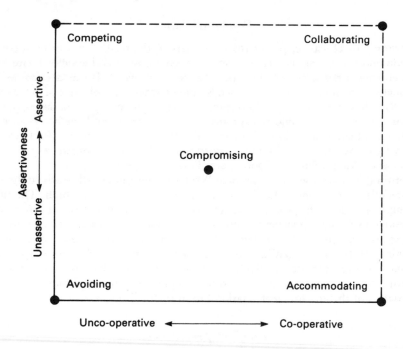

Figure 3.2 The Thomas model of conflict handling styles

Source: Adapted from Thomas, 1976

unco-operative. Collaborating is an assertive and co-operative approach where one party attempts to work with the other party in an effort to find an integrative and mutually satisfying solution. Avoiding occurs when one is unassertive and yet unco-operative. Interests are not articulated and the conflict is postponed to resurface at a later stage. Accommodating represents a mix of co-operativeness and unassertiveness and occurs when one neglects one's own concerns in order to satisfy the concerns of the other party. Compromising represents an intermediate position in terms of both assertiveness and co-operation and a situation where both parties satisfy at least some of their concerns.

It has been suggested (Kirkbride et al., 1991) that Chinese people have a high preference for the adoption of compromising and avoiding behaviours and a low preference for competing and assertive styles, and that these preferences are a function of key traditional Chinese values, such as collectivism, and the importance of harmony, conformity, and 'face'. These hypothesized preferences have been empirically confirmed by a study (Tang and Kirkbride, 1986) which reports research into cultural differences in conflict handling styles between Chinese and Western government executives in Hong Kong. The data showed a contrasting Western preference for the more assertive collaborating and competing styles.

Bargaining and negotiation

Obviously such clear cross-cultural differences in relation to power, authority, and conflict handling preferences are bound to have serious implications for bargaining and negotiation behaviours. At least four such implications are suggested for Chinese negotiating style (Kirkbride et al., 1991). First, the greater Chinese expectation of a compromise solution in a negotiation will tend towards the need to increase the room available for manoeuvre and thus to the setting of higher initial demands, which results in wider bargaining ranges. This would contrast with those, such as Americans and British, who generally adopt more confrontational styles and thus retain greater expectations of reaching agreement at or near their own desired settlement points (Graham and Herberger, 1983). In the case of the PRC, several commentators have noted how Chinese negotiators often engage in extreme opening offers/demands or even in the issuing of 'non-negotiable' demands (Pye, 1982).

Second, the greater proclivity for avoiding will tend to make the negotiation process slower than would be expected in the West, as the 'real' issues will take longer to surface. Since the opening up of the PRC in 1976, there have been many documented tales of American and European business people becoming extremely frustrated at the protracted nature of negotiations and the absence of any time frame (Frankenstein, 1986; Pye, 1986; Reeder, 1987). Whilst this occurs for a number of reasons, including Chinese conceptions of time and the bureaucracy of PRC institutions, we may trace the origins back to an unwillingness to engage in confrontation and fear of loss of 'face'.

Third, following on from the above, it may be argued that the relative neglect by the Chinese of collaborating is the result of a general tendency for such cultures to see power as a 'zero-sum' or 'win-lose' game (Hofstede, 1980). As we have suggested, the Chinese preferences for avoiding and compromising are concerned to elide the negative aspects of losing in such situations. Chinese negotiators therefore tend to adopt a 'defensive' attitude, with the key task being to avoid loss.

Finally, the Chinese respect for authority and hierarchy, and their acceptance of high power distance naturally leads to a situation where the relative status of the parties to the negotiation becomes a key variable (Pye, 1982). Chinese negotiators are concerned to ascertain the authority and status of their negotiating opponents, which is taken as both a measure of the seriousness in which the other party is approaching the negotiation and a reflection of the level of respect being shown. Another associated feature stemming from a hierarchical tradition is the importance of ritual in social interactions generally, and negotiations in particular (Pye, 1982). It may be argued that ritualization, by restricting behaviour to required forms and patterns, is yet another way for the Chinese to contain overt conflict. Such formalism and ritualized behaviour can be confusing and difficult for the non-Chinese negotiator. For example, Graham and Herberger (1983) note that the American stress on informality and equality, encapsulated in a 'just call me John' mentality, blinds Americans to the importance of such status differences and formal rituals.

Compared to their counterparts in the West, Chinese staff are less likely to challenge superiors, less likely to trust other employees, and more likely to use avoiding and compromising styles of conflict resolution. As a result, their preferred negotiation style tends to be slower, more defensive and more formalized. This obviously has implications for the patterns of employee relations in Chinese societies. For example, the relatively low union density and almost total absence of strikes and other forms of industrial action in Hong Kong can be partly explained by such cultural factors (England and Rear, 1981; England, 1989). Similar arguments could also be made in respect of the 'non-adversarial' and 'congenial' labour relations scene in Singapore (Anantaraman, 1984; Krislov and Leggett, 1984). One can also imagine the problems which exist in firms containing staff from both cultures. Again, examples would include Hong Kong, Singapore, and Taiwan, where often indigenous Chinese staff are managed by Western expatriates.

Conclusion

Power, as we have seen, is an inherent feature of the employment relationship. Indeed, it may be argued that this relationship is as much 'political' as it is economic, in that it represents the temporary marking of the contested frontier of control. Despite this universality, both the ways in which power is exercised by the dominant actor and the responses to such exercise by the subordinate actors can be seen to vary cross-culturally, thus creating very different power dynamics in the employment relationship and its processes. Power thus becomes a central explanatory variable in comparative employee relations.

Restricting ourselves to the capitalist world economy, we can suggest that management, as representatives of capital, are generally the dominant party in the employment relationship. Employees, as a result of having to sell their perishable labour power, are usually weaker, although they can increase their power by collective organization. The analysis of power, on this level, would not be very illuminating. For example, outcome perspectives would report that management were able, even on a one-dimensional analysis, to exert control over most important (and a myriad of unimportant) issues (Edwards, 1983). Resource perspectives would enable us to audit the superior resource strength of employers and to identify situations where union resources are likely to be maximized (Mishel, 1986).

However, such material resource disparities must be continually reproduced. In the employment relationship neither side can constantly mobilize its forces and resources. Most issues are decided within the framework of material resource distribution but not necessarily by direct reference to it. Instead, power is often exercised by the more subtle processes of rhetoric, argument, and ideological control. To the extent that such processes are successful, the more simple and overt use of material resources will be obviated. As Clegg has eloquently argued, 'it is only when control slips, assumptions fail, routines lapse and "problems" appear that the overt exercise of power is necessary' (1979, p. 147). Our understanding of power processes in employment relations will be greatly increased by further research work on these linguistic and ideological processes.

Notes

1 For similar but expanded power typologies see Hamilton (1976, 1977) and Wrong (1979).

References

Anantaraman, V. (1984) The significance of the non-adversarial union–management relationship in Singapore. *Singapore Management Review*, 6, 1, 35–50.

Armstrong, P. J., Goodman, J. F. B. and Hyman, J. D. (1981) *Ideology and Shop-floor Industrial Relations*. London: Croom Helm.

Astley, W. G. and Sachdeva, P. S. (1984) Structural sources of intraorganizational power: a theoretical synthesis. *Academy of Management Review*, 9, 1, 104–13.

Bacharach, S. B. and Lawler, E. J. (1981) *Bargaining: Power, Tactics and Outcomes*. San Francisco: Jossey-Bass.

Bachrach, P. and Baratz, M. S. (1962) The two faces of power. *American Political Science Review*, 16, 947–52.

Beynon, H. (1973) *Working for Ford*. Harmondsworth: Penguin.

Clegg, S. R. (1979) *The Theory of Power and Organization*. London: Routledge.

Clegg, S. R. (1989) *Frameworks of Power*. London: Sage.

Cook, K. S. (1977) Exchange and power in networks of intraorganizational relations. *Sociological Quarterly*, 18, 62–81.

Craypo, C. (1986) *The Economics of Collective Bargaining: Case Studies in the Private Sector*, Washington DC: Bureau of National Affairs.

Czarniawska-Joerges, B. and Joerges, B. (1988) How to control things with words: organizational talk and control. *Management Communication Quarterly*, 2, 2, 170–93.

Dahl, R. A. (1975) The concept of power. *Behavioral Science*, 2, 201–15.

Dunlop, J. T. (1958) *Industrial Relations Systems*. New York: Holt, Rinehart & Winston.

Edwards, C. (1978) Measuring union power: a comparison of two methods applied to the study of local union power in the coal industry. *British Journal of Industrial Relations*, 16, 1, 1–15.

Edwards, C. (1983) Power and decision making in the workplace: a study in the coal mining industry. *Industrial Relations Journal*, 14, 1, 50–69.

Edwards, C. (1987) Formal industrial relations and workplace power: a study on the railway. *Journal of Management Studies*, 24, 1, 63–90.

Emerson, R. M. (1962) Power–dependence relations. *American Sociological Review*, 27, 31–41.

England, J. (1989) *Industrial Relations and Law in Hong Kong* (2nd ed.). Hong Kong: Oxford University Press.

England, J. and Rear, J. (1981) *Industrial Relations and Law in Hong Kong*. Hong Kong: Oxford University Press.

Etzioni, A. (1961) *A Comparative Analysis of Complex Organizations*. New York: Free Press.

Flanders, A. (1970) *Management and Unions*. London: Faber & Faber.

Foucault, M. (1979) *Discipline and Punish: The Birth of the Prison*. New York: Random House.

Frankenstein, J. (1986) Trends in Chinese business practices: changes in the Beijing wind. *California Management Review*, 29, 1, 148–60.

French, J. R. P. and Raven, B. (1968) The bases of social power. In D. Cartwright and A. Zander (eds), *Group Dynamics*, New York: Harper & Row, 259–69.

Friedman, A. (1977) *Industry and Labour: Class Struggle at Work and Monopoly Capitalism*, London: Macmillan.

Giddens, A. (1976) *New Rules of the Sociological Method*. London: Hutchinson.

Giddens, A. (1979) *Central Problems in Social Theory*. London: Macmillan.

Giddens, A. (1984) *The Constitution of Society*. Cambridge: Polity Press.

Goldman, P. and Van Houten, D. R. (1977) Managerial strategies and the worker: a marxist analysis of bureaucracy. *Sociological Quarterly*, 18, 108–25.

Gowler, D. and Legge, K. (1983) The meaning of management and the management of meaning: a view from social anthropology. In M. Earl (ed.), *Perspectives on Management: A Multidisciplinary Analysis*, Oxford: Oxford University Press, 197–233.

Graham, J. L. and Herberger, R. A. (1983) Negotiators abroad – don't shoot from the hip. *Harvard Business Review*, July/August, 160–8.

Gronn, P. C. (1983) Talk as the work: the accomplishment of school administration. *Administrative Science Quarterly*, 28, 1, 1–21.

Gronn, P. C. (1984) I have a solution . . . administrative power in a school meeting. *Educational Administration Quarterly*, 20, 2, 65–92.

Hamilton, M. (1976) An analysis and typology of social power – Part 1. *Philosophy of the Social Sciences*, 6, 4, 289–313.

Hamilton, M. (1977) An analysis and typology of social power – Part 2. *Philosophy of the Social Sciences*, 7, 1, 51–65.

Hardy, C. (1985) The nature of unobtrusive power. *Journal of Management Studies*, 22, 4, 384–99.

Hickson, D. J., Hinings, C. R., Lee, C. A., Schneck, R. E. and Pennings, J. M. (1971) A strategic contingencies theory of intra-organizational power. *Administrative Science*

Quarterly, 16, 2, 216–29.
Hofstede, G. (1980) *Culture's Consequences: International Differences in Work-Related Values*. Beverly Hills: Sage.
Hyman, R. (1975) *Industrial Relations: A Marxist Introduction*. London: Macmillan.
Inkeles, A. and Levinson, D. (1969) National character: the study of modal personality and sociocultural systems. In G. Lindzey and E. Aronson (eds), *The Handbook of Social Psychology (vol. 4)*, Reading, Mass: Addison-Wesley, 418–506.
Kirkbride, P. S. (1986a) The rhetoric of power: the case of Bettavalve Placid – Part 1. *Employee Relations*, 8, 2, 1986, 13–16.
Kirkbride, P. S. (1986b) The rhetoric of power: the case of Bettavalve Placid – Part 2. *Employee Relations*, 8, 4, 1986, 23–6.
Kirkbride, P. S. (1988a) The one that got away: rhetoric in negotiation. *Employee Relations*, 10, 1, 17–21.
Kirkbride, P. S. (1988b) Legitimising arguments and worker resistance. *Employee Relations*, 10, 2, 28–31.
Kirkbride, P. S., Tang, S. F. Y. and Westwood, R. I. (1991) Chinese conflict preferences and negotiating behaviour: cultural and psychological influences. *Organization Studies*, 12, 3.
Kluckhohn, F. and Strodtbeck, F. (1961) *Variations in Value Orientations*. Evanston, Ill: Row, Peterson.
Krislov, J. and Leggett, C. (1984) The impact of Singapore's 'congenial' labour relations ethic on its conciliation service. *Singapore Management Review*, 6, 2, 95–106.
Levinson, H. M. 1966: *Determining Forces in Collective Bargaining*. New York: Wiley.
Lewis, H. G. (1963) *Unionism and Relative Wages in the United States*. Chicago: Chicago University Press.
Lukes, S. (1974) *Power: A Radical View*. London: Macmillan.
Marchington, M. (1975) Sources of workgroup power capacity. University of Aston Management Centre Working Paper, 41. Birmingham: University of Aston.
Mintzberg, H. (1983) *Power in and around Organizations*. New York: Prentice-Hall International.
Mishel, L. (1986) The structural determinants of union bargaining power. *Industrial and Labor Relations Review*, 40, 1, 90–104.
Nichols, T. and Armstrong, P. J. (1976) *Workers Divided*. London: Fontana.
Pye, L. W. (1982) *Chinese Commercial Negotiation Style*. New York: Oelgeschlager, Gunn & Hain.
Pye, L. W. (1986) The China trade: making the deal. *Harvard Business Review*, July/August, 74–80.
Reeder, J. A. (1987) When west meets east: cultural aspects of doing business in Asia. *Business Horizons*, Jan/Feb, 69–84.
Rees, A. (1977) *The Economics of Trade Unions*. London: University of Chicago Press.
Schienstock, G. (1981) Towards a theory of industrial relations. *British Journal of Industrial Relations*, 19, 2, 170–89.
Somers, G. G. (1969) Bargaining power and industrial relations theory. In G. G. Somers (ed), *Essays in Industrial Relations Theory*, Ames: Iowa State University Press, 39–53.
Tang, S. F. Y. and Kirkbride, P. S. (1986) Developing conflict management skills in Hong Kong: an analysis of some cross-cultural implications. *Management Education and Development*, 17, 3, 287–301.
Taylor, F. W. (1911) *Principles of Scientific Management*. New York: Harper & Row.
Thomas, K. (1976) Conflict and conflict management. In M. D. Dunnette (ed.), *Handbook of Industrial and Organizational Psychology*, Chicago: Rand McNally, 889–935.

Weber, M. 1947: *The Theory of Social and Economic Organisation.* (Translated by T. Parsons and A. M. Henderson). New York: Free Press.
Wrong, D. (1979) *Power: Its Forms, Bases, and Uses.* Oxford: Blackwell.

Further reading

Bacharach, S. B. and Lawler, E. J. (1980) *Power and Politics in Organizations.* San Francisco: Jossey-Bass. For mainstream views from the field of organizational theory see also Mintzberg (below).
Clegg, S. (1989) *Frameworks of Power.* London: Sage. A masterly and encyclopaedic review of power at the macro level, which introduces his concept of circuits of power.
Hofstede, G. (1984) *Culture's Consequences: International Differences in Work-Related Values* (abridged ed.). Beverly Hills: Sage. Contains the best discussion of cross-cultural differences in relation to the exercise of power and reactions to it.
Lukes, S. (ed.) (1986) *Power.* Oxford: Blackwell. A neat and accessible introduction to a selection of the classical views on power from sociologists and political scientists.
Mangham, I. (1986) *Power and performance in Organizations.* Oxford: Blackwell. Although operating from a dramaturgical/social interactionist perspective, which has been criticized for neglecting power, this provides a lively and provocative view of micro level power processes in the boardroom.
Mintzberg, H. (1983) *Power in and around Organizations.* New York: Prentice-Hall.

Part II

Managing Employment Relations

4

Constructing Control

Tom Keenoy

Introduction

Most of us are singularly inconsiderate of the humble hamburger, that quintessential leitmotiv of fast food. In the 1960s, the pop-artist Oldenburg proclaimed its social and cultural significance with the construction of a giant sculpture of a hamburger. More recently, some have pleaded we boycott this icon of modern capitalist culture since its manufacture can be linked to the destruction of the rain forests. (Others can think of far less noble reasons for avoiding the consumption of such fare.) In particular, consider the total production process required before that ground-beef concoction, coated with instant onions and delivered in a papier mâché bun, arrives in your mouth accompanied by a gelatinous dollop of tomato ketchup.

It starts life running around in South America being herded by gauchos not too far from the rain forest which has previously been cut down and burnt by lumberjacks, at the behest of some anonymous American multinational, in order to provide grasslands. Subsequently having been slaughtered by butchers, it is loaded into refrigerated ships by dockers and spends three weeks at sea being cosseted by merchant seamen before being unloaded by more dockers at Southampton. Thence by road to Smithfield market in London where, at about three in the morning, the carcases will be unloaded from the lorry by 'pullers-back', carried onto the market by 'pitchers' and delivered to a meat wholesaler's stall. There it will dressed by a 'cutter' and tastefully displayed by a 'humper' for onward sale. Once purchased by a buyer from a meat-processing company, it will be carried out of the market by 'bummarees' and loaded on to a lorry for delivery to a factory where, perhaps prior to reconstitution, it undergoes an unspeakable process of cutting, grinding, mincing, mashing, mixing and testing before it emerges the other end as sparkling fresh quarter-pounders, ready to grace laminated table-tops throughout the land.

At the heart of these complex logistics lie the employment relationships of several thousand people whose interdependent work activities are essential for us to have an uninterrupted supply of hamburgers. Similar arrangements exist for the production, processing, marketing and distribution of many products and services in modern society. For this to be accomplished effectively, work has to be designed, programmed, costed, organized and co-ordinated. All such tasks, conventionally deemed to be the work of managers, involve the exercise or imposition of control over behaviour. In short, managers, in attempting to persuade, cajole or coerce employees to do as they are told, are responsible for constructing, operating and maintaining a bewildering array of control mechanisms designed to ensure each individual actually performs their designated work.

The limits of managerial control

Initially, the managers' task appears deceptively straightforward, for they start with a number of distinctive advantages. As has already been indicated (see Chapter 3), in terms of the societal distribution of power, employers enjoy a distinct power advantage. In market economies their basic claim to authority rests on the long established rights of private property and, in what remains of the planned economies, employers' rights are legitimized by the state. These, in turn, provide the bases of managerial prerogatives: it is management which decides whether or not there will be work and management which enjoys the right to decide how work will be organized (Storey, 1983). Such rights are usually underpinned by legal statutes. In addition, at the level of organization, the superior position of management and the scope for managerial control are reinforced by the conventional hierarchy of authority and supervision and buttressed by work rules and procedures; production and quality control systems; wage-payment and reward systems—which are often directly linked to output or productivity targets—and by the work technology itself which, as in the case of assembly-line production, may operate as an impersonal control mechanism on employee behaviour.

These 'situational' control mechanisms are invariably supported by a variety of ideological pillars. At a general level, as evidenced by the promulgation of the 'enterprise culture' in the UK in the 1980s, these may be designed not only to legitimize managerial authority but also to proclaim the reinvigorating qualities of a particular form of economic organization. More specific managerial ideologies, which are seen to promote managerial objectives and to integrate the individual into the employing organization, are associated with particular schools of management thought (Bendix, 1974; Child, 1969). Ultimately, or ideally as Anthony (1977, p. 228) has observed, 'the end result is achieved when the application of authority and power is no longer necessary to assist in the achievement of the organisation's goals because the goals have been internalised by those who are to pursue them.' In recent years, with the hype of the 'excellence syndrome' (Peters and Waterman, 1982) and the stress on corporate cultures, human resource management and transformational leadership, managerial ideologies have come to be associated with particular companies. (See below and also chapter 5.)

None the less, despite this formidable armoury and the initial capacity to determine the ground rules of employment, the transformation of management's initial power advantage into specific and effective forms of control is limited by a number of factors. In addition to the pervasive impact of the historical context,[1] managerial control may be constrained by a vast range of other contextual and operating conditions. For example, among the most important are the level and competitiveness of economic activity, unemployment, the governmental political complexion and economic and social policies, the condition of local labour markets, and the legal context – which may impose restrictions on how labour can be treated – can all limit the choices available to management. In addition, managerial control strategies are subject to internal factors, such as the character of their labour force – more skilled and professional employees invariably expect (and get) a greater degree of autonomy; the degree and effect of trade union organization; the sensitivity of production to disruption and the history of employee relations. All of these features may close off certain control options to management.

The important analytical point to emerge from this discussion is that, despite power imbalances, control mechanisms and processes are inherently fragile, being vulnerable not only to a bewildering array of dynamic historical and situational constraints but also to the withdrawal of consent by those over whom control is exercised. This is why regulation of the employment relationship is both a continuing preoccupation and a permanent problem for contemporary management. Control has to be constructed in a fashion which also 'manufactures' consent. This latter point must be explored further before considering the nature of more specific forms of control.[2]

The Management Problem: Manufacture of Consent

The manufacture of consent is problematic for two major reasons: the first relates to the nature of work in industrial society and the second to the nature of the employment relationship itself.

The nature of work

Contemporary work and work organization have been subject to the twin historical processes of the *division of labour*, which, as illustrated by the hamburger production process, has engendered ever increasing specialization, and *bureaucratization*, which has engendered the construction of ever more systematic impersonal controls over work behaviour. Both these processes can be shown to have directly facilitated the extension of managerial control over work and employee behaviour. But they have also had other consequences. Production processes have become ever more interdependent and thus more sensitive to even minor disruptions: a stoppage in a car component factory can result in the complete shutdown of car manufacture in the companies it supplies. And, with the introduction of the more cost-effective 'just-in-time' manufacturing systems, which minimize the stocks of such components held on the main manufacturing site, the production process has become even more vulnerable to disruption (Wilkinson and Oliver, 1989). Thus, the methods used to extend managerial control have also, paradoxically, increased the potential power of employees.

In addition, the progressive reduction – or destruction – of work activities into their component elements, in order to increase control and industrial efficiency, has had the effect of creating jobs which are unremittingly repetitive and intrinsically banal. Boiling an egg is intellectually more demanding than many modern industrial work activities. The net effect, to cut a long and complex story perilously short, is that employees have tended to become increasingly instrumental in their attitudes to work: in some circumstances their psychological involvement is focused on the cash nexus to the detriment of all else (see also chapter 2). Workers have such minimal responsibilities that money dominates or even replaces all other motivations, for financial reward is the only possible satisfaction (Goldthorpe et al., 1968; Thompson, 1983). One incisive commentary has suggested that this progressive elimination of automony and discretion from work has generated a downward spiral of alienating low trust in contemporary employment relations (Fox, 1974). Hence deskilling – one of the consequences of managerial efforts to increase control over work – has also had the effect of minimizing the potential for employee involvement and commitment. This becomes a problem as soon as management expect more than mute acquiescence from their employees (see chapter 6).

The employment relationship

Fundamentally, the employment relationship is an institutionalized structure facilitating processes of social exchange. On the surface, we are accustomed to regard it as an economic exchange of labour for money although it also embodies social, psychological and political exchanges.

Despite the conventional shorthand that everyone works for money, by now (see chapter 2) it should be clear that work is associated with a far more complex set of social meanings and expectations. Work not only provides money to exchange for goods and services but is also a key indicator of social status and social identity. This may exacerbate the managerial dilemma, since, if work provides only minimal status and identity, the pursuit of instrumental rewards – which can supply the external accoutrements of status and identity – may become a surrogate. The contemporary fashion for increasing participation and involvement can be seen as one managerial strategy designed to mediate such difficulties, though it has to be handled with care (Cressey et al., 1985; see also Strauss, this volume). And the employment relationship is intrinsically political not only because an individual's position within it may determine their social class and social expectations but also because control of the employment relationship tends to be associated with significant access to political power in society. Thus, the pivotal social significance of work and the way it is organized is one reason why the employment relationship is, conceptually, best seen as one of socio-economic and not merely economic exchange.

It has long been recognized that socio-economic exchange processes involve the mediation of different interests: at the most simple level, it is in the interest of the employer to minimize the cost of labour and in the interest of the employee to maximize the price of labour. Hence, employment relationships engender bargaining – which can be either individual or collective – and the mobilization of power in order to protect or advance such interests. Since the market can impose fierce penalties on those who cannot control it, employers established employers' associations while employees formed trade unions to provide institutional bases for both the pursuit of their respective interests and the 'management' of potential conflict. Thus, the employment relationship is characterized by endemic – though not necessarily overt – conflicts of interest.

In addition, since the exchange of labour necessarily involves employee acceptance – however reluctant, of the employer's right to direct that labour, the employment relationship is also characterized by superior–subordinate authority relations. This constitutes an additional source of endemic conflict, since the employment contract rarely specifies the precise terms of the exchange. Despite the use of job descriptions – which can never be in any sense 'complete' – such specificity is not only very difficult but, in some circumstances, impossible to achieve. In practice, the employer usually purchases only very vague 'quantities' of labour: the measurement may be in terms of time – 'a hamburger gristle-grinder works five eight-hour shifts each week' – or in terms of fulfilling a particular function: 'as the assistant marketing manager you will be responsible for promoting McDoggie's hamburgers throughout the Isle of Man'. Such generality means that what constitutes a legitimate instruction is often a matter for negotiation *after* the contract of employment has been signed. If a supervisor instructed our gristle-grinder to sweep the floor at the end of the shift, the response might be: 'That's not my job.'

This may be a particular source of difficulty when management are seeking to change working arrangements and habits, for many employees develop notions not only of what 'work' belongs to a particular 'job' but also of what constitutes a 'fair day's work'. Such notions become social norms and, particularly in long-established industries, often occupy a powerful moral role in the employee sub-culture. They are usually deep-rooted and resistant to change. Hence, when management seek to change the work-content of a job or to increase control over employees in order to improve productivity or otherwise increase efficiency, such developments – especially if they involve a loss of autonomy or extra effort from employees for no additional reward – are often resisted. If the proposed changes are regarded as excessive they may produce de-motivation, absenteeism and poor work or generate demands – in the form of a wage claim – to revise the contract of employment.

Analytically, these endemic sources of conflict highlight the symbiotic nature of the relationship between the controllers and the controlled: their exchange means that they are dependent on each other and, however imbalanced the distribution of power, the controlled always have some leverage on the terms of exchange. No matter how extensive the controls, in the final analysis, management is reliant on employee co-operation.

Finally, it should be evident that the employment relationship is a specific form of power relationship. As chapter 3 has indicated, power is implicated both in the social structures we create, such as organizations, and in the social processes, such as bargaining, which are used by organizational members to regulate their relations and behaviour. Power is thus a property of the structure, processes and actions characteristic of employment relationships and, in common with all power relationships, a central and enduring feature is the contest for control. This is not to imply there is permanent war between employer and employee – far from it – but to insist that the potential for conflict always exists and that the maintenance of order is a permanent problem (Keenoy, 1981).

It should now be clear why management are faced with a perpetual dilemma: in constructing control they have to cope with the paradox of what might be called the 'motivation–control' equation. On one side is the need to ensure the active involvement and positive participation of the workforce in the pursuit of business objectives – something which may be critical where the quality of the product or service is directly dependent on employee performance. This implies treating employees with respect, rewarding them fairly or even generously and, perhaps, seeking to elicit responsibility and trust. On the other side is the need to control work-behaviour in the light of the economic realities of competition and the profit-motive. These imply treating the employee as an economic resource to be made as economically efficient as possible: in the practice this may require extracting additional productivity for no additional cost, minimizing wages and rewards and declaring redundancies. As Hyman (1987) observes of this contradiction, 'employers require workers to be both dependable and disposable'.

Regulating Employment and Constructing Control

Given the dynamic and diverse nature of work and work-organization, it is unsurprising to find management have resort to a multitude of historically contingent control mechanisms and strategies. Indeed, the analysis of management practice and thought can be interpreted as the historical quest to resolve this unresolvable paradox (Rose, 1988). Attempts to impose a panoramic theoretical order on management practice have been instructive but over-simplistic. Edwards (1979), examining the American experience, concluded that managerial strategy had developed from the autocratic 'bossing' of *simple control* through *technical control* – in which workers are constrained by the pace of the production technology – to *bureaucratic control* which relies on rules and procedures. In contrast, Friedman (1977), who analysed British developments, identified *direct control* and *responsible autonomy* as alternative strategies available to management. This distinction echoes the motivation–control dilemma, since the exercise of direct control militates against employees enjoying responsible autonomy.

Management style

Others, less ambitious or perhaps more realistic, have merely sought to distinguish the types of managerial style which can be associated with different employee relations strategies. Purcell and Sisson (1983), for example, drawing on the seminal work of Fox (1974), identify five major control patterns: the *traditionalists*, who are the epitome of the exploitative capitalist, exercise strict control and reject trade unionism; the *sophisticated paternalists*, who also refuse to recognize unions but invest a great deal of time and money in 'people-management' in the belief that such investment is good for the company; the *sophisticated moderns*, who acknowledge that conflict is endemic to the employment relationship and, in consequence, attempt to regulate that conflict by consulting and bargaining with unions, comprise *constitutionalists*, who insist on a clear demarcation of union and management interests, and *consultors*, who, while they engage in bargaining, seek to pre-empt disputes by extensive consultation and attempt to transform conflicts of interest into 'joint problems'; and finally, the *standard moderns*, who, having no clearly articulated strategy, are essentially pragmatic, reactive and opportunistic: industrial relations only becomes a consideration when it becomes a problem.

A particular weakness of this classification is that the last type – which contains the largest number of companies – is something of a dustbin category. More recently, Purcell (1987) has developed a more restricted and refined analysis by insisting that management style must be based on a coherent and articulated set of guiding principles linked to business policy. He argues for the greater sensitivity of a dimensional rather than a type approach and identifies two dimensions: *individualism*, reflecting policies which lay greatest stress on workers' individual rights and capabilities, and *collectivism*, which reflects the extent to which management encourages employees to have a collective voice in regulating employment.

At best, such classification schemes provide useful discriminations and general guidelines. Given the embedded legacy of the historical context and a vast range of situational control mechanisms, no two companies – even if they operate with similar production systems and manufacture comparable products – are likely to be able to construct precisely the same set of controls. Hence, few companies fit neatly into any of the necessarily crude categories.

Since, as suggested above, the contest for control is an enduring feature of the employment relationship, one way of imposing conceptual coherence on these various approaches to the control problem is to locate the various strategies, types and dimensions in relation to the dispersion of power. This produces three relatively distinctive *control syndromes* which appear to provide reasonably comprehensive coverage of the possibilities: *unilateral control*, where one actor, invariably but not always management (see below), is dominant; *bilateral control*, where independent employee organizations exercise a variable degree of constraint on managerial dominance; and *co-operative control*, where power is nominally shared between the members. It is theoretically possible for companies to shift between categories over time and to operate different control syndromes in different parts of the organization.

All of which may seem somewhat daunting to someone whose ambition is to manage a hamburger joint. However, the range of possibilities reflects a sensitivity both towards the motivation–control problem and towards the complexity of the dynamic socio-economic contexts which constrain managerial choice. In the examples which follow, we shall attempt to both illustrate and elaborate this conceptual jungle. But first it is essential to outline one critical feature of the historical context which is ever present and which plays a dominant role in shaping control-strategy choices.

Politico–legal context

Government–created legal frameworks constitute the scaffolding within which management and workers construct control. In social democracies, the 'legal rules' represent the quintessential bureaucractic means of social control. Their distinctive quality is that such rules are generally vested with the virtually unquestionable legitimacy of our value commitment to the 'rule of law': the theory is that no one is 'above the law' and, in liberal democracies, any challenge to the prevailing 'legal rules' can be condemned as an attempt to 'undermine the law' or set oneself 'above the law'. However, despite the rhetorical claim to even-handed neutrality, the law is inseparable from and often subordinated to broader governmental policies and political ideologies (Keenoy, 1985).

This finds clear reflection in the fact that the precise legal specification of the contract of employment and the laws regulating employment vary significantly from country to country. For example, in the UK, under Common Law, an employee has a duty to obey reasonable orders and to take reasonable care of the employer's property; in the Soviet Union, the worker's constitutional guarantee of a right to work is balanced by the citizen's duty to work (Pravda and Ruble, 1986). In general, the legal provisions cover individual rights and duties; trade union rights and duties; procedures and public institutions – such as industrial tribunals and arbitration agencies – to regulate industrial conflict, and aspects of health and safety at work (Thomason, 1988; Lewis, 1986). Less generally, the law may set minimum wages and, from time to time, even Western governments may use the law to regulate prices and incomes. Two brief examples should illustrate the pervasive influence of governmental legal constraints on the employment relationship.

First, the British experience. From 1945, trade unions enjoyed a slow but progressive influence and social legitimacy. Successive governments remained committed to full employment, a growth economy and the expansion of the welfare state (Crouch, 1977). Indeed, the degree of agreement was such that the 1960s and 1970s were characterized as a period of 'consensus politics'. This facilitated the steady growth of trade union and employment rights: trade union leaders enjoyed significant political influence, collective bargaining and incomes policies were the primary means of regulating the employment relationship and employees had access to a floor of employment rights and welfare benefits.

However, the election of 1979 heralded Thatcherism and the radical attempt to recast this dominant social philosophy: monetarist ideology de-legitimized trade unionism, public expenditure, the provision of public services and the commitment to full employment. Employment rights have been reduced and there has been a significant reduction in the relative value of unemployment benefits. Although there remain serious doubts as to the real impact of this dramatic political change on the character of employment relations (McInnes, 1987; Batstone, 1984), trade union rights have been reduced, the range of legal actions more narrowly confined and membership and influence have significantly declined. Managerial control capacity has expanded and new forms of employment relationship have been popularized (Bassett, 1986; Brewster and Connock 1985; Atkinson, 1984). While global economic forces have clearly contributed to these changes, Thatcherite ideology has facilitated their growth and development.

Second, in contrast, the German experience. The reconstruction of West Germany after 1945 has been achieved by a succession of governments which have, broadly, remained loyal to the social democratic legacy of 1945. Although there have been difficulties (Streeck, 1984), the system of co-determination, which enshrines the legal rights of workers' councils at company level, has been maintained. Although this system has been criticized (von Beyme, 1980) and has been affected by global economic forces, the combination of industrial unionism and co-determination has arguably played a key role in achieving the objectives of providing a near-comprehensive employee voice and minimizing both unemployment and overt conflict between capital and labour. Whether this 'success story' can be sustained with the unification of the two Germanies remains to be seen.

Employees in the former German Democratic Republic have grown up with no experience of the sometimes harsh consequences of labour market forces. Employment relations in the GDR were regulated according to the canons of another kind of conservatism: one where all major resource allocation decisions were taken according to the Leninist political principles of democratic centralism which posits a unity of purpose between workers, managers and the state. In the ideological absence of conflicts of interest between management and workers, employment relationships were regulated by a constitutional authoritarianism flowing from the ruling communist party, in which the role of trade unions was to promote worker co-operation, output and productivity while ensuring that management abided by the labour codes protecting employees. In practice, since union officialdom was dominated by the communist party, the unions invariably supported management objectives in preference to the interests of workers (Rueschemeyer and Scharf, 1986).

These brief examples illustrate the fundamental conditioning impact of the prevailing *politico-legal context* on the policies and practices which regulate and control the employment relationship. The colour and tone of the dominant political values and philosophy not only are embedded in the legal frameworks within which employers and employees construct their control strategies but also establish a political climate defining the parameters of employer and employee action which are considered socially legitimate.

The Control Syndromes

From unilateral pretensions...

Conceptually, unilateral regulation refers to those situations where one actor enjoys the authority or has the power to set all or most of the employment rules.

As noted above, the employers' initial power advantage permits them to set the initial ground rules and gives them an overwhelming capacity for unilateral initiatives. However, in practice, given the historical context and the nature of the motivation–control equation, the scope for unilateral control is always a matter of degree. (Having 'total' control over the employment relationship might seem to represent the achievement of managements' wildest fantasy. However, the evidence suggests that such control is only effective when it flows from normative commitment – as is sometimes found in religious sects or political parties. Total control based on coercion, as in forced labour camps, may be effective but is highly inefficient.)

One of the most quoted examples of unilateral regulation is that practised by IBM. This company has such a distinctive and apparently effective managerial style that it is identified as the archetypal *sophisticated paternalist*. The key to understanding 'the IBM way' lies in the proactive personnel policy which underpins and continually reinforces the corporate culture. It is comprised of six elements. First, the managerial commitment to full employment means that if jobs disappear through technological change or if a plant is shut down then the company will offer alternative employment elsewhere and pay for relocation.[3] Second, long before it came into fashion, IBM minimized 'them–us' attitudes by having a 'single status' policy: from the chairman down, everyone shares the same sickness benefit scheme and all eat in the same dining rooms. Third, a critical control mechanism is the system of rewards. There are no automatic annual increases but, with the use of salary surveys, IBM is careful to ensure their rates are among the very best in the industry. Pay is determined through a sophisticated job-evaluated scheme and increases are based on regular perform-ance reviews: individuals are rewarded and move up the scales on merit in a system which is perceived to be fair. While this illustrates a stress on *responsible autonomy* and *individualism*, progress is measured through the flexible but none the less *bureaucratic* job-evaluated scales.

Managerial concern to pre-empt employee dissatisfaction is reflected in the other three elements. The IBM Appraisal and Counselling Scheme ensures an annual statement of each employee's performance against set objectives: this would include an assessment of progress, career ambitions and consideration of possible training, with everything being carefully monitored by the Personnel Department. Fifth, there is an effective company-wide communication system and, finally, there are well-trodden procedures for individuals or groups to raise grievances. The 'Open Door' scheme permits individuals to take a grievance to the highest level – Peach (1983) estimates that 25 per cent of these cases find in favour of the employee. In addition, there are the 'Speak Up' and 'Multiple Speak Up' procedures through which individuals or groups can anonymously ask questions, complain or register a grievance and receive a reply within 10 days.

Of course, life at IBM is by no means as smooth as this brief account might imply and nor should the policies be seen as necessarily altruistic. Overall labour costs, at 18 per cent, and market leadership suggests that IBM has chosen a cost-effective strategy which minimizes the turnover of highly trained labour. At the same time, the level of job security, excellent terms and conditions of employment, and the preventative care-taking to meet employee aspirations, in the context of an organizational climate which ostensibly values investment in people as a matter of principle, represents a powerful stimulant to employee loyalty and commitment. Alternatively, a critical perspective might suggest that a system where everyone seems to be watching everyone else provides management with an insidious and manipulative set of controls. However, employees do not seem to object. In an ACAS ballot of 13,000 employees to see if trade union recognition ought to be recommended, 95 per cent voted against.

Other non-union multinational companies, such as Hewlett-Packard, 3M, Marks and Spencer, and Kodak, operate with comparable control strategies which place a premium on the proactive management of discontent. Whether such approaches should be regarded as genuine attempts to construct a socially legitimate consensual core to employee relations or as a covert and expensive form of 'union avoidance' remains contentious. The issue is complicated by the possibility that once the initial objective – say, to pre-empt union recruitment – has been achieved, it slips from memory and, as management derive the undoubted benefits of positive employee relations, the strategy becomes transformed into the organizational culture. Through experience, management come to believe their own propaganda. This highlights the important fact that control strategies have unintended consequences.

However, alternative unintended consequences are possible if management are economical with the truth. Thomas (1988) discusses a case study by Grenier (1988) of how Johnson and Johnson, the multinational proprietary medicine and baby powder company, set about establishing a new plant on a green–field site in Mexico. Lower labour costs and the absence of unions are likely to have been among the reasons for the choice of location. Grenier, a social psychologist, was employed as an internal consultant to assist in the start-up process. This included extensive pre-hiring psychological testing to screen prospective employees, intensive exposure to the corporate culture, and setting up semi-autonomous work teams to solve production and quality troubles and to evaluate worker acclimatization and performance. Part of his work was secretly to tape-record these team meetings and keep detailed notes on who spoke and what they said, in order to monitor the process of socialization, assess how the groups were developing their capacity for responsible autonomy, and gauge employee satisfaction. All appeared to be caring and progressive.

However, when a group of dissatisfied workers sought to bring in a union, the whole tone and temper was transformed. According to Grenier, these same tools were enlisted in the battle against unionization: socialization became indoctrination, team meetings were used to put peer pressure on individuals and isolate those with pro-union attitudes, and Grenier was asked to construct a test to measure employee support for unionism. Forced to take sides, he exposed all to the union and was, in turn, subjected to the same surveillance, harassment and intimidation that had been used against employees. The result was his book, which seeks to elaborate the ideological and coercive potential of techniques used to construct consensus. As Thomas (1988, p. 392) perceptively observes, 'intimacy and intimidation are sometimes difficult to distinguish from one another'.

Unilateral strategies are not, of course, the preserve of large multinationals with the financial resources to employ the occasional naïve or rogue social psychologist.

Far from it; indeed, in rare instances some employee groups, for example printers and boilermakers, at the expense of public opprobrium, have enjoyed extensive unilateral control over limited aspects of work organization, such as manning levels and job demarcation. More generally, *traditionalists*, who hold anti-trade union views and invariably legitimize their control with reference to conventional managerial prerogatives derived from property rights, are predisposed to regard unilateral regulation as a normal component of such rights. Union members may find themselves passed over for promotion and activists may be sacked. Nor should such practices be regarded as a hangover from the nineteenth century (Bain, 1970). If employers can avoid depending on employee motivation by taking advantage of favourable labour market conditions, utilising *direct* or *technical* control mechanisms and preventing unionization, they can continue to take an exploitative approach to employees. Even small enterprises may be able to defend such traditional rights. For example, in a famous dispute over union recognition, Grunwick, a photo-processing company with a workforce of immigrant female labour, was able to continue production by recruiting a replacement non-union labour force. This was maintained despite the combined opposition of the TUC and a two-year 'strike' of sacked employees (Rogaly, 1977; Dromey and Taylor, 1978).

A contrasting alternative – although it appears to sit uneasily in the unilateral category – is the Oriental equivalent of *sophisticated paternalism*: the now famed 'Japanese management' syndrome. It characterizes about one-third of indigenous Japanese companies and, in the light of the competitive advantages it appears to bestow on Japanese multinationals, has become increasingly influential in the West. It comprises three core elements (Dore, 1973; Hanami, 1980) and a number of subsidiary elements (McKenna, 1988). The three fundamental controls are: lifetime employment (for male employees) – once employed the normal expectation of both company and employee is long-term commitment; seniority wages – rewards are primarily linked to length of service rather than being task specific; and enterprise unionism, which is company-dependent since membership is confined to the company and union officials are elected from the workforce.

Typically, a range of supportive controls is also present. Initial employment is highly competitive and is based on carefully screened selection to ensure the correct attitudes. Training is intensive and company specific. While it acclimatizes the employee to the company's expectations and idiosyncracies – the Geordies selected as supervisors for the new Nissan plant in Sunderland were sent to Japan for intensive exposure to Nissan's production control techniques and managerial methods – it also reduces the value of the employee in the labour market. Although seniority is usually the key to promotion, it also depends on satisfactory periodic assessment by superiors of ability, attendance, and attitude. Predictably, employment opens the way to an extensive range of welfare benefits: these may include sickness benefits and medical care, sports and leisure facilities, subsidized shopping and outings – work groups are often expected to socialize together. In Japan, there are even marriage-arranging services. Such elements increase the employees' dependence on the company. Various work practices are also designed to build and continually reinforce teamwork: collective participative decision-making processes are combined with quality circles to engender a collective identity and an individual sense of responsibility for the product.

Although the presence of enterprise unions appears to demarcate clearly what is often called Japanese *welfare paternalism* from the nascent IBM's of this world, such unions invariably enjoy a very close relationship with the company and should be regarded as constituting a supportive rather than an alternative source of authority in the company. In this respect they appear to fulfil similar functions to the staff associations much beloved by British banks and insurance companies. The fundamental difference in the two patterns of managerial control lies in the relative stress laid on *individualism* and *collectivism*. While, to some extent, this reflects differences in more general societal cultural values, as a catalyst of organizational cohesion, the Japanese approach, which channels and subordinates individualism to team objectives, appears to constitute a more coherent approach to the motivation–control dilemma. Within the sophisticated paternalist approach there remains an inherent tension between the stimulus to meritocratic individualism and the promotion of employee collaboration. Japanese management practice appears to overcome this tension.

. . .Through bilateral accommodations. . .

The term 'bilateral accommodation' is used to distinguish those forms of control which involve employee representatives or their organizations in constructing motivation and control. One central differentiating feature of bilateral control is the role of *external* organizations, such as trade unions and professional associations. Hence, by definition, staff associations and Japanese enterprise unions, which can be regarded as managerial surrogates for independent representation, would be excluded. The major mode of bilateral control is collective bargaining, which comes in diverse forms and is frequently bolstered by a range of supportive arrangements, such as joint consultation, worker directors, workers' councils, and a variety of joint participative and productivity committees. The other major difference between unilateral and bilateral control is the *de facto* managerial recognition of the inherent conflict of interests in the employment relationship.

Conceptually, collective bargaining is usually seen as a joint rule-making process, involving the mobilization of power, which provides a socially acceptable means of institutionalizing the inherent conflicting interests which characterize the employment relationship (Flanders, 1970; Watson, 1980). It not only functions to regulate employment and work relations but also, in permitting employees a voice, assists in the process of legitimizing managerial authority (Kerr et al., 1973). Such legitimacy is, of course, dependent upon employees continuing to perceive the exchange as 'fair'. Each country has its own historically conditioned bargaining structures; there are varying legal and ideological contexts and distinctive patterns of management and union organization. This makes generalization hazardous, but each 'system' has a differentiated *structure* and the *bargaining process* has certain generic features (Clegg, 1976; Bean, 1985; Sisson, 1987; see also chapters 9, 10, 13)

Collective bargaining extends the constraints on management choice in two major ways. First, the agreements are subject to revision at the initiative of external agencies, such as trade unions and employers' associations. Second, the formal agreement, where it regulates terms and conditions throughout an industry, such as engineering or road haulage, has to be tailored to meet the diverse needs of all the companies in that sector. Hence, particularly in the private sector, 'national' agreements often specify only minimum terms and conditions. Such multi-employer bargaining is one of the reasons why the *standard modern* fire-fighting approach has been so prevalent in the UK: since wages and dispute resolution are subject to the external authority of trade unions and employers' associations, employment relations are not regarded as a managerial priority. Bargaining at plant and workshop level, which, if the company uses incentive based wage-payment systems, can take place almost daily, has been left to personnel and industrial relations specialists in conjunction with union representatives. There is evidence, considered below, that this pattern is now changing.

Such externalization of managerial responsibility for employment relations can be even greater in most of the public sector, where national agreements specify the actual terms and conditions of employment and have led to the creation of a highly *bureaucratized constitutionalist* set of controls. Managerial responses to problems are necessarily reactive for all they can do is look up the appropriate 'national' procedure, phone the relevant officials and let events take their course. Such inflexibility – in particular, the fact that national wage rates make local labour markets irrelevant – is the major reason why, in the 1980s, Thatcher governments, in attempting to impose the discipline of the market throughout society, consistently attempted to break up national bargaining arrangements in the public sector (Mailly et al., 1989).

Increased flexibility and more appropriate control were also the objectives of the increasing number of larger companies which, from the 1960s onwards, decided to withdraw from multi-employer bargaining and establish their own corporate approach to employment policy. The Ford Motor Company, which had never been a member of the relevant employers' association, provided one model for the nascent *sophisticated modern* strategies. Ford came to the UK in 1911, resisted recognizing unions until 1941 and subsequently sought to minimize union influence by developing a distinctive hardline *constitutionalist* approach. Hence, Ford's collective agreements display detailed rules covering every issue subject to joint regulation. Interests are clearly demarcated and anything not included in the agreement is deemed to be the prerogative of management. Not surprisingly, such a rigid approach not only generated suspicion and instrumental attitudes but also promoted reactive and defensive postures from both management and unions.

A study by Friedman and Meredeen (1980) illuminated the internal contradictions of this control strategy. Ford's overriding stress on formalization, designed to stabilize control over employee relations and work organization by ensnaring them within strict rules, also led to an inability to adapt. Reliance on the rules sometimes exacerbated conflicts, reinforced 'them–us' attitudes and bred a low-trust organizational culture resistant to the introduction of more participative and integrative modes of control. An attempt to introduce quality circles failed and the less ambitious employee involvement programme which replaced it has yet to be accepted by manual workers (Starkey and McKinlay, 1989). In terms of the motivation–control dilemma, Ford's historical emphasis on control remains a singular barrier to the generation of employee commitment.

As Purcell and Sisson (1983) note, few chose to follow Ford's lead in detail and most sophisticated moderns are *consultors*. They try to minimize the morass of bureaucratic constraint and display more concern to create positive relations with trade unions, develop effective means of consultation and an atmosphere in which issues are defined as 'problems' to be solved rather than as 'conflicts' to be fought. Thus, they construct the 'motivational space' for the growth of co-operative attitudes in which managerial initiatives designed to increase productivity, change working practices or introduce new technology, are more likely to succeed. The conventional model *consultors* are companies such as ICI, Esso, Shell and BP. However, similar if less consistent managerial control strategies increasingly characterize unionized multinational and multi-plant companies in a range of industrial sectors.

More recently, in the wake of recession in the early 1980s and the bite of international competition, there is evidence suggesting that a variety of more integrative practices, such as joint consultation, increased information sharing, participative problem-solving and a generalized concern to increase employee involvement, may be starting to take root in an even wider range of enterprises (Edwards, 1987; Marginson et al., 1988). Edwards sees this as the emergence of 'enlightened managerialism' and, in the USA, where the process appears to have gone further, such neo-pluralist strategies (Keenoy, 1990) are claimed to be transforming employment relations (Kochan et al., 1986). It would be unwise to equate such developments with the demise of adversarial bilateral strategies, since increases in participation appear to follow economic cycles (Ramsey, 1977). The test will be whether such practices retain their legitimacy once the economic pressures ease.

Hence, the abstract logic which suggests that the best bilateral strategy is one which minimizes the control capacity of the other actor may be deeply misleading. Empirically, the most effective strategy depends upon an accurate reading of the pattern of situational constraints. Such glibness must be heavily qualified, managerial choice is invariably limited not only by external factors but also by previous choices. As the case of Ford illustrated, the attempt to mimic the Japanese success with quality circles, while it may have been distinctly 'progressive', demanded too much of management and employees habituated to a more bruising culture.

One final example – significantly on a green-field site – underlines this important point and also shows that some forms of collective bargaining seem to be little more than ritual conformity to surface appearances. When the Nissan company decided to invest some £400 million in a new plant in Sunderland, the plan included meticulous concern to minimize the role of unions. The possibility of either an enterprise union or no union at all was politically unrealistic, so Nissan insisted on having a 'single union' arrangement. The promise of at least 3,000 jobs in an area of very high unemployment ensured there was little resistance and the pressures to submit to Nissan's requirements were reflected in the eventual formal agreement signed with the engineers' union, the AEW. This includes so many restrictive clauses – there is not even specific provision for union representatives on the key bargaining mechanism, the Company Council – that it is difficult to envisage how effective bargaining can ever develop (Crowther and Garrahan, 1988). Japanese companies in the UK have been at the forefront of the new-style 'single union, no strike' deals. (Burrows (1986) lists 21 such agreements of which seven are in Japanese companies.) It is hardly surprising that the Nissan corporate strategy attempts, where possible, to replicate their indigenous managerial practice.

...To co-operative alternatives

Despite their economic insignificance, a brief examination of co-operative management approaches to constructing control can be instructive in illuminating the all-pervasiveness of the motivation–control dilemma. The genuine co-operative enterprise, which is collectively owned and democratically managed by the members, appears to have resolved this problem by eliminating the fundamental structural causes of differential interests.

A major difficulty in assessing the potential of co-operative organizations to create alternative forms of control lies in the fact of their economic fragility[4] (see also chapter 13). Since most are formed either out of the ruins of a failing enterprise or as a self-help response to unemployment, the problems of under-capitalization and an often hostile product market mean that generally all energies are focused on survival. Instead of practising worker control, the co-operative is often forced down the degenerative road to 'worker capitalism' and 'self-exploitation', for their first lesson is that principled convictions are no defence against the dull compunction of economic life. The available evidence clearly indicates that effective survival depends upon access to protected markets, the cushion of co-operative federations, and governmental support agencies. Unsurprisingly, the most successful co-operatives do not always conform to the co-operative blueprint but pragmatically accommodate capitalist institutions and ideologies. For example, the Scott-Bader Commonwealth in the UK was formed after the original owner transferred the shares to an employee trust fund and created a system of genuine participative decision-making; and the expansion of the Mondragon co-operatives in Spain has been critically dependent on the continued financial support of the *Caja Laboral Popular*, a savings bank (Bradley and Gelb, 1983).

In their analysis, Mellor et al. (1988) detail a daunting list of issues which must somehow be resolved to ensure continued co-operation and commercial effectiveness. The management process is a veritable minefield made all the more treacherous by inexperience, deeply rooted suspicions about the apparent non-productiveness of management as an activity and previous socialization which conditions us to hierarchy and patriarchy. Most co-operatives are ill-prepared for participative decision-making which, to be effective, requires time and sensitivity. With no clear-cut lines of authority, the potential for conflicts is greater. The absence of management skills makes forward planning, external relations and routine administration problematic and working-class attitudes to borrowing may seriously impede financial planning and control.

Production and personnel functions can be similarly troublesome. In a situation where self-motivation is the norm, supervision and quality control may be presumed to be superfluous, but 'them–us' attitudes often carry over from previous work socialization. In addition, production still needs to be planned and co-ordinated: having an equal share in ownership does not necessarily mean members know how to organize their own work. Job-rotation offers a means of demystifying managerial activities but may not always be appropriate or commercially desirable. Relations with trade unions are often ambiguous because the co-operative may expect the union to adopt the role of an arbitrator rather than a representative. In a situation where someone is being disciplined or dismissed, this means an inevitable conflict of interest between the individual and the collective.

Perhaps curiously, all this suggests that, far from resolving the motivation–control issue, the management of co-operative employment relationships becomes even more problematic. In contrast to conventional capitalist enterprise, a co-operative consciously pursues far more complex goals in the context of far more vulnerable organizational relationships but invariably with far fewer resources. Success is measured on compound criteria and will depend not only on a user-friendly economy but also on more subtle and sophisticated managerial skills. Such a conclusion is not to denigrate co-operative enterprise in any way but merely to re-emphasize the perpetual enigmas of constructing control.

Conclusion

This chapter has sought to elaborate the nature of the conceptual and practical problems relevant to understanding how the employment relationship is regulated. In so far as it is meaningful to talk in terms of findings, three points merit emphasis. First, regulation involves exercising control, which is a dynamic interactive power process; control mechanisms and processes take a kaleidoscopic variety of forms. Second, regulation is permeated by contradictions which reflect the competing and irreconcilable demands made of the employment relationship: efficiency requires that labour be controlled like any other economic input, while effectiveness requires that employees display a positive motivation in the pursuit of organizational objectives. This means that managerial control strategies can never be anything other than variable, contradictory and incomplete; hence control has to be continuously constructed and reconstructed. And third, in consequence, the social legitimacy of managerial control is inherently precarious and ephemeral. Despite the undoubted impact of social and managerial ideologies as means of securing social order and psychological acceptance in employment relations, they are merely surface phenomena on the underlying structure of endemic conflicting interests.

Notes

1 This is an all-embracing and, in consequence, somewhat vague term which is often used to cover a lot of ground. At the most general level, it refers to the constraints imposed on action by the societal context. Thus, the nature of the economic and political system, the legal framework, the role of religion or any other significant contextual feature, such as climate, may severely limit decision-making. More specifically, it may be indicative of the particular form of organization – such as public or multinational or co-operative – under discussion or, more prosaically, it may refer to the particular history of an industry or company.

2 The concept of management control is the subject of a voluminous and contentious theoretical debate beyond the scope of this chapter. For an excellent examination of the key issues see Reed (1989) and for a critical assessment of the historical developments in managerial attempts to construct control see Rose (1988).

3 The halo enjoyed by IBM for so long slipped in December 1989 when the American parent company, in response to intensified competition, announced a 'restructuring' programme which will result in 100,000 redundancies (4.5 per cent of the US workforce).

4 The following section draws extensively on Mellor et al. (1988) which provides an excellent summary of the literature. See also chapter 13.

References

Anthony, P. D. (1977) *The Ideology of Work*. London: Tavistock.

Atkinson, J. (1984) *Flexibility, Uncertainty and Manpower Management*. Report No. 89. London: Institute of Manpower Studies.

Bain, G. S. (1970) *The Growth of White Collar Trade Unionism*. Oxford: Clarendon Press.

Bassett, P. (1986) *Strike Free: New Industrial Relations in Britain*. London: Macmillan.

Batstone, E. V. (1984) *Working Order: Workplace Industrial Relations over Two Decades*. Oxford: Blackwell.

Bean, R. (1985) *Comparative Industrial Relations*. London: Croom Helm.

Bendix, R. (1974) *Work and Authority in Industry*. Berkeley: University of California.

Bradley, K. and Gelb, A. (1983) *Cooperation at Work, the Mondragon Experience*. London: Heinemann.

Brewster, C. and Connock, S. (1985) *Industrial Relations: Cost-Effective Strategies*. London: Hutchinson.

Burrows, G. (1986) *No-Strike Agreements and Pendulum Arbitration*. London: Institute of Personnel Management.

Child, J. (1969) *British Management Thought*. London: Allen & Unwin.

Clegg, H. A. (1976) *Trade Unionism under Collective Bargaining*. Oxford: Blackwell.

Cressey, P., Eldridge, J. T. and McInnes, J. (1985) *Just Managing: Authority and Democracy in Industry*. Milton Keynes: Open University Press.

Crouch, C (1977) *Class Conflict and the Industrial Relations Crisis: Compromise and Corporatism in the Policies of the British State*. London: Heinemann.

Crowther, S. and Garrahan, P. (1988) Corporate Power and the Local Economy. *Industrial Relations Journal*, 19, 1, 51–9.

Dore, R. (1973) *British Factory, Japanese Factory*. London: Allen & Unwin.

Dromey, J. and Taylor, G. (1978) *Grunwick: the Workers' Story*. London: Lawrence & Wishart.

Edwards, P. K. (1987) *Managing the Factory*. Oxford: Blackwell.

Edwards, R (1979) *Contested Terrain*. London: Heinemann.

Flanders, A. (1970) *Management and Unions*. London: Faber & Faber.

Fox, A. (1974) *Beyond Contract: Work, Power and Trust Relations*. London: Faber & Faber.

Friedman, A.L. (1977) *Industry and Labour*, London: Macmillan.

Friedman, H. and Meredeen, S. (1980) *The Dynamics of Industrial Conflict: Lessons from Ford*. London: Croom Helm.

Goldthorpe, J. H., Lockwood, D., Bechofer, F. and Platt, J. (1968) *The Affluent Worker: Industrial Attitudes and Behaviour*. Cambridge: Cambridge University Press.

Grenier, G. J. (1988) *Inhuman Relations: Quality Circles and Anti-unionism in American Industry*, Philadelphia: Temple University Press.

Hanami, T. (1980) *Labour Relations in Japan Today*. London: Martin.

Hyman, R. (1987) Strategy or Structure?: Capital, Labour and Control. *Work, Employment and Society*, 1, 1, 25–55.

Keenoy, T. (1981) The Employment Relationship as a Form of Socio-Economic Exchange. In G. Dluglos and K. Wieiermair (eds), *Management Under Differing Value Systems*, New York: de Gruyter, 405–46.

Keenoy, T. (1985) *Invitation to Industrial Relations*. Oxford: Blackwell.

Keenoy, T. (1990) HRM: A Case of the Wolf in Sheep's Clothing? *Personnel Review, 19*, 2, 3–9.

Kerr, C., Dunlop, J. T., Harbison, F. and Myers, C. A. (1973) *Industrialism and Industrial Man*. Harmondsworth: Penguin.

Kochan, T. A., Katz, H. and McKersie, R. B. (1986) *The Transformation of American Industrial Relations*. New York: Basic Books.

Lewis, R. (ed.) (1986) *Labour Law in Britain*. Oxford: Blackwell.

MacInnes, J. (1987) *Thatcherism at Work*. Milton Keynes: Open University Press.

McKenna, S. (1988) 'Japanisation' and Recent Developments in Britain. *Employee Relations*, 10, 4, 6–12.

Mailly, R., Dimmock, S. J. and Sethi, A. S. (1989) *Industrial Relations in the Public Services*. London: Routledge.

Marginson, P., Edwards, P. K., Martin, R., Purcell, J. and Sisson, K. (1988) *Beyond the Workplace*. Oxford: Blackwell.

Mellor, M., Hannah, J. and Stirling, J. (1988) *Worker Cooperatives in Theory and Practice*. Milton Keynes: Open University Press.

Peach, L. H. (1983) Employee Relations at IBM. *Employee Relations*, 5, 3, 17–20.

Peters, T. J. and Waterman, R. H. (1982) *In Search of Excellence: Lessons from America's Best-Run Companies*. New York: Harper & Row.

Pravda, A. and Ruble, B. (eds) (1986) *Trade Unions in Communist States*. Winchester, Mass: Allen & Unwin.

Purcell, J. (1987) Mapping Management Styles in Industrial Relations. *Journal of Management Studies*, 24, 5, 533–48.

Purcell, J. and Sisson, K. (1983) Strategies and Practice in the Management of Industrial Relations. In G. S. Bain (ed), *Industrial Relations in Britain*, Oxford: Blackwell, 95–120.

Ramsey, H. (1977) Cycles of Control: Worker Participation in Social and Historical Perspective. *Sociology*, 11, 3, 481–6.

Reed, M. (1989) *The Sociology of Management*. London: Harvester Wheatsheaf.

Rogaly, J. (1977) *Grunwick*. Harmondsworth: Penguin.

Rose, M. (1988) *Industrial Behaviour*. Harmondsworth: Penguin.

Rueschemeyer, M. and Scharf, C. B. (1986) Labour Unions in the German Democratic

Republic. In A. Pravda and B. Ruble (eds), *Trade Unions in Communist States*, Winchester, Mass: Allen & Unwin, 53–84.

Sisson, K. (1987) *The Management of Collective Bargaining: An International Comparison.* Oxford: Blackwell.

Starkey, K. and McKinlay, A. (1989) Beyond Fordism? Strategic Choice and Labour Relations in Ford UK. *Industrial Relations Journal*, 20, 2, 93–100.

Storey, J. (1983) *Managerial Prerogative and the Question of Control.* London: Routledge & Kegan Paul.

Streeck, W. (1984) *Industrial Relations in West Germany.* London: Heinemann.

Thomas, R. J. (1988) What is Human Resource Management? *Work, Employment and Society*, 3, 2, 392–402.

Thomason, G. (1988) *A Textbook of Human Resource Management.* London: Institute of Personnel Management.

Thompson, P. (1983) *The Nature of Work.* London: Macmillan.

Von Beyme, K. (1980) *Challenge to Power.* London: Sage.

Watson, T. J. (1980) *Sociology, Work and Industry.* London: Routledge & Kegan Paul.

Wilkinson, B. and Oliver, N. (1989) Power, Control and the Kanban. *Journal of Management Studies*, 26, 1, 47–58.

Further Reading

Anthony, Peter (1986) *The Foundation of Management.* London: Tavistock. Anthony, somewhat provocatively, but never perversely, argues that management have consistently failed to take proper responsibility for managing the employment relationship. A useful supplement to Fox (below).

Fox, Alan (1974) *Beyond Contract: Work, Power and Trust Relations.* London: Faber. Perhaps no one has explored the motivation-control dilemma in more depth than Fox. This book remains one of the most incisive and sensitive analyses available.

Kioke, Kazo (1988) *Understanding Industrial Relations in Modern Japan.* London: Macmillan. Kioke has been researching Japanese management practice for over twenty years and this book provides an insider's view of the Japanese phenomenon.

Reed, Mike (1989) *The Sociology of Management.* Hertfordshire: Harvester Wheatsheaf. The theoretical and empirical complexities of coming to an understanding of management control are elaborated on.

Rose, Michael (1988) *Industrial Behavior.* (2nd edition). Harmondsworth: Penguin. For a general and critical history of the way management practice in constructing control has developed this is invaluable.

Shibagaki, K., Trevor, M. and Abo, T. (1989) *Japanese and European Management.* Tokyo: Tokyo University Press. An edited collection of papers which explore the application of such practices in Europe.

Storey, John (1989) *New Perspectives on Human Resource Management.* London: Routledge. With respect to dramatic emergence of human resource management in the 1980s, this is the best available account of this to be found.

5

Employee Commitment and Control

David E. Guest

Introduction

Faced by rapid change and growing competition, many organizations are being forced to reassess the basis on which they manage their workforce. In particular, they have been searching for new and more effective systems of motivation and control. This chapter examines one such approach, namely attempts to develop a new relationship with workers which is based on policies designed to create commitment to the organization. It will examine the assumptions underlying organizational commitment, evaluate the impact of these policies, consider some of their implications for industrial relations and explore the conditions under which they are likely to be successful. In doing so, it will set commitment in the wider context of human resource management.

Systems of Control and Motivation

Recent developments

Reasons for seeking a more effective utilization and control of the workforce are not hard to find (see Guest, 1987; Kochan et al., 1986; Walton, 1985). Foremost among them is the increasingly competitive business environment, be it local, national or international, facing many organizations and the resultant need to find new ways of competing effectively. One source of competitive advantage is through a more effective use of employees. Support for the benefits of such a strategy can be found in the research on successful organizations. Perhaps the most obvious example is Peters and Waterman's (1982) *In Search of Excellence*. This seemed to show that policies designed to make full use of human resources were a key feature of American companies with a long term record of success. Subsequent studies in the UK and elsewhere, admittedly not always of a very high quality, have nevertheless confirmed this central finding.

During the 1980s, two important factors facilitated the application of human resource management. One was the considerable advance made by organizational psychologists in the development of relevant techniques. These range from selection techniques and methods of socialization and training to leadership and goal setting. For organizations wishing to adopt human resource management, they provide some of the means to implement it. It is also worth noting that psychologists, often working as consultants, became much more proficient at marketing these techniques. A second factor, in the UK in particular, was the political and economic climate of the 1980s which encouraged employers to explore new systems of motivation and control.

Successive pieces of legislation in the 1980s sought to reduce the power of trade unions. At the same time there was explicit encouragement of mechanisms to increase employee involvement in the organization, implicitly bypassing or marginalizing the unions. This was most notably manifested in the encouragement of various forms of employee share ownership and profit sharing.

Historical background: compliance versus commitment

The mechanisms of control that operate in an organization reflect the underlying assumptions about work, workers and the nature of organizations that are held by those at the top of the organization who shape the systems of manpower control. The main choices of control system have been given various labels but all capture essentially the same issues. Etzioni (1961), for example, distinguishes between alienative involvement, calculative involvement and moral involvement. Kelman (1961) describes the choice between compliance, identification and internalization, where internalization is defined as a congruence between individual and organizational values. Fox (1974), looking more explicitly at industrial relations, uses rather different dimensions labelled radical, pluralist and unitarist.

Returning to the assumptions of those at the top of organizations, McGregor (1960) contrasted two types of 'theory' about the workforce which senior managers might hold and which would be likely to determine their preferred system of control. Theory X views workers as lazy and essentially disinterested in work. They do not identify with the goals and values of the organization and are therefore likely to require tight management control. Theory Y accepts that workers can identify with organizational goals and therefore, if given responsibility and autonomy, will display high motivation and commitment to the task and to the organization. Working more explicitly within the context of human resource management, Walton (1985) has made a similar distinction which he defines as a contrast between management philosophies of control and commitment.

The possibility of a highly committed workforce holds obvious attractions for many managers. However, it often requires a fundamental shift in their underlying assumptions about the nature of the workforce and about how best to manage it. The contrast between the traditional, and currently still dominant, system of control based on compliance and the newer approach based on commitment is highlighted in table 5.1.

The traditional and still dominant system of control throughout UK industry is based on compliance. Because managers seek compliance from the workforce, they are concerned, as table 5.1 indicates, with obtaining standard performance

Table 5.1 Possible bases for workforce policy

Aspects of policy	Compliance	Commitment
Psychological contract	Fair day's work for a fair day's pay	Reciprocal commitment
Locus of control	External	Internal
Employee relations	Pluralist	Unitarist
	Collective	Individual
	Low trust	High trust
Organizing principles	Mechanistic	Organic
	Formal/defined roles	Flexible roles
	Top–down	Bottom–up
	Centralized	Decentralized
Policy goals	Administrative	Adaptive/ Effectiveness
	Standard performance	Improving performance
	Cost minimization	Maximum utilization

rather than maximum or continually improving performance. One of the merits of this system is its concern for fairness; but mechanisms for ensuring fairness, such as job specifications and job evaluation-based payment systems, can become mechanisms for reinforcing rigidity. As a result, the system as a whole comes under challenge for being inefficient and inflexible.

Managerial assumptions about the need to operate a compliance based system have strong support. They are based on beliefs about differences of interest which, according to recent research, still persist (Guest and Dewe, 1991). They also assume that both sides have power. Traditionally the power of the workforce has often been collectively represented through the trade union movement. Increasingly, attempts have been made to limit this to individual power exerted through the market. In other words, workers possess non-substitutable skills which they can transfer in the labour market. Managers possess power through their ability to offer incentives and to impose punishment and through control of communication and therefore possibly through ideology.

Katz and Kahn (1978) have identified five conditions for the operation of compliance based models. The first is what they term 'normative socialization' or acceptance of the structure of authority. The second is the use of legitimate authority or the acceptance of the right of supervisors to give instructions/orders. A third is clear authorization; in other words, each worker should know precisely what is expected of him or her. Fourth, there should be the ability to enforce punishments and sanctions. This entails some expectation of being caught and punishment for misdemeanours. Finally, there must be opportunities to expel non-conformers. They might have added a sixth factor, incentives to perform correctly. This would reinforce pay-offs for compliance of the correct sort, possibly reflected in regular attendance but more likely in high performance. They cite a range of psychological evidence (for example, Milgram, 1965; Tannenbaum, 1974) to support the first key condition, acceptance of the legitimacy of organizational authority.

Given that these conditions can often be met, what has gone wrong with this approach and why are companies looking to alternative means of motivating and controlling their workforce? A first response is to challenge whether it has gone wrong. It certainly reflects the still dominant approach to management of the workforce. More importantly, it may still be the most feasible system to operate in many contexts. As the evidence we shall review later suggests, only a small minority of companies have in fact moved away from this system.

The answers can be found partly in the control systems that the approach requires. Because compliance is based on low trust, it requires firm external control mechanisms, such as clocking on, tight supervision and careful inspection of work. Mintzberg (1983), adopting a rather different perspective from Katz and Kahn, argues that any management must impose some system of control to ensure standardization of performance. He cites five main mechanisms: informal communication between workers, direct supervision, standardization of work processes, standardization of outputs and standardization of knowledge and skills. A system of control based on compliance is likely to emphasize direct supervision, work processes and outputs. This requires bureaucratic systems, including hierarchy, inspectors, and mechanisms for standardization, which are all reflected in their most refined form in the traditional assembly lines of large organizations. These represent both inefficiencies, in that top management, if they believed that they had a trustworthy and competent workforce, could dispense with many of the controls, and inbuilt inflexibilities, in that workers are typically given standard, clearly delimited tasks for which they are paid a carefully calculated wage and any change is likely to become a matter of protracted negotiation. These may not matter in the context of a stable market environment and a mechanistic organization structure. However, for an increasing proportion of organizations, the environment has become less stable, requiring a capacity for rapid adjustment and an ability to respond flexibly to specific and varied customer demands. To meet these demands swiftly and effectively, organizations require a workforce which is more than merely compliant. It requires their active help and the use of considerable local initiative. The assumptions on which the design of managerial jobs was based must therefore be extended to more of the workforce. Tom Keenoy developed this analysis in Chapter 4 where he highlights the problems for managers of reconciling the need for control and the need for a motivated workforce.

Despite the potential attractions of applying human resource management to obtain a more committed workforce, the problems are formidable. First, the policy may founder on the unenthusiastic response of a workforce reluctant to display commitment to the organization. Second, the workforce and in particular trade unions may be deeply suspicious of management's motives. By strengthening workers' attachment to their employer, human resource management policy may weaken their attachment to their union. This may therefore represent a challenge to traditional industrial relations, a challenge which those suspicious of management's motives and anxious about their long term job security may oppose. Third, presenting perhaps even more of an obstacle, are the ingrained assumptions of managers at all levels about workers and about how best to manage them. Fourth, there is a certain lack of clarity about the steps necessary to obtain a committed workforce. To understand these problems and issues more fully, we need, as a starting point, some analysis of the concept of commitment.

The Concept of Commitment

As interest in commitment has grown, so too has the number of definitions. In practice these can be broadly reduced to three groups concerned with attitudinal, exchange and behavioural commitment. In this section we briefly examine each of these approaches and evaluate the status of the concept of commitment.

Three approaches to commitment

The concept of attitudinal commitment can be traced to the work of Buchanan (1974) who defined organizational commitment as:

> a partisan, affective attachment to the goals and values of an organization, to one's role in relation to goals and values, and to the organization for its own sake, apart from its purely instrumental worth. (p. 533)

This definition is specifically concerned with commitment to an organization and focuses on attitude rather than behaviour. Mowday et al. (1982), in what is probably the most widely used definition, adopt a more active view and extend Buchanan's definition to suggest that organizational commitment is:

> the relative strength of an individual's identification with and involvement in a particular organization. It is characterized by at least three factors:
>
> 1 A strong belief in and acceptance of an organization's goals and values.
> 2 A willingness to exert considerable effort on behalf of the organization.
> 3 A strong desire to maintain membership of the organization. (p 27)

This implies that organizational commitment has both an affective and behavioural component. While this may be appealing to policy-makers, it presents researchers with a major problem, since the definition conflates the process and outcome. It is difficult to relate variations in levels of commitment, defined and measured in this way, to dependent variables such as effort, performance and labour turnover, since these are contained in the definition. Nevertheless, this definition has become the most widely used. There are a number of reasons for this. Mowday et al. (1982) have built a theory around it, outlining plausible antecedents and consequences of commitment; they have also developed a convenient measure of commitment and used it to provide a baseline of research for others to build on.

A second approach to commitment has been outlined by Becker (1960) and subsequently developed and operationalized by, among others, Hrebiniak and Alutto (1972). They view commitment as the result of an exchange between two parties. It may apply to the employer and employee but it extends into all kinds of social exchange. As defined by Hrebiniak and Alutto this type of commitment, known as exchange commitment is:

> a result of individual–organizational transactions and alterations in side bets or investments over time. The more favourable the exchange from the participants' point of view, the greater the commitment to the system. (p. 556)

This implies that satisfaction and identification with the organization is less important than a sense of being tied to it through investments such as pay, pensions, promotion expectations and social relationships. Commitment to an organization will result for as long as an individual believes that membership provides him or her with the best exchange available.

Some of the more recent work on commitment has acknowledged the distinction between these two types of commitment and measured them both. Meyer and Allen (1984), accepting that each provides valid but different bases for commitment, have devised separate scales to measure each type. They have labelled the two concepts 'affective' and 'continuance' commitment and have presented encouraging evidence of the validity of their scales. McGee and Ford (1987) have supported the validity of the affective commitment scale but suggest that continuance commitment comprises two separate components, one concerned with the various types of investments made by an individual in the present organization and the other with the lack of attractive alternatives. They report a positive correlation between sunk costs and affective commitment and a negative correlation between lack of alternatives and affective commitment. One reason why Meyer and Allen's work could be important is their suggestion that each type of commitment has different behavioural consequences. Affective commitment will be linked to effort while continuance commitment, as its name implies, will be linked to low labour turnover.

The third major type of commitment is more explicitly concerned with behaviour and has rather different psychological roots. Indeed, it can be traced back to some of Lewin's (1947) early work on social influences on behaviour. Salancik (1977) describes this third type of commitment, known as behavioural commitment, as follows:

> The degree of commitment derives from the extent to which a person's behaviors are binding. Four characteristics of behavioral acts make them

binding, and hence determine the extent of commitment: explicitness; revocability; volition; and publicity.

(1977, p.4)

This definition points to the factors that need to be taken into account to obtain behavioural commitment. It is worth nothing that they share a number of features with goal setting (Locke and Latham, 1984), for which one requirement is a clear individual commitment to pursue a specified goal. Behavioural commitment therefore represents a potentially powerful technique to influence performance. However, it is probably best seen in this context as an important technique rather than a basis for employee relations policy. Therefore, while noting it as another important dimension of the general concept of commitment, we will not explore it in detail in this chapter.

Criticisms of the concept of commitment

From the preceding analysis it will have become clear that commitment is a difficult and rather elusive concept. Not surprisingly it has attracted its fair share of criticism. Most of that criticism has been directed at the concept of attitudinal organizational commitment as defined by Mowday et al. (1982). One theme in the criticisms has been the risk of concept redundancy. There appears to be potential overlap between their version of organizational commitment, job involvement, work as a central life interest, the Protestant work ethic and possibly professionalism (Morrow, 1983; Blau, 1985). Relevant studies show intercorrelations of about 0.5 between job involvement, job satisfaction and organizational commitment. However, in one of the few studies to explore this explicitly, Brooke et al. (1988) concluded that they are empirically distinct concepts.

From a different perspective, criticism has been directed at the concept of organization (Coopey and Hartley, 1991). It is far from clear to what organization, to what section or level of the organization, the concept is intended to refer or does refer in practice when data are collected. Reichers (1985, 1986) has empirically demonstrated the existence of multiple and potentially competing attachments, for example to a profession, a work group and a company. This raises the question of whether an individual can be committed to both company and trade union, an issue to which we return later.

A further focus of criticism has been the measures of commitment. Meyer and Allen (1984) have argued convincingly that the main measures of attitudinal and exchange commitment contain elements of both concepts. Indeed, most research which has bothered to investigate this has shown that the Occupational Commitment Questionnaire (Mowday et al. 1979) contains two factors (Angle and Perry, 1981; Dimitriadis, 1990). Question-marks over the validity of the scales should be borne in mind when considering the findings of empirical studies of the causes and consequences of commitment, which are described here.

Virtually all of the work described so far is North American. There has been little theoretical or empirical work on commitment in the UK. Nevertheless, Cook and Wall (1980) have developed and validated a British measure of commitment which has been quite widely used. From a rather different perspective, Oliver (1990) has explored commitment among workers in a co-operative.

In summary, this review of work on the nature and status of organizational commitment indicates that it can be justified as an independent concept. However, there are problems in dealing with issues such as multiple commitments. There also appear to be two dimensions to organizational commitment, with rather different behavioural consequences, and this has not been sufficiently taken into account by those using the dominant measure of commitment, the Organizational Commitment Questionnaire, developed by Mowday et al. (1982).

Despite these conceptual and operational problems, there is evidence that policy-makers are attracted by the possibility of using organizational commitment to improve performance, to reduce labour turnover and possibly to weaken collective links to trade unions. If organizational commitment is to achieve these goals, it must operate through certain policy levers, the mechanisms necessary to achieve increased organizational commitment. There is at least one book which presents a number of cases of companies which have pursued policies designed to increase workforce commitment to the organization and which provides detailed advice to employers who might wish to embark on this course (Martin and Nichols, 1987). There is also extensive evidence that companies are using employee involvement policies as a mechanism to influence commitment. We can therefore review the impact of commitment and the shift in policy that it implies through an analysis of the impact of employee involvement. This brings organizational commitment firmly into an area of central concern to the wider field of employee relations.

The rationale for using employee involvement as a means of increasing organizational commitment rests upon a set of assumptions about the causes and consequences of commitment. More specifically, it assumes that the practices associated with employee involvement will increase commitment and that increased commitment will have an impact on employee behaviour.

Before exploring the impact of employee involvement, and as a basis for better understanding its impact, we need first to review the evidence on the antecedents and consequences of organizational commitment. At this point it is worth emphasizing again that almost all of the research is concerned with attitudinal organizational commitment based on the definition and measure offered by Mowday et al. (1982), and has been conducted almost entirely in North America.

The Causes of Organizational Commitment

There have been many studies exploring the assumed antecedents or causes of commitment (for an early review, see Mowday et al. 1982). However, most are correlational (for exceptions see, for example, Bateman and Strasser, 1984; Stumpf and Hartman, 1984; Meyer and Allen, 1988) and therefore can do no more than offer hypotheses about cause and effect relationships.

Mowday et al. (1979) suggest that the causes of commitment fall into four categories: personal/individual characteristics, role related experiences, work experiences and structural factors. It may be helpful to add a fifth category of personnel policies, such as job security and single status. In the present context there is no space to review the range of studies and to provide a full evaluation of their findings. Instead, a summary is provided in table 5.2. This identifies the main factors which have been found to be associated with variations in commitment. More weight has been given to the findings of the longitudinal studies and the causal factors emerging from these studies are presented in italic.

For policy-makers and more particularly for advocates of employee involvement, the results of this review are not very encouraging. Two sets of variables with clear policy implications emerge with some consistency. It appears that a job which meets expectations encourages higher commitment. Furthermore, some people have a greater propensity than others to display commitment through work involvement. This implies that one important path to high commitment is for management to take great care at the stages of recruitment, selection and socialization (see also Chapter 2). Caldwell et al. (1990) have provided empirical evidence in support of this contention. The second major element is job design.

Table 5.2 Antecedents of high Organizational commitment

Categories	*Factors*
Personal characteristics	*Work involvement*
	Lower education
	Age (older)
Work role	*Job scope/Responsibility*
	Opportunity for self-expression
	Low role stress
Experiences in the organization	*Confirmed expectations*
	Positive leadership/Supervision
	Commitment norm
	Feeling socially involved
Structural characteristics	Scope for ownership
	Decentralization
	Interdependence within organization
Personnel policies	Security/Ability to count on organization
	Fair treatment/Equitable pay

Commitment appears to be higher among those whose job provides scope for responsibility and for self-expression.

Taken as a whole, the results of the extensive literature on presumed antecedents of commitment raise doubts about the extent to which it is feasible to use company policy, and more particularly employee involvement policies, to influence commitment.

The Consequences of Commitment

The appeal of organizational commitment for managers and researchers lies largely in its assumed impact on behaviour. Indeed, as noted above, the definition provided by Mowday et al. (1982) embraces behavioural consequences. It is therefore plausible to expect that there will be a link, more especially when use is made of the Organizational Commitment Questionnaire which they devised on the basis of their definition and which has been the dominant measure adopted in research. The consequences of commitment are usually considered in terms of the impact on labour turnover, absenteeism and job performance. Implicit in this ordering is the assumption that the most direct impact should be on labour turnover followed by absence. Job performance is usually heavily influenced by a number of other factors and in any case is mediated through effort.

Industrial action and union membership

Commitment might also be expected to have an impact on industrial relations, since high commitment implies loyalty to and identification with the values of the organization. This would presumably be measured through indices of collective action, ranging from restriction of output to strikes. We might hypothesize that those committed to their employing organization would be reluctant to engage in any form of individual or collective action which jeopardized the interests and goals of that organization. Organizational commitment should also be a variable which helps to predict which workers will choose to engage in collective action or which workers will cross the picket line. No research on commitment has directly addressed these questions. Stepping back from industrial action, organizational commitment should also predict trade union membership. This raises a set of more complex issues to which we return in the next section. Meanwhile, it is worth noting that future research might usefully focus on the link between commitment and industrial action and union membership.

Labour turnover

In the early studies summarized by Mowday et al. (1982), a clear and consistent correlation between commitment and lower labour turnover was reported. These correlations typically averaged around 0.40 and they could be interpreted as showing the important influence of organizational commitment. However, recent more thorough analyses questioned this.

Models of labour turnover have become increasingly sophisticated. For example, Mobley et al. (1979) have presented a very complex model which, at its core, predicts that labour turnover will be a function of job satisfaction, expected utility of alternative roles internal to the organization, expected utility of external roles, and a variety of non-work values and contingencies. In a test across a number of longitudinal studies, Mowday et al. (1984) found general but unstable support for the model. More importantly in the present context, both commitment and job satisfaction were related to labour turnover but only indirectly through their influence on intention to quit. In this as in many other studies, intention to quit was the best predictor of actual labour turnover. Job satisfaction and commitment added no independent additional explanatory power.

Testing another model of labour turnover developed by Steers and Mowday, Lee and Mowday (1987) found that commitment correlated -0.35 with intention to quit and -0.10 with actual turnover. Regression analyses showed that job satisfaction explained 12.4 per cent of the variance in intention to quit while commitment explained just 4.1 per cent. Only intention to quit predicted actual turnover.

Farkas and Tetrick (1989) reached a similar conclusion. Over time it was not possible to arrive at a confident causal ordering of job satisfaction and commitment but, looking at the early phase of employment in the military, when commitment seemed to develop, their research supported a model in which satisfaction was a determinant of commitment which was in turn a determinant of intention to stay.

Finally, Price and Mueller (1986) explicitly tested Price's model which hypothesizes causal linkages from antecedents to job satisfaction to commitment to intention to quit to quitting. They did not look at the possibility of reverse causality between job satisfaction and commitment. Their results generally supported the model. A range of factors, of which job satisfaction was the most important, explained 42 per cent of the variance in commitment. Furthermore, a range of variables including job satisfaction and commitment explained 27 per cent of the variance in intention to quit. Finally, a range of factors, of which by far the most important was intention to quit followed by job satisfaction and then some way behind by commitment, explained 12 per cent of the variance in quitting behaviour. Interestingly, the findings support the model but show that it is very weak when it comes to predicting actual turnover.

These longitudinal studies show that we need to be very cautious in claiming a link between commitment and labour turnover. All of the studies show that there is a link, because commitment is one important predictor of intention to quit which is invariably by far the best predictor of actual labour turnover. Commitment provides at best no more than a modest additional independent explanation of labour turnover. All of the studies also show a complex relationship between satisfaction and commitment. They are strongly correlated, but the causality is not clearly from satisfaction to commitment; in at least one study (Price and Mueller, 1986) satisfaction appears to have more independent explanatory power than commitment. Nevertheless, commitment is important because of its consistently significant role as a predictor of intention to quit.

We have dealt at some length with the link between organizational commitment and labour turnover. There are three reasons for this. First, it illustrates the complexity of work in this area and the difficulty of disentangling the role of commitment. Second, labour turnover is generally acknowledged to be the outcome that is most likely to be affected by commitment and consequently has been the most extensively researched. Finally, as we shall see, labour turnover has a key role in the theory of human resource management.

Absenteeism

Although a link between commitment and absenteeism has often been assumed, the rationale for this link is seldom made explicit. Models of absence and attendance behaviour, like those for labour turnover, have become increasingly sophisticated but even an approach such as that presented by Steers and Rhodes (1978) suggests that attendance is a function of motivation to attend and of ability to attend. Commitment may affect motivation but will have little effect on ability. It will also be necessary to take into account competing commitments in the family. These factors suggest that, at best, the link between organizational commitment and absence will be weak. The evidence supports this view.

Mowday et al. (1982), in their review of the evidence, cite four studies. Two show significant negative correlations and two show insignificant positive correlations. More recently, Brooke and Price (1989) testing the Steers and Rhodes (1978) model, found no support for any link between commitment and absence. Nor was any link found in the longitudinal study conducted by Price and Mueller (1986). More research is clearly called for, but at this stage the evidence does not support any link between organizational commitment and absence.

Job performance

Mowday et al. (1982), in their overview of the impact of commitment, suggest that 'clearly, the least encouraging finding that has emerged from studies of commitment is a rather weak relationship between commitment and job performance' (p. 35). They themselves report eight correlations from two studies. Only two of these correlations are marginally significant. Since then, a number of studies have reported correlations between commitment and performance. For example, Lee and Mowday (1987) found that supervisory ratings of performance among financial institution employees correlated 0.09 with commitment and 0.11 with job satisfaction. Shore and Martin (1989), using a sample of bank tellers, found that supervisory ratings of performance correlated 0.24 with job satisfaction but only 0.03 with commitment. However, a more objective measure, the dollar value of bank tellers' errors, correlated -0.11 with job satisfaction and -0.27 with commitment.

Meyer et al. (1989) found a positive relationship between affective commitment and performance ratings and a negative relationship between these ratings and continuance commitment. Their sample size was small but the results suggest that if future research separates out the two dimensions of organizational commitment, then stronger links to performance might be found.

The available evidence shows a small, positive and marginally significant correlation between performance, typically measured using supervisory ratings, and commitment. Generally, these same studies show that satisfaction has a stronger relationship with performance. Furthermore, the presence of a marginally significant correlation does not tell us anything about the relative importance of commitment as a predictor of performance. It should be noted that, as with absence, it may not be wise to expect a strong link between commitment and performance. Commitment may result in greater effort. The extensive literature on expectancy theory reminds us that the link between effort and performance is mediated by a range of factors and is often weak.

In the same way that we need to be more careful about how we measure commitment, there is also scope for refining and extending the measures of performance. At present, performance is defined from a managerial perspective but usually uses ratings. Alternatives, such as suggestions, participation in quality circles or volunteering for overtime and weekend work, might fruitfully be utilized in future research. There is clearly a need also to consider the range of industrial relations outcomes, referred to earlier, such as grievances, collective action and attendance at union meetings.

In summary, the research on the outcomes associated with commitment is disappointing for those who believe that commitment should be a positive influence on employee behaviour. It may be that expectations about the influence of commitment are too high. It is certainly difficult to reach confident conclusions about anything other than labour turnover, mainly because there has been so little reported research. The more extensive evidence on turnover indicates that commitment is an important predictor of labour turnover but that its impact is indirect, mediated by the more important variable of intention to quit. Furthermore, commitment usually appears to be a less important predictor than job satisfaction.

Commitment to Company and Trade Union

One of the factors that might explain why policies to enhance organizational commitment do not always have the expected impact and why even highly committed employees do not behave in ways that appear to conform with that commitment is the possibility that more powerful competing commitments exist for these individuals. If we are to take seriously the concept of commitment, it would be most unwise to assume that the employer is the only significant potential focus of commitment. Employees may have equal or more powerful commitments to their family, profession, trade union, and to a range of leisure and non-work activities. These may have an important influence on behaviour and more particularly on labour turnover and absenteeism. In the context of employment relations it is the possibility of a competing commitment to a trade union that is of particular interest. Indeed, a major impetus behind attempts by some organizations to promote commitment through employee involvement is the desire to weaken links between workers and their trade union. At the same time, trade unions are becoming more aware of this possibility and have recognized the need to develop policies which will ensure that they retain the loyalty of their members. This has led to research on union commitment and on the possibility of dual commitment to both company and trade union.

Research on union commitment has followed a somewhat similar path to research on company commitment. Gordon et al. (1980) have developed and validated a measure of union commitment which has subsequently been extensively used. Heavily influenced by the work of Mowday, Porter and Steers, they identified four factors: loyalty to the union, responsibility to the union, willingness to work for the union, and belief in unionism. This indicates that union commitment is multi-dimensional and that it shares with the Mowday et al. (1982) version of company commitment an inbuilt action or behavioural component. Subsequent research has focused on the antecedents, the dimensions and the consequences of union commitment (see, for example, Thacker et al., 1990). There is as yet an insufficient body of research on which to base any general conclusions, more particularly on the consequences of union commitment, although Thacker et al. do report positive associations with attendance at union meetings, voting behaviour and other forms of union activity.

The feasibility of dual commitment

One of the underlying research questions is whether the models predicting company and union commitment are similar. Fukami and Larson (1984) concluded that they were similar, to the extent that the same variables predicted commitment to both company and union. Thacker et al. (1990) concluded that the underlying model might be similar but that the actual variables within the model will differ for union and company commitment. Barling et al. (1990). representing what is probably the dominant view, found that company and union commitment are caused by different factors. This raises interesting questions about the feasibility of dual commitment. Logically, if commitment to company and to trade union are caused by different extremes of the same variables, then dual commitment is not possible. If they are caused by the same dimension of particular variables (for example, a high potential for work involvement, older rather than younger workers), then dual commitment is possible. Finally, if they are caused by different variables, then dual commitment is also possible. More research is needed before we can unravel which of these possibilities is closest to reality.

Interest in what was initially known as dual allegiance was first displayed by American researchers at the time when union membership was growing in the 1950s and there was some concern among managers about the ability of companies to retain the commitment of their workforce. More recently it has re-emerged in the context of the decline in trade union membership and concern about whether trade unions will be able to retain the loyalty of their members. There is now an extensive body of research, most of which indicates that dual commitment is possible. A key mediating factor appears to be organizational climate or, to be more specific, industrial relations climate (Angle and Perry, 1986). Where it is co-operative and conflict free, dual commitment is likely to be more feasible. Where it is more hostile and adversarial, workers may be forced to make a choice and to opt for company or union, or else they may display commitment to neither. The study by Barling et al. (1990) is interesting because it was conducted in the wake of an industrial dispute. They reported a correlation of -0.25 between company and union commitment. This varied between 0.06 among those who perceived a positive organizational climate and -0.52 among those who judged the organizational climate in negative terms. Questions could be asked about the causal directions of these associations but they do reinforce the existence of a link between dual commitment and industrial relations climate.

An important applied issue is the extent to which dual commitment is actually displayed. Caution must be exercised in interpreting correlational results, since a positive correlation might reflect either dual commitment or low commitment to both company and union. The more careful research, including the study by Angle and Perry (1986) which used three separate measures of company, union and dual commitment, has generally found a low level of dual commitment.

Recent comparative research using a modified measure of commitment, based more on Buchanan's (1974) concept of identification with company and union, showed important variations across workers in the same industrial sector in different countries (Guest and Dewe, 1991). Results for some of the main countries included in the study are presented in table 5.3.

These results appear to provide indirect support for the importance of industrial relations climate. In those countries with a reputation for co-operative industrial relations, such as Sweden and West Germany, dual commitment is higher than in countries such as Italy and the UK. However, the generally high proportion in the sample, in a country such as the UK, showing commitment to neither company nor trade union suggests that both companies and trade unions have a long way to go to generate higher commitment.

Consideration of dual and competing commitments raises questions about the benefits of commitment for individuals rather than organizations. Randall (1987) has presented the case against commitment, arguing that it may provide opportunities for individuals to be exploited and could represent a loss of individuality, and Kanter (1989) has explored the problem of excessive commitment to an organization for family life. Set against these concerns, Romzek (1989), in a longitudinal study, found a positive link over time between a measure of organizational involvement and both non-work and career satisfaction. This implies that it may not be appropriate to consider most potentially competing sources of commitment in 'either – or' terms. An alternative explanation raised by Romzek is that a dispositional factor, perhaps some persisting trait associated with a greater or lesser willingness to become involved in any kind of activity, shapes levels of commitment to all kinds of activity (Staw and Ross, 1985).

Table 5.3   Current levels of commitment of workers in consumer electronics

	Total number Union members	Non-union	Dual allegiance Union members	(%) Non-union	Union allegiance Union members	(%) Non-union	Company allegiance Union members	(%) Non-union	No allegiance Union members	(%) Non-union
UK	329	168	17	3	27	1	11	36	45	61
W. Germany	215	168	39	45	39	17	10	21	11	17
Sweden	710	22	29	–	20	–	15	–	37	–
Italy	544	392	10	6	40	17	5	13	45	65

Source: Guest and Dewe, 1991

Employee involvement as a path to high commitment

'Employee involvement' is a term which is used rather loosely to describe a range of company policies and procedures. They share the goal of increasing employees' commitment and contribution to an organization. Five main forms of involvement can be distinguished: improving the provision of information to employees, for example through briefing groups and company employee reports; improving the provision of information from employees, for example through suggestion schemes and quality circles; changing the structures and arrangements of work, perhaps through greater delegation and the redesign of jobs; changing the incentives, typically through employee share ownership programmes or performance related pay; and finally, changing relationships through more participative leadership and greater informality. Looking back to the evidence on the antecedents of commitment, it seems plausible to expect that some but not all of these approaches, if carefully designed and consistently implemented, might improve commitment. In so far as they improve the industrial relations climate, they might also increase the scope for dual commitment.

During the 1980s, many companies in the UK pursued policies of employee involvement. The 1984 Workplace Industrial Relations survey (Millward and Stevens, 1986) noted that 31 per cent of organizations claimed to have taken some sort of initiative to increase employee involvement. The most popular mechanism was two-way communication. Other surveys have confirmed the widespread development of employee involvement initiatives (e.g. Edwards, 1987; Marginson et al., 1988).

There has been very little research on the link between employee involvement policies and company commitment, so it is not possible to reach any firm conclusions about the validity of the assumptions underlying these policies. There has, however, been extensive research on the impact of some of the specific policies. We know, for example, that employees generally welcome these initiatives and that they can increase job satisfaction. But at the individual and group level there is no consistent evidence of any impact on motivation, performance or industrial relations outcomes (Kelly and Kelly, 1991). At a more general level, and allowing for a few specific and notable exceptions, no relationship has been found between the use of employee involvement initiatives and company or plant performance (Edwards, 1987; Marginson et al., 1988). Furthermore, the life expectancy of many of these initiatives is short. This has been most thoroughly investigated with respect to quality circles (see, for example, Bradley and Hill, 1987; Campbell and Campbell, 1988).

Despite the inadequate research base, it is possible tentatively to conclude that all too often employee involvement in the UK and in North America fails to achieve the objectives set for it by management: namely, increased commitment and thereby improved performance, reflected directly in better quality and quantity of goods and services and indirectly through various forms of co-operative behaviour and more positive industrial relations outcomes. In the light of the preceding review of the causes and consequences of commitment, the limited impact of the employee involvement initiatives should not come as a surprise. If commitment is being used as the intervening variable between employee involvement policies and expected improvements in performance, this may reflect a faulty model of the part that organizational commitment can play. Its link to performance has not been convincingly demonstrated.

A second factor which might explain the limited impact is the method of introduction and implementation. Often techniques are introduced in a piecemeal way, more as the 'flavour of the month' than as part of a coherent strategy. One consequence of this is that they are not sufficiently embedded into company systems and quickly fall into disuse, especially in those contexts where line managers are less than enthusiastic about some of the initiatives.

The failure of personnel techniques, derived largely from organizational psychology, to have the expected impact in organizations has been noted before. Organizational development and leadership training are two relevant examples. Staw (1986) attributes this to the understandable resistance of many workers to efforts to change their underlying values and preferences. He suggests that it needs a much more concerted effort to bring about such changes. Lawler (1986), writing from a slightly different perspective, reaches a similar conclusion. To achieve what he terms a 'total involvement organization' requires a long term coherent strategy involving a combination of techniques and, by implication, a far reaching commitment to the overall strategy on the part of all managers. This perspective has been one influence on the growing interest in a more broadly based approach, such as human resource management.

Human Resource Management

A feature of the 1980s was the growing number of writers advocating more effective management of human resources as a path to competitive advantage. By implication this represented something new and distinct from what went before. All too often this was not the case; human resource management meant little more than a re-titling of a personnel department or a re-statement of the importance of human resources. However, human resource management can be much more than this. Indeed, it can be presented as a quite different approach (Guest, 1987). The roots of this approach can be found in theory and techniques derived from organizational psychology, combined with the use of business strategy. This results in the kind of model presented in Figure 5.1.

The assumptions underlying this model of human resource management are the same as those associated with the commitment based system of control presented earlier in the chapter and they are an important feature of its distinctiveness. Briefly, it proposes that careful use of the policy levers on the left-hand side of figure 5.1 can lead to the human resource outcomes listed in the middle of the figure. If these are achieved, and it is essential that all four are achieved, then the outcomes on the right-hand side could be expected. The three elements at the bottom of the figure, leadership, culture and strategy are the 'cement' that binds the human resource system together and ensures that it is taken seriously within a given organization. Although this is presented as a model, it can quite easily be developed into a set of theoretical propositions once

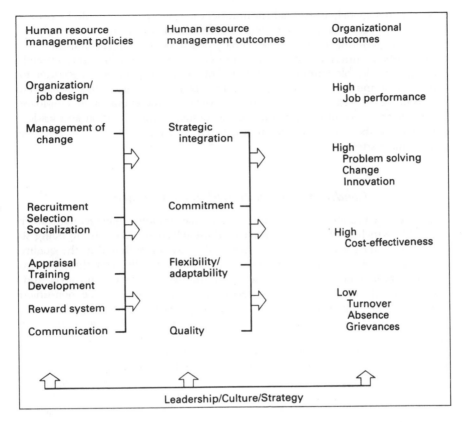

Figure 5.1 A model of human resource management

the particular characteristics of the policy levers have been specified more clearly (for example, the type of job design and the characteristics sought in those selected for employment).

In the present context, a key feature of the model is its acceptance that commitment to the company is not in itself enough to obtain the kind of improvements that many organizations seek. Indeed, commitment is just one of four key human resource policy goals, the others being flexibility, quality, and strategic integration. Flexibility refers to the content of jobs and the skills required to perform them and also to the structure of the organization. Quality in this context covers the quality of the work, the quality of the workforce, which is usually reflected in some investment in training and development, and the quality of treatment of the workforce by management. Strategic integration is concerned with the fit between business strategy and human resource management, with the way in which human resource policies cohere and with the extent to which line managers accept the values associated with human resource management.

Within this model, attitudinal commitment to the company should be complemented by behavioural commitment. Behavioural commitment can help to enhance job performance, while the primary benefit of attitudinal commitment is to limit labour turnover and therefore justify the investment in highly trained, high quality, flexible employees. A range of personnel policies is necessary to achieve these and considerable emphasis must be given to selection, socialization and training as well as to mechanisms which are more linked to employee involvement and commitment, such as job design, communication and leadership style. In short, they amount to a coherent and integrated human resource management strategy.

Conditions for successful implementation

Very few organizations achieve this set of human resource management policy goals. Nevertheless, there is evidence that those which are successful in doing so achieve superior performance from their staff. This is manifested in the quality and quantity of employee performance and will normally feed through into company profitability. It is also discernible through low labour turnover and, more especially in the USA, in a tendency for such firms to be non-union (Foulkes, 1980). Furthermore, there is some evidence (Purcell et al., 1987) that in the UK those organizations most enthusiastically pursuing a range of employee involvement policies, in a manner likely to lead to the kind of human resource management policy goals outlined above, are typically foreign owned. Many of these are newly established 'green-field' plants and are also non-union.

It has proved much more difficult for companies to introduce significant changes towards employee involvement in established plants (Guest, 1989). The constraints of technology, worker attitudes, management attitudes and lack of financial resources have often proved insurmountable. Too often, existing production systems are designed to provide simple jobs and the workforce have become used to the existing job content and associated relationships (see also chapter 2). Both workers and management may be suspicious of attempts to change established patterns. To invest both in major new technology, altering job design and working arrangements, and in a new or retrained workforce is simply too expensive and too much trouble. The result is some chipping away at the edges of existing systems, producing at best some marginal improvements in working arrangements. Currently this is most likely to be achieved by some sort of quality improvement programme. Indeed, partial changes can create new problems. In particular, they can cause anxiety and resistance among managers if they become attempts to move away from the old system of compliance based control without satisfactorily replacing it with a new commitment based system.

There is a clear association between human resource management and non-union plants. This approach, with commitment at its core, poses a threat to trade unions. In the UK it has rarely proved a threat in practice, except in the new 'green-field' plants; and there the absence of a trade union may be less keenly felt because there was no prior union system. Another factor, which is both reassuring to unions and perhaps an explanation of lack of change, is that many personnel managers seem comfortable with the existing collective bargaining arrangements. Where they have introduced new forms of employee involvement, they have done so alongside the existing arrangements rather than instead of them. Some may possibly hope for a withering away of the traditional collective system but this has seldom happened. Indeed, its persistence helps to explain the limited impact of attempts to enhance commitment to a company.

Summary and Conclusions

This chapter has outlined the pressures behind industry's interest in employee commitment, an interest which is typically manifested in policies of employee commitment. A closer analysis of psychological theorizing and research revealed that the benefits that were often assumed to flow from high levels of organizational commitment may have been overestimated. There have been problems in conceptualizing and operationalizing commitment. Furthermore, research has shown that commitment has only a very weak link to performance, although it does seem to be associated with lower labour turnover. Nor has research revealed any clear association between most forms of employee involvement and commitment to a company. Despite this, there are policy implications in the consistent findings that commitment can be enhanced through careful policies of recruitment, selection and socialization and through job design. Together these can help to create a fit between a person's expectations and the realities of organizational life.

One of the conceptual problems in commitment theory concerns the feasibility of multiple commitments and therefore the potential for conflict between commitment to a company and to a trade union. Dual commitment appears to be possible where the industrial relations climate is co-operative and based on integrative bargaining. The limited evidence on levels of commitment in the UK indicates that commitment to both company and union is generally low.

An important part of the explanation for the limited impact of attempts to increase commitment through employee involvement can be found in the failure to integrate the innovations into a wider, coherent human resource strategy. Where this can be achieved, and where company commitment can be combined with behavioural commitment, there may be pay-offs for the company. At the same time, an effective strategy of this sort can marginalize trade unions and thereby pose a threat to them. However, the formidable constraints on introducing a coherent human resource strategy in anywhere other than green-field sites indicates that this threat is rarely realized.

References

Angle, H. and Perry, J. (1981) An empirical assessment of organizational commitment and organizational effectiveness. *Administrative Science Quarterly*, 26, 1–14.
Angle, H. J. and Perry, J. L. (1986) Dual commitment labor–management relationship climates. *Academy of Management Journal*, 29, 31–50.

Barling, J., Wade, B. and Fullager, C. (1990) Predicting employee commitment to company and union: divergent models. *Journal of Occupational Psychology*, 63, 49–61.

Bateman, T. S. and Strasser, S. (1984) A longitudinal analysis of the antecedents of organizational commitment. *Academy of Management Journal*, 27, 95–112.

Becker, H. S. (1960) Notes on the concept of commitment. *American Journal of Sociology*, 66, 32–42.

Blau, G. J. (1985) The measurement and prediction of career commitment. *Journal of Occupational Psychology*, 58, 277–88.

Bradley, K. and Hill, S. (1987) Quality circles and managerial interests. *Industrial Relations*, 26, 68–82.

Brooke, P. P. and Price, J. L. (1989) The determinants of employee absenteeism: an empirical test of a causal model. *Journal of Occupational Psychology*, 62, 1–19.

Brooke, P. B., Russell, D. W. and Price, J. L. (1988) Discriminant validation of measures of job satisfaction, job involvement and organizational commitment. *Journal of Applied Psychology*, 73, 139–45.

Caldwell, D. F., Chatman, J. A. and O'Reilly, C. A. (1990) Building organizational commitment: a multifirm study. *Journal of Occupational Psychology*, 63, 245–61.

Campbell, J. P. and Campbell, R. J. (1988) *Productivity in Organizations*. San Francisco: Jossey-Bass.

Cook, J. and Wall, T. (1980) New work attitude measures of trust, organizational commitment and personal need non-fulfilment. *Journal of Occupational Psychology*, 53, 39–52.

Coopey, J. and Hartley, J. (1991) Reconsidering organizational commitment. *Human Resource Management Journal* 1, 3, 18–32.

Dimitriadis, Z. S. (1990) Commitment to work: an empirical study of construct validity. Mimeo. Graduate Industrial School of Thessaloníki.

Edwards, P. K. (1987) *Managing the Factory*. Oxford: Blackwell.

Etzioni, A. (1961) *A Comparative Analysis of Complex Organizations*. New York: Free Press.

Farkas, A. J. and Tetrick, L. E. (1989) A three-wave longitudinal analysis of the causal ordering of satisfaction and commitment on turnover decisions. *Journal of Applied Psychology*, 74, 855–68.

Foulkes, F. (1980) *Personnel Policies in Large Non-Union Companies*. Englewood Cliffs, NJ: Prentice-Hall.

Fox, A. (1974) *Beyond Contract: Work, Power and Trust Relations*. London: Faber & Faber.

Fukami, C. V. and Larson, E. W. (1984) Commitment to company and union: parallel models. *Journal of Applied Psychology*, 69, 367–71.

Gordon, M. E., Philpot, J. W., Burt, R. E., Thompson, C. A. and Spiller, W. E. (1980) Commitment to the union: Development of a measure and examination of its correlates. *Journal of Applied Psychology*, 65, 479–99.

Guest, D. (1987) Human resource management and industrial relations. *Journal of Management Studies*, 24, 503–21.

Guest, D. (1989) Human resource management: its implications for industrial relations and trade unions. In J. Storey (ed.), *New Perspectives on Human Resource Management* London: Routledge, 41–55.

Guest, D. and Dewe, P. (1991) Company or trade union: which wins workers' allegiance? A study of commitment in the United Kingdom electronics industry. *British Journal of Industrial Relations*, 29, 75–96.

Hrebiniak, L. G. and Alutto, J. A. (1972) Personal and role-related factors in the development of organizational commitment. *Administrative Science Quarterly*, 17, 555–73.

Kanter, R. M. (1989) *When Giants Learn to Dance*. London: Simon & Schuster.

Katz, D. and Kahn, R. L. (1978) *The Social Psychology of Organizations* (2nd ed.). New York: Wiley.

Kelly, J. and Kelly, C. (1991) Them and us: social psychology and 'the new industrial relations'. *British Journal of Industrial Relations*, 29, 25–48.

Kelman, H. C. (1961) Processes of opinion change. *Public Opinion Quarterly*, 25, 57–78.

Kochan, T. A., Katz, H. and McKersie, R.B. (1986) *The Transformation of American Industrial Relations*. New York: Basic Books.

Lawler, E. E. (1986) *High Involvement Management*. San Francisco: Jossey-Bass.

Lee, T. W. and Mowday, R. T. (1987) Voluntarily leaving an organization: an empirical investigation of Steers and Mowday's model of turnover. *Academy of Management Journal*, 30, 721–43.

Lewin, K. (1947) Group decision and social change. In T. M. Newcomb and E. L.Hartley (eds), *Readings in Social Psychology* New York: Holt.

Locke, E. A. and Latham, G. (1984) *Goal Setting: A Motivational Technique That Works*. Englewood Cliffs, NJ: Prentice-Hall.

McGee, G. W. and Ford, R. C. (1987) Two (or more?) dimensions of organizational commitment: re-examination of the affective and continuance commitment scales: *Journal of Applied Psychology*, 72, 638–41.

McGregor, D. (1960) *The Human Side of Enterprise*. London: McGraw-Hill.

Marginson, P., Edwards, P. K., Martin, R., Purcell, J. and Sisson, K. (1988) *Beyond The Workplace: Managing Industrial Relations in the Multi-establishment Enterprise*. Oxford: Blackwell.

Martin, P. and Nichols, J. (1987) *Creating A Committed Workforce*. London: Institute of Personnel Management.

Meyer, J. P. and Allen, N. J. (1984) Testing the 'side-bet theory' of organizational commitment: some methodological considerations. *Journal of Applied Psychology*, 69, 372–8.

Meyer, J. P. and Allen, N. J. (1988) Links between work experiences and organizational commitment during the first year of employment: a longitudinal analysis. *Journal of Occupational Psychology*, 61, 195–210.

Meyer, J. P. Paunonen, S. V. Gellatly, I. R., Goffin, R.D. and Jackson, D. N. (1989) Organizational commitment and job performance: It's the nature of the commitment that counts. *Journal of Applied Psychology*, 74, 152–6.

Milgram, S. (1965) Some conditions of obedience and disobedience to authority. *Human Relations*, 18, 57–76.

Millward, N. and Stevens, M. (1986) *British Workplace Industrial Relations 1980–1984*. Aldershot: Gower.

Mintzberg, H. (1983) *Structure in Fives: Designing Effective Organizations*. Englewood Cliffs, NJ: Prentice-Hall.

Mobley, W. H., Griffeth, R. W., Hand, H. H. and Meglino, B. M. (1979) Review and conceptual analysis of the employee turnover process. *Psychological Bulletin*, 86, 233–50.

Morrow, P. C. (1983) Concept redundancy in organizational research: the case of work commitment. *Academy of Management Review*, 8, 486–500.

Mowday, R. T. Koberg, C. S. and McArthur, A. W. (1984) The psychology of the withdrawal process: a cross-validational test of Mobley's intermediate linkages model of turnover in two samples. *Academy of Management Journal*, 27, 79–94.

Mowday, R. T., Porter, L. W. and Steers, R. M. (1982) *Employee–Organization Linkages: The Psychology of Commitment, Absenteeism and Turnover*. New York: Academic Press.

Mowday, R. T., Steers, R. M. and Porter, L. W. (1979) The measurement of organizational commitment. *Journal of Vocational Behavior*, 14, 224–47.

Oliver, N. (1990) Rewards, investments, alternatives and organizational commitment: empirical evidence and theoretical development. *Journal of Occupational Psychology*, 63, 19–31.

Peters, T. and Waterman, R. (1982) *In Search of Excellence*. New York: Harper & Row.

Price, J. L. and Mueller, C. W. (1986) *Absenteeism and Turnover Among Hospital Employees*. Greenwich, CT: JAI Press.

Purcell, J., Marginson, P., Edwards, P. K. and Sisson, K. (1987) The industrial relations practices of multi-plant foreign-owned firms. *Industrial Relations Journal*, 18, 130–7.

Randall, D. M. (1987) Commitment and the organization: the organization man revisited. *Academy of Management Review*, 12, 460–71.

Reichers, A. E. (1985) A review and reconceptualization of organizational commitment. *Academy of Management Review*, 10, 465–76.

Reichers, A. E. (1986) Conflict and organizational commitments. *Journal of Applied Psychology*, 71, 508–14.

Romzek, B. S. (1989) Personal consequences of employee commitment. *Academy of Management Journal*, 32, 649–61.

Salancik, G. R. (1977) Commitment and the control of organizational control and belief. In B. M. Staw and G. R. Salancik (eds), *New Directions in Organizational Behavior*, Chicago: St Clair Press, 1–54.

Shore, L. M. and Martin, H. J. (1989) Job satisfaction and organizational commitment in relation to work performance and turnover intentions. *Human Relations*, 42, 625–38.

Staw, B. M. (1986) Organizational psychology and the pursuit of the happy/productive worker. *California Management Review*, 28, 4.

Staw, B. M. and Ross, J. (1985) Stability in the midst of change: a dispositional approach to job attitudes. *Journal of Applied Psychology*, 70, 469–80.

Steers, R. M. and Rhodes, S. R. (1978) Major influences on employee attendance: a process model. *Journal of Applied Psychology*, 63, 391–407.

Stumpf, S. A. and Hartman, K. (1984) Individual exploration of organizational commitment or withdrawal. *Academy of Management Journal*, 27, 308–29.

Tannenbaum, A. S. (1974) *Hierarchy in Organizations*. San Francisco: Jossey-Bass.

Thacker, J. W., Fields, M. W. and Barclay, L. A. (1990) Union commitment: an examination of antecedent and outcome factors. *Journal of Occupational Psychology*, 63, 33–48.

Walton, R. E. (1985) From control to commitment in the workplace. *Harvard Business Review*, 63, March–April, 76–84.

Further reading

All of the titles listed below are American and, although there has been some good British and European material, are the most seminal pieces.

Foulkes, F. (1980) *Personnel Policies in Large Non-Union Companies*. Englewood Cliffs, NJ: Prentice-Hall.

Gordon, M. E., Philpot, J. W., Burt, R. E., Thompson, C. A. and Spiller, W. E. (1980) Commitment to the union: Development of a measure and examination of its correlates. *Journal of Applied Psychology*, 65, 479–99. Describes the rationale for, and development of, a measure of union commitment.

Lawler, E. E. (1986) *High Involvement Management*. San Francisco: Jossey-Bass. This along with Foulkes contains good illustrations of the potential benefits of achieving high organizational commitment in the context of a human resource strategy.

Mowday, R. T., Porter, L. W. and Steers, R. M. (1982) *Employee–Organization Linkages: The Psychology of Commitment, Absenteeism and Turnover.* New York: Academic Press. For those wanting to understand the development and operationalization of the concept of commitment, this is still the best background book.

6

Pay and Payment Systems

Henk Thierry

Introduction

Employment conditions are high on the list of topics at conferences. Many workshops, seminars and training sessions are regularly being organized for managers, union officials and employees. Subjects for discussion include job evaluation schemes, wage rates, payment by results systems, flexible payment strategies, and so forth. Let us assume that one of the lecturers in a symposium, after making some introductory remarks, requests each member of the audience to write down on a piece of paper how much she or he earns. What will happen? Usually, a rather uncomfortable silence besets the audience. Some participants even have doubts about whether or not they have subscribed to the right seminar. But the lecturer provides some background information: it is not his intention to make individual earnings data public. He is just curious to learn whether most participants have accurate knowledge concerning their pay. The participants' misgivings disappear: the lecturer may now continue his presentation, having everybody's undivided attention.

Are employees and managers indeed accurately informed about their income? Research data, as well as experiences gained at seminars of this type, show time and again that the majority is not. Regardless of education and job level, some assess their net income level to be 10 per cent or more lower or higher than it actually is. Many more people are misinformed about their gross income. With respect to the level of benefits (in the case of sickness, unemployment, retirement, and so forth), most employees and managers merely have some vague ideas; only the actual recipients of benefits know better.

Yet, this *petite histoire* has another important implication. The income that we earn has a special, personal meaning to us. Our income reflects how others are evaluating us; it indicates the value, not only in economic terms, that others ascribe to the individual. Consequently, the person's income touches on her or his own ideas and attitudes regarding her or his value – in short, the self-concept – and thus reveals something about her or his *personal identity*. In most European cultures, people are not inclined to disclose, without restriction, information within this private domain: hence the temporary uncomfortable climate when the question of personal income is raised.

But if our income conveys meanings which are important to us, both materially and symbolically, why do we have such inadequate knowledge about it? Usually, this is not because of an inadequate (weekly or monthly) wage or salary slip. Even slips which contain detailed information both about all allowances received and about all premiums and taxes paid by an individual, in order to explain the difference between gross and net earnings, do not lead to an increase in knowledge *per se*. This is true also in the case of the, as yet few, European companies which provide their employees with a *Personal Benefit Statement* (Vinke and Keizer, 1988). This Statement contains an individualized overview of all employment conditions (exact salary; detailed allowances; specified acquired benefits, and so on) which apply to the employee. It is the *passive* character of such information that seems to be the vital point: it does not play a role in any process of decision-making which is significant to the individual employee. Most employees cannot materially influence their level of income or the design of their income package. However, when employees have to decide regularly (say, annually) how to allocate a specified amount of money to various options, they need detailed information about short and long term effects of alternative choice patterns. Then their level of knowledge is very high (Vinke and Thierry, 1984). Such is the case when the so-called Cafeteria Plan, or flexible benefits plan, is applied: options relate to, for example, extra vacation, additional insurance, training courses, and cash pay (see p.155).

This brief exposition highlights two related points. First, the meanings that are conveyed to each employee in a company by the payment systems that apply to him or her essentially determine the degree of (positive or negative) impact of pay on his or her behaviour at work. Second, in order to affect work behaviour, the characteristics of these payment systems should, as a minimum requirement, be known to the employees concerned and understood by them. On the one hand, this suggests that current organizational payment practices are much less meaningful to many employees than they might be. On the other hand, managers receive an inadequate return on their monetary investment in the pay systems that they use, to the extent that employees are not aware of their existence and/or evaluate them negatively.

These related themes determine the design of this chapter. In the next section there is a review of some psychological theories regarding how payment acquires, maintains or loses meanings. In the third section we categorize these meanings in four clusters, after which various payment objectives (or managerial 'functions' of pay) are differentiated. These objectives derive their operating capacity from the psychological meanings of pay. In the fourth section we turn to a discussion of some major payment systems, with an emphasis on relevant research data, since the system of payment is one of the determinants of the meanings of pay. In the final section we summarize our main points and suggest how to avoid payment systems lagging behind, as they often do, when incisive organizational changes are taking place. The extent to which payment policy is tuned to policy-making in the personnel and organization area at large is actually another important determinant of meanings of pay.

Psychological Theories of Pay

The essential issue that a psychological theory on pay should address is how and in which respects pay affects the work behaviour of the individual employee. That is: the theory should explain how pay acquires, maintains and also loses meanings for employed people. The theory should also deal with major determinants of these meanings. Actually, there are no theories in psychology which are designed in particular to describe or to predict attitudes and/or behaviours regarding compensation. Rather, more general theories on work motivation and on behavioural learning have been applied to payment strategy and payment practice. Common to all is a concern with *behaviour–outcome relationships*, in particular with the connections between individual performance on the one hand and material as well as non-material rewards (or sanctions) on the other.

Some theories are *cognitive* in nature: they focus on the perceptions, attitudes, ideas and intentions of the employee that represent her or his employment situation. Behaviour is considered to be purposeful, intentional and determined by conscious thought processes; payment is usually conceptualized as one of the important rewards of (performance) behaviour. Its importance is seen to be determined, first, by the perceived clarity and strength of the relationship with specified behaviours and, second, by the extent to which it provides the means to satisfy salient motives.

Other theories stress processes of learning by *reinforcement*. Outcomes that are positive for the individual reinforce preceding behaviours (habits are formed), and negative outcomes cause 'extinction'. Thus, responses of an individual which prove to be effective in a particular setting tend to be given again when that setting recurs. Essentially the individual is conceived to be a passive organism, subject to processes of reinforcement. Payment is seen as a 'learned' reinforcer, the effectiveness of which generalizes to many situations.

The two approaches suggest two opposing models of the employee. The cognitive perspective may give rise to the metaphor of the autonomous, enacting individual, continuously creating his or her own 'subjective' working environment. The reinforcement perspective on the contrary suggests an 'ecological machine' metaphor: the employee just reacts mechanically to conditions of employment. We think it to be more useful to conceptualize both approaches as complementary, and not as mutually exclusive (Thierry, 1989). Regulatory mechanisms (such as cues, habits, experience) appear to affect our cognitions in various ways. Conversely, human beings are capable of changing reinforcement processes intentionally (e.g. Bandura, 1986) and of adding selected reinforcers. Most human behaviour, including employee behaviour, is structured by reinforcement processes *interacting* with individual constructs and cognitions. Both approaches converge in stressing the vital importance of behaviour–outcome relations, and a combined perspective helps us to understand how payment affects employees' behaviour at work.

Expectancy theory

This motivation theory, also known under the name of its core concepts – Valence, Instrumentality, Expectancy (VIE) – has dominated research and practical applications for some 25 years (Vroom, 1964; Lawler, 1973; Mitchell, 1982; Thierry, 1984; Petri, 1986; Ilgen and Klein, 1989). Its basic assumption is that each human being is faced regularly with the opportunity or the necessity of choosing between alternative actions. Which action will be selected? Let us assume that an employee may emphasize either the quantity or the quality of production in his or her work. First, the employee will consider how likely it is that spending (more or less) effort on the job will result in a high quantity or a good quality (that is, *expectancy*). Second, the employee will assess the probable consequences occurring when he or she produces more or performs very well (*instrumentality*). It may seem to him or her that emphasizing the quantity of products or services might cause some envy on the part of his or her workmates. But it might also slightly increase the level of group earnings (according to the payment system in use). Yet the employee wonders whether each group member ought to profit from his or her extra effort. When he or she chooses to stress the quality of the work to be done, the supervisor is expected to notice that and to give some verbal recognition to the employee. Moreover, performing well may in the long run improve the employee's craftmanship and thus, according to expectation, increase his or her opportunities for promotion. Finally, the employee takes into account the degree of attractiveness (*valence*) of each of these potential outcomes.

Expectancy theory now holds that the interaction between these three components, expectancy, instrumentality and valence, determines the choice of action. The employee will favour the alternative that will *reward* him or her, according to *expectation*, with the *best* results. Thus, a line of action may be selected whose outcome is more uncertain than that of another alternative; yet the rewards to be gained clearly outweigh those resulting from other lines of action, and so forth.

Lawler (1971, 1981, 1987) has applied this theory to the domain of payment. Pay in itself has no importance. It becomes important to the extent that it is seen as *instrumental* in satisfying salient (*valent*) motives. Let us assume that somebody has a strong motive to be as secure and safe as possible. Thus, being on the lookout for situations in which risks can be minimized, pay may become very important. Pay may provide the person with the means to insure her or himself in various respects, to provide for shelter, perhaps for comfort, and so forth. Moreover, pay may probably be a good means of satisfying other motives, e.g. gaining recognition from others, acquiring more autonomy, gaining specific competence through additional education. It may also result in negative outcomes for the person, such as when she or he expects to be seen by colleagues as a 'friend of the boss' instead of as 'one of them'. Pay may be instrumental to an outcome and yet be neutral to an employee. This would occur, for example, when she or he expects that more pay would lead to achieving more status, while she or he is indifferent to (more) status; then pay would have no importance in this respect.

Consequently, when, for example, questionnaire data reveal that pay is important (in our terms: meaningful) to an employee, it may signal various things. At the very least we know that pay is seen as a means of satisfying one or more salient motives. The more alternatives (other than pay) an employee has at his or her disposal to gain what he or she wants, the less important pay will be (other things being equal). The less alternatives and/or the more motives to which pay is instrumental, the more important pay is. This may explain why lower paid employees often rate payment to be still more important than higher paid employees do. Another implication of expectancy theory is that employees who deem pay to be important and who expect their performance to be instrumental in gaining more pay will be the better performers.

Interest in expectancy theory has shown a revival in the recent past, since its predictions and results fit in very well with the outcomes of one of the strongest motivational techniques: *goal setting* (Locke and Latham, 1984, 1990; Thierry, 1989). Goals originate in values, according to Locke and Latham, and consist of particular actions to be pursued and targets to be reached. Thus, the goal for today or this week may relate to the number of orders to be gained from customers, the quality of maintenance work, and so forth. Goal setting theory holds that an employee's motivation to perform will be highest when:

1 Task goals are set at a high level.
2 Task goals are made very specific.
3 Task goals are accepted by the employee as realistic.
4 Frequent feedback is provided.

Concerning the meanings that pay may acquire, expectancy theory stresses the *instrumental* nature of pay: it satisfies motives. Goal setting theory is in accordance with this but adds an important feature: pay may feed back to the employee how well she or he has been performing. Pay may inform the employee about his or her position *relative* to the goal set and to workmates. It is this latter aspect which stands out in the next theory.

Equity theory

Each human being has a basic need to evaluate his or her opinions and abilities, according to Festinger (1954). When objective norms are absent, each person will tend to compare him or herself with a 'comparison other' who is in similar circumstances. With respect to opinions, the person strives for uniformity with others. In the case of an ability (or another valued characteristic), the person wants to be slightly better than the comparison other. A successful comparison process results in consonance: the person is satisfied. When not successful, dissonance occurs which will stimulate the person to bring about changes.

Adams (1963, 1965) has specified this general motive in a theory of psychological equity. Within an exchange relationship, each person is motivated to achieve *balance* between his/her contributions ('inputs') and his/her inducements ('outcomes') in comparison with the other's input–outcomes ratio as perceived by the person. Contributions are, for example, education, experience, effort, intelligence. Inducements are achievement, pay, recognition, and so on. A 'comparison other' can be another employee, a category of workers, a professional group, and so forth; but it can also be, say, the employment policy of a company, or the person's own past record, or how well off he or she expects to be in the near future (cf. Goodman, 1974). All sorts of attributes may potentially act as input or outcome variables. Whether they actually do depends upon the person's recognition of a variable and its estimated relevance to an exchange relationship. Similar criteria determine the choice of the comparison other(s) among many potential referents. When inputs (e.g. effort) and outcomes (e.g. pay) balance, relative to the other's input–outcomes ratio, then equity (consonance) will be perceived. But when there is no balance, feelings of inequity (dissonance) will prevail.

Various forms of consonance and dissonance are possible. Table 6.1 summarizes the major ones. Thus, forms 1, 4 and 5 are equitable in nature, since the relative input–outcome ratio is perceived as equal (by the person). Form 2 shows inequity as a result of underpayment: the person will try first, according to Adams, to increase the outcomes. If that is impossible or unsuccessful, the person may decrease the level of effort. The inequity of Form 3 may, at least in principle, be solved either by raising the person's effort (which would result in the kind of consonance illustrated by Form 5), or by decreasing the person's payment. The latter kind of consonance – low/low; low/low – is conceptually equivalent to Form 1. Yet, the person may have trouble in raising his or her efforts, e.g. when the outcome would be a still higher payment. Likewise, it may be difficult to lower his or her pay in cases where this may be achieved only by means of a very low level of effort; this would still result in a low/high ratio for the person. Thus, the person might consider, in this case as well as with respect to other forms of

Table 6.1: Consonance and dissonance

	Effort	*Payment*	*Result*
1. Person	High	High	Consonance
Other	High	High	
2. P	High	Low	Dissonance (underpayment)
O	High	High	
3. P	Low	High	Dissonance (overpayment)
O	Low	Low	
4. P	High	Low	Consonance
O	High	Low	
5. P	High	High	Consonance
O	Low	Low	
6. P	High	Low	Dissonance (maximum)
O	Low	High	

dissonance, the use of other potentially inequity – reducing strategies, such as a cognitive 'relabelling' of inputs and/or outcomes, a change of comparison other, or withdrawal behaviour (e.g. absenteeism). These strategies will not concern us further here (cf. Syroit, 1984; Thierry, 1989).

The extent to which equity (consonance; satisfaction) is felt by the person actually operates as a feedback mechanism within a regulatory system. The more the relative input–outcome ratio is out of balance, the more the person will try to restore it. Payment plays an important role in this respect, since it is almost always considered to be an important outcome within an employment relationship. Equity theory emphasizes the *relative* (comparison) *meaning* of payment. First, pay is valued in terms not of sheer amount but of balance with one or more comparison others: in addition to the others' pay, the inputs (of others and of the person) are at stake. Second, others may impact upon how the person 'translates' his or her inputs into required outcomes, such as pay, in order to achieve equity. This characteristic has important implications for collective or individual labour agreements (e.g. Belcher and Atchison, 1976). Third, as in expectancy theory (p.139), the less outcomes afforded to a person within an exchange relationship, the more important pay will be (other variables being constant).

In expectancy theory, behaviour – outcome relations were stressed; that is, behaviour is considered to originate from cognitive processes, leading to preferred outcomes (such as payment). Pay derives its meaning from its perceived relationship with specified preceding performance behaviours as well as from its perceived instrumentality to satisfy salient motives. Equity theory also focuses upon behaviour-outcome relationships: yet the emphasis is upon the regulatory, feedback function of (in)equity. The meaning of payment is relative in nature: it indicates the position of the person in comparison with other(s). In the next section we will discuss a theory that deals with this relationship in the reversed order: outcome–behaviour connections.

Partial reinforcement

In the introduction to this section we briefly alluded to the basic tenets of theories of reinforcement. Behaviour is determined by its consequences: effective responses tend to recur in similar settings; ineffective reactions will not. Such mechanisms may explain the regulatory, 'systemic' characteristics of our behaviour. Often, human beings act automatically: their habits reveal that certain behaviours proved to be successful repeatedly on earlier occasions. Their experience teaches them that particular reactions were usually effective in the past and are so now. When faced with novelty, they still tend to look for routine programmes (cf. March and Simon, 1958). Even when new information must be processed, unmet challenges faced, and different goals pursued, our 'wired-in' programmes still play a role.

Yet, not all regulatory behaviours, such as habits, routine programmes, taken-for-granted perceptions, are effective, although they persist. Some outcome–behaviour connections may have been established by chance or erroneously. Other connections may have become dysfunctional, such as when changes in work behaviour are required in response to the introduction of new technology, the adoption of another managerial philosophy, a different way of organizing the work process, and so forth. To the extent that former, 'unwanted' behavioural patterns tend to persist, these are apparently reinforced by outcomes of which the person is usually not aware. This suggests that we should analyse closely the conditions under which these behaviours occur, in order to establish new outcome–behaviour connections. It is this approach, in which major concepts of operant conditioning theory (Skinner, 1953, 1971, 1990) are integrated, which characterizes organizational behaviour modification (OB-mod.; see for a review: Luthans and Kreitner, 1985; Luthans and Martinko, 1987). Applied to payment (as well as to various other outcomes), OB-mod. implies that a specified amount of money (e.g. a bonus) should be tied immediately and unambiguously to 'functional' behaviours each time that these behaviours are manifested (functional behaviours are acts of an employee, instrumental to the performances of crucial components of his or her task). Dysfunctional behaviours should not be reinforced or ought to be tied to negative outcomes.

But is it really necessary to reward immediately desired behaviours, such as a specified level of performance, each time that they occur (called *continuous reinforcement*)? Extensive animal research shows that animal 'performance' improves remarkably when behaviour is *partially* reinforced. Partial reinforcement refers to variation in the amount of responses or in the time interval that precedes a reward. Thus, pigeons coo more often when deprived of food every now and then. When hungry, rats run faster to the centre of a maze. Compared to continuous reinforcement, partial reinforcement leads also to a much slower rate of extinction of the behaviours concerned when the reward is missing for a long time or is even withdrawn (as an effect of 'counter-conditioning': see Amsel, 1972; Petri, 1986). Do these findings also apply to human beings?

In forestry, harvested areas must be replanted with seedlings. Unfortunately, some types of animals may gnaw on these and feed themselves, as do small beavers in the north-west part of the USA. In the latter half of the 1970s Latham and Dossett (1978) carried out an experiment on partial reinforcement, involving beaver trappers who were employed in the summer season. After intensive talks with the union, two experimental conditions were established. The first prescribed that one dollar would be paid for each beaver caught (*continuous reinforcement*: CR). The second condition required that a trapper, after having caught a beaver, had to guess the colour (out of four) of a marble. A correct guess paid him $4; a wrong guess paid him nothing (partial, also called *variable reinforcement*: VR4). Two groups were randomly formed, each of which worked for four weeks under one condition and then changed to the other for the same period of time. Prior to the experiment, individual performance figures had been measured, also during four weeks: the groups did not at that time differ significantly from one another. Each trapper received the normal hourly wage rate during the full 12-week period. It is important to note that, with an appropriate number of trials, probability estimates indicate that earnings will be the same in both conditions.

What happened? Interestingly, inexperienced trappers did best in the CR condition, while experienced trappers did best in the VR4 condition. Most trappers favoured this variable treatment, since it provided them with challenge and a lot of fun; it reduced boredom and it introduced some variety in their work. The experiment was repeated each year (cf. Saari and Latham, 1982) until, in the latter part of the 1980s, it was stopped, owing to a change in employment strategy of the company.

In later years, other partial reinforcement conditions were installed for the trappers, such as having two, three or five alternatives, with a correct guess paying $2, $3 or $5. Other groups have been involved and other performance behaviours have been stressed, such as planting seedlings (Yukl and Latham, 1975); scoring punch cards (Berger et al., 1975); selling retail goods (Luthans et al., 1981). Data from many studies show mixed results: both continuous and partial reinforcement schedules usually lead to higher/better performance scores than hourly wage rates. VR schedules are often, but not always, better than CR ones. One of the problems in comparing data is that partial reinforcement should be operationalized along at least three dimensions (which it is usually not): the *frequency* (amount of responses; time interval) with which the reinforcer is provided; the *inclusiveness* of the performance measure (is one behavioural segment or a series of acts rewarded?); and the *size* of the reinforcer.

Thus, results are to some extent ambiguous. A usual interpretation would be to point to differences in operationalizing the major concepts, in research design, and in data handling, as the main sources for such a lack of clarity. Yet, we favour another perspective: we question the tenability of the *continuous* reinforcement concept in the case of more complex human behaviours. Is it an exception or is it the rule that behaviours are immediately followed by rewards in settings outside the laboratory? Consider the event of reading a difficult text: sometimes we fail to grasp the full content of a mathematical formula or of an argument. Do we throw the text away, never to take it up again? Not so; often we try again after a while, perhaps even harder. Why? Because we know from earlier experience that continued activity may pay off every now and then. Such a situation is also faced by an author, having problems in finding correct arguments or in stating these understandably. Usually the manuscript is repeatedly reworked and redesigned because eventually a 'satisfying' result is gained. Similarly, a commercial representative continues to visit potential customers, although failures are frequent. Likewise, an entrepreneur often tries to do better when faced with a loss; more often than not it has proved successful in the past. Indeed, it is probably very hard to find examples of continuous reinforcement relating to more complex human behaviour in practice. In other words, partial much more than continuous reinforcement may explain the motivation of complex human behaviour (see also Mawhinney, 1986).

It is interesting to note that CR did not even apply strictly to the series of experiments with beaver trappers, described earlier in this section. During a private visit to their site, the former foreman explained to us that the trappers, in later years of the experiment, were not placed in an experimental (or control) condition *prior* to any period of performance. At the *end* of each working week, each trapper decided which reinforcement schedule would apply to reward him for the amount of beavers already caught during that week.

Thus, there are strong indications that cognitive factors cannot be neglected. As outlined earlier, reinforcement and cognitive processes jointly structure human behaviour. Particular performance behaviours do persist, not only because they have been rewarded previously but also because of 'learned' expectations and intentions. Thus, payment will affect the individual's performance behaviour more when it is more closely and unambiguously tied to vital aspects of performance. It is not necessary, however, to provide for an immediate reward: some 'uncertainty', within specified rules of the game, may even elicit more effort. Payment may thus acquire an *instrumental* meaning for the employee: a means by which the satisfaction of salient motives is made possible. Its feedback function allows the assessment of *relative position*, a factor which is also important in the perception of equity.

All of the theories discussed in this section focus upon behaviour–reward connections, but each of them does so from a particular point of view. They converge in stating that payment will affect the individual's performance behaviour more effectively, to the extent that it is related more closely to that behaviour. Thus, as performance outcomes (or perhaps efforts) vary, payment — but not necessarily its size — should vary too. It is vital that each employee should easily understand the performance–pay relationship. Yet, some (variable) delay in receiving pay may motivate an employee more strongly and be more meaningful than when pay is provided after a fixed amount of performance outcomes or on fixed dates.

Neither theory assumes that the individual employee is located in a social or societal vacuum. On the contrary, expectancy theory takes into account all sorts of group and organizational opportunities as well as constraints impacting upon the employee. Yet, the theory's major point is that these conditions are relevant, to the extent that they influence the *content* of the employee's expectations – e.g. which particular behaviour will lead to which particular outcome – as well as the *probability* of these connections. Equity theory emphasizes the way in which these conditions affect the effectiveness of achieving *balanced* cognitions and the possibilities for solving perceptions of *dissonance*. Finally (partial), reinforcement theory ascribes a determining force to group and organizational conditions in *shaping* and *controlling* the employee's behaviour.

It is important to keep this in mind when practical implications of these theories are considered. Since the performance–pay relationship is the core theme, task, group and organizational characteristics should be analysed from the perspective of how this relationship is furthered or impeded. Thus, it has been shown that tasks which allow more discretion to the employee provide more meaningful relations, while tasks which are dependent upon group input and group decision-making often obscure these. Likewise, the larger the work group, the more difficult to understand the relation between performance and pay; this would necessitate additional sources of feedback, e.g. supplied by the manager. Furthermore, group norms and values affect the variance in performance, and thus the performance–pay relationship. More standardized and formalized organizational procedures for getting the work done often restrict the opportunities for adapting performance–pay relations to changing circumstances (see also Lawler, 1987).

We now turn to the meaningfulness of pay, both for the employee and from the manager's viewpoint.

Meanings of Pay

Four categories

In the preceding section we touched on some specific meanings of pay to the individual employee. In general, we differentiate between four main categories of meaning (Thierry et al., 1988; Thierry, forthcoming). Essentially, pay is meaningful to the employee because it conveys information about important domains other than pay. Thus, an employee 'reads' into her/his pay more or less access to material welfare, or a lack of recognition for work contributions particularly valued by the employee, and so forth. For some employees pay has a lot of meanings, for others it is less revealing. Also, pay reflects many meanings in particular situations, while it is almost meaningless in other settings (why this is so will be discussed in the next sections). In general, however, pay can refer to four domains, as follows.

1 *Salient motives.* Pay is meaningful because the employee expects that it will allow him or her to satisfy important motives and to reach relevant goals. Because of this instrumental nature, pay may stand for example, for avoidance of insecurity, for feelings of competence or for opportunities for self-realization. This domain relates to Lawler's extension of expectancy theory (p.139); we will call it the *motivational properties* of pay.

2 *Relative position.* First, pay provides feedback on how the employee's task performance is progressing (or has progressed) with respect to the *goals* or targets set. In giving information about the effectiveness of the contributions made to his/her work (such as care for quality; setting adequate priorities) as well as about the impact of external events (e.g. machine breakdown; loss of a customer), pay may call for the employee's redirection of efforts during (or after) task performance. Second, pay provides feedback about the employee's effectiveness in comparison with *others*, such as co-workers, other employees up or down the hierarchy, or professional colleagues. Both components constitute the second category: relative position.

3 *Control.* Pay is meaningful because it signifies to the employee the extent to which she or he has been successful in *influencing* others, such as the supervisor, workmates, people in other departments, or customers, during task performance, in order to reach her/his goals. Also, characteristics of the particular payment systems in use reflect the degree of control exerted by and upon the employee. This relates to the employee's impact upon the total amount of pay, the variation in pay from time to time, the composition of the pay package, the principles upon

which payment systems are based, etc. It is remarkable that this category – the degree of active and passive control mirrored by pay – has been mostly neglected in the literature (see, however, White, 1976).

4 *Spending*. Pay is meaningful because it reflects the products and services that the employee can afford to purchase. In this, it also mirrors the easiness with which this is done. Consequently, pay is perceived in terms of individual welfare.

As mentioned before, a particular payment system may score low on some or all four meanings, for example because its content does not match the technology of most tasks, or because employees do not trust the way in which it is applied in practice.[1] This would indicate that the very system appears to be rather meaningless to the employees concerned. The point is, however, that the four categories are *conceptually* distinct. *Empirically*, they may correlate in some instances and not in others. Correlations are expected to occur, for example, when actual spending (4) embodies the pursuit of motivational properties (1), or when a low amount of active control (3) relates to a rather poor relative position (2). But motivational properties will seldom be correlated with relative position.

It is our hypothesis (Thierry, forthcoming) that a payment system, to the extent that the employee understands its operative ('technical') part, will affect the employee's behaviour at work more incisively when this system is more meaningful (in terms of the four categories) to the employee. In the previous section on psychological theories, the issue of how payment may acquire (or lose) meanings was discussed. One of the conclusions held that when performance results change, one or more payment components should mirror that change (but not necessarily immediately). We can extend this conclusion now in stating that when relevant aspects of an important domain (to which payment refers) undergo change, payment ought to reflect these changes in order to remain meaningful.

Managerial functions of pay

Up until now the significance of pay has been analysed from the perspective of the recipient: the individual employee. The characteristics of payment systems which are actually used in a company shape these meanings to a considerable degree. Therefore, we turn now to the objectives (or 'functions') that managers, in their role as allocators and distributors of pay, may pursue by using particular payment systems. For each of the six managerial functions mentioned in table 6.2 (cf. Thierry et al., 1988), one example of a relevant payment system or form will be given. By means of pay, a manager may try to accomplish the objectives shown in table 6.2.

Managers have not always clearly outlined the objectives that they would like to meet by using a particular payment strategy. More importantly, payment systems or forms in use often do not match the objectives pursued, such as when employees have to learn new behaviours (e.g. as an effect of the introduction of new technology) under a job salary system. This may be one reason why payment systems frequently fail to be particularly effective. But even when objectives and

Table 6.2   Managerial functions (objectives) in respect of pay systems

Objective	System/Form
To *attract* employees.	Job salary (levels derived from wage surveys).
To *keep* qualified employees.	Bonus to stay (e.g. shares; options for shares; labour market allowance).
To *stimulate* effective performance.	Payment by results (when related to critical performance factors).
To *teach* employees new behaviours at work.	Multi-skill bonus.
To *compensate* for inconvenient work conditions.	Allowance, separate from job salary.
To *prevent/solve* labour conflicts.	Job evaluation (related to job salary).

systems do match, the result may still be unsatisfactory if employees are not able to grasp how the systems are operating (e.g. as an effect of poor feedback).

Why is it possible to affect the behaviour of employees at all by means of pay, in accordance with any of the objectives outlined in table 6.2? The answer is, basically, because of the meanings – the four categories mentioned earlier – that are evoked by the use of payment systems. It is now time to take a closer look at frequently used payment systems. We start with a note on processes of decision-making.

Systems of Payment

Pay dynamics

Decision-making about payment issues – strategies, systems, pay rises – is a rather complicated matter, which shows considerable differences not only between European countries but also often among industries and companies within countries. First, in the UK and the Republic of Ireland, a rather decentralized system of industrial relations prevails, in which shop floor bargaining plays a crucial role. A description of the decision-making process that is typical of continental North-West European countries would start with the issue of whether or not there is any national agreement on labour conditions between the main employers' federations and the major unions. If there is such an agreement, it would specify the rules of the game in global terms as well as the priorities to be elaborated in negotiations per trade, sector or company. An example would be the demarcation of the margins of an acceptable average increase in labour costs, along with a preference on how to split this, allowing a part for collective provisions and a part for wage and salary rises. Second, almost every country in West, North and Central Europe has one or more laws in which the formal power of industrial democracy institutions, such as the Works Council in a company, is detailed, e.g. concerning payment issues. In most cases, trade union officials on a trade or local level negotiate the major terms of a new contract with the entrepreneur, leaving secondary issues to be elaborated by the Works Council.

Third, several industries, such as the metal trade in various countries, traditionally apply particular systems of payment (e.g. job evaluation). As this is usually agreed upon by the trade unions and the employers' organization, most of the time there is quite strong pressure on individual companies to comply. Fourth, some trades or larger companies take the lead in negotiating new labour conditions, the results of which are laid down in a Collective Labour Agreement. This operates as a reference point for collective agreements in many other trades and sectors. Fifth, the degree of unionization is important: this is often higher in traditional industries and lower in sectors in which the impact of new technologies has created many new jobs. The less unionized is a company, the more important are managerial considerations in deciding upon payment issues. Finally, labour conditions for civil servants and the non-profit sector are derived in most countries from agreements made in various industrial trades and sectors.

This general sketch leaves out important aspects, such as the unions' prevailing ideology (e.g. the sharing of power versus the control of power), or factors determining wage and salary increases, or bodies and institutions impacting upon negotiations and the making of agreements. Yet, it helps us to understand the dynamics of creating consensus or at least temporary agreement between the parties concerned in many West, North and Central European countries. It may also explain why there are relatively few strikes about payment matters in that part of the continent. If there are such strikes, they are usually not addressed in particular against an individual company (unless a 'leading' Agreement is in the making), but are concerned with subjects at national or trade level. There is a growing trend in many European countries towards more decentralized bargaining and, consequently, more local – that is, company specific – agreements. An interesting question is whether this will lead to more local strikes and arbitration procedures in the near future.

We have classified the payment systems in four categories. The first bears upon the value (the 'level') of the job to be done, while the second focuses upon one or more characteristics of job performance. The third category includes individual options regarding a modest part of the income package, while category four relates to paying for incidental performance.

Rewarding job level

In West European countries and in the USA, wage or salary surveys are used on a large scale to help companies to determine the salary rates for managerial and specialist jobs. Consultancy agencies usually survey large samples of companies annually in order to determine comparative earnings data. Although statistics are not available, we assume that salary rates for most managerial jobs are primarily set on this basis. It implies that the 'market rate' is considered to be the right or fair salary level.

Yet, there is a growing tendency in some countries (e.g. the Netherlands, Germany) to apply systems of job evaluation to managerial jobs. Job evaluation systems are used widely to set the rates for blue collar workers in some countries (such as Germany, France, Belgium, Switzerland, Denmark, the Netherlands). Unfortunately, reliable statistics are not available. The basic objective of job evaluation is to order all jobs within a company according to their relative value. The concept of job value refers to what is needed, in terms of work requirements or worker characteristics, to fulfil the job under normal conditions; thus, actual performance features, such as the quantity or quality, are omitted from consideration.

Various procedures may be used to achieve a relative value order of jobs, such as ranking total jobs or classifying these in categories. One of the most systematic, and probably mostly used, job evaluation procedures is the *point-rating method*. First, several bench-mark jobs are selected, the contents of which are laid down in a job description. Second, jobs are analysed in terms of key characteristics, e.g. required knowledge, responsibility, and social skills. Points are then allocated to each characteristic (taking the weight – the relative importance – of each characteristic into account), after which the total job value is set by adding all points together. The value of all other jobs is derived by comparing these, per characteristic, with the nearest bench-mark job. After ordering all jobs according to their value, categories (job classes) are made. The wage or salary rate for each category is usually negotiated by unions and employers and is laid down in a Collective Labour Agreement (see de Jong and Thierry, 1984).

In some countries job evaluation is used primarily on a company basis. In others it is institutionalized in trade, sectorial or even national structures of labour relations between employers' federations, unions and the government. In the Netherlands, companies started in the mid-1960s to eliminate differences in employment conditions of blue and white collar workers (the so-called 'harmonization'). Thus, job evaluation systems there have applied, since the early 1970s onwards, to most or all employees within a company (at first only to non-managerial employees, later also to categories of managers). Comparable developments occurred later on in France and Germany (e.g. the metal trade); they are now beginning to take place in the UK and the USA. Moreover, job evaluation data have been used in the Netherlands to achieve a national incomes policy (relating, for example, the earnings of professions to those of comparable civil servants). Several countries use these data to further equal opportunities for female employees as compared to males.

It is surprising that research data on the effectiveness of job evaluation systems and their outcomes are rather scarce (see, for a recent review, Thierry and de Jong, 1989). However, during the past few years, there has been an upsurge in research studies originating in complaints from (categories of) female employees against 'unequal' pay. As these cases have been brought to courts in various countries, specialists (often psychologists) have been asked to perform supportive research. This relates not only to particular forms of possible bias, i.e. gender related, in all phases of job evaluation but also to more general aspects of reliability and validity.

Part of this research supports earlier evidence that job analysis often has a variety of serious shortcomings. A thorough job analysis is very time consuming and necessitates, on the one hand, a detailed scrutiny of attributes of the work to be done and, on the other, a thoughtful translation of these atributes in terms of aptitudes, abilities and skills required (e.g. McCormick, 1976; Spector et al., 1989). In practice, however, the bench-mark jobs are analysed – systematically but not thoroughly – in terms of some characteristics (usually between 5 and 20) which tend to confuse work attributes with psychological requirements. Moreover, most other jobs are hardly analysed at all.

It has also been shown more than once that job value or job earnings data are not always reliable and valid (construct-wise and empirically). Employees whose salaries are set on the basis of job evaluation often appreciate the security and the fairness of their earnings. However, they often resent the full predictability of their pay and, when no other major payment system is applied, the fact that their performance level is not taken into account. Which meanings of pay will be evoked by applying a job evaluation system for rewarding the level of a job? Unfortunately, there are not yet sufficient data available to give an empirically based answer. With some speculation we expect this system to have a moderate score on the first category: motivational properties. Job level reward may be rather instrumental in satisfying security motives, but hardly instrumental in meeting, for example, achievement, esteem and power motives. It will score rather low on relative position: job level reward contains no information regarding the degree of progress towards goals set. But the reward level may be considered to be fair in comparison which other employees (the second aspect of relative position). Also, we expect a low score on control, since the reward level signifies to the employee that his or her degree of influence over others is not taken into account. Finally, the score on spending will be rather high, since job level reward determines the major part – in some countries around 90 per cent – of final take-home pay.

Rewarding job performance

The strategy of paying people for the results of their work dates far back, probably to ancient Greece and the Roman empire. Nowadays, the use of such a strategy differs considerably between countries and across time. Around 1980, a survey held within the countries of the European Community (1981) showed that the highest rates were found in the UK and in the Irish Republic (45–50 per cent of all employed workers). The Netherlands had by far the lowest rates (19 per cent) and still have so. Estimates indicate that around 35 per cent of the US working force is subject to a payment by results system. Traditionally, East European countries apply these systems on a very large scale: at least 75 per cent of the workers; it is an open issue whether these figures will change in the coming years.

One of the oldest systems is *piecework*: first, an estimation is made of the number of products or pieces a worker can produce per day; second, the (market) price for the worker is taken to settle the wage rate. By combining both data, the piece rate is established. Although modern technology has made it virtually impossible in many instances to conceive of pieces or separate products, this system is still in use, in particular in most East European countries.

With the coming of age of industry, *bonus systems* were developed. They are also called 'tariff' systems, since the term tariff means 'prior announcement', in this case concerning the rate for the job. First, the kind of work to be done is studied extensively. By means of an analysis of work methods, sometimes also of bodily movements, of the division of work in task components, and of the sequence of all phases of work, norms are designed that indicate what is understood to be a 'normal' performance level. Norms may bear upon pace or quantity (as mostly in earlier decades of this century), or upon quality, use of raw materials, scrap produced, etc. If systematic work study is difficult or impossible, as in the case of ship maintenance or repair, experience with comparable jobs or best estimates provides the normative basis. Second, the relation between performance in excess of the norm and bonus pay is established, e.g. proportional or decelerating.

Quite different systems and forms are grouped under the umbrella of payment by results systems. The use of *merit rating*, both for employees and managers, is fairly widespread. Usually, the results of the annual individual performance assessment is taken as the 'index' of performance. A moderate or average 'merit' assessment results in some additional pay in many instances but, in general, the better the merit, the higher the pay. For employees this may imply a salary increase, a bonus, or an additional month of pay, etc. Managers may also receive one of these or else receive shares, options for shares, profit shares, and so forth. More generally, payment by results systems may be applied on an individual or a group basis (the latter, for example, in the case of group tasks or a group project). They may also bear upon a major division or a company at large, such as when the Scanlon Plan is applied. This plan combines a system of employee participation, in which departmental committees encourage the generation of ideas and suggestions for achieving more effective results, with a share for all in the financial results gained by these improvements (e.g. Frost et al., 1975; Thierry and de Jong, 1979).

Many research studies have been done on the effectiveness of payment by results and flat payment systems. Elsewhere, we have reviewed the data of several thousands of studies (Thierry, 1987). Table 6.3 summarizes the gross outcomes of this review. Only empirical research studies were included in these reviews. The row entries indicate the variables of concern to the researchers, regardless of the theory or the hypothesis they espoused. Performance and satisfaction were frequently assessed criteria, while understanding and co-operation rank second. More than 40 separate studies relate to the system of piece rate (the first column): consistently, performance levels increased and the quality of the organization of work improved. Many more studies bear upon the bonus system, with mixed results: weak spots relate to difficulties in understanding how the core part of the system 'the performance–pay relationship' works, as well as to deficient task norms. A summary, of course, cannot catch the many detailed findings that ought to be described when making evaluative comments. However, these findings indicate that there is not something like 'the winning system' or 'one best

Table 6.3 Summary of review of research on payment systems

Factors studied	Piece rate	Bonus	Merit rating	Individual PBR[a]	Group PBR[a]	Scanlon Plan	PBR[a] in general	Fixed pay
Performance	9[b]	8		9	7	9	8	5
Organization of work	9							
Satisfaction (with pay, work, etc.)			3		6	8	6	9
Co-operation vs. conflict		9			3	8		
Fairness		7						
Understanding performance–pay relation		4	3		3		3	
Task norms		4						
Generation of ideas						8		

[a]PBR = Payment by Results.
[b]9 = excellent; 6 = moderate; 3 = very negative.

Source: Adapted from Thierry, 1987

system', although the Scanlon Plan (in addition to piece rate) comes out pretty strongly. Yet, there is a consistent loser: merit rating. Employees fail to understand how their pay (increase?) is related to the annual assessment results, which causes dissatisfaction, for example. Some data indicate that this relationship actually hardly exists, at least for individual employees (e.g. Markham, 1988). Again, turning to the row entries, payment by results systems score very low on understanding and pretty high on performance effects. Detailed data concerning flat payment (such as hourly pay or job salary) show that performance levels *increased* in some 30 studies but *decreased* in more than 50 cases.

This overview shows that payment by results systems may work effectively, but not necessarily so. Among important considerations are, first, the *objectives* to be pursued by means of pay. From the managerial perspective, these functions (p.147) ought to be integrated within the strategic business plan of the company. Some research shows that *participation* by employees in this process is vital: this offers the opportunity not only to bring forward different opinions and values but also to trace weak spots or errors when a system is actually designed (cf. Bowey et al., 1982). This implies that when the majority of employees does not eventually favour the implementation of a payment by results system, management should not insist on it. The quality of the *social climate* is a vital second issue: distrust and continuous conflict between departments, supervisors and employees often prevent payment by results systems from operating effectively. Like many other personnel strategies, these systems are too vulnerable to survive such stresses.

Third, performance factors that are fed into the payment system should be *relevant* to the job of the employee and be largely *controllable* by him or her. This may also explain why merit rating comes out so badly: most performance assessment systems use (semi-) psychological characteristics, such as responsibility, instead of outcome or behavioural variables. The relevance as well as 'influenceability' of these are questionable, especially as complicated processes of translation (from outcome or behaviour to psychological trait) are needed. Moreover, modern technology makes group work important or even unavoidable.

Traditionally, pay for performance systems focus upon individual employees (except, of course, when a system such as the Scanlon Plan is applied). We think that they ought to be tailored more to groups of workers, departments or even an organization at large. Returning to our review of some psychological theories on pay (p.139), the core theme in these theories was identified as the relationship between behaviour (performance) and reward (pay). We stated that task, group and organizational characteristics consequently ought to be considered in terms of how this relationship may be facilitated or impeded. One of the most vital conditions that have to be met when larger numbers of employees are subject to a payment by results system is the provision of adequate feedback. When this condition is fulfilled, there is no major reason to be hesistant (as the Scanlon Plan practice has repeatedly shown).

Again with some speculation, we would expect payment by results systems, at least in principle, to score high on most categories of meaning of pay. Pay for performance recognizes vital contributions that have been made, which motivates an employee (category 1), positions him or her relative to goals set and other employees (category 2), and takes the amount of control exercised into account (category 3). Spending (category 4) may score high when the bonus is seen as an (unexpected?) extra amount; it may score rather low when it is perceived as an acquired right. Of course, deficiencies in the design and/or the administration of any pay for performance system in practice may result in a low score in various categories.

Rewarding individual options

For most employees and managers in industrialized countries the income package is predetermined. The composition of the primary and secondary income depends fully upon the agreement negotiated between employers and unions, or upon the nature of the organization's compensation philosophy. Usually, employees and managers – in their role of recipients of pay – have no impact at all upon the design of the package of their total compensation. This is remarkable, from at least three different points of view. First, many companies (and unions) favour some degree of participation, or industrial democracy, involving employees in matters of individual, group and/or organizational concern. It is hardly consistent to exclude matters of pay, since it is an important concern. Second, the usefulness of provisions and benefits to employees varies considerably, e.g. as an effect of individual differences, phase of life, and kind of work. For instance, it has been shown repeatedly that when employees are allowed to make a choice, an unmarried male worker in his early twenties will opt for more time off, while his married colleague of the same age prefers to have more cash. Third, as we outlined in the introductory section, the return that a company receives from its monetary investment in pay is far less certain when particular components are not valued very high by employees (or are not even known by them).

By means of the so-called Cafeteria Plan, also named flexible payment or Flexi-Plan, each organization member is given the opportunity to make a choice from among a given set of options. Many options often bear upon 'time for pay', such as when an employee favours a free afternoon each fortnight, or an extended summer vacation, or a reservoir of 'spendable time units' to be consumed after several years (e.g. sabbatical leave) or some years prior to retirement. Other options relate to 'pay for time', e.g. when some vacation days have not been spent. Still other options refer to (additional) benefits, such as more extensive health care, retirement pension, or a savings plan. All options offered should have been checked regarding their feasibility (to the organization) and their average attractiveness (to the employees). In many cases, cash pay is also provided as an option (e.g. for those to whom the value of all other options is lower). The amount of pay that each employee may spend annually on making options is usually determined by the estimated productivity increase and/or reduction in costs and/or cost of living compensation. In some cases, employees can exchange some allowances and/or a small part of their current pay for options which they prefer more.

The Cafeteria Plan was introduced in the late 1960s in some companies in the

USA. After a very slow start its application gained momentum, in particular in the second part of the 1980s. West European companies have adopted the Plan on a rather modest scale, partly because fringe benefits are provided much more extensively to employees in most West European countries.

Although much experience is available, research data are still rather scarce. Most US research dates back to the early 1970s; some Dutch studies were done in the first part of the 1980s (for a review of both: Thierry and Croonen, 1980; Vinke and Thierry, 1984) and some are continuing. Some of these data show that employees gain very accurate knowledge of their income, since they need that in order to make adequate decisions. Other results reveal that biographical and attitudinal data, which are relevant to members of a particular company, allow quite accurate predictions to be made of choice patterns. The direct spin-off to a company is not fully documented yet, although some companies mention the use of the Plan in their personnel advertisements.

In terms of pay meanings, we would guess that the effective use of a Cafeteria Plan would result in high scores on active control and on spending, and in moderately high scores on motivational properties.

Rewarding incidental performance

Managers as well as employees in many companies throughout Europe and the USA often complain that organizational compensation policies are too rigid to reward 'outstanding' contributions adequately. These contributions relate to, for example, individuals who have worked long hours in order to complete a large order, or a group of employees that has solved a product quality problem or has made an unusual effort to satisfy a customer with particular demands. To deal with this problem, managers may reward individuals or groups of employees immediately after their achievement (or effort) with a ticket for a lunch, a dinner for two persons, a stay in a hotel for one night, an expensive conference, a study tour (with some vacation days), and so forth. Characteristically, these rewards are intended to provide the manager with more symbols to express his or her recognition of employees' contributions than are usually at his/her disposal. In some exceptional cases, when rewards represent a lot of money, this strategy is used in order to keep qualified employees engaged to the firm.

Although such reward systems are quite widely used, we are not familiar with any empirical study in this area. We would guess that incidental rewards would score rather high on relative position and moderately high on motivational properties.

Conclusion: Organizational Change and Pay

Paradoxically, change is becoming a constant, if not stable, phenomenon in organizational life. There is almost no company or service institution that is not facing any process of change. Moreover, there is usually not one single event which necessitates organizational adaptation but rather quite a few, often seemingly unrelated, developments which need to be handled. Also, many changes are not simply confined to a few departments, specialists or areas of company policy-making but reverberate throughout the organization. This is what usually happens when a company faces, say, a take-over, a buy out, a changing consumer market, the introduction of advanced technology, the adoption of another managerial philosophy, the need for a better quality of products and services, the need for more profitable activities, or the need for a reduction in overhead costs.

The subject which interests us here is at which phase of a change process payment matters (strategy, system, wage and salary level) are explicitly considered. Throughout this chapter we have emphasized that an appropriate use of pay may have considerable positive effects on the motivation, performance and satisfaction of employees. In order to achieve this, payment strategy, i.e. managerial objectives to be reached through pay, and concomitant payment systems must be consistent with the business plan of the company. While taking account of relevant employees' attitudes and opinions, this implies that payment matters are not treated as belonging to a separate, rather isolated, section but are integrated into the general policy of the company. This will facilitate consistency in motivating employees through the various company policy areas. On the other hand, employees must perceive a clear relationship between their pay and their performance. In order to be meaningful, pay should reflect the changes in four domains to which it may refer: *salient motives; relative position; control; spending.* If these requirements are not met, pay is primarily a great cost to the company, without adequate return on investment, and is not very meaningful, if not a matter of regular disappointment and conflict, to employees.

Unfortunately, the role of payment is usually not very well understood in processes of organizational change. When the subject of change explicitly refers to matters of payment — like the introduction of job evaluation — it is of course taken care of. But in most other organizational changes it is not (e.g. Strauss, 1975; Fein, 1976; Harrison, 1987). Payment issues appear to lag behind: very often they are addressed in the final phase of a change process, when most important decisions have been taken already. Lawler (1981, 1987) proposes on the contrary to introduce pay changes very early and to use this as a 'leading subsystem'. This coincides with the core message of this chapter: pay is more important in organizational life than is often recognized.

Notes

1 Tentative scales have been developed as part of a larger research programme at the Department of Work and Organizational Psychology, University of Amsterdam (e.g. Miedema et al., 1988; Miedema, 1990).

References

Adams, J. S. (1963) Toward an understanding of inequity. *Journal of Abnormal and Social Psychology*, 67, 422–436.

Adams, J. S. (1965) Inequity in social exchange. In L. Berkowitz (ed.), *Advances in Experimental Social Psychology* (vol. 2), New York: Academic Press.

Amsel, A. (1972) Behavioral Habituation, Counter Conditioning, and a General Theory of Persistence. In A. H. Black and W. F. Prokasy (eds), *Classical conditioning II: Current Research and Theory*, New York: Appleton-Century Crofts.

Bandura, A. (1986) *Social Foundations of Thought and Action*. Englewood Cliffs, NJ: Prentice-Hall.

Belcher, D. W. and Atchison, T. A. (1976) Compensation for work. In R. Dubin (ed.), *Handbook of Work, Organization and Society*, Chicago: Rand McNally, 567–611.

Berger, C. J., Cummings, L. L. and Heneman, H. G. (1975) Expectancy Theory and Operant Conditioning Predictions of Performance under Variable Ratio and Continuous Schedules of Reinforcement. *Organizational Behavior and Human Performance*, 14, 227–43.

Bowey, A. M., Thorpe, R., Mitchell, F. H. M., Nichols, G., Gosnold, D., Savery, L. and Hellier, P. K. (1982) *Effects of Incentive Payment Systems United Kingdom 1977–1980*. Department of Employment Research Paper 36. London: HMSO.

European Foundation For the Improvement of Living and Working Conditions (1981) *Spread and Characteristics of Wage Payment Systems: Summary Report*. Dublin.

Fein, M. (1976) Motivation for work. In R. Dubin (ed.), *Handbook of Work, Organization and Society*, Chicago: Rand McNally, 465–530.

Festinger, L. (1954) A Theory of Social Comparison Processes. *Human Relations*, 7, 117–40.

Frost, C. F., Wakeley, J. H. and Ruh, R. A. (1975) *The Scanlon Plan for Organization Development: Identity, Participation, and Equity*. East Lansing: Michigan State University Press.

Goodman, P. S. (1974) An Examination of Referents used in The Evaluation of Pay. *Organizational Behavior and Human Performance*, 12, 170–95.

Harrison, M. I. (1987) *Diagnosing Organizations*. London: Sage.

Ilgen, D. and Klein, H. J. (1989) Organizational Behavior. *Annual Review of Psychology*, 40, 327–51.

Jong, J. R. de and Thierry, Hk (1984) Job Evaluation. In P. J. D. Drenth, Hk Thierry, P. J. Willems and Ch. J. de Wolff (eds), *Handbook of Work and Organizational Psychology*, Chichester: John Wiley, chapter 2.11.

Latham, G. P. and Dossett, D. L. (1978) Designing Incentive Plans for Unionized Employees: a Comparison of Continuous and Variable Ratio Reinforcement Schedules. *Personnel Psychology*, 31, 47–61.

Lawler, E. E. (1971) *Pay and Organizational Effectiveness*. New York: McGraw-Hill.

Lawler, E. E. (1973) *Motivation in Work Organizations*. Monterey, Calif: Brooks/Cole.

Lawler, E. E. (1981) *Pay and Organization Development*. Reading, Mass: Addison-Wesley.

Lawler, E. E. (1987) The Design of Effective Reward Systems. In J. W. Lorsch (ed.), *Handbook of Organizational Behavior*, Englewood Cliffs, NJ: Prentice-Hall, 255–71.

Locke, E. A. and Latham, G. P. (1984) *Goal setting: a motivational technique that works*. Englewood Cliffs, NJ: Prentice-Hall.

Locke, E. A. and Latham, G. P. (1990) *A Theory of Goal Setting and Task Performance*. Englewood Cliffs, NJ: Prentice Hall.

Luthans, F. and Kreitner, R. (1985) *Organizational Behavior Modification and Beyond*. Glenview: Scott, Foresman.

Luthans, F. and Martinko, M. (1987) Behavioral Approaches to Organizations. In C. L. Cooper and I. Robertson (eds), *International Review of Industrial and Organizational Psychology*, Chichester: Wiley, 35–60.

Luthans, F., Paul, R. and Baker, D. (1981) An Experimental Analysis of the Impact of Contingent Reinforcement on Salespersons' Performance Behavior. *Journal of Applied Psychology*, 66, 314–23.

McCormick, E. J. (1976) Job and Task Analysis. In M. D. Dunnette (ed.), *Handbook of Industrial and Organizational Psychology*, Chicago: Rand McNally, 651–96.

March J. G. and Simon H. A. (1958) *Organizations*. New York: Wiley.

Markham, S. E. (1988) Pay-for-Performance Dilemma Revisited: Empirical Example of the Importance of Group Effects. *Journal of Applied Psychology*, 73, 172–80.

Mawhinney, T. C. (1986) Reinforcement Schedule Stretching Effects. In E. A. Locke (ed.), *Generalizing from Laboratory to Field Settings*, Lexington: Heath, 181–6.

Miedema, H. (1990) Voortgangsrapport (Progress Report on Meanings of and Satisfaction with Payment). Internal Report. Amsterdam: Department of Work and Organizational Psychology, University of Amsterdam.

Miedema, H., Rotting, W. and Thierry, Hk (1988) *Some Empirical Data on Two Psychological Meanings of Compensation*. Scheveningen: Seventh International Work and Pay Conference. September.

Mitchell, T. R. (1982) Expectancy-Value Models in Organizational Psychology. In N. T. Feather (ed.), *Expectations and Actions: Expectancy-Value Models in Psychology*, Hillsdale, NY: Lawrence Erlbaum.

Petri, H. L. (1986) *Motivation: Theory and Research (2nd ed.)*. Belmont: Wadsworth.

Saari, L. M. and Latham, G. P. (1982) Employee Reaction to Continuous and Variable Ratio Reinforcement Schedules involving a Monetary Incentive. *Journal of Applied Psychology*, 67, 506–8.

Skinner, B. F. (1953) *Science and Human Behavior*. New York: Free Press.

Skinner, B. F. (1971) *Beyond Freedom and Dignity*. New York: Bantam.

Skinner, B. F. (1990) Can Psychology be a Science of Mind? *American Psychologist*, 45, 1206–10.

Spector, P. E., Brannick, M. T. and Coovert, M. D. (1989) Job Analysis. In C. L. Cooper and I. T. Robertson (eds), *International Review of Industrial and Organizational Psychology*, Chichester: John Wiley, 281–328.

Strauss, G. (1975) Job Satisfaction, Motivation, and Job Redesign. In Strauss, G. e.a. (eds), *Organizational Behavior: Research and Issues*, Madison: Industrial Relations Research Association.

Syroit, J. E. M. M. (1984), *Interpersonal Justice: a Psychological Analysis Illustrated with Empirical Results*. Tilburg: Catholic University Brabant. Doct. published dissertation.

Thierry, Hk (1984) Motivation and satisfaction. In P. J. D. Drenth, Hk Thierry and Ch. J. de Wolff (eds), *Handbook of Work and Organizational Psychology*, Chicago: John Wiley, chapter 2.1.

Thierry, Hk (1987) Payment by Results Systems: A Review of research 1945–1985. *Applied Psychology: an International Review*, 36, 91–108.

Thierry, Hk (1989) Motivatie en satisfaktie (Motivation and satisfaction). In P. J. D. Drenth, Hk Thierry and Ch. J. de Wolff (eds), *Nieuw Handboek Arbeids- en Organisatiepsychologie*, Deventer: van Loghum Slaterus (to appear in English), chapter 2.1.

Thierry, Hk (forthcoming) *Beloning en Arbeidsgedrag* (Payment and Behaviour at Work). Alphen a/d Rijn: Samsom.

Thierry, Hk and Croonen, J. J. F. (1980) Does The Cafeteria Plan pay off? An Empirical Research Study. *Management Decision*, 18, 303–12.

Thierry, Hk and Jong, J. R. de (1979) *Naar participatie en toerekening: theorie en praktijk* (Towards Participation and Gain Sharing: Theory and Practice). Assen: Van Gorcum.

Thierry, Hk and Jong, J. R. de (1989) Functiewaardering (Job Evaluation). In P. J. D.

Drenth, Hk Thierry, and Ch. J. de Wolff (eds), *Nieuw Handboek Arbeids- en Organisatiepsychologie*, Deventer: van Loghum Slaterus (to appear in English), chapter 2.13.

Thierry, Hk, Koopman-Iwema, A. A. and Vinke, R. H. W. (1988) *Toekomst voor Prestatiebeloning?* (Any future for Payment by Results Systems?) Scheveningen: Stichting Maatschappij en Onderneming.

Vinke, R. H. W. and Keizer, W. A. J. (1988) *Effectief communiceren over het belonings pakket* (Effective communication about the income package). Deventer: Kluwer.

Vinke, R. H. W. and Thierry, Hk (1984) *Flexibel belonen: van Cafetariaplan naar praktijk* (Flexible compensation: from Cafeteria Plan towards practice). Deventer: Kluwer.

Vroom, V. H. (ed.) (1964) *Work and Motivation.* New York: Wiley.

White, M. (1976) *Employees' Attitudes to Pay Methods.* Noordwijkerhout: European Federation of Productivity Services/European Association of Personnel Management Pay Methods Research Conference. (September)

Yukl, G. A. and Latham, G. P. (1975) Consequences of Reinforcement Schedules and Incentive Magnitudes for Employee Performance: Problems Encountered in an Industrial Setting. *Journal of Applied Psychology*, 60, 294–8.

Further reading

Readers interested in payment techniques, procedures and practical results in general are referred to Wallace and Fay, and White. Those who are interested in payment theory and research as well as consultant's perspectives may profit from Lawler and Thierry.

Lawler, E. E. (1987) The Design of Effective Reward Systems. In J. W. Lorsch (ed.), *Handbook of Organizational Behavior*, Englewood Cliffs, NJ: Prentice-Hall.

Thierry Hk (1990) Beloning van de arbeid (Compensation of Work). In P. J. D. Drenth, Hk. Thierry, Ch. J. de Wolff, (eds), *Nieuw Handboek Arbeids- en Organisatiepsychologie*, Deventer: van Loghum Slaterus (English text forthcoming).

Wallace, M. J. and Fay, C. H. (1988) *Compensation Theory and Practice.* Boston: PWS-Kent.

White, M. (1981) *Payment Systems in Britain.* Aldershot: Gower.

Part III

Organizing Employees

7

Joining a Trade Union

Jean F. Hartley

Introduction

Why do some employees choose to join trade unions while others in similar circumstances do not? How do employees make the decision to be a union member? Why, within some organizations, are there areas or departments with a high level of union density while others have lower density?[1] What do we know about what motivates people to join? What do employees want or expect from their trade unions?

Such questions, with their social psychological focus, have become especially pertinent in the 1990s as trade unions face considerable challenges to their size, power and purpose. The 1980s saw a large decline in union membership numbers and density in Britain, the USA and most other European countries (Visser, 1988; Kochan, 1988; Fiorito and Greer, 1982). The traditional bases of union membership – in large manufacturing plants and in the public sector – are being eroded by recession and restructuring, technological and demographic change, and legislative and managerial initiatives (see also Introduction). There is a tendency for new jobs to be in smaller workplaces and in the service sector. More new jobs are being offered on a part-time or contract basis. These are employment contexts where unionization is not strong and where the advantages of collective bargaining are not so evident.

An understanding of why workers join trade unions can be valuable in understanding employment relations and in facing some of the challenges of the future. In this chapter we look systematically at some of the evidence – and some of the assumptions and unresolved questions – about union joining. This chapter takes a social psychological perspective on union membership and joining. However, it is also important to understand the broader context of union joining, so that we can develop an awareness of the relationships between structural forces in society and individual choice and motivation.

Trade Unions and the Decision to Join

There is a wide variety of goals, purposes and values which trade unions (and other employee associations) may pursue. The legal constraints within which they operate are also different. In the USSR (currently), a trade union member gains access to childcare, holidays and other social welfare benefits, but collective bargaining is as yet unknown. In contrast, a trade union member in the USA, who is accustomed to 'business unionism', will gain benefits from and perhaps have a role in the fixed term collective bargaining contract and little else. In Britain, union members may be drawn into an active role in the workplace; by contrast, in the former West Germany trade unionists are involved in little shopfloor activity. Thus, across the world, trade unions have varied functions which may affect potential employees' assessments about the value of joining. This suggests that generalizing from research findings in one country to another may be problematic. This is particularly relevant where we consider the American literature on union joining, which focuses almost exclusively on the union certification election.[2] In addition, within each country, unions can vary so considerably that Blackburn (1967) coined the term 'unionnateness' to describe a continuum of unions from those expressing traditional union values (such as the importance of collective bargaining, independence from the employer, the use of strikes and other industrial action) to those with fewer of these values.

Finally, in this consideration of variation, we examine the degree of voluntariness that an individual has in becoming a union member. In some workplaces and occupations, union membership is obligatory. For example, in Britain, some engineering plants operate an informal union membership agreement.[3] In such cases, searching for social psychological explanations of union joining is unnecessary; membership is an institutional fact. Social psychology will be most useful in understanding voluntary union joining.

In understanding the decision to become a voluntary union member, we can draw on several sources of information about union membership and activities, including research on aggregate union growth and decline, union joining, differences between union members and non-members, potential members, such as school-leavers, and, to a lesser extent, research on union activity and union leaving. The reader may wish to explore the degree of similarity in the theories and outcomes explored in this chapter and those on union participation (chapter 8) and industrial action (chapter 11).

This chapter will attempt to provide a systematic account of the contextual forces influencing union membership before focusing on social psychological factors which help to explain individual and group variation in joining behaviour. An understanding of the context (macro-economic and institutional factors) is essential for two reasons: first, because these theories involve assumptions about employee perceptions, cognitions, attitudes and behaviour which are amenable to testing at a social psychological level and thereby provide empirical data about macro-economics and institutional factors; second, because an appreciation of the value of social psychological analysis will occur when the range of appropriateness is fully understood.

The Context
Aggregate union growth and decline

Considerable work has been undertaken on the macro-economic and institutional factors influencing aggregate union membership levels, both over time and across occupations and industries. This research has been undertaken in a number of countries, notably in Britain (e.g. Bain and Price, 1980; Bain and Elsheikh, 1976; Disney, 1990), in the USA (Ashenfelter and Pencavel, 1969; Fiorito and Greer, 1982) and in Europe (Visser, 1988). This level of analysis is currently an area of vigorous debate. The factors which appeared to explain union growth for Britain in the 1970s were less useful as union membership plummeted in the 1980s.

Kochan (1980, 1988) argues that changes in aggregate union membership are best understood by considering the economic and political environment of trade unions. The business cycle has a considerable effect on union growth, although researchers differ in their assessment of its impact on decline. The business cycle has three components: price and wage inflation, and the threat of unemployment (e.g. Bain and Elsheikh, 1976). The significance of these factors has been tested empirically using multiple regression analyses on large time-series data. Bain and Elsheikh (1976) suggest that both wage and price inflation act as separate factors encouraging union membership. They also suggest that unemployment has a curvilinear relationship, with lower levels of unemployment encouraging employees to have the security of union membership while higher levels discourage union joining.

Bain and his co-workers describe their theory as an aggregate theory, stating that they are *not* concerned with individual decision-making about joining a trade union. Nevertheless, some of their assumptions concern individual behaviour and are untested. For example, Bain and Price (1983) state that 'there can be little doubt that the behaviour of prices and earnings during the period 1969–1979 encouraged large numbers of workers . . . to unionise in an attempt to defend or to improve their standards of living' (p. 16). Their explanation of one of the influences of unemployment is that 'workers who are not in unions may be reluctant to join unions in periods of high unemployment for fear of antagonising their employers and thereby losing jobs' (p. 17). Although Bain and others have identified empirical relationships between macro-economic factors and union membership, their approach is weaker in determining whether the explanations that they offer are accurate. Is this how employees perceive their situation?

Researchers have also identified an important role for the political and social climate (e.g. Ginsberg, 1970; Bain and Price, 1983), especially the role of government both as legislator and as employer. Periods of rapid expansion of union membership in the USA and Britain have coincided with periods of facilitative legislation, for example in Britain in the mid-1970s. And, since 1979, when membership declined sharply, the Conservative government has enacted legislation which has made it more difficult for unions to recruit members and to organize effectively (Dickens, 1990).

Employer policies and behaviours also affect aggregate union levels (Terry, 1983; Kochan, 1980; Brown, 1981). Bain and Price (1983) partly attribute union growth in the 1970s to the increasing preparedness of employers to formalize industrial relations and to professionalize personnel management. The importance of employer attitudes and behaviour helps to explain the dramatic rise in union membership in the public sector in Britain in the 1970s. On the other hand, in the 1980s and early 1990s, many employers' attitudes towards unions became less positive or even hostile. This has resulted in some union derecognition (Claydon, 1989; Lawler, 1986) or in the establishment of more unitarist human resource management approaches in the hope of union avoidance (e.g. Guest, 1987) or in the bypassing of unions without dismantling industrial relations procedures (Marginson et al., 1988).

Union joining is also influenced by enterprise and industry characteristics. For example, larger establishments are more likely to be unionized. Bain and Price (1983) suggest that employees there are more likely 'to feel the need to unionise because of the bureaucratic manner in which they are managed on the job' (p. 27) and because unions have a stronger incentive to recruit there. However, this explanation again makes assumptions about employee perceptions and motivations. There is some evidence that size of establishment affects both attitudes to work (Ingham, 1970) and perceptions of management (Allen and Stephenson, 1983) but any assumption about the impact on membership needs to be investigated.

Industrial sectors vary in the density of union membership. For example, Bain and Price (1983) calculated that, in Britain, union density was high in coal mining (97.1%), engineering (79.6%), national government (91.3%) and local government (77.5%). These figures contrast with, for example, distribution (14.9%), agriculture (22.7%) and construction (36.7%). There are considerable variations by industrial sector in other countries too (Fiorito and Greer, 1982; Visser, 1988). It is not clear whether these empirical findings represent size, employment concentration, age of the industry, labour costs or characteristics of employees in these industries. More fundamental than the industrial sector, however, is the distinction between public and private sector: in a recent national survey, Gallie (1989) found that 69 per cent of employees in the public sector were in unions compared with 31 per cent in the private sector and a similar effect has been found in other research.

Trade union availability and trade union membership

Economists such as Green (1990) and Disney (1990) propose that union joining is determined by two sets of factors:

> At the first stage there are certain factors which determine whether there is a recognised union or staff association within the establishment for the individual to join. The outcome of this stage can loosely be termed 'the determinants of coverage'. . . . Second, there is a question of whether the individual chooses to join a union that is recognised. This can be termed the 'determinants of individual membership'.
>
> (Disney, 1990, p. 171)

Disney (1990) indicates the key role of the business cycle as an influence on coverage, thereby supporting the work of Bain and others. However, in understanding individual variation in union joining, he argues that the availability or otherwise of a union at the workplace needs to be taken into account, otherwise our interpretations of individual motivation are seriously flawed. This can be well illustrated using some data analysed by Green (1990). Drawing on data in the 1983 General Household Survey, he analysed responses to two questions: 'Is there a trade union or staff association at your place of work, which people can join if they want to?' and 'Are you currently a member of (that or) any trade union or staff association?' Table 7.1 is reproduced from Green and shows that, where a union is available at work, the differences between groups appear less than among workers overall.

For example, from the data about all employees it might appear that female part-time workers are reluctant trade unionists, since only 29.4 per cent overall are members. However, it is clear that they have a considerably higher membership level where there is a union available (61.2 per cent). Thus, low levels of union density among female part-time workers is more likely to be an attribute of either their job or their work environment than the motivation or characteristics of the individual. Similarly, the difference between men and women in union density reduces when coverage (union availability) is taken into account. In the detailed regression analyses undertaken where a union was present at work, Green found no statistically significant difference between men and women in union joining.

The distinction between factors influencing union coverage and factors affecting individual choice is supported by other work. For example, Cregan and Johnston (1990) and Spilsbury et al. (1987) show the powerful influence of union availability on the joining behaviour of young entrants to the labour market. Also, for currently employed workers, the most important reason for no longer being a union member is moving to a job without a union (Gallie, 1989; van der Veen and Klandermans, 1989).

Table 7.1 Trade union membership

	Percentage of trade union membership	
	All employees	Employees who have a union available at work
Males	62.2	81.1
of whom: Manual	65.0	83.9
Non-manual	55.9	74.6
Females	40.7	69.6
of whom: Full-time	50.4	74.5
Part-time	29.4	61.2

Source: Green, 1990, using data from the 1983 General Household Survey

The two-factor approach to union membership requires still further work before it provides a clear link between structural factors influencing union availability and those which influence the individual decision to join at a particular workplace where a union is available. The dimension of coverage is conceptualized as dichotomous: whether a union is available or not rather than the variation in what a workplace union might provide or be perceived (by potential members) to provide. The two-factor approach still does not examine individual attitudes and motivations. Nevertheless, it suggests that the context of much individual choice is union availability. It also shows that a social psychological theory of union joining which ignores factors influencing union availability is bound to be incomplete and even misleading (just as a solely structural approach cannot explain disaggregated data).

We might also note that, although no evidence is available, a social psychological analysis may also be valuable in explaining some circumstances where coverage is non-existent and workers press for union recognition. However, this is a rarer occurrence and there is no psychological literature available on this other than in the context of the American union certification election, for which see Brett (1980) and Getman et al. (1976) for summaries.

Union recruitment strategies

Union joining is affected by the recruitment strategies of the trade unions and the vigour with which recruitment is pursued. Lawler (1986) in the USA and Kelly and Heery (1989) and Beaumont and Harris (1990) in Britain have examined union strategies from an organizational perspective. Kelly and Heery found that full-time officials of several major national unions were encouraged to place a strong emphasis on recruitment but that the organizational structure did not reward endeavours to recruit new workers. The officials, already burdened by long hours and a range of negotiating responsibilities, had little time for recruitment. Nor was there a reward structure, in pay or career terms, for attention to recruitment. Furthermore, there were some differences in declared priority between national policy and district committee strategy. However, despite this, some unions in Britain are taking important initiatives in recruitment, such as developing specific and varied campaigns to foster recruitment and to reduce barriers to joining by generating more 'user-friendly' union activities. The TUC has also become more involved in recruitment (TUC, 1989). If unions are to run successful recruitment campaigns, then this will be considerably facilitated by a careful analysis of what potential members want and expect from joining.

Individual and social influences on union joining

An assortment of variables has been put forward as influencing union joining at the level of the individual. These can be bewildering in range and, as Brett (1980) and Premack and Hunter (1988) note, empirical rather than theoretical.

We shall commence by teasing out the principal variables which have been proposed as affecting union choice. In the following section we attempt to progress beyond this to examine some ideas about the *processes* of union joining.

Personal and occupational characteristics

Personal characteristics independent of the job have been researched but the results are largely negative. Age, marital status, gender, race and full- or part-time working have been explored (see Bain and Elias, 1985; Bain and Price, 1983; Green, 1990; Youngblood et al., 1984; Poole et al., 1983; De Witte, 1989; Kochan, 1980; Maxey and Mohrman, 1980). Although, at an aggregate level, older workers are somewhat more likely overall to be union members (Bain and Price, 1983), this is difficult to separate from the fact that older workers are more likely to work in traditional industries (where unions are more likely to be recognized).

Although women's attitudes have sometimes been put forward as a significant factor in explaining their lower propensity to join, we have already seen that a more compelling explanation lies in structural factors, notably union availability but also industrial sector and size of establishment. Although the principal explanation of gender differences is not attitudinal, an interesting study by Snyder et al. (1986) did find some differences in job attitudes. The lack of gender difference in willingness to join (Kochan, 1980; Gallie, 1989) suggests that trade unions can be optimistic about their ability to recruit women members in the future, although their employment location may cause difficulties. Kochan (1988) found a similar structural explanation for the relationship between race and union membership. Overall, we can rule out personal characteristics as a basis for explaining propensity to join a trade union. Any effect is small compared with structural explanations of membership.

The search for occupational characteristics to explain union membership has not fared much better. Skill level has not been found to be related to membership, for example (Bain and Price, 1983). And although white collar workers are generally less well unionized than blue collar workers (Gallie, 1989; de Witte, 1989), this can be largely explained by the preparedness of employers to recognize white collar unions, and by size of establishment (Bain, 1970; Bain and Price, 1983; Poole et al., 1983).

Job attitudes

Are union members more disenchanted with their working life and therefore more prepared to join a union? This has been a favourite research theme of US research, where considerable effort has gone into examining the relationship between attitudes and vote (intended or actual) in a union certification election. Dissatisfaction with wages has been related to unionization in US research (e.g. Farber and Saks, 1990; Schriesheim, 1978; Kochan, 1980; Youngblood et al., 1984). Dissatisfaction with other terms and conditions has also been found (as above and also De Cotiis and Lelouarn, 1981; Snyder et al., 1986). Snyder et al.

(1986) found in a study of US social service employees that women were significantly more dissatisfied than men with promotion prospects and women union members especially so. Although less research has been carried out in Europe, similar findings exist regarding dissatisfaction with terms and conditions (Guest and Dewe, 1988) and with wages (Kerr, 1990), and a concern about job security (Guest and Dewe, 1988; van der Vall, 1970). However, satisfaction with intrinsic aspects of the job shows only a modest relationship with unionism (e.g. Schriesheim, 1978; De Cotiis and Lelouarn, 1981) and less than with satisfaction with terms and conditions (for example, Schriesheim in a small study of 59 production workers found a correlation of -0.74 with economic and -0.38 with non-economic satisfaction).

Some aspects of administration and involvement seem important. Guest and Dewe (1988) found that union members were more dissatisfied with aspects of involvement in managerial decision-making and with opportunities for training and personal development. Premack and Hunter (1988) and Kochan (1980) also found dissatisfaction with administration to be important predictors of union membership.

Overall, job satisfaction (i.e. covering both intrinsic and extrinsic factors) is indeed related to unionization in the US but it is not as simple to explain what this means. Youngblood et al. (1984) suggest that job attitudes while they may be a *trigger* for union joining (in the US context), need *augmentation* by other attitudes and beliefs to be a cause of actual behaviour. Kochan (1980) makes a similar point: dissatisfaction with 'bread and butter' issues does not mean that joining a union is the behavioural outcome: remaining dissatisfied or leaving that employment are also logical possibilities. Thus, a theory of union joining needs to explain *why* dissatisfaction should be translated into behaviour (even assuming that this is the causative path: it is also quite plausible that joining a union makes employees more dissatisfied with their terms and conditions). Gordon and Nurick (1981) suggest that the relationship between work attitudes and union joining may be more salient in the context of a union certification election than where an employee is joining an union already established at the workplace.

Social and instrumental beliefs

How far are employees motivated to join because of strongly held beliefs, or how much is joining a more pragmatic decision? Are certain beliefs about unions and their power and purpose (perhaps less strongly held) necessary to become a union member?

Joining a union on ideological grounds (i.e. having a strong belief in the value and purpose of trade unions) is not a major reason. Some employees may be predisposed to join regardless of the costs and benefits incurred, but this is not a large group: in van der Vall's (1970) study, 7 per cent of blue collar and 3 per cent of white collar union members cited moral duty as their reason for joining. (However, such employees may have some influence on the joining behaviour of their colleagues.) Guest and Dewe (1988) investigated whether union members were more class conscious than non-union members but found that the claim for class and occupational solidarity on membership was not supported (see also Gallie, 1989). De Witte (1989) found that young trade unionists were more likely to place themselves on the left of the political spectrum.

Are more pragmatic beliefs important? Researchers have argued that union joining is increased where employees believe that the union will be *instrumental* in helping them to obtain outcomes. Van der Vall (1970) notes this in his study of Dutch union members: 'The viability of a voluntary organization will depend on the presence of deeply felt needs among its members and their conviction that nothing will satisfy these better than the organization' (p. 80). Guest and Dewe (1988) found that the belief that the union best represents the employee's interest was the most important variable in a multiple regression analysis (with another significant variable being the perception of union success in the plant).

Maxey and Mohrman (1980), in a study of 182 white collar employees, found that union members were less likely to believe that they could influence their working conditions through channels such as talking to their superior, through high work performance or through networking. Kochan (1980) found that the belief that conditions could be changed through union action was correlated with membership and he argues that this belief might well form a means by which employees might direct their dissatisfaction into union joining rather than, say, turnover or absenteeism (see also Youngblood et al., 1984; Zalesny, 1985; Premack and Hunter, 1988).

Of related interest is the evidence that union joining is partly motivated by the provision of protection against adversity, whether that be managerial arbitrariness, unfair treatment or accusations of misconduct. Van der Vall (1970) found that the highest single motive for joining was 'conflict insurance', that is, the provision of material and legal assistance in the possible event of individual grievances and problems. He found that 76 per cent of blue collar and 65 per cent of white collar employees gave this as their primary motive for joining. Kerr (1990) found, in a public sector union, that members appreciated having access to legal and safety advice. Among nurses, the Royal College of Nursing's professional indemnity insurance was especially welcome among members (Carpenter et al., 1990).

Some US research has also found a correlation with the 'labour union image' held by employees (e.g. Youngblood et al., 1984; Kochan, 1980), although this variable is often rather vague, consisting of four or five items concerning whether unions in general are too corrupt, too powerful, unnecessary, and so on. It seems to indicate a positive or negative attitude to unions in society, though quite how one interprets this variable is not entirely clear.

Overall, then, we find that instrumental beliefs are important, with those who perceive themselves as unable to influence their work environment through more informal, individualistic or employer-initiated activities being more likely to unionize. However, the instrumental beliefs may perhaps be more important in the US context, given the research which takes place at the time of a union election (when it is likely that an employee will consider whether the union can help to create change in the plant). The social and instrumental beliefs of potential union members could be a significant area for social psychologists to explore further. The perceptions of the relationship between cause and effect (for example, union joining and changes in work conditions) could be explored, using the theoretical frameworks of causal attribution and locus of control. This relates also to questions about the extent to which employees feel empowered by joining the union and whether this changes as a result of *being* in the union. We might also ask questions about the origins of beliefs about power, efficacy and instrumentality both in the family (see also chapter 1) and in the workplace (chapter 2).

Social networks

So far we have considered the employee making a decision about the trade union as though he or she were acting in social isolation, but we also need to consider the influence of other people on the individual's decision to join. This might take place in a variety of ways: for example, inside or outside the workplace, through social pressure or through socialization, through argument and discussion, or through identification.

Socialization outside the workplace may well influence union joining, since it has an impact on so many aspects of economic life (see also chapter 1). It has been found that union members are more likely to have had union-active parents (e.g. De Witte, 1989; Gallie, 1989; van der Vall, 1970). (In fact, many studies have researched only the father's union activity.)

For young people entering the labour market, peers and colleagues are more important than parents (De Witte, 1989), suggesting that the group climate is significant for young people as they are socialized into the workplace. In a study of school-leavers, Cregan and Johnston (1990) found that 4 per cent of union members had joined for family reasons and 15 per cent because 'everyone else is in it' or 'for social reasons'. A further 14 per cent were union members because they were 'expected to'.

Adults too, are susceptible to social influence. Van der Vall (1970) found that:

> many workers join the union in order to occupy a psychologically safe position among the members of their group, i.e. in order not to be isolated or despised as a 'parasite'. Evidence of this is that 82% of blue-collar and 81% of the white-collar workers mentioned persons in their immediate environment who had influenced their decision to join. Since 32% and 38% respectively gave such influence as their basic motive, it may be concluded that at least one-third join mainly on account of the convictions of others. (1970, p. 136)

However, we may note that the pervasiveness of social influence, as recorded above, does not mean that it is necessarily motivated by the desire to avoid isolation or hostile attitudes. Social influence can, of course, be more benign than this, involving exposure to arguments about the role and purpose of trade unions, or increasing the attractiveness of social group membership and social identity.

One role for social influence is provided by reasons for non-membership. In the Cregan and Johnston (1990) study, 40 per cent of non-members said that they had not been asked, and in Kerr's (1990) study the figure was 39 per cent. The TUC found that the most prevalent reason for not being a union member was not having been asked (TUC, 1989).

The role of colleagues, union members and others in the workplace still requires further clarification. Brief and Rude (1981) suggest that salient referent others, such as the immediate supervisor and co-workers, are important (see also Youngblood et al., 1984; Beaumont and Elliott, 1989). Some research (e.g. Brief and Rude, 1981; Youngblood et al., 1984) has drawn explicitly on the theory of reasoned action of Ajzen and Fishbein (1980), which assumes that a person's intention to act in a particular way is modified by the subjective norm (the employee's judgement of the likelihood that relevant others, such as co-workers and friends, would expect the employee to behave in a particular way). Action is shaped also by the employee's motivation to comply (or not) with these relevant other's expectations.

The use of the Ajzen and Fishbein model takes us further than the simple dissatisfaction–action model of much of the job attitude research. However, there is still much to learn about how other people, such as co-workers, family, employer, union activists, affect both the motivation and the decision to be a union member. Does the employee make a one-off decision or is joining a more gradual process as the employee becomes more engaged in group interactions and group identity? Do referent others shape perceptions of instrumentality or of the costs and benefit of joining? Or is joining a union a procedure involving social information processing (Salancik and Pfeffer, 1978), such that joining is a behavioural act and the reasons and meaning develop *after* the action as a consequence of it? There is certainly evidence that socialization processes continue within the trade union after joining (Gordon et al., 1980; Gallie, 1989; van der Veen and Klandermans, 1989). Gallie (1989) found that only about half (47 per cent) of those who felt that they had been coerced into joining believed later that this was still the case.

Perhaps comparison with the membership of other voluntary organizations, such as the church, environmental and other pressure groups, could be helpful in understanding union joining decisions. There is still much that we could explore about *how* social influence occurs and about whether some employees are more susceptible to social factors than others.

Structural and individual levels of analysis: summary

We can summarize the preceding work by pointing to the value of both structural and individual level analyses. From a psychological perspective, structural factors are the context within which individual decisions are constrained. These structural variables may themselves be examined in terms of the subjective perceptions and expectations of employees. The variables that we have examined so far are listed below; those in brackets have not had a strong relationship with union joining. The structural variables largely have their impact on union availability, while individual and social variables are thought to affect joining where a union is available (though some structural variables, such as the 'business cycle', have been predicated partly on individual employee behaviour).

The context of individual decisions: structural factors	*Individual decisions* (Personal characteristics: age, gender,
Business cycle: wage and price	race).
inflation,	(Occupational characteristics: skill, status,
unemployment.	class).
Employer behaviour.	Aspects of job satisfaction.
Government action.	Social and instrumental beliefs:
Public vs. private sector.	(ideology), union effectiveness.
Industrial sector.	Social networks.
Establishment size.	

Process theories of union joining

So far we have looked at *variables* which foster or inhibit union joining but some do not tell us much about the *processes* of becoming a union member. Can we propose theories of union joining which explain the social and individual processes of perception, cognition, expectation and choice, whether conscious or not, that underlie the behavioural act of joining a union? Some of the analyses that we have looked at have implied processes of union joining. For example, in exploring the role of job dissatisfaction in becoming a member, there is a view that the underlying process is of frustration leading to membership. Or, in exploring the role of work colleagues and family, there is a presumed set of social processes, such as socialization, the development and expression of group identity, and the role of social representations. The number of process theories of union joining are rather limited. While others exist, we shall concentrate here on three such approaches.

Sequential decision processes: Premack and Hunter

Premack and Hunter (1988) present a model of individual unionization decisions, based on US research. Their framework is shown in figure 7.1.

Their model is built on meta-analysis, which is able to compare statistically several existing studies of union joining. Twelve US studies were used in the analysis, and the variables considered were wage level, extrinsic satisfaction, satisfaction with administration, union instrumentality, intention to become a union member, and the person's report on his or her vote (the last two being similar enough to be called the unionization decision). There are two paths to unionization: either through the sequential steps of the predictors (see figure 7.1) or through one of the predictors alone. If an individual is satisfied (with wages, with other terms and conditions, with company administration), then unionization will not occur. Where the individual is dissatisfied, then a search process begins to explore alternatives such as quitting. If the alternatives are limited, then

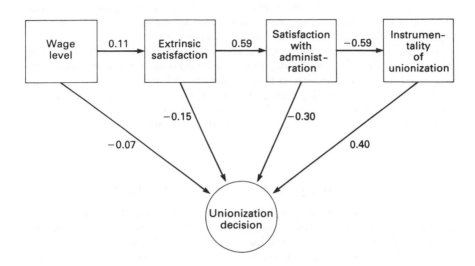

Figure 7.1 Premack and Hunter's (1988) model of the unionization decision

Source: S. L. Premack and J. E. Hunter (1988) Individual unionization decisions *Psychological Bulletin*, 103, 223–34. c 1988 American Psychological Association.

unionization may occur if the individual perceives the union as being able to change important aspects of the work environment (i.e. union instrumentality).

Premack and Hunter's model is a statistically complex approach to understanding union joining as a series of steps. The model suggests that employees may use different decision steps and different criteria for union membership, and therefore that the search for a single, universal path of decision-making is inappropriate. The precise model allows for replication in future studies (although the actual sequence of steps could be open to debate and testing). The model is also useful in suggesting alternatives to union joining (such as quitting or remaining dissatisfied). These have not been explored in the statistical analysis because of lack of empirical data but it would be straightforward to collect such data (Zalesny, 1985). An interesting development would be to try to specify which employees might be involved in all of the steps while others are not.

However, this model and others from the USA are weak in that they concentrate on dissatisfaction as the prime motivator of joining, while under-emphasizing social influences. The idea of dissatisfaction as a motivation for membership is rather crudely built on frustration–aggression theory (see also Klandermans, 1986), which implicitly involves a restricted and negative view of the role and function of trade unions (if organizations cared for their employees, unions would be unnecessary). There is also the problem of causation: does dissatisfaction cause union joining or vice versa? And there is the problem of using dissatisfaction to explain union belonging as opposed to union joining (since if the source of dissatisfaction is removed or lessened, the employee ought presumably to quit the union). The dissatisfaction approach is more popular and more extensively researched in the USA than elsewhere.

The model also seems to propose that the US employee makes his or her decision in isolation from social influences inside and outside the workplace. Yet, even in the USA, the evidence is that employers and unions conduct vigorous campaigns to influence voting choice (Lawler, 1986) and it is highly likely that informal social influence occurs too. Even in the USA, the argument for exploring social influence is compelling; in countries with a stronger collective culture it is imperative.

Categories of motivation: Van der Vall

Van der Vall (1970) proposed, on the basis of Dutch research, that there are three categories of motivation for union joining. He argued that the social environment (work, family and leisure) interacted with personal needs and the image of the union to affect the employee's motives for joining. The typology of motives is:

1 Egocentric motives: employees join because they believe that they will benefit personally (e.g. for protection against employer arbitrariness; the need for security; access to union services).
2 Sociocentric motives: employees join for reasons based on their social and political beliefs and a collective interest (e.g. idealism, collective interest, a sense of solidarity).
3 Social control motives (e.g. influence of parents, fellow workers, superiors, friends).

Van der Vall's own work suggested that egocentric motives were the most prevalent but that sociocentric and social control motives were also important. Employees could be motivated by more than one reason and he found that manual workers gave an average of 3.8 motives for joining (there were several possibilities in each category).

Van der Vall's framework is not rigorous and has not attracted much empirical testing (but see De Witte, 1989). Although motivations have been categorized, it is not clear how motivation is presumed to drive behaviour. Nevertheless, despite its conceptual and empirical weakness, it is a framework which is amenable to empirical enquiry. One of its strengths is that it gives weight to both collective (sociocentric) and social influence motivations, which have been neglected, especially in US research, and only weakly tested in research such as that of Guest and Dewe (1988). There is clearly scope for research which broadens out from solely instrumental (egocentric) motivations for union membership (see also Booth, 1985). The implicit model of the trade unionist, in Van der Vall's work, is much more social and active than in American research. Joining is about belonging to a voluntary organization and pursuing personal and social goals rather than simply a passive means for expressing discontent.

However, much more theoretical and empirical work is required on this framework.

Rational choice: Klandermans

Klandermans' (1984) model builds on a value expectancy approach to motivation, which states that a person will be motivated to engage in certain actions to the extent that he or she *expects* his or her behaviour to lead to an outcome and to the extent that he or she *values* that outcome. The model was originally developed to explain union participation and industrial action (see also chapters 8 and 11) but has also attracted some interest for its potential application to understanding union joining. It is more fully explained in chapter 11 on industrial action. It is outlined here (though in less detail) because it offers an analysis of how employees make decisions about membership.

In the context of union joining, Klandermans' model has three sets of expectancies and values for what he calls action mobilization. First, there is the expectancy that the action (in this case, joining) will achieve the goals of the action (which may be social, instrumental, political or whatever; for example, that joining will contribute to increasing wages or to reducing vulnerability to employer arbitrariness), combined with the value of that goal for the individual. A second expectancy–value concerns the expected reaction of significant others to joining and not joining (this builds on the work of Ajzen and Fishbein, 1980). The value to the individual of these expected reactions is also involved. Third, there is the expectancy–value concerned with the costs and benefits of joining or not joining (for example, the expectancy that union dues or time required for meetings are a cost but that the benefits are the security offered by union membership or social contact). These three motivations are believed to combine additively in such a way as to predict the employee's *willingness* (or intention) to join the union. It does not predict actual action, since that may be governed also by the context (as we have seen earlier). The schematic representation of the model is given in figure 11.1 (p. 250). Chapter 11 also engages in an evaluation of the model in its application to industrial action, and some of those comments are relevant here to union joining.

In empirical terms, the theory has not been tested in the context of union joining, except for one small study of hotel workers which is not reported in English (mentioned in Klandermans, 1986). There is clearly room for further research. On theoretical grounds, it has some attractions. As it is based on subjective perceptions, beliefs and values, it can help to explain variation in union joining where employees are in similar objective circumstances. It incorporates instrumentality beliefs and includes the impact of others on the decision. It allows for the influence (and testing) of some of the structural, context variables through subjective perceptions (for example, the role of the employer in encouraging or discouraging union membership could be explored through examining the expected reaction of the employer and the value placed on that by the employee).

However, like all motivation theory based on the expectancy framework, it implies a rational weighing up of a range of possible actions by the individual which is then followed by rational decision-making. Do employees act in this way? The evidence for rational decision-making is not strong in many contexts, including this one (Brett and Hammer, 1982). And it is also possible that individuals join through being socially influenced and then *rationalize* or come to understand their decision (Salancik and Pfeffer, 1978). The theory also implies that employees have sufficient *knowledge* about the pros and cons of membership, whereas many members are likely to be unaware of many aspects of these until after they have joined. The theory is more genuinely social than, for example, that of Premack and Hunter, but it is still markedly individualistic. More emphasis could be given to interaction processes among employees (see also chapter 11).

Klandermans' theory may be more useful in certain contexts than in others; for example, where the costs and benefits are salient or visible, such as in union certification elections, or where the costs and benefits of joining or not joining are fairly equal. However, there may well be contexts where union joining is not a weighing up of expectancies and values. Indeed, one area where it may be less relevant is in explaining union joining in the context of a union recognition dispute. For the Tolpuddle Martyrs, and for the union members at Grunwick in the 1970s (for which see Rogaly, 1977), the value of Klandermans' work may be less relevant than it is in more everyday contexts.

Process theories: future research

Theories of why and how employees join unions still have a number of problems. First, there are only a few such theories (though the recent increased interest in union joining may change this). In addition, they are restricted in the range of variables that they employ, they are still weak on how motivation occurs and decisions are taken, and they are still largely individualistic. Furthermore, insufficient evidence has been gathered to support or refute them. There are some very promising lines of enquiry, however.

Future research ought to focus on two further issues. The first is to allow a genuinely social influence on union joining. We need to know much more about aspects of group influence on joining; for example, the prevailing union culture in the workplace, how joining contributes to social identity, how far perceptions of needs and expectations are socially transmitted, how much socialization occurs within the workplace. Second, longitudinal research designs would be valuable in exploring the views and values that employees bring to the workplace and how these are changed by social influence both before and after becoming a union member. Beaumont and Elliott (1989) have made a start by looking at social influences on potential union members during their training as nurses.

Conclusion

This chapter has looked at a range of structural and psychological factors to explain variations among employees in their opportunities and preparedness to become union members. The work illustrates the necessity, in the field of employment relations, to use multiple levels of analysis to produce satisfactory explanations of events. Neither a structural nor a social psychological analysis is sufficient on its own. Structural explanations such as the business cycle, employer and government behaviour, and features of the industry and organization are important determinants of union coverage, that is, whether or not a union is recognized. However, a structural analysis is inadequate where it makes assumptions about individual and social motivations but does not test these. Here, a psychological level of enquiry is needed. Whether objective conditions match subjective reality could be investigated. A social psychological analysis is particularly pertinent in explaining differences between employees in contexts of voluntary membership where unions *are* recognized (though it could also be used to explore why and how employees establish unions). However, there is much further research to be done: there exists a range of variables without an adequate theoretical base, and process theories are prominent by their scarcity.

The work reviewed has important implications for both trade unions and management in their efforts to recruit members/staff. The 1990s will continue to see great changes in employment and trade unions need to find out about the needs, values and expectations of their current and potential members if they are to continue recruitment. Booth (1989) notes the dilemmas for unions in offering improved services to members as a way to increase union recruitment: this might increase egocentric motivation but weaken collective motivation and group identity. Further detailed analysis of member motivation and its implications for both individual members and the total organization is needed. Furthermore, if employer attitudes to unions continue to be lukewarm or even hostile, how far should trade unions adjust to these new circumstances? There has been plenty of controversy over the 'beauty contest' approach to gaining union recognition at green-field sites, whereby interested trade unions offer themselves to the employer before recruitment has begun, and where it is the *employer* who decides which union will be granted recognition in a single union agreement.

The current situation, with its declining union membership, has been represented in some circles as an improvement for managers in their management of labour, but is that actually the case? How far have large firms in the past relied on union recognition and collective bargaining procedures to ensure consistent personnel practices? The move in the 1980s to bypass unions or decentralize collective bargaining has not been without its problems for management (see, for example, Legge, 1988; Marginson et al., 1988). The development of human resource management may be unitarist and may express no need or desire for unions (Guest, 1987) but there are problems with this approach. Not all organizations can aspire to the level of resourcing required for such an approach. As Lawler (1986) notes, this may involve a costly union substitution strategy. Also to what extent, in trying to avoid unions, must managements provide the very services for which unions campaign, such as above average remuneration, consistent and fair personnel practices, and access to a grievance procedure (see also chapter 4, and Bassett, 1986)?

Thus, the 1990s are a time of challenge and change for trade unions and for managements. Recruiting new union members is a key step for unions in the development of their industrial and political power. Union membership is an area of increasing academic interest, and it is not at all surprising that this is a developing area of theory and practice.

Notes

1 Union density refers to the percentage of employees who are union members compared with the total potential membership. It can be calculated nationally, by industry, and so forth. There is some variation in the basis of calculation and therefore the figures can vary by a few percentage points. For example, Disney (1990) calculates density of union members as a percentage of the employed workforce, while Bain (1970) uses as the denominator both the employed and unemployed workforce. Generally those who are self-employed and those in the armed services are excluded.

2 The USA union certification election involves a federally regulated legal procedure whereby employees at a plant are asked to vote for or against becoming union members. If over 50 per cent of the workforce vote for membership, then a union contract will be established and certain rights and responsibilities will be conferred on both management and union. The data collection possibilities of having all employees in an organization express their views about work and unionism at the same time has proved highly attractive to psychologists. However, there has been less emphasis on the antecedents of unionization and the social influences on the decision. In Europe, it is much more likely that a potential union member will be joining an established union. (For descriptions of the US procedures, see Getman et al., 1976; Lawler, 1986.)

3 The existence of formal pre- and post-entry closed shop arrangements has been increasingly restricted in Britain during the 1980s as a result of legislation. They were made unlawful in the 1988 Employment Act. However, they continue informally in some workplaces, where social pressures to join may be considerable.

References

Ajzen, I. and Fishbein, M. (1980) *Understanding Attitudes and Predicting Social Behaviour*. Englewood Cliffs, NJ: Prentice-Hall.

Allen, P. T. and Stephenson, G. M. (1983) Intergroup understanding and size of organizations. *British Journal of Industrial Relations*, 21, 312–29.

Ashenfelter, O. and Pencavel, J. H. (1969) American trade union growth: 1900–1960. *Quarterly Journal of Economics*, 83, 434–48.

Bain, G. (1970) *The Growth of White-Collar Unionism*. Oxford: Clarendon Press.

Bain, G. and Elias, P. (1985) Trade union membership in Great Britain: an individual level analysis. *British Journal of Industrial Relations*, 23, 71–82.

Bain, G. and Elsheikh, F. (1976) *Union Growth and the Business Cycle: An Econometric Analysis*. Oxford: Blackwell.

Bain, G. and Price, R. (1980) *Profiles of Union Growth*. Oxford: Blackwell.

Bain, G. and Price, R. (1983) Union growth: dimensions, determinants and destiny. In G. Bain (ed.), *Industrial Relations in Britain*, Oxford: Blackwell, 3–33.

Bassett, P. (1986) *Strike Free: New Industrial Relations in Britain*. London: Macmillan.

Beaumont, P. B. and Elliott, T. J. (1989) Individual employee choice between unions: some public sector evidence from Britain. *Industrial Relations Journal*, 20, 119–27.

Beaumont, P. B. and Harris, R. I. (1990) Union recruitment and organising attempts in Britain in the 1980s. *Industrial Relations Journal*, 21, 274–86.

Blackburn, R. (1967) *Union Character and Social Class: A Study of White Collar Unionism.* London: Batsford.

Booth, A. (1985) The free rider problem and a social custom theory of trade union membership. *Quarterly Journal of Economics*, 99, 253–61.

Booth, A. (1989) What do unions do now? *Discussion paper in economics 8903.* Uxbridge: Brunel University.

Brett, J. B. (1980) Behavioral research on unions and union-management systems. In B. M. Staw and L. L. Cummings (eds), *Research in Organizational Behavior* vol 2. Greenwich, Conn: JAI Press, 177–213.

Brett, J. B. and Hammer T. H. (1982) Organizational Behavior and Industrial Relations. In T. A. Kochan, D. J. Mitchell, and L. Dyer (eds), *Industrial Relations Research in the 1970s: Review and Appraisal.* Madison, WI: Industrial Relations Research Association, 221–81.

Brief, A. and Rude, D. (1981) Voting in union certification elections: a conceptual analysis. *Academy of Management Review*, 6, 261–7.

Brown, W. (1981) *The Changing Contours of British Industrial Relations.* Oxford: Blackwell.

Carpenter, M., Elkan, R., Leonard, P. and Munro A. (1990) Professionalism and unionism in nursing and social work. Unpublished paper. Department of Applied Social Studies, University of Warwick. Coventry.

Claydon, T. (1989) Union derecognition in the 1980s. *British Journal of Industrial Relations*, 28, 214–24.

Cregan, C. and Johnston, S. (1990) An industrial relations approach to the free rider problem: young people and trade union membership in the UK. *British Journal of Industrial Relations*, 28, 85–104.

DeCotiis, T. A. and LeLouarn, J. (1981) A predictive study of voting behavior in a representation election using union instrumentality and work perceptions. *Organizational Behavior and Human Performance*, 27, 103–18.

De Witte H. (1989) Why do youngsters join a trade union? Paper presented to Fourth West European Conference on the Psychology of Work and Organization. Cambridge, UK, April.

Dickens, L. (1990) Learning to live with the law? The legislative attack on British trade unions since 1979. *New Zealand Journal of Industrial Relations*, 14, 37–52.

Disney, R. (1990) Explanation of the decline of trade union density in Britain: An appraisal. *British Journal of Industrial Relations*, 28, 165–77.

Farber, H. S. and Saks, D. H. (1990) Why workers want unions: the role of relative wages and job characteristics. *Journal of Political Economy*, 88, 349–69.

Fiorito, J. and Greer, C. (1982) Determinants of US unionism: past research and future needs. *Industrial Relations*, 21, 1–32.

Gallie, D. (1989) Trade union allegiance and decline in British urban labour markets. *Working paper 9.* ESRC Social Change and Economic Life Initiative. Oxford: Nuffield College.

Getman, J., Goldberg, S. and Herman, J. (1976) *Union Representation Elections: Law and Reality.* New York: Basic Books.

Ginsberg, W. L. (1970) Union growth, government and structure. *Review of Industrial Relations Research*, 1, 207–60.

Gordon, M. E. and Nurick, A. J. (1981) Psychological approaches to the study of unions and union–management relations. *Psychological Bulletin*, 90, 293–306.

Gordon, M. E., Philpot, J. W., Burt, R. E., Thompson, C. A. and Spiller, W. E. (1980) Commitment to the union: development of a measure and an examination of its correlates. *Journal of Applied Psychology*, 65, 479–99.

Green, F. (1990) Trade union availability and trade union membership in Britain. *Manchester School of Economic and Social Studies*, 58, 378–94.

Guest, D. (1987) Human resource management and industrial relations. *Journal of Management Studies*, 24, 503–21.

Guest, D. and Dewe, P. (1988) Why do workers belong to a trade union?: a social psychological study in the UK electronics industry. *British Journal of Industrial Relations*, 26, 178–94.

Ingham, G. K. (1970) *Size of Industrial Organization and Worker Behaviour*. Cambridge: Cambridge University Press.

Kelly, J. and Heery, E. (1989) Full time officers and trade union recruitment. *British Journal of Industrial Relations*, 27, 196–213.

Kerr A. (1990) Trade union recruitment in the public sector. Unpublished MSc thesis. London: London School of Economics.

Klandermans, B. (1984) Mobilization and participation in trade union action: a value expectancy approach. *Journal of Occupational Psychology*, 57, 107–20.

Klandermans, B. (1986) Psychology and trade union participation: Joining, acting, quitting. *Journal of Occupational Psychology*, 59, 189–204.

Kochan, T. A. (1980) *Collective Bargaining and Industrial Relations*. Homewood, Ill: Irwin.

Kochan, T. A. (1988) The future of worker representation: an American perspective. *Labour and Society*, 13, 183–201.

Lawler, J. J. (1986) Union growth and decline: the impact of employer and union tactics. *Journal of Occupational Psychology*, 59, 217–30.

Legge, K. (1988) Personnel management in recession and recovery: a comparative analysis of what the surveys say. *Personnel Review*, 17, 1–72.

Marginson, P., Edwards, P. K., Martin, R., Purcell, J. and Sisson, K. (1988) *Beyond the Workplace: Managing Industrial Relations in Multi-Establishment Enterprises*. Oxford: Blackwell.

Maxey, C. and Mohrman, S. A. (1980) Worker attitudes toward unions: a study integrating industrial relations and organisational behavior perspectives. *Proceedings of the 33rd Annual Convention of the Industrial Relations Research Association*, 33, 326–33.

Poole, M., Mansfield, R., Frost, P. and Blyton, P. (1983) Why managers join unions: evidence from Britain. *Industrial Relations*, 22, 426–44.

Premack, S. L. and Hunter, J. E. (1988) Individual unionization decisions. *Psychological Bulletin*, 103, 223–34.

Rogaly, J. (1977) *Grunwick*. Harmondsworth: Penguin.

Salancik, G. R. and Pfeffer, J. (1978) A social information processing approach to job attitudes and task design. *Administrative Science Quarterly*, 23, 224–53.

Schriesheim, C. A. (1978) Job satisfaction, attitudes toward unions, and voting in a union representation election. *Journal of Applied Psychology*, 63, 548–52.

Snyder, R. A., Verderber, K. and Morris, J. H. (1986) Voluntary union membership of women and men: differences in personal characteristics, perceptions and attitudes. *Journal of Occupational Psychology*, 59, 205–16.

Spilsbury, D., Hoskins, M., Ashton, D. J., and Maguire, M. J. (1987) A note on the trade union patterns of young adults. *British Journal of Industrial Relations*, 25, 267–74.

Terry, M. (1983) Shop steward development and managerial strategies. In G. Bain (ed.), *Industrial Relations in Britain*, Oxford: Blackwell, 67–91.

TUC (1989) *Special Review Body Second Report: Organising for the 1990s*. London: Trades Union Congress.

Van der Vall, M. (1970) *Labor Organizations*. New York: Cambridge University

Van der Veen, G. and Klandermans, B. (1989) Exit behavior in social movement organizations. In B. Klandermans (ed.), *Organizing for Change: Social Movement Organizations in Europe and the United States*, Greenwich, Conn: JAI Press, 179–98.

Visser, J. (1988) Trade Unionism in Western Europe: present situation and prospects. *Labour and Society*, 13, 125–82.

Youngblood, S. A., De Nisi, A. S., Molleston, J. L. and Mobley, W. H. (1984) The impact of work environment, instrumentality beliefs, perceived labor union image, and subjective expected norms on union voting intentions. *Academy of Management Journal*, 27, 576–90.

Zalesny, M. D. (1985) Comparison of economic and non-economic factors in predicting faculty vote preference in a union representation election. *Journal of Applied Psychology*, 70, 243–56.

Further reading

Bain, G. S. and Price, R. (1983) Union growth: Dimensions, determinants and destiny. In G. S. Bain (ed), *Industrial Relations in Britain*. Oxford: Blackwell. A valuable summary of the research about the structural factors affecting union membership.

Guest D. E. and Dewe, P. (1988) Why do workers belong to a trade union? A social psychological study in the UK electronics industry. *British Journal of Industrial Relations*, 26, 178–94. An empirical study of the differences between union members and non-members which examines several frameworks for explaining union membership.

Klandermans, B. (1986) Psychology and trade union participation: Joining, acting, quitting. *Journal of Occupational Psychology*, 59, 189–204. A review of the whole field of union membership activity, which covers much of the literature on union joining and which draws out some of the links between joining and participation.

Kochan, T. A. (1980) *Collective Bargaining and Industrial Relations*. Homewood, Ill: Irwin. Chapter 5 (pages 124–76) covers the American literature on structural and individual factors affecting union joining.

Premack, S. L. and Hunter, J. E. (1988) Individual unionization decisions. *Psychological Bulletin*, 103, 223–34. A meta-analytic study covering a number of American studies of the decision to join a union in the context of the union certification election.

8

ːade Union Participation

Bert Klandermans

Introduction

The fact that people join trade unions does not tell us about the extent of their participation in these organizations. Some members spend a lot of time and effort on union affairs; others pay their dues and do nothing more. In the previous chapter, we looked at the reasons why people join trade unions; here our focus shifts to the question, 'What do people *do* in trade unions?' The answer contributes significantly to the psychology of employment relations because, after all, unions are dependent on their members for their survival. They are, of course, financially dependent on their membership for the maintenance of the organization but they also depend on their members as a pool of potential activists and paid officials and, in the case of industrial action, as a pool of participants in collective action. More generally, the impact of a union is contingent upon the proportion of the workforce that it organizes, the degree to which the union and its membership are prepared to engage in industrial action, and the financial strength of the union (Gene et al., 1986; Müller-Jentsch, 1985).

Trade unions as organizations: representation and administration

In unions, as in other voluntary organizations, there is an in-built tension between a 'representative rationality' and an 'administrative rationality' (Child et al., 1973): on the one hand unions have to represent their members' interests, on the other hand they have to carry out their tasks effectively (see also Crouch, 1982). Michels (1962) stated that, in voluntary organizations, the administrative rationality inevitably gains the upper hand, a development that leads to oligarchic and undemocratic structures. Others (e.g. Batstone et al., 1977; Hartley, 1989; Hemingway, 1978) have suggested a less deterministic course and have proposed that voluntary organizations have to manage the tensions between the two rationalities.

Recently, several writers have argued that the actions of union organizations over the last few decades reveal a swing away from the 'representative rationality'. In writing about the European trade unions, both Sabel (1983) and Müller-Jentsch (1985), for example, observed that concentration and expansion had led to the development of ever more encompassing unions which became concerned with whole sectors of the economy. Consequently, the unions found it increasingly difficult to reconcile the interests of members in different sectors, such as government vs. market, growth industries vs. declining industries, and minorities vs. dominants. Indeed, what is in the interest of one membership group may not necessarily be in the interest of the others, and agreements that meet the demands of one sector of the membership may produce dissatisfaction in another. Therefore Müller-Jentsch (1985) foresees a new power base for trade unions, namely, the capability of a union to negotiate benefits and to gain influence with employers in exchange for controlling its membership. This change may well result in the generation of procedures with no other objective than the reduction of membership influence on a union's policy-making. Sabel (1983) even saw in these developments a revival of an old dilemma: 'how to make subordinates part of the organization without sharing power with them' (p. 230). The unions' dependence on the membership has not only continued but increased, because the more complex organizations need more financial resources and because the leadership is more dependent on the rank and file for information. These developments have been accompanied by an increasing bureaucratization and professionalization of the organization (see also Jonker-gouw, 1982), which has made preserving the stability of the organization more important as an objective. Although these observations are restricted to the situation on the European continent, Cornfield (1987) observed similar transformations in his discussion of the consequences of diversification in trade unions in the USA. The American unions, in response to their decline, sought to broaden their domains by expanding the number of industries within which they were operating. This diversification produced unions which were much more heterogeneous than they had been before and therefore generated co-ordination problems of the kind mentioned above.

Acquiring vs. allocating resources: influence of the membership

The general trend which these authors observe reduces the members' influence over the leaders. Union members, however, may resist reduced influence and, because the leadership is ultimately dependent on the membership, members do have significant leverage. This is not to say that they make frequent use of it. In fact they do not, not least because, as we shall see, on many occasions they agree with the union's policy. Nevertheless, members do have several options if they want to put pressure on the leadership: they can participate in existing decision-making procedures; they can refuse to take part in collective action; they can withdraw support; they can resign as members; they can participate in protest against their union; they can resort to external forces such as courts, committees of appeal, and the Press (Akkermans, 1985; Benson, 1986; Hancké, 1986; Nicholson et al., 1981).

Nicholson et al. (1981) have categorized these different options according to three main modes of influence: opposition (protest), negative control (withdrawal of support or participation), and participation. Participation and opposition require more effort from an individual than does negative control, hence the latter method is the most frequently used. One significant factor is the the 'pay-off from participation' (Strauss, 1977, p. 233). Participation and opposition sometimes demand substantial effort from the individual. Under normal circumstances, people are willing to make this effort if they are committed to the organization (Hirschman, 1970) and if they have some expectation of success (Klandermans, 1984a, 1989b). If, however, members have only a weak commitment to the organization and/or very low expectations of success, they may decide to withdraw their support (Van der Veen and Klandermans, 1989).

In sum, what people do in trade unions is in one way or another related to control over policy. Members provide resources; leaders decide on the use of resources. This situation inevitably produces tension because the need for integration, control, and discipline requires both strong leadership and, at the same time, member involvement (Hartley, 1989).

Like any other organizations, unions are 'goal-directed, boundary-maintaining, activity systems' (Knoke, 1985, p. 221). Management of organizations centres on the acquisition and allocation of resources for the purpose of realizing the organization's goals. To the extent that a union's goals aim at social change, its resources include those of political power. Not all the resources available to a union are intended for external use; a relatively large proportion goes towards accommodating members' needs and maintaining and strengthening the organization. Decisions to apply the available resources externally or internally are of crucial importance to the union's policy-making.

If we apply Knoke's (1985) analysis in this context, we see that unions, like all other influence associations, are confronted with two types of actors: potential supporters (workers, the unemployed) and authorities (employers or government). *Interaction with supporters* leads the organization to acquire resources. Through *interaction with authorities* the organization exerts its influence.

Union members decide whether they will provide the required resources (money, time, activism, participation in industrial action). Their decisions to make resources available are presumed to be contingent on their evaluation of the way in which the resources are employed by the organization. And it is the organization (and its members) that determine how the acquired resources are to be put to use: that is, what portion will go into activities involving authorities (including representation, collective bargaining, and industrial action), what part will be used to maintain the organization (its officials, staff, buildings, equipment), and what part will be reserved for publicity and public relations and for securing a continued influx of resources (by way of public relations, information and persuasive communication, membership services, etc.). Members participate to a greater or lesser extent in these decision-making processes. The remainder of this paper will be devoted to these two forms of participation: the provision of resources and influencing the union's policy.

The Provision of Resources

Trade unions are largely dependent on their membership for their resources. Members pay their dues, occupy positions and undertake tasks within the organization, and participate in industrial action. Without these efforts, unions would not be able to survive. This section will examine the factors that make union members willing to provide these resources.

Participation in the organization

Members can participate in a union in many different ways, and many more members than is often assumed take part in the organization's affairs. Klandermans et al. (1976), for instance, found that three-quarters of union members in their study had undertaken at least one of a number of possible activities in the past year, and the research of Nicholson et al. (1981) yielded a figure as high as 85 per cent. Union participation appears to be multidimensional (McShane, 1986). Here we need to distinguish between those members who are active but do not hold office (i.e. they may disseminate information, recruit new members, attend meetings, read union papers, and so on) and members who hold a position in the union (shop stewards, representatives to national or regional boards, members of councils, members of special task forces or working committees, and so on).

The active union member

Several studies reveal that 50 per cent or more of union members are in some way actively involved in the organization (Klandermans et al., 1976; Nicholson et al., 1981; Van Teeffelen, 1988). Recent studies (Hancké 1986; Hoyman and Stallworth, 1987; Van Teeffelen, 1988; Van Rijn, 1990; see also Kryl, 1990) confirm Klandermans' conclusion (1986), in his review article on union participation, that demographic variables such as age, education, income, and gender seem to have little relation to the distinction between active and non-active members. The same finding holds for job satisfaction, for which correlations with participation in the union are in general weak. Nor is there a simple relationship between union satisfaction and union participation. (As we have already seen in chapter 7, these demographic variables bear a similar relation – or lack of relation – to workers' decisions to join a union). According to Klandermans' review, socialization variables were more important than demographic factors. Variables such as political preference, class consciousness, and ideology are strongly related to an individual's degree of activism in the organization. In addition, union participation appears to have a pay-off structure. Individuals are active because participation satisfies important needs, such as meeting other people, engaging in interesting activities. But it turns out that this intrinsic value of participation is less important to workers than the expectation that participation will help them to achieve some valued goals, such as improving their situation, maintaining a strong union (Hoyman and Stallworth, 1987; Nicholson et al., 1981). Equally important seems to be 'a sense of plant, job or occupational community' (Strauss, 1977, p. 222) or 'a culture of solidarity' (Fantasia, 1988). Both Strauss and Fantasia demonstrated that such cultural factors strongly promote union participation. Without denying the relevance of these findings, we must realize, however, that a sense of community or solidarity among the workforce will promote union participation only if the collectivity values participation positively (Hoyman and Stallworth, 1987; De Witte, 1988). If the workforce regards union participation negatively, a strong sense of community will discourage active involvement in the union.

Holding a position

De Witte (1988) points to the simple but important fact that in order for someone to take up a particular position, he or she must have been asked to do so, although occasionally individuals do put themselves forward. And in order to be asked to take up a position, an individual must be known to the people who are recruiting and must fit the profile that they have in mind. Consequently, as De Witte reports, recruiters are most likely to ask those individuals who are visible, who have been members for a long time and thus have many contacts in the union. Similarly, individuals with a more militant profile, who believe in the union as an organization and in the necessity and effectiveness of collective action, are more likely to be asked.

De Witte's study is a recent example of research into the recruitment of lay officials. Most of this research has investigated the recruitment of shop stewards (Batstone et al., 1977; Chinoy, 1950; Nicholson, 1976). Nicholson (1976) undertook an extensive survey of the different ways in which employees become shop stewards, distinguishing between the external and internal forces through which individuals become stewards. He divided the internal factors into forces defined by tasks, ideology, and ambition; the external forces he identified as: (a) a crisis in which the least apathetic employee takes the task upon him or herself; (b) selection by one's colleagues because of one's popularity or prestige; and (c) nomination by current stewards or officials. Like De Witte (1988), Nicholson found that the most common routes to the position of steward were the last two. Nicholson also found no systematic differences between shop stewards who were recruited in different ways. Rather, different modes of working arise from a complex interaction of initial orientation, subsequent on-the-job-experience, and consequent dealings with management and constituency. Several typologies have been developed to describe the differences in the way that various stewards operate. Batstone et al. (1977), for instance, developed a typology based on two factors: the pursuit of union principles and the emphasis that stewards place on either a delegate or representative role. Eighty-five per cent of the stewards in their study conformed to two of the four types defined by these two factors: 'leaders' (50 per cent), for whom the constituency is not the primary reference point but who feel that union policy and their fellow stewards are at least equally important (their union principles are high, and they stress a representative role), and 'populists' (35 per cent), who feel a primary responsibility to their constituency (their union principles are low; they stress a delegate role). Martin et al. (1982) distinguished shop stewards who have just as strong a commitment to the company as to the union from shop stewards who have a stronger commitment to the union. Differences in ways of working may have something to do with distinct types of shop steward positions. Both Batstone et al. (1977) and Nicholson et al. (1981) pointed to the existence of a 'quasi-elite' of experienced stewards, who are in close contact with the conveners and who play an important role in decision-making. Laterveer (1972) revealed how high-ranking lay officials, for example members of the council of the Dutch union of metal workers, were more similar to paid officials than to other lay officials.

Numerous studies have compared lay officials/shop stewards with rank-and-file members (Anderson, 1979; De Witte, 1988; Hancké, 1986; Izraeli, 1982; Klandermans et al., 1981; Laterveer, 1972; McShane, 1986; Nicholson et al., 1981; Strauss, 1977). The most important differences between officials and members appeared in attitudes, values, and behaviour *vis-à-vis* the union. Lay officials took part in more union activities, had a stronger class consciousness, and were more positive about radical, political union issues than were ordinary members, who tended to give priority to traditional issues such as wages and terms of employment. Lay officials differed from ordinary members in relation to a few demographic variables: they were more often male, they were older, they were better educated, they had been with the company and in the union longer, and they had a higher income. Research has not revealed any *systematic* differences between the degree of job satisfaction and company commitment of members and lay officials, but, when it indicates a relationship, it shows that lay officials report greater satisfaction and a stronger commitment to the company than do ordinary members (Nicholson et al., 1981; Klandermans et al., 1976, 1981). Laterveer (1972), Chacko (1985), and McShane (1986) did find, however, that lay officials more often felt that the company was not making full use of their abilities. This finding would seem to be an answer to the question that Strauss (1977) raised: perhaps an individual chooses a union career because a career in the company is difficult? But, on the whole, the number of similarities between members and lay officials was greater than the number of differences.

Instrumentality, interaction, and commitment: The psychology of sustained participation

In the previous sections we have examined why workers become active or take up a position in a union, but we have not yet explained why they *stay* active. Indeed, very little research has addressed this question. Commitment to the union, perceived union instrumentality, and social integration into the union seem to be key factors (Fullagar and Barling, 1989; Van der Veen and Klandermans, 1989; Van Teeffelen and Klandermans, 1989). Commitment to the union, as Gordon et al. (1980) define it, refers to the individual's wish to remain a member, to his or her willingness to invest energy in the organization, and to a belief in union values. Participation is perceived as instrumental if the benefits of participation outweigh the costs (Van der Veen and Klandermans, 1989; Van Teeffelen and Klandermans, 1989), and perceived union instrumentality refers to the union's effectiveness in achieving its goals (Kryl, 1990). Both Klandermans and his colleagues and Fullagar and Barling (1989) point to the way in which perceived instrumentality, interaction, and commitment have a mutually reinforcing effect on sustained participation. Commitment to the union promotes participation, since the stronger an individual's commitment to a union, the more likely it is that he or she will stay actively involved (Gordon et al., 1980; Klandermans, 1989a). Commitment, on the other hand, evolves over time, as members interact with others in the organization. Consequently, one can argue that, over time, active members become more committed to their union. The perceived instrumentality of union participation, in its turn, encourages participation and reinforces commitment to the union (Fullagar and Barling, 1989; Van Teeffelen and Klandermans, 1989). Commitment to the union leads to increased participation, and participation strengthens commitment. Hence, the circle is closed. This description suggests a dynamic model of sustained participation in which instrumentality and interaction with others in the organization combine to strengthen or weaken commitment. In a similar way a downward spiral may evolve: reduced perceived instrumentality leads to reduced commitment and reduced interaction with others in the organizations. Reduced interaction further weakens commitment, and eventually commitment may become so weak that the individual member withdraws active support.

Participation and the allocation of resources

We can assume that an individual's inclination to provide resources to an organization depends on his or her appreciation of the way in which those resources have been employed in the past. On the whole, unions may allocate resources to one of the following domains (cf. Hochner et al., 1980): collective bargaining (including strike funds), services to individual members (including handling grievances, legal aid, assistance with tax or social security affairs), representation in societal institutions (including social security and unemployment services, health services, governmental advisory boards), political activities (putting pressure on policy-makers, party or candidate endorsement, lobbying), and organizational maintenance (including finance, administration, membership recruitment, and public relations).

We may assume, too, that the way in which an organization distributes its resources among its various obligations determines its image. In discussing the policies of Dutch unions, Teulings (1987), for example, criticizes the unions for allocating resources to their different domains in an unbalanced way. In Teulings's eyes, the unions allocate a disproportionate share of their resources for representation and organizational maintenance. Studies of unions in other countries seem to arrive at a similar conclusion (Crouch, 1982; Benson, 1986; Müller-Jentsch, 1985; Perline and Lorenz, 1970). According to Teulings, if the unions want to retain their membership, they should spend much more of their resources on services to individual members. At least in the Netherlands, studies of the reasons that workers give for resigning from a union seem to support Teulings, inasmuch as one reason given for leaving the organization is dissatisfaction with services to individual members (Industriebond NVV, 1981; Teulings, 1983; Van der Veen, 1985; Veltman, 1985).

Research among union members invariably reveals that, in the eyes of the membership, collective bargaining is a trade union's most important task (cf. Crouch, 1982; Van Teeffelen and Klandermans, 1989; Van Rijn, 1990). A union which neglects this function will sooner or later find its members opposing its policy, as the Dutch civil service unions discovered when workers in the health care system protested after the unions had failed to incorporate the workers' demands into the bargaining package.

Members rank services to individual members below collective bargaining but, as mentioned above, the lack of such services is often the reason why members quit the union, if in their opinion the organization fails to operate appropriately.

The few studies on the political activities of unions seem to indicate that union members do not object to these activities but do not give them a high priority (Masters and Delaney, 1987; Leopold, 1986, 1987; Strauss, 1977). The same seems to hold for representation and organizational maintenance (Crouch, 1982; Müller-Jentsch, 1985). The UK, where the government forced unions to organize ballots to decide whether they should have 'political funds', provides some interesting data on the degree of support for political activities by the unions. To the surprise of most observers, union members voted overwhelmingly in favour of establishing such funds.

Together these results suggest that, as long as unions take their major obligation – collective bargaining – seriously and as long as they function effectively in providing membership services, members will have few complaints. In general, then, satisfaction with European and American unions is rather high (Klandermans, 1989a; Strauss, 1977). This fact may help to explain why so few union members participate in decision-making. After all, most members believe that unions exist to relieve them of work, not to give them work. And as long as they feel that the union is doing its job correctly, they see no reason to change. But what if members disagree with their union's policy? What opportunities do they have to amend or discard that policy or even to push through an alternative policy?

Influencing the Union's Policy

Union members who want to influence their union's policy have three different options: participation in existing decision-making procedures, withdrawal of support, or protest against the union leadership – or, in the terms that Nicholson et al. (1981) use: participation, negative control, or opposition.

Participation in existing decision-making procedures

Not surprisingly, the more deeply union members are involved in union affairs (through holding office, attending meetings, voting, reading union newspapers, and so on) and the more positive their attitudes towards the union, then the more extensive their participation in decision-making (Anderson, 1979; Hochner et al., 1980).

The membership meetings provided by the union are an important means of giving members the opportunity to influence the organization's decision-making. Several decades ago, Lipset et al. (1956), in discussing attendance at meetings, remarked that, rather than ask why union members do not attend meetings, we should ask why they do. 'What is the benefit of attending?', these authors wonder. Their answer is: very little. According to most members, union meetings are boring, the content is difficult to grasp, and members have little influence anyway.

Recent Dutch studies demonstrate that attitudes toward union meetings have changed little in the past few decades (Van Rijn, 1990). Such negative attitudes are the more problematic because it is not unusual for union meetings to be held after working hours. In other words, attendance at meetings must compete with other leisure activities. Thus, it is not enough for a meeting to have important issues on the agenda; the issues must be so important that they take precedence over a favourite television programme, a sports event, a party, or domestic responsibilities (e.g. childcare). Such a competition is difficult to win. Consequently, a large proportion of the membership never attends a union meeting at all. (In the case of the Dutch unions, for instance, this proportion may be anywhere from two-thirds to three-quarters of the membership; cf. Klaassen, 1986; Klandermans, 1984b; Van Teeffelen, 1988; Van Rijn, 1990. Similar percentages were found in the UK by Nicholson et al., 1981).

These statistics draw attention to the costs and benefits of participation as a determinant of attendance at union meetings. Nicholson et al. (1981), Klandermans (1984b), Klaassen (1986), and Hoyman and Stallworth (1987) have shown that the most important determinants of participation are the need to exert influence and the member's expectation that by attending a meeting he or she will indeed be able to exert some influence. The nature of the meeting may affect these variables. For instance, meetings which provide opportunities to exert influence will attract more members for whom this factor is important than will meetings which do not offer such opportunities (Klaassen, 1986). For that matter, Klaassen's research revealed that both the members' expectations about the extent to which they could affect a meeting's decisions and their assumption about the influence that the meeting would have on union policy were important determinants of participation.

Aside from fostering democratic values within the union organization, a single membership meeting necessarily has only a limited impact on the union's policy. Unions make policy for different levels in industrial relations and within various arenas of decision-making, at both the national and local levels, and these multiple policies are not always compatible. Therefore tensions between policies inevitably arise from time to time. In principle, union members can participate in decision-making at each level, but a meeting of members of a specific company or region can have only limited influence, especially on those aspects of a union's policy which reach beyond the local level (Müller-Jentsch, 1985). Yet, national or sectoral policy often influences conditions at the local level, reducing the room for negotiation at that level. The way in which Dutch unions conduct national policy-making may serve as an example of this relationship between the national and local levels (Klandermans, 1982; Klandermans and Terra, 1981). In the Netherlands, national or sectoral union policies define the limits for local bargaining. At the stage in the policy-making process where the membership becomes involved, however, so much of the nationwide or sectorwide policy has already been established that it is very difficult for individual meetings to amend or transform it. Indeed, because the votes of all the meetings are taken together, the votes of a specific meeting are lost in the grand total. Unless some countermobilization takes place – a very unlikely development and one often discouraged by the leadership when it does occur – it is certain that the proposed policy will be approved. This procedure presents no trouble as long as it can be assumed that the majority of the membership in fact supports the policy but, if it does not, nothing in such procedures can prevent the union from entering the collective negotiations with a policy that does not have the members' support. The consequence is that the union discovers membership discontent in a different way; for instance, through a membership which refuses to engage in any collective action in support of that policy.

Although the relationship between nationwide and sector-wide bargaining and local bargaining will vary in different countries, we may assume that in every union tensions between policy levels will arise now and then. The example from the Netherlands illustrates that, given such tensions, it is not easy to influence the national policy from below.

Withdrawal of support

The preceding discussion makes it clear that the opportunities to influence a union's policy through membership meetings are limited. This is not to say that union members have no influence whatsoever. There are other ways to influence the union's policy rather than through participation in decision-making. As we mentioned earlier, one of these ways is negative control: withdrawal of support, or non-participation (Nicholson et al., 1981). Although analysts assume that negative control occurs frequently (Nicholson et al., 1981), they find it difficult to distinguish negative control from withdrawal of support or non-participation for other reasons. Hence, although resigning as a member is a well known form of negative control (Akkermans, 1985), the reasons for resigning are so manifold that it is difficult to ascertain whether a member left the union because of dissatisfaction with the union's policy or for a different reason. In fact, in most instances the reasons why union members resign are simply unknown and, of those which are known, only a minor proportion is related to dissatisfaction with the union's policy (Klandermans, 1986; Van der Veen, 1985; chapter 7). To the leadership, the difficulties of replenishing membership losses are perhaps more telling than attrition through negative control because they indicate that the organization is losing its attractiveness to the workers in specific sectors or is failing to attract workers in newly growing sectors (Cornfield, 1986).

Non-participation in collective action, like resignation, can stem from reasons other than dissatisfaction with union policy. Free riding, for instance, is a form of non-participation which is based on an individual's assumption that he or she will benefit from the results of collective action whether or not he or she participates in it (Klandermans, 1988). But whatever the source of a member's unwillingness to participate, in times of conflict with employers, a union organizer faced with a membership which is reluctant to engage in any collective action must realize that the union's policy is flawed in terms of either its demands or the means of action that it has chosen. This assertion could be substantiated with illustrations from many countries but, for the sake of economy, only two typical examples from the Netherlands are noted here.

In the late 1970s, Dutch unions tried to develop a policy in response to soaring unemployment. In 1978 the engineering union (IB-FNV), inspired by its British counterpart, tried to introduce manning agreements (that is, agreements about a guaranteed number of jobs for a fixed period). From the very beginning the employers adamantly opposed this move. Thus, the negotiations quickly became deadlocked, and the union had to choose whether to mobilize for industrial action or to compromise. To give an initial demonstration of its determination, the union organized protest meetings of the membership but the turnout at these meetings was so conspiciously low that further militant action was inconceivable. No manning agreement at all was made at that time, nor was there any more talk of manning agreements afterwards. Research conducted at that time revealed that less than one-fifth of the membership and only half of the union's lay officials in the companies had any idea of what manning agreements were like (Klandermans, 1982).

In the following year, 1979, shortening the working week was the unions' answer to the ever-increasing unemployment in the Netherlands. As the discussion about the pros and cons of reducing the working week unfolded, the unions were soon on the defensive. Before long, the consequences of this position became clear. In the course of the negotiations, an increasing number of the union members came to doubt that reducing working hours would lower the unemployment level. Consequently, the members were less and less willing to engage in collective action (Klandermans, 1984a).

Protest against the union's leadership

Sometimes union members see no other option than to mobilize against the union leadership itself. In the Netherlands in 1989, for example, nurses and workers in the health care system engaged in mass action in protest against their employers and the government. At the same time, their protests were directed against their unions, because the protestors were striving to win a much higher wage increase than employers, government *and* unions had in mind. These demands for higher wages came as a complete surprise to the union leadership because, just a few weeks earlier, membership meetings had agreed to more modest increases. Only after it became clear that the action group might evolve into a competing union did the unions increase their demands to the level of that of the protestors. In the

Netherlands, collective action directed against unions is not very common, although in the 1960s and 1970s a number of wildcat strikes radicalized the Dutch unions. These strikes were especially effective in changing the unions' policies because they came in a period when the unions' leadership was divided and substantial minorities within the leadership were supported by the strikes (Teulings, 1985; see also Müller-Jentsch, 1985, on West Germany).

Protests by the membership are not always as effective as they were in the case of the Dutch health care workers (Akkermans, 1985; Teulings, 1985). In America, Benson (1986) suggests, such protests became effective only after legislation was passed which gave the rank and file of American trade unions the legal opportunity to fight against undemocratic procedures in their unions. Whether Benson is right or not, legislation can facilitate or hinder internal protest against union leadership (consider also recent legislation in the UK which enables union members to prosecute their own unions on a wider range of issues than previously).

Trade unions in the UK have had their revolts as well. In surveying the period between World War II and the early 1970s, Hemingway (1978, pp. 174–5) counted no less than 41 breakaway unions in the UK. According to Hemingway, unions face a fundamental dilemma about discipline and democracy: 'Leaders of any political hue may stress discipline and subordination to collective unity. But whenever members feel their interests are being ignored they are likely to challenge their leaders and assert a right to democratic control' (p. 176). A few unions, however, do generate organized opposition, as Lipset et al. (1956) describe in *Union Democracy*. Participation in regular decision-making processes may fail to give membership the control that it desires. Consequently, if the membership wants to change policy, it has no options other than factional opposition, coercion, and direct action. Both Hemingway and, later, Benson (1986) argued that these elements are necessary to the process of government, not indications of a breakdown in that process.

Conclusion

Membership participation in unions is determined by the fundamental processes of resource acquisition, resource allocation, and decision-making. Because providing resources is the responsibility of the membership, while allocating those resources falls to the leadership, relations between the membership and the leadership are inherently a source of tension. Naturally, members want to see results in exchange for the resources that they provide, and leaders want to have leeway to decide on the allocation of resources according to their own insights. Although union leaders may intend that decision-making procedures should be democratic, in most unions these procedures do not strengthen the position of the membership. In fact, the literature reviewed here suggests that, as a rule, decision-making procedures favour the leadership. Therefore, the membership's opportunities to influence the allocation of resources, or more generally the union's policy, are limited. Yet, without dues-paying members, without active members, and without lay officials, no union would be able to maintain its organization or achieve its goals. Thus, paradoxically, it is not participation but the opportunity to withdraw support that gives members control over the organization. The very fact that participation is a necessary condition for organizational survival makes withdrawal of support a powerful means of control. If members stop providing resources for the union, the union will not be able to survive as an organization either in 'peacetime' or in conflict. This is not to say that it is easy for members to use withdrawal of support as a concerted action. Indeed, as soon as members initiate an organized withdrawal of support, the leadership will in all likelihood define their action as rebellion and respond to limit its impact.

Although only a few members take part in a union's decision-making processes, since participation does not give members any significant influence, the union's policy does not necessarily diverge from what the membership wants. Indeed, the membership more often supports union policy than not. As long as the leadership functions to the members' satisfaction, members do not really take much interest in union democracy and have no reason to frequent membership meetings. After all, most workers become union members in order to have their interests represented rather than to represent their interests themselves. If, however, they are dissatisfied with their union, members may begin to care about union democracy and, as they try to make changes, they will discover how difficult it is to have an impact on the union's policy.

References

Akkermans, M. J. W. M. (1985) *Beleidsradicalisering en ledendruk: Een studie over de Industriebond-NVV in de periode 1968–1975*. Nijmegen: Instituut voor Toegepaste Sociologie.

Anderson, J. C. (1979) Local union participation: A re-examination. *Industrial Relations*, 18, 18–31.

Batstone, Eric, Boraston, Ian, and Frenkel, Stephen (1977) *Shop Stewards in Action: The Organization of Workplace Conflict and Accommodation*. Oxford: Blackwell.

Benson, Herman (1986) The fight for union democracy. In Seymour Martin Lipset (ed.), *Unions in Transition: Entering the Second Century*, San Francisco: ICS Press, 323–72.

Chacko, T. J. (1985) Member participation in union activities: Perception of union priorities, performance, and satisfaction. *Journal of Labour Research*, 6, 363–73.

Child, J., Loveridge, R. and Warner, M. (1973) Towards an organizational study of the trade unions. *Sociology*, 7, 71–91.

Chinoy, E. (1950) Local union leadership. In A. W. Gouldner (ed.), *Studies in Leadership*, New York: Harper & Row.

Cornfield, Daniel B. (1986) Declining union membership in the post World War II era: The united furniture workers, 1939–1982. *American Journal of Sociology*, 91, 1112–53.

Cornfield, Daniel B. (1987) Decline and diversification: Causes and consequences for organizational governance. *Research in Sociology*, 5, 187–216.

Crouch, C. (1982) *Trade Unions: The Logic of Collective Action*. London: Fontana.

De Witte, H. (1988) Waarom worden jongeren lid van een vakbond? *Tijdschrift voor Arbeidsvraagstukken*, 4/3, 18–35.

Fantasia, Rick (1988) *Cultures of Solidarity. Consciousness, Action, and Contemporary American Workers*. Berkeley: University of California Press.

Fullagar, C. and Barling, J. (1989) A longitudinal test of a model of the antecedents and consequences of union loyalty. *Journal of Applied Psychology*, 74, 213–27.

Gene, A., Slomp, H. and van Snippenburg, L. B. (1986) Vakbondskracht en vakbondsinvloed in Nederland en België. *Tijdschrift voor Arbeidsvraagstukken*, 2/4, 5–13.

Gordon, M. E., Philpot, J. W., Burt, R. E., Thompson, C. A. and Spiller, W. E. (1980) Commitment to the union: Development of a measure and an examination of its correlates. *Journal of Applied Psychology*, 65, 479–99.

Hancké, B. (1986) Vakbondsleden en vakbondsdemocratie. *Tijdschrift voor Arbeidsvraagstukken*, 2/4, 30–43.

Hartley, Jean (1989) Leadership and decision making in a strike organization. In Bert Klandermans (ed.), *Organizing for Change: Social Movement Organizations in Europe and the United States. Vol. 2, International Social Movement Research*, Greenwich, Conn: JAI Press, 241–66.

Hemingway, J. (1978) *Conflict and Democracy: Studies in Trade Union Government*. Oxford: Clarendon.

Hirschman, Albert O. (1970) *Exit, Voice and Loyalty: Responses to Decline in Firms, Organizations and States*. Cambridge, Mass: Harvard University Press.

Hochner, A., Koziara, K. and Schmidt, S. (1980) Thinking about union democracy and participation in unions. *Proceedings of the 32nd Annual Meeting of the Industrial Relations Research Association*, IRRA, Madison, Wisconsin.

Hoyman, Michele M. and Stallworth, Lamont (1987) Participation in local unions: A comparison of black and white members. *Industrial and Labor Relations Review*, 40, 323–35.

Industriebond NVV (1981) *Onderzoek Ex-leden*. Amsterdam: NVV.

Izraeli, Dafna N. (1982) Avenues into leadership for women: The case of union officers in Israel. *Economic and Industrial Democracy*, 3, 515–29.

Jonkergouw, Theo (1982) Vakbondsleiders in Nederland: Van indringer tot bondgenoot en steunpilaar. Unpublished dissertation. University of Tilburg.

Klaassen, Rob (1986) Participate van kaderleden in besluitvormings-processen van de vakbond. Doctoraalscriptie, Vakgroep Sociale Psychologie, Vrije Universiteit, Amsterdam.

Klandermans, Bert (1982) Arbeidsplaatsenovereenkomsten: Waarom de mobilisatiecampagne voor een vernieuwing mislukte. *Tijdschrift voor Agologie*, 11, 23–36.

Klandermans, Bert (1984a) Mobilization and participation: Social psychological expansions of resource mobilization theory. *American Sociological Review*, 49, 583–600.

Klandermans, Bert (1984b) Membership meetings and decision making in trade unions. Paper presented at the Egos colloquium on Trade Unions in Europe: The organizational perspective, Amersfoort, The Netherlands, 11–13 October.

Klandermans, Bert (1986) Psychology and trade union participation: Joining, acting, quitting. *Journal of Occupational Psychology*, 59, 189–204.

Klandermans, Bert (1989a) Union commitment: Replications and tests in the Dutch context. *Journal of Applied Psychology*, 74, 869–75.

Klandermans, Bert (1989b) Grievance interpretation and success expectations: The social construction of protest. *Social Behaviour*, 4, 113–25.

Klandermans, Bert and Terra, Nico (1981) Een vakbond mobiliseert: De beleving van de CAO-onderhandelingen in 1979. Vakgroep Sociale Psychologie, Vrije Universiteit, Amsterdam.

Klandermans, Bert, Huisman, Wouter and Messelink, Bert (1976) Participatie in de vakbond: Een kwestie van bewustzijn. Vakgroep Sociale Psychologie, Vrije Universiteit, Amsterdam.

Klandermans, Bert, Terra, Nico and Oegema, Dirk (1981) Een vakbond mobiliseert: Vakbondsbewustzijn en vakbondsparticipatie. Vakgroep Sociale Psychologie, Vrije Universiteit, Amsterdam.

Knoke, David, (1985) The political economies of associations. In Richard D. Braungart (ed.), *Research in Political Sociology (vol. 1)*, Greenwich, Conn: JAI Press, 211–42.

Kryl, Ilona Patricia (1990) Union participation: A review of the literature. In P. J. D. Drenth, J. A. Sergeant and R. J. Takens (eds), *European Perspectives in Psychology (vol. 3)*, Chicester: Wiley, 147–66.

Laterveer, R. (1972) Met ander ogen. Rapport van een attitude-onderzoek onder leden, kaderleden, bondsraadsleden en bezoldigde bestuurders van de metaalbedrijfsbond NVV. Amsterdam: Metaalbedrijfsbond NVV.

Leopold, John W. (1986) Trade union political funds: A retrospective analysis. *Industrial Relations Journal*, 17, 287–303.

Leopold, John W. (1987) Moving the status quo: The growth of trade union political funds. *Industrial Relations Journal*, 18, 286–95.

Lipset, S. M., Trow, M. A. and Coleman, J. S. (1956) *Union Democracy: The Internal Politics of the International Typographical Union*. Glencoe, Ill: Free Press.

McShane, Steven L. (1986) The multidimensionality of union participation. *Journal of Occupational Psychology*, 59, 177–87.

Martin, J. E., Magenau, J. M. and Peterson, M. F. (1982) Variables related to patterns of commitment among union stewards. Wayne State University, Detroit.

Masters, Marick F. and Delaney, John Thomas (1987) Union political activities: A review of the empirical literature. *Industrial and Labor Relations Review*, 40, 336–54.

Michels, Robert (1962) *Political Parties*. New York: Free Press.

Müller-Jentsch, Walther (1985) Trade unions as intermediary organizations. *Economic and Industrial Democracy*, 6, 3–33.

Nicholson, Nigel (1976) The role of the shop steward. *Industrial Relations Journal*, 7, 15–26.

Nicholson, Nigel, Ursell, Gill and Blyton, Paul (1981) *The Dynamics of White Collar Unionism: A Study of Local Union Participation*. London: Academic Press.

Perline, M. M. and Lorenz, V. R. (1970) Factors influencing member participation in trade union activities. *American Journal of Economics and Sociology*, 29, 425–37.

Sabel, Charles F. (1983) The internal politics of trade unions. In Suzanne D. Berger (ed.), *Organizing Interests in Western Europe: Pluralism, Corporatism, and the Transformation of Politics*, Cambridge: Cambridge University Press, 209–48.

Strauss, George (1977) Union government in the US: Research past and future. *Industrial Relations*, 16, 215–42.

Teulings, A. W. M. (1983) Strijd en Zekerheid: Een onderzoek naar ledenverloop en ledenbinding van een vakbeweging in crisistijd. Amsterdam: Universiteit van Amsterdam.

Teulings, A. W. M. (1985) Teloorgang van pluralistisch radicalisme in de vakbeweging. *Tijdschrift voor Arbeidsvraagstukken*, 1/3, 5–15.

Teulings, A. W. M. (1987) Het gebouw van de vakorganisatie. Een renovatievoorstel. *Tijdschrift voor Arbeidsvraagstukken*, 3/4, 5–15.

Van der Veen, Gerrita (1985) Leden werven en leden binden: Een onderzoek naar de mogelijkheden voor een vakbond om leden te winnen en het ledenverloop te verlagen. Vakgroep Sociale Psychologie, Vrije Universiteit, Amsterdam.

Van der Veen, Gerrita and Klandermans, Bert (1989) Exit behavior in social movement organizations. In Bert Klandermans (ed.), *Organizing for Change: Social Movement*

Organizations in Europe and the United States, Vol. 2, International Social Movement Research Greenwich, Conn: JAI Press, 179–98.

Van Rijn, Ingrid (1990) Vervoer en Vakorganisatie. Onderzoeksprogramma CNV/VU, Vrije Universiteit, Amsterdam.

Van Teeffelen, Lex (1988) CFO-Ledenonderzoek. Vakgroep Sociale Psychologie, Vrije Universteit, Amsterdam.

Van Teeffelen, Lex and Klandermans, Bert (1989) Tussen rationele afweging en interactie. Ledenbinding en het opzeggen van het vakbondlidmaatschap. *Tijdschrift voor Arbeidsvraagstukken*, 5/4, 4–15.

Veltman, J. (1985) Je bent jong en je wilt wat. *Tijdschrift voor Arbeidsvraagstukken*, 1/3, 54–62.

Further reading

Batstone, Eric, Boraston, Ian, and Frenkel, Stephen 1977: *Shop Stewards in Action: The Organization of Workplace Conflict and Accommodation.* Oxford: Basil Blackwell.

An extensive study of local industrial relations in British industries. Shop steward organizations are described and a typology of shop stewards is employed to explain differences inbetween branches in the organization.

Lipset, Seymour Martin (ed.), 1986, *Unions in Transition: Entering the Second Century,* San Francisco: ICS Press.

An anthology with papers addressing diverging issues with regard to changing industrial relations in the United States.

Crouch, C. 1982: *Trade Unions: The Logic of Collective Action.* Fontana: London.

A theoretical discussion of unions as collective actors. A discussion of industrial action from a rational choice viewpoint.

Hemingway, J. 1978, *Conflict and Democracy: Studies in Trade Union Government,* Oxford: Clarendon.

A study in trade union government. Based on analyses of a number of major conflicts between union leadership and rank and file in Great Britain.

Nicholson, Nigel, Ursell, Gill and Blyton, Paul 1981. *The Dynamics of White Collar Unionism: A Study of Local Union Participation.* London: Academic Press.

An extensive study of union participation among white collar workers based on solid theorizing.

Journal of Occupational Psychology, 1986, 59. Special Issue on Psychology and Industrial Relations, edited by John Kelly and Jean Hartley.

One of the rare attempts to bring together a number of psychologically oriented papers on industrial relations.

Part IV

Dynamics of Intergroup Relations

Part IV

Dynamics of Intergroup Relations

9

Intra-organizational Bargaining

Ian E. Morley

Introduction

The term 'intra-organizational bargaining' was brought into common use by
Walton and McKersie (1965) as a sub-process of 'social negotiation'. By 'social
negotiation' they meant those 'systems of activity' involving 'complex social
units' in an attempt to define or redefine the 'terms of their interdependence'.
They identified four such systems of activity (which are also described in Chapter
10). Three of them dealt with relations between the social units, namely:
'distributive bargaining', in which negotiators dealt with the 'issues' which
divided them; 'integrative bargaining', in which negotiators worked through
'problem areas of joint concern'; and 'attitudinal structuring', in which negotiators attempted to change the 'basic bonds' between the units. The fourth,
however, dealt with relations within each of the social units. The function of
'intra-organizational bargaining' was to achieve an internal consensus about the
ends and means of the external negotiation between the units.

Walton and McKersie's major contribution has been to treat union–
management negotiations as a paradigm case of social negotiations. They have
also shown the importance of dilemmas in negotiation, thus revealing that
negotiation skill is not just a matter of learning which tactics are available
(Morley, 1981, 1986). Some critics have taken the view, however, that their
framework may fit labour negotiations in America but may not apply (or has
'had little application') in the UK (Friedman and Meredeen, 1980, p. 314).
Others believe that the distinctions between the four sub-processes need to be
revised in more or less fundamental ways (Anthony, 1977; Morley, 1984; Tracy
and Peterson, 1986).

The most fundamental critique has come from Anthony (1977) who has
argued that almost all collective bargaining is distributive bargaining, so that
integrative bargaining is simply distributive bargaining in which the parties adopt
a collaborative rather than a competitive approach. He has also argued that
neither attitudinal structuring nor intra-organizational bargaining represent
separate 'systems of activities'. In his view the former is a set of tactics available
to those who wish to adopt a collaborative approach, while the latter is an

'environmental characteristic of the total field within which bargaining takes place'. Quite simply, 'it takes place within organisations rather than between them'. He argues that in so far as internal negotiation is an essential part of the negotiating process we would expect it to be explained in 'precisely the same terms as the external process which takes place between organizations' (Anthony, 1977, pp. 227–8).

We may have a great deal of sympathy with this point of view. Walton and McKersie (1965) themselves use the term 'intra-organizational bargaining' to refer to the various problems of adjustment which occur because Party and Opponent contain people with very different interests and very different views. For example, both internal and external negotiations may need to bring in people who belong to the same company but are drawn from different sites. For these reasons, the annual negotiations between the British Steel Corporation and the Iron and Steel Trades Confederation used to allow for up to 100 people on the union side (Hartley et al., 1983). There may also be teams which contain representatives of several companies or several unions. Such configurations are by no means uncommon in British industrial relations (Brown, 1981).

Given such obvious coalitions of interest, it is easy to see the force of Anthony's point of view. Internal negotiations within the Party or Opponent coalition may not be very different from external negotiations between Party and Opponent. For example, Kochan (1980) has reported that the internal negotiation is often 'every bit as intense' as the external negotiation. Furthermore, others have raised the interesting possibility that the 'major action' occurs within rather than between the sides, since internal negotiations last longer than external negotiations and involve discussions in which there is 'real give-and-take' (Chamberlain and Kuhn, 1986, p. 97).

The subject of internal negotiation has received very little notice compared with the subject of external negotiation. Nevertheless, quite considerable attention has been paid to the possibility that internal conflict is a major cause of impasse in external negotiations, frequently leading to industrial disputes which are won by the other side (Kochan, 1980; Meredeen, 1988). There are three main reasons for this. When internal conflict 'spills over' into negotiations between the sides, it becomes much harder to see what each regards as minimum acceptable terms. Negotiators also find it harder to see whether commitments made at the 'bargaining table' will be approved by those whom they represent. Finally, a side which cannot agree a policy is likely to find that internal divisions are exploited fully by other parties. In some cases, such as those where there is no clear hierarchy of control, bilateral bargaining between the parties may turn into multilateral bargaining. This seems to be characteristic of city government bargaining in the USA, where the management coalition is characterized by diversity of goals and by dispersion of power. Apparently, management loses its ability to provide co-ordinated responses to union demands as union officials expand the scope of external negotiations in order to bring in more and more officials from the management side (Kochan, 1980). Quite clearly, each organization must find its own ways of developing an effective political process to manage the process of 'internal adjustment' (Anthony, 1977).[1]

Walton and McKersie themselves pay rather more attention to problems which arise when members of a negotiating team have to report back to reference groups within their own organization. They use the term 'intra-organizational bargaining' to refer to 'the system of activities which brings the expectations of principals into alignment with those of the chief negotiator' (Walton and McKersie, 1965, p. 5). Such a system of activities is needed because those remote from the process of external negotiation frequently develop quite unrealistic views of what can be achieved in those negotiations (also see Winkler, 1974). Accordingly, Walton and McKersie spend a very great deal of time analysing the power[2] of the chief negotiator to modify or ignore the expectations of his or her reference groups. This has led some critics to argue that their picture of intra-organizational bargaining is somewhat unbalanced because it has much less to say about the process whereby members of the reference groups influence the chief negotiator (Tracy and Peterson, 1986).

We are not persuaded that this second set of problems is fundamentally different from the first. The central problem is that of achieving consensus within the management or the union organization (also see chapter 10). We shall therefore attempt to understand the process of internal negotiation by using the same sort of framework which was previously applied to the analysis of external negotiation (Morley, 1981, 1986; Hosking and Morley, 1991). The main elements of that framework are set out below.

Internal Negotiation and External Negotiation

Negotiation begins when someone sees change, or the possibility of change, in the status quo (Morley, 1986). This suggests immediately that there are two central problems in negotiation. The first is to describe the change. It is important that group members reach a working consensus that the changes are changes of a certain kind. The second is to forge commitments to collective action based on those descriptions. Without such commitment any agreements reached are unlikely to 'stick'. This perspective is sometimes described as a language–action perspective (Hosking and Morley, 1991). It suggests that the most important function of internal negotiation is to find a dominant interpretation of the issues and to use it to plan for external negotiations between the sides.

It should be evident from this that negotiations cycle through stages involving internal adjustment (intra-organizational bargaining) and external adjustment (usually distributive bargaining). The internal negotiations affect the external negotiations, and vice versa.[3] The two processes are linked because they are the intra-group and the inter-group stages of a collective process which allows the participants to make sense of change and to decide collectively how to manage it. This means, of course, that negotiations, whether internal or external, cannot be understood apart from the historical contexts of which they form a part, and which they help to produce.

From a socio-historical perspective, what is important about the external negotiations is not that the negotiators reach agreements but that the agreements can be justified as rules, defining the terms on which the parties will do business in the future. The negotiations are conducted in the context of existing rules. The effect of the negotiation is to add some new rules or to change some of the old ones. This is why negotiators have been described as writing social history (Morley, 1986; Morley et al., 1988).

The internal negotiations function to provide the participants with a collective rationale, linking what is happening now to what has happened in the past and what needs to happen in the future. The external negotiations function to find agreements which make sense to each of the sides, because they may be seen to follow from just such a collective rationale. Without such a rationale the process of external negotiation is likely to be prolonged, or to break down. Because of this it is not uncommon for opposing negotiators to help each other to handle problems of internal adjustment (Warr, 1973; Batstone et al., 1978).

To make sense of change, the participants must organize a collective process in which they handle certain *core problems*. These are the identification of issues, the development of solutions, the choice between alternatives, and the implementation of policies. The core problems set negotiators cognitive and political problems. The cognitive problems arise because the negotiators have to make sense, intellectually, of what is happening and why. The political problems arise because different people have different views about which kinds of policies make sense, and are more or less willing to commit themselves to particular lines of action.

The ability of negotiators to deal with these problems depends on the success with which they have developed social networks, which help them to gather organizational intelligence, and which help them to generate commitments to policies. Even so, the cognitive and political problems lead to dilemmas in negotiation, whether internal or external.[4] Unless the dilemmas are properly handled, negotiation is unlikely to be successful, whether internal or external. Finally, it is assumed that effective negotiations require effective leadership. Without this, the process of negotiation, whether internal or external, will not be structured so that the participants are able to forge a set of agreements which make collective sense.

Essentially, we are proposing that participants need to understand the issues, and to understand why the policies they propose are practical solutions to the political problems. Without such understanding, and without genuine commitment to action based on that understanding, any agreements obtained are unlikely to 'stick'.

The framework summarized above is rather different from that extant in most of the social psychological literature on bargaining and negotiation (e.g. Rubin and Brown, 1975; Pruitt, 1981). Most of that literature has been 'individualistic' in orientation (Morley, 1988; Morley et al., 1986; Hosking and Morley, 1991). It has provided inadequate models of people, processes, and contexts. The model of people has been inadequate because people have not been given the respect to which they are due as intelligent social actors. The model of social process has been inadequate, not only because communications have been treated as moves in games of strategy rather than as sequences of messages and meanings but also because the social process has been treated as an individual process rather than as a collective process (through which collective cognitive images are created and changed). Finally, the model of social context has been inadequate because it has lacked a socio-historical perspective (which shows, for example, how social contexts are constructed from social processes).

It may be thought, therefore, that the theoretical framework to be presented requires some justification. We shall attempt to provide this justification by first illustrating the main themes with a number of concrete examples. We shall then say a little more about the kinds of theory necessary to provide an adequate treatment of intra-organizational bargaining in particular, and negotiation in general. Compared with the treatment of Carnevale and Keenan (chapter 10), the treatment given here is much more obviously in the tradition of work which may be called social and constructivist (Hosking and Morley, 1991).[5]

Five Examples of Intra-organizational Bargaining

First example

The first example has been taken from Kochan's (1980) description of how one American company prepared for contract negotiations with 'the major bargaining unit in its largest manufacturing facility' (p. 203). It illustrates the two sets of problems identified by Walton and McKersie (1965): of finding a working consensus with a management coalition; and of having the policy that was developed by that coalition ratified by the chief executive of the firm.

In this case, management makes every attempt to bring multiple perspectives to bear on the problem, expanding the membership of the initial group both laterally and vertically. This makes it harder for the coalition to agree a policy, because the different participants have very different views, but it makes it more likely that the policy selected is based on information which has been quite carefully authenticated (see Goldhaber et al., 1979). If the process is properly organized, the members of the negotiating team will become committed to a policy which they are all able to understand and which they are all able to accept.

> Preparation began at the plant level when local industrial relations staff systematically reviewed problems in the existing contract and collected information about the local labour market. They discussed problems with supervisors and with the plant manager. The object of the exercise was to decide items to be placed on the negotiating agenda and to rank the issues in order of importance for improving the operation of the plant.
>
> Subsequent discussion expanded 'laterally' (to include industrial relations specialists from different plants) and 'vertically' (to include other functional specialists at the divisional level and perhaps even the vice-president for finance). Outside industrial relations consultants were also involved. There was also a high level review of national economic trends. At this stage, intra-organizational bargaining was particularly visible because representatives of the different plants held different views about the 'expected benefits of contractual changes'. There was also considerable debate

about suggestions to replace 'discrepancies' in the language of local contracts with clauses preferred by higher management. The outcome of the negotiation was a document setting out what changes needed to be made in the existing contract, for what reasons, and with what priorities. Economic parameters for the wage settlement were also established at this stage.

The final stage was to have the policy approved by the chief executive officer and the board of directors. Kochan has reported that this meeting is sometimes delayed until after the first formal negotiating session with the union.[6] (pp. 202–6)

Second example

Warr (1973) has provided a very clear case study of a comprehensive pay and productivity agreement in which local management negotiated with five local trade unions. His work illustrates the cognitive problems which arise when negotiations are technically complex.[7] It also illustrates the political problems which arise when the union team is made up of shop stewards from several different trade unions. The members of the union team were also inexperienced. This made it imperative that they had a leader who was able to help them to solve the cognitive and political problems, by helping them not only to identify the salient issues but also to reach a working consensus within the team. The case study identifies two dilemmas central to the political process. It shows that, to reach a satisfactory agreement, management had to resist the temptation to exploit disunity in the union side. Instead, management realized that they had to help the shop stewards to reach a working consensus. They also had to help them to persuade their constituents that the general lines of action being proposed actually made sense.

> The negotiation was 'essentially a domestic matter' (p. 85), although outside officials were consulted from time to time. Management was represented by five people (two plant managers, the company administration manager, the industrial relations manager, and the personnel officer). The union team consisted of 19 people drawn from the 32 members of the Joint Shop Stewards' Committee (JSSC).
>
> The initial management proposals were carefully prepared and extremely complex, covering 65 typewritten sides of A4 paper. However, 'most of the negotiators were quite unused to agreements of this complexity' (p. 85). Consequently, their immediate task was to organize themselves to 'handle the complicated situation and reach some sort of group opinion' (p. 93).
>
> Warr has found it convenient to divide the negotiations into four phases. At the end of the first stage, the union side had apparently 'gained a good understanding of the company's proposals and had picked out the issues of immediate concern' (p. 100).
>
> The second stage was one in which the union side faced major problems of internal adjustment. The team lacked a clear impartial leader

who was able to grasp the salient issues. There was also considerable (and sometimes bitter) conflict within the negotiating team. Most were sympathetic to the idea of a company-wide agreement and seem to have accepted the proposals in principle, whilst realizing that much remained to be sorted out in practice. Nevertheless, very few were willing positively to assert that they were coming round to management's point of view. One group of stewards were completely opposed to the proposals, however, and demanded 'new negotiations which were quite unrelated to national agreements for the engineering industry' (p. 117). Their position was clearly not going to be unpopular with their members since it was, essentially, a demand for more money. Furthermore, it was much easier to argue their case because it was much easier for them to say exactly what that case was. They carried the day, and the union side demanded new negotiations.

Management's response was that they would have to register a failure-to-agree and move negotiations through an agreed procedure involving full-time union officials and representatives of the employers' association. The union team appear not to have known of this procedure, although it was part of a national agreement, and 'dispersed in some confusion'. Negotiations were formally suspended.

Warr had commented that during this stage the union side were attempting to resolve two 'central dilemmas': whether decisions required unanimity or whether they could be made by majority rule; and whether Stewards should take a leader or a delegate role ('own-versus-members'-decisions'). These issues had been there from the beginning but 'had not mattered too much during the first phase'. Now they had come to the fore 'because there were mixed opinions and the dilemmas . . . ground the negotiating team into indecision' (Warr, 1973, p. 113).

During the interval, union district officials suggested that the unions form a much smaller negotiating team (with 11 members). Management suggested that the unions employ two 'fact-finders' who would be given their own office and have access to financial information so that they could check management claims. Negotiations resumed with each side concentrating upon factual questions. The object of the exercise was to keep talks going so that the two sides could gain a better understanding of what each thought was important, and why. The union side remained opposed to management on many points of detail but 'were coming to agree with them about the general way in which the problems should be handled' (p. 126). At this stage, management actions were designed to preserve discipline and unity within the union side and to help union negotiators to convince the shop floor that negotiations were proceeding along the right lines.

In the final stage, disagreement between union stewards was again evident. However, union organization had now evolved to the point where it was accepted as legitimate to handle such disputes by the judicious application of a majority voting rule.

Third example

Putnam has described the process of negotiation by tracking the evolution of issues within and between teams representing a teachers' union and a school board (Putnam, 1985; Putnam and Sotirin, 1985). The example shows that different negotiators may have very different relationships with the groups they represent, best described in terms of the contrast between leader and delegate roles. It shows the importance of adopting some sort of language–action perspective in which people build collective interpretations of the issues and commit themselves to actions on the basis of those interpretations. Much of the behaviour of the negotiator who was allowed to take a leader role was designed to influence the ways in which his constituents described the issues. The object of the exercise was to provide a collective rationale for his various actions, some already past, some yet to come.

The union team met in a library, and consisted of eleven teachers representing high school teachers, middle school teachers, or elementary school teachers. The management team consisted of eight members who met in a central office. External negotiations took place *in private* ('in a coffee room down the hall') with one professional negotiator representing the employer and one representing the employees.[8]

Apparently, 'the teachers placed few demands on their negotiator and allowed him to function as their autocratic leader while the board held their negotiator to more stringent monetary and language items' (Putnam and Sotirin, 1985, p. 18). The teachers' negotiator acted as a 'gatekeeper who manipulates information' (Putnam, 1985), controlling the 'overall shape of the package' but involving other representatives in 'hassles over minor issues' (Putnam and Sotirin, 1985, p. 18). More specifically, 'he was able to manipulate the language codes and interpretive schemes of his constituents' by 'holding back information on concessions until a timely moment. . . . Then when he received other concessions from the board, he bargained with his team to make official concessions in the areas he had already dropped' (Putnam and Sotirin, 1985, p. 20). The board negotiator, on the other hand, accurately reported information to the management team and acted to 'facilitate' the process of internal adjustment.

The teachers were happy with the settlement, although, according to Putnam and Sotirin, the changes were only cosmetic and allowed the Board to keep more fundamental issues 'below the surface' (p. 24).

Fourth example

Batstone and his associates have been much concerned with the processes whereby social action is collectively defined in ways which lead to a settlement or in ways which lead to a dispute. The example chosen concerns the effect of the domestic organization on a near-strike by a section of indirect workers (Batstone et al., 1978, pp. 89–95). It shows the importance of building close relationships with people who may provide organizational intelligence, social support, or suggestions for action. Batstone et al. have shown that the conveners rely heavily on a group of experienced shop stewards known as the 'quasi-elite'. The quasi-elite are shop stewards who take a leader role. They are opinion leaders who were in close touch with other opinion leaders. They are respected because they 'embody proven expertise, a certain consensus upon the broad nature of trade unionism, and a concern with the maintenance of unity at the level of the domestic organization' (Batstone et al., 1977, pp. 45–6).

The historical context was one in which the section felt let-down by conveners and full-time officials who had failed to secure their demands for a new incentive scheme. One man had been suspended, leading to a strike which produced 'a major lay-off in assembly'. The section went on to impose further restrictions on work which would delay management stocktaking. There was opposition from other union officials because such action would jeopardise the lay-off pay of workers from assembly.

The section stewards discussed the restrictions with 'opinion-leaders' in the work group. There was general support for the view that indirect workers were ignored until stocktaking came round because 'the domestic organization was dominated by pieceworkers'. Consequently, the conveners did everything they could 'to keep assembly happy'. Evidently, 'such articulations of their feelings' encouraged the section stewards seriously to consider the possibility of a total stoppage, knowing the section would support it.

The conveners realized that management intended to refuse lay-off pay because it would 'hurt the company' to pay it, and could do so quite legitimately under existing agreements. They debated the issues informally with the section stewards and urged them formally to lift the restrictions at a meeting of the JSSC.

The section stewards agreed to consult their members and persuaded a respected opinion leader to propose the motion that they should continue their restrictions and threaten a strike. The conveners attended the section meeting but were unable to carry the day. The vote was two to one against lifting the action.

Experienced assembly stewards who were part of a 'quasi-elite' group demanded, and got, a further meeting of the JSSC, at which the section stewards were 'strongly criticized'. The stewards were told to go back to their section and to persuade them to reverse their decision. Otherwise, the JSSC would meet again and consider taking the matter to a mass meeting.

The subsequent meeting was 'very subdued' except for one somewhat aggrieved comment that 'You represent us and not the JSSC'. Nevertheless, the section agreed to lift the restrictions, and the workers from assembly received lay-off pay.

Fifth example

The fifth example is taken from Friedman and Meredeen's analyses of the Ford Sewing Machinists' strike for equal pay in 1968 (Friedman and Meredeen, 1980; Meredeen, 1988). Friedman was the convener of the plant where the machinists worked. Meredeen was part of the Ford management negotiating team.

To understand the dispute it is important to place it in its social and historical setting. Two factors seem to have been especially important. The first was Ford's record as an equal opportunity employer. It was realized that employers discriminated massively against women in a very large number of ways, and that Ford had been one of the worst offenders. The second was that Ford had been making major efforts to correct a number of fundamental weaknesses in its industrial relations policies (anticipating some of the proposals of the Donovan Commission).

One set of changes was of particular significance. After an extensive exercise in job evaluation, Ford proposed a two-year pay and productivity deal designed to bring its wage structure up to date. Negotiations were conducted through the institution of a Shop Stewards' National Joint Negotiation Committee (NJNC). The union members of the NJNC raised the question of equal pay for women, but the company would only agree to pay 85 per cent of the rate for men. It was clearly understood, however, that women would be paid the same rates as men when the Factories Act was amended to remove restrictions on women's hours of work. Five months later the pay and productivity agreement was implemented nationwide.

The dispute began with a claim that the jobs of some women sewing machinists should have been given a higher grade in the job evaluation exercise which preceded the negotiations. Subsequently, the strikers 'displayed an admirable unity of purpose and action', and showed what could be achieved by the 'intelligent choice and consistent application of relevant and realistic strategies and tactics' (Meredeen, 1988, pp. 290–1).

The leadership displayed by Friedman was crucial to the strikers' success. He made two extremely important decisions. The first was not to progress the dispute through procedure, because he felt that it was an example of discrimination against women. This allowed him to convert the dispute into one about equal pay. The second was to limit strike action to the women directly involved. This had the effect of 'insulating the strike from any undermining influence' (limiting the scope of the bargaining within the wider union coalition) because it was difficult for other people to 'feel entitled to a voice in determining what should happen next' (Friedman and Meredeen, 1980, pp. 198–9; Meredeen, 1988, p. 57). One effect of the strike was to show Ford management that they could no longer rely on the views expressed by trade union members of the NJNC as 'accurately reflecting those of the shop floor' (Meredeen, 1988, p. 58).

The way in which the company saw the issues also depended on the way in which the women's claim was linked to the pay and productivity negotiations. Essentially, the management were prepared to risk losing a great deal of production, valued at about £1 million per day, to defend the principles behind their industrial relations strategy. They were anxious not to compromise the pay and productivity negotiations, and to preserve the status of the NJNC.

On the management side, the major problems of internal adjustment concerned the differences between the 'hawks' and the 'doves'. Such differences do not seem to have prevented management from taking effective action, although it is clear that they were extremely surprised by the action of the women. Nevertheless, they were able clearly to identify the main issues. They realised that, from their point of view, any reasonable settlement would have to satisfy certain major constraints. They were then able to construct a peace formula,[9] which allowed them to satisfy those constraints, and which allowed the strikers to justify a return to work.

> As a result of its job evaluation exercise, Ford set up two grades of sewing machinists, production sewing machinist (the lower grade) and prototype sewing machinist (the higher grade). Some time later, nearly 200 production sewing machinists at the Dagenham River Plant, all women, protested that their job justified the higher grade. Management investigated the matter, but confirmed their original gradings.
>
> Shop stewards from the Trim Shop made a formal protest and raised the matter at meetings of the Joint Works Committee (JWC). The plant convener (Friedman) argued that the women had been discriminated against, and that their job profiles, which had been agreed by the union, had subsequently been marked down, without consultation, to hold them at the lower grade, or had perhaps simply been ignored. Because of this he refused to put the complaint through the new grading grievance procedure. The production sewing machinists voted to impose an overtime ban, to be followed, after seven days, by a one-day strike.
>
> The day before the strike was due, Meredeen met the shop stewards who sat on the union side of the JWC. He discovered that the sewing machinists' shop stewards were convinced that the company had 'done the girls down' (Friedman and Meredeen, 1980, p. 82). After some discussion it was agreed that Meredeen would try to place the problem before a meeting of the Profile Review Committee, which was already in session. He was not able to have the problem discussed and all of the sewing machinists at the Dagenham River Plant stopped work and walked off the job.
>
> When the sewing machinists returned to work they each received a letter, warning them that their action was in breach of contract; would do nothing to help their case; and might have serious personal consequences. However, the women refused to accept the letters, reaffirmed their ban on overtime, and voted to stage a further one-day strike.
>
> Management realized that the dispute was becoming serious and arranged a series of meetings with Dagenham shop stewards and with union district officials. They began increasingly to see Friedman's position 'as an attack on the fundamental basis of the job evaluation and wages structure' (Friedman and Meredeen, 1980, p. 85). They also took the view that 'Any departure from the agreed Grievance Procedure would bring the whole New Wage structure into disrepute' (Friedman and Meredeen,

1980, p. 85). Apparently, the company's main concern was to maintain confidence in the NJNC as a viable negotiating body. At the end of extensive discussions, the union district officials registered a failure to agree. The sewing machinists voted to begin an all-out strike.

Friedman has written that 'The sewing machinists' resolve to take issue with the company stemmed from their conviction that sex discrimination had denied them their rightful grade' (Friedman and Meredeen, 1980, p. 140). However, because the issue of grading was not one which would receive official support, the union leadership decided to make a stand on the basis of equal pay. There were thus four clear issues: a grievance over grading; sex discrimination; the refusal of the union to follow procedure; and equal pay.

Most of the sewing machinists belonged to the National Union of Vehicle Workers (NUVB). Some belonged to the Transport and General Workers Union (TGWU); some to the General and Municipal Workers Union (GMWU); and some to the Amalgamated Union of Engineering and Foundryworkers (AEF). All of the unions were willing to make the strike official on the basis of the grievance about the grading. The AEF were willing to make the strike official simply to support the principle of Equal Pay.

It is important to realize that the claim for equal pay had not been presented in the normal way, through the NJNC. Ford wanted the disputes over grading and over sex discrimination to be pursued through procedure. They were supported by those members of the NJNC who had negotiated the Pay and Productivity Agreement. This meant that 'there was no difficulty about establishing an alliance between the company and the majority of the national trade union officials at NJNC level' (Friedman and Meredeen, 1980, p. 145) and confirmed the women's determination to use the NJNC machinery.

According to Meredeen, the financial costs of acceding to the women's demands were small. However, the failure of the unions to follow Procedure seems to have convinced Ford management that they had to take a hard line. They made it clear that the strike, if it continued, would lead to the complete closure of the Dagenham body and assembly plants. They also asked the Secretary of State for Employment (Barbara Castle) to help them to settle the dispute.

Car production at Dagenham came to a standstill and the company laid off over 5,000 body and assembly plant workers. Barbara Castle was afraid that a long strike would harm not only Ford but also the country, and so announced that she was setting up a Court of Inquiry, to be chaired by Sir Jack Scamp. The Court announced publicly that its task would be much easier if the machinists returned to work. At a mass meeting the sewing machinists decided to stay on strike and agreed not to meet again for a further week. Ford's Managing Director sent a telegram to the Prime Minister (Harold Wilson), pointing out that the dispute threatened some 40,000 jobs throughout the UK, with a very major loss of export earnings.

As a result of this telegram, the members of the strike committee were invited to meet Barbara Castle at the Ministry. She suggested that the way to resolve the dispute was to let Jack Scamp's Court of Inquiry look into the issue of sex discrimination. The issue of grading should be handled through the normal procedure. The way to handle the issue of equal pay within the firm was to agree an increase in the women's rate (to bring it in line with that paid at General Motors' Vauxhall plant). In addition, she pledged that the Government would also move quickly to introduce legislation to give men and women the same rate for the same job.

The company agreed to increase the women's rate to 90 per cent of that of the men but stipulated that, 'in order not to humuliate the NJNC', the offer had formally to be made at a specially convened meeting of the NJNC (Friedman and Meredeen, 1980, p. 166). After some internal discussion the strike committee accepted this formula. The company offer was presented at the NJNC and the women's rate was increased from 85 per cent to 92 per cent of the men's rate.

When the sewing machinists' claim was taken through procedure, the sewing machinists lost their case for upgrading, although it was clearly a close run decision. The sewing machinists were extremely upset, although their increased wages meant that they soon recouped what they had lost during the strike. With respect to the issue of equal pay, the Strike Committee felt that they had won a victory which would be recognized as historically significant.

The company felt that the formula which was agreed satisfied a number of major constraints which it had quite clearly identified during the process of internal adjustment. In particular, it had preserved its new wage structure and it had defended itself against charges of discrimination against women, since the Court of Inquiry was satisfied that 'nothing of this sort happened' (Friedman and Meredeen, 1980, p. 220).

Both sides felt that they had learned important lessons from the dispute, which would affect their future conduct of industrial relations (see Friedman and Meredeen, 1980; Meredeen, 1988).

The Process of Internal Adjustment

The five examples of intra-organizational bargaining are very different in kind. Two describe American experience. Three describe industrial relations in the UK. Three of the cases were technically complex. Two were not. Each was taken from a text which seemed to make a serious theoretical contribution to the study of collective bargaining, although the contributions are of very different kinds. It would be foolish to make any serious claims about the generality of the cases. We would claim only that the points that are made below are not idiosyncratic. For the most part they are illustrated in more than one of the cases. Where they are not, other evidence is available, although detailed case studies of intra-organizational bargaining are extremely difficult to find.

We trust that the examples go some way towards illustrating four main points. The first is that internal negotiation is a process which functions to forge collective commitments to policies which make sense to the participants. The second is that those who have built strong social networks are better able to handle the cognitive and political aspects of the internal (or the external) negotiation tasks. The third is that the cognitive and political problems lead to dilemmas in the process of internal negotiation. The fourth is that the process of internal negotiation needs to be properly organized and led. We shall consider each of these points in turn.

Forging Collective Commitments which Make Sense

From a language–action perspective, internal negotiation has two aspects. The first is intellectual, and arises because social actions are inherently ambiguous and because they cannot be completely described (Bennett and Feldman, 1981; Hosking and Morley, 1991). Consequently, we have always to work out what is going on, and why, on the basis of evidence which is fragmentary and incomplete. The second is political, and arises because people are required to commit themselves to forms of collective action which they can justify to those whom they represent. To justify our actions we have to show that they may be seen as following a particular line (Harré, 1979). This means that we must be able to give a *rationale* which links what is happening now to what has happened in the past, and to what will happen in the future, showing that we have learned our lessons from the past and are using them to guide appropriate action (see Fifth Example). Such a rationale helps people to judge which are the most salient issues. This is why inexperienced negotiators are at such a disadvantage. They have not been able to learn from past experience what is important, and why (see Second Example).

The two problems are related because people are unlikely to keep their commitments unless they reach a working consensus about what is happening, and why. We suspect that this is one main reason why bilateral negotiations sometimes turn into multilateral negotiations (see p. 204). Broadly speaking, the process of internal adjustment should be designed to promote policies which all participants understand and all participants accept.

From an intellectual point of view it would seem important to have our cognitions socially validated so that we are confident that they are free from various kinds of personal bias. Most textbooks of social psychology describe the process as one in which people validate their ideas by comparing them with those held by people similar to themselves. However, there is a very real risk that teams of like-minded people may fail to see warning signs that the policies they prefer are likely to go wrong when put into effect. This is particularly likely to occur when a cohesive group operates under stress and follows procedures which lead to biased processing of information (Janis, 1982).[10] The result is that the participants commit themselves prematurely to interpretations which are plausible, but false or incomplete. This seems to have happened in the Ansell's brewery dispute when strike leaders held over-optimistic views about the level of domestic support (Waddington, 1987).

This is why writers such as Linstone (1984) have argued that the process of social comparison needs to be opened up to include people with very different views. This is what the management negotiators who are described in the First and Fifth Examples attempted to do (although the first group had much more time available than the second). It seems likely that building teams who engage multiple perspectives is a necessary, but not sufficient, condition for the success of various kinds of collective work (Hosking and Morley, 1991). Multiple perspectives mean that the team is in a better position to develop *viable* policies, because people with different points of view are likely to point to different reasons for and against any particular line of action.

Of course, as more and more people are added to the group it becomes more and more difficult to build a working consensus. It is almost as if there were a dialectical contradiction between the requirement to build multiple perspectives into a team and the need to build a working consensus. Participants may have difficulty in reaching agreement because there are too many conflicting points of view (as in the Second Example).

Building Social Networks

There is evidence that those who wish to succeed in organizational life need to build relationships with many other people (Hosking and Morley, 1991). Those with more extensive networks and with the ability to ask the right kinds of question are more likely than others to obtain authentic information, because they are more likely to talk to those close to the action, and because they are able to 'triangulate' different points of view.

At the same time, they are more likely to be able to promote their own language codes or interpretive schemes (see Third Example). One reason why some people are more influential than others is that they are linked into 'networks of relationships through which arguments can be promoted' (Batstone et al., 1978, p. 6). The conveners described in the Fourth Example relied heavily on the members of a quasi-elite group of shop stewards to mobilize support for their interpretations of what should be done, and why. In return, the conveners listened carefully to what the members of the quasi-elite had to say. The members of the quasi-elite were able to influence other shop stewards because of their experience and because they were opinion leaders in the domestic organization. As Batstone et al. (1978) have pointed out, relationships of this kind quite clearly serve 'to bolster the power of some rather than others and to facilitate the identification and pursuit of some kinds of issues as against others' (p. 7).

Batstone and his associates have also shown that it is particularly important for negotiators to build close bargaining relationships with members of the opposing teams. The relationships are exchange relationships in which participants help each other to understand what has happened, what is happening, what is likely to happen, and why. Such understanding is likely to increase their influence when they meet internally to plan for negotiation between the sides.

Dilemmas in the process of negotiation

Cognitive and political problems lead to dilemmas in internal and external negotiations. The way in which these are handled has a major impact on negotiation process and outcomes (Walton and McKersie, 1965; Morley, 1986; Hosking and Morley, 1991). Negotiations may even 'grind into indecision', as the Second Example has shown. Not surprisingly, therefore, negotiators attempt to learn from the past in such a way that solutions to those dilemmas can be used productively in the present (Sarason, 1972).

The two dilemmas identified in the Second Example deserve some further comment since, as Warr (1973) has said, they are 'the central ones of any negotiating group' (p. 113). Certainly, any negotiating team must face the question of how to make a group decision, given a distribution of opinion within the group. This question has received surprisingly little attention in the social psychological literature on negotiation, except for the work of Mannix et al. who have argued that a simple majority rule 'may discourage the trade-offs that are critical to integrative decision making' (Mannix et al., 1989, p. 510).

Much more attention has been paid to the dilemma of whether to take a leader or a delegate role. On the union side, it raises quite fundamental questions about the nature of democracy because the need for the rank-and-file membership to participate in decision-making is set against the need for strong leadership (Hartley et al., 1983). Without strong leadership it may be impossible for a union to achieve sufficient unity and purpose for negotiators to work out a coherent point of view. However, this means that the leader will sometimes have 'to win his members over', sometimes tell them 'they're not on', and sometimes 'stir them to action'. Some stewards are unable or unwilling to take this role. They act as 'populists' rather than 'leaders' (Batstone et al., 1977, 1978).

Quite clearly, there will be times when the expectations of negotiators do not match those of their domestic organization. In the Second Example, many stewards began to feel that their more militant members did not really understand the issues: 'Surely they as a negotiating team were responsible for deciding how negotiations should develop?' (Warr, 1973, p. 112). Management negotiators frequently take a similar view, and there is evidence that senior management frequently develops quite 'unreal expectations' about external negotiations (Anthony, 1977, p. 57). Intra-organizational bargaining is needed to bring the misplaced optimism[11] of senior management into line with the more realistic views of those in the negotiating team (Walton and McKersie, 1965; Anthony and Crichton, 1969; Anthony, 1977).

The Second Example also illustrates a third dilemma. It arises in the following way. On the one hand, it might be thought that an ideal planning process would be one in which people become increasingly committed to plans as they move from broad formulations to specific proposals (Levin, 1976).

Furthermore, there are many reasons to delay making commitments until the various threats and opportunities have been clearly defined. Leaders, for example, 'hope that situations will unfold in an orderly enough way that their worst doubts will be past before the situation requires a public voice' (Huff, 1984, p. 262). However, it is costly to delay too long because it may allow other people to articulate their own definitions of the situation and seek support for partisan positions, perhaps very narrowly defined (Huff, 1984). This is essentially what happened when the JSSC decided to break off negotiations on pay and productivity. The situation had not become sufficiently orderly for those sympathetic to a company-wide agreement to frame the issues and to provide a dominant definition of the problem. They were not yet sure what represented 'success' in the negotiations, and temporarily lost support to what was, essentially, a minority point of view.

Leadership

Hosking and Morley have argued that leadership is central to the dynamics of organizational groups (Morley and Hosking, 1984; Hosking, 1988; Hosking and Morley, 1988, 1991). One reason is that successful leaders are better able to negotiate a social order that facilitates what Kanter (1984) has called the 'creative' and 'political' aspects of change. The 'creative' aspects arise because leaders have a special responsibility to manage meanings by providing 'pictures' or 'frames' for other people (Smircich and Morgan, 1982). Indeed, they acquire power to the extent that other people rely on them to do these jobs because they have the relevant expertise. The political aspects arise because policies compete for support and because leaders cannot simply direct the actions of the led. Their influence has to be accepted. Furthermore, it is most important that those who are led continue vigorously to express their own point of view. To be effective, external negotiation must be linked to a process in which participants build shared interpretations of what is going on, and why, what can be negotiated, how it can be negotiated, and when it can be negotiated. Given that this is itself a process of negotiation, it is quite astonishing that the literature on leadership has paid so little attention to leadership considered as a form of negotiation (Hosking and Morley, 1988; Smith and Peterson, 1988). To quote one of the Chief Executive Officers interviewed by Hosking, 'it's what I do all day long' (Hosking and Morley, 1991).

It is quite clear that the process of negotiation, whether internal or external, needs to be properly organized (see First, Second and Fifth Examples). This may raise different problems for the management and the union sides.

On the management side, the leader of the domestic organization may not be the leader of the management negotiating team. When there is too little direction from top management, the team will face problems working out what to do. There are some very clear examples of this in the arena of international relations (Morley, 1982), but there is no reason to suppose that problems are confined to that domain. For example, there is evidence that many directors construct 'an isolated social world' in which 'their own employees become part of the psychological environment' (Winkler, 1974, p. 196). Whilst this may have some short term advantages as a mechanism for coping with a stressful environment, it is now clear that effective leaders spend a lot of their time building effective networks (Hosking and Morley, 1991). They realize that they have been 'placed in the middle of a system of relationships out of which [they] must fashion an organization that will accomplish [their] objectives' (Sayles, 1964, p. 27).

It is equally important that the leader of the negotiating team keep top management informed of what is happening, and why. In this respect it is worth noting evidence that external negotiations may break down because of failures in communication within the management side. Winham and Bovis (1978) used State Department Training Simulations to show, for example, that successful teams gave more adequate information to their principals, particularly in the later stages of negotiation. They sent them more information and took greater pains to put that information in an appropriate context. This minimized confusion[12] and made it easier to handle problems of internal adjustment. There was evidence that this made it easier for negotiators to link 'roughly equivalent issues' in external negotiations, thus increasing the likelihood that agreements would be obtained.

On the union side, there are considerable problems of co-ordination within the coalition. One reason is what Hartley et al. (1983) have identified as the conflict between the need for leadership and the need for democracy. They have argued that:

> the potential for conflict between leadership and democracy is a real one for all unions, driven by contrasting pressures. On the one side are those of oligarchy: the tendency for selective self-qualification for leadership roles, and for power to coalesce around informal elites, formal structures or bureaucratic processes. On the other side are those of participation: the legitimation of leadership by democratic process, the ideology of equal rights and membership sovereignty, and the moral imperative of the positive high levels of membership involvement. Hartley et al., 1983 (p. 15)

Unless this dilemma is resolved, negotiators may face considerable uncertainty over how to act. For example, when it became obvious that there was going to be a national strike against the British Steel Corporation, one local Strike Committee raised problems of how to deal with safety cover; of whether to allow dispensations so that some firms could continue working; of whether to encourage participation from the private sector; of who was eligible for social security benefit; and so on. Such questions require urgent answers. They are most likely to be raised and dealt with by leader stewards, particularly conveners or members of the 'quasi-elite', because these are the people most likely to see the central dilemmas and to give them most careful consideration. They are also the people most able to mobilize support from the membership and from other stewards.

Conclusion

Negotiations in organizations involve management and union coalitions. They cycle through stages of internal adjustment (intra-organizational bargaining) and external adjustment (inter-organizational bargaining). The two stages are dynamically linked, so that what happens in the internal negotiation affects what happens in the external negotiation, and vice versa. Careful attention to the process of intra-organizational bargaining shows the weakness of much of the traditional literature and confirms the conclusion of Morley et al., (1988, p. 118) that 'we must shift the emphasis from models which are individualistic and economic to models which are social and contextual'. Negotiation is a form of intelligent social action in which participants organize response to change, or the possibility of change, in the status quo. To understand this form of action it is important to consider those cognitive and political processes whereby participants make sense of their world, forge collective commitments, and handle the central dilemmas of group life. Leaders have a special responsibility to fashion organizations which will accomplish these objectives. To do so they have to be skilful negotiators themselves. Thus, the study of intra-organizational bargaining also has much to offer the literature on leadership.

Notes

1 According to Evan and MacDougall (1967), the idea that internal divisions within a party will always be exploited is a piece of folk psychology which is not confirmed by experimental evidence. In contrast, it is quite clearly supported by systematic analyses of industrial disputes, such as those of Meredeen (1980). A compromise position is that internal differences will often be exploited fully, but not always, depending on factors such as the bargaining relationship between the negotiators, the complexity of the issues, and the experience of the negotiators (Morley, 1981; Warr, 1973).

2 This power is based on the combination of specific information, based on direct relationships with members of those parties, and general expertise about the nature of employment relations. The question of what knowledge negotiators require has been neglected in the psychological literature, although see Morley (1986).

3 This is a central assumption of Tajfel's (1981) theory of intergroup relations. Tajfel has argued that we cannot understand what happens within groups if we abstract those groups from the context of their relations with other groups. Equally, we cannot understand what happens between groups unless we understand what happens within groups. For further discussion see Hosking and Morley, 1991, ch. 4.

4 Walton and McKersie (1965) had a clear appreciation of the importance of dilemmas. This aspect of their work has not, in our opinion, received the attention it has deserved.

5 The difference between these emphases has been set out with very great clarity by Putnam (1985). Much of what Carnevale and Keenan (Chapter 10) have said relates to negotiation as strategy rather than negotiation as concerned with messages and meanings. To see the difference in emphasis it is worth noting that, whereas Carnevale and Keenan speak of scripts as strategies which contain sets of tactics, Hosking and Morley (1991) speak of scripts as one of several cognitive constructs (such as narratives,

stories, and sagas) which situate general lessons about threats and opportunities in specific contexts where negotiation takes place. Our view is that the different approaches have different strengths and weaknesses. The approach described by Carnevale and Keenan has been the dominant one. Other approaches now need to be given much more serious consideration than they have received so far.

6 The decision to delay ratifying the policy until after the first formal meeting with the union side may be construed in various ways. One advantage is that it gives the management team more time to learn what the union really want this time, and why.

7 See Morley (1982) for a review.

8 Experimental studies of intra-organizational bargaining have shown that the process and outcomes of external negotiations are affected by the nature of the relationship between a negotiator and his or her constituents. The general idea has been that negotiators will have more room to manoeuvre when they are trusted by their constituents; when negotiations are less visible; when there is less time pressure; and when they are confident in their ability to do well in future negotiations, whether internal or external (Wall, 1975; Adams, 1976; Putnam, 1985).

9 According to Morley et al. (1988), the major problem in external negotiations is to find a formula linking what is happening now to what has happened in the past, and to what will happen in the future. Once participants accept a formula, they know the general form that an agreement will take, *and why*. The rest is detail. Very similar views have been expressed by Zartman (1977), in the context of international negotiations.

10 The structural faults identified by Janis include faulty leadership, lack of methodical procedures for information search and information appraisal, and the 'insulation' of the group from other parts of the domestic organization. For a more detailed discussion, see Hosking and Morley 1991, ch. 4.

11 The case studies of Meredeen (1988) contain some quite striking examples of misplaced optimism on the part of senior management. This may lead the unions to believe that a dispute has been engineered quite deliberately (Hartley et al. 1983).

12 A similar point may be made by saying that one major responsibility of the leader of the management team is to protect top management from surprises (Kouzes and Posner, 1987).

References

Adams, J. S. (1976) The structure and dynamics of behaviour in organizational boundary roles. In M. D. Dunnette (ed.), *Handbook of Industrial and Organizational Psychology*, Chicago: Rand McNally, 1175–99.

Anthony, P. D. (1977) *The Conduct of Industrial Relations*. London: Institute of Personnel Management.

Anthony, P. and Crichton, A. (1969) *Industrial Relations and the Personnel Specialists*. London: Batsford.

Batstone, E., Boraston, I. and Frenkel, S. (1977) *Shop Stewards in Action*. Oxford: Blackwell.

Batstone, E., Boraston, I. and Frenkel, S. (1978) *The Social Organization of Strikes*. Oxford: Blackwell.

Bennett, W. L. and Feldman, M. S. (1981) *Reconstructing Reality in the Courtroom*. London: Tavistock.

Brown, W. (ed.) (1981). *The Changing Contours of British Industrial Relations*. Oxford: Blackwell.

Chamberlain, N. W. and Kuhn, J. W. (1986) *Collective Bargaining* (3rd ed.). New York: McGraw-Hill.

Evan, W. M. and MacDougall, J. A. (1967) Interorganizational conflict: a labor–management bargaining experiment. *Journal of Conflict Resolution*, 11, 398–413.

Friedman, H. and Meredeen, S. (1980) *The Dynamics of Industrial Conflict*. London: Croom Helm.

Goldhaber, G. M., Dennis, H. S., Richetto, G. M. and Wiio, O. (1979) *Information Strategies: New Pathways to Corporate Power*. Englewood Cliffs, NJ: Prentice-Hall.

Harré, R. (1979) *Social Being*. Oxford: Blackwell.

Hartley, J. Kelly, J. and Nicholson, N. (1983) *Steel Strike* London: Batsford Academic.

Hosking, D. M. (1988) Organizing, leadership and skilful process. *Journal of Management Studies*, 25, 147–66.

Hosking, D. M. and Morley, I. E. (1991) *A Social Psychology of Organizing*. London: Harvester Wheatsheaf.

Huff, A. (1984) Situation interpretation, leader behavior, and effectiveness. In J. G. Hunt, D. M. Hosking, C. A. Schriesheim and R. Steward (eds), *Leaders and Managers: International Perspectives on Managerial Behavior and Leadership*, Oxford: Pergamon, 253–62.

Janis, I. L. (1982) *Groupthink: Psychological Studies of Policy Decisions and Fiascoes*. Boston: Houghton-Mifflin.

Kanter, R. M. (1984) *The Change Masters: Corporate Entrepreneurs at Work*. London: George Allen & Unwin.

Kochan, T. A. (1980) *Collective Bargaining and Industrial Relations*. Homewood, Ill: Irwin.

Kouzes, J. M. and Posner, B. Z. (1987) *The Leadership Challenge: How to Get Extraordinary Things Done in Organizations*. San Francisco: Jossey-Bass.

Levin, P. H. (1976) *Government and the Planning Process*. London: George Allen & Unwin.

Linstone, H. A. (ed.) (1984) *Multiple Perspectives For Decision Making: Bridging the Gap Between Analysis and Action*. Amsterdam: North Holland.

Mannix, E. A., Thompson, L. L. and Bazerman, M. H. (1989) Negotiation in small groups. *Journal of Applied Psychology*, 74, 508–17.

Meredeen, S. (1988) *Managing Industrial Conflict: Seven Major Disputes*. London: Hutchinson.

Morley, I. E. (1981) Negotiation and bargaining. In M. Argyle (ed.), *Social Skills and Work*, London: Methuen, 84–115.

Morley, I. E. (1982) Preparation for negotiation: conflict, commitment and choice. In H. Brandstätter, J. H. Davis and G. Stocker-Kreichgauer (eds), *Group Decision Making*, New York: Academic Press, 387–419.

Morley, I. E. (1984) Bargaining and negotiation. In C. Cooper and P. Makin (eds), *Psychology For Managers*, London: Macmillan/British Psychological Society, 214–34.

Morley, I. E. (1986) Negotiating and bargaining. In O. Hargie (ed.), *A Handbook of Communication Skills*, London: Croom Helm, 303–24.

Morley, I. E. and Hosking, D. M. (1984) Decision-making and negotiation: leadership and social skills. In M. Gruneberg and T. Wall (eds), *Social Psychology abd Organizational Behaviour*, Chichester: Wiley, 71–92.

Morley, I. E., Webb, J. and Stephenson, G. M. (1988) Bargaining and arbitration in the resolution of conflict. In W. Stroebe, A. W. Kruglanski, D. Bar-Tal and M. Hewstone (eds), *The Social Psychology of Intergroup Conflict*, Berlin: Springer-Verlag, 117–34.

Pruitt, D. G. (1981). *Negotiation Behavior*. New York: Academic Press.

Putnam, L. (1985) Collective bargaining as organizational communication. In P. K.

Tomkins and R. McPhee (eds), *Organizational Communication: Traditional Themes and New Directions*, Newbury Park: Sage.

Putnam, L. and Sotirin, P. (1985) Structural contradictions in a teachers' bargaining context. Paper presented at the annual convention of the International Communication Convention, Honolulu, Hawaii, May.

Rubin, J. Z. and Brown, B. R. (1975). *The Social Psychology of Bargaining and Negotiation*. New York: Academic Press.

Sarason, S. B. (1972) *The Creation of Social Settings and the Future Societies*. San Francisco: Jossey-Bass.

Sayles, L. R. (1964) *Managerial Behavior: Administration in Complex Organizations*. New York: McGraw-Hill.

Smircich, L. and Morgan, G. (1982) Leadership: the management of meaning. *Journal of Applied Behavioral Science*, 18, 257–73.

Smith, P. B. and Peterson, M. F. (1988) *Leadership, Organizations and Culture*. London: Sage

Tajfel, H. (1981). *Human Groups and Social Categories*. Cambridge: Cambridge University Press.

Tracy, L. and Peterson, R. B. (1986) A behavioral theory of labor negotiations: how well has it aged? *Negotiation Journal*, 2, 93–108.

Waddington, D. P. (1987) *Trouble Brewing: A Social Psychological Analysis of the Ansell's Brewery Dispute*. Aldershot: Avebury.

Wall, J. A. (1975) The effects of constituent trust and representative bargaining visibility on intergroup bargaining. *Organizational Behaviour and Human Performance*, 14, 244–56.

Walton, R. E. and McKersie, R. B. (1965) *A Behavioral Theory of Labor Negotiations*. New York: McGraw-Hill.

Warr, P. B. (1973) *Psychology and Collective Bargaining*. London: Hutchinson.

Winham, G. R. and Bovis, H. E. (1978) Agreement and breakdown in negotiation: report on a State Department Training Simulation. *Journal of Peace Research*, 15, 285–303.

Winkler, J. T. (1974) The ghost at the bargaining table: directors and industrial relations. *British Journal of Industrial Relations*, 12, 191–212.

Zartman, I. W. (1977) Negotiation as a joint decision process. In I. W. Zartman (ed.), *The Negotiation Process: Theories and Applications*. Beverly Hills: Sage.

Further Reading

Walton, R. E. and McKersie, R. B. (1965). *A Behavioral Theory of Labor Negotiations*. New York: McGraw-Hill. Treats intra-organizational bargaining as one sub-process of social negotiations. Still the best known work on the topic, perhaps because it contains so many examples of different kinds of problem.

Kochan, T. A. (1980). *Collective Bargaining and Industrial Relations*. Homewood, Ill: Irwin. This is an advanced text which summarises a great deal of theory and research.

Warr, P. B. (1973). *Psychology and Collective Bargaining*. London: Hutchinson. This is very much an introductory text, and explains some important psychological aspects of negotiation in the context of a detailed description of a particular case.

Anthony, P. D. (1977). *The Conduct of Industrial Relations*. London: Institute of Personnel Management. Argues that internal negotiation is to be understood in the same way as external negotiation.

10

The Resolution of Conflict: Negotiation and Third Party Intervention

Peter J. Carnevale and Patricia A. Keenan

Introduction: Negotiation and Conflict

This chapter concerns the attempts to resolve the conflicts that occur between workers and employers in organizations. In organizations, workers and employers often depend on each other to attain important organizational and personal goals. Sometimes workers and employers see their interests as entirely opposed, which can produce misunderstandings, poor relationships, and destructive conflicts (Deutsch, 1973). However, through negotiation, workers and employers can reach agreements which resolve some of their differences and strengthen their relationship. The resolution of organizational conflict through negotiation is a central topic of interest to organizational researchers, and is the central focus of this chapter.

Worker–employer conflicts can be highly complex, for example, when the issues involve pensions, insurance, lay-off and recall procedures, flexibility in assigning employees to jobs, and grievance procedures (cf. Freeman and Medoff, 1984; Kochan and Katz, 1988). How issues get resolved has considerable significance not only for the individuals involved in the conflicts but also for the organization as a whole. Worker–employer conflicts often have broad impact. A teachers' strike, for example, has a direct effect on the teachers, school administrators, and children; it also has effects on the community of parents who must arrange for children to be cared for when school is not in session.

Collective bargaining is an organizational mechanism for handling worker-employer conflicts. In collective bargaining, the employees' representatives negotiate directly with management on matters that ultimately define the terms of employment. A well-known example in the UK is the role of the union 'shop steward' (Goodman and Whittingham, 1969; Stephenson, 1981a). The shop steward, who represents the workers, handles workplace bargaining with representatives of the employers when conflicts arise over pay, and in bargaining over grievances and disputes about work conditions.

This chapter is based in part upon work supported by the National Science Foundation under Grant No. BNS-8809263 to Peter Carnevale. The authors are grateful to Jean Hartley, Geoffrey Stephenson and Andrea Hollingshead for their very helpful comments.

It is important to note that conflicts in organizations go beyond the formal negotiations between management and workers. Conflicts between workers and employers on issues such as pay and conditions comprise only a sub-set of the broader set of conflicts that can occur in organizations. Any manager in an organization can be involved in resolving conflicts between or within departments, in a union or non-union setting, in any situation where there are conflicting interests. There is evidence that managers spend a significant portion of their time handling conflicts, more than 25 per cent (Thomas and Schmidt, 1976).

Conflict and negotiation defined

Following Putnam and Poole (1987), conflict is 'the interaction of interdependent people who perceive opposition of goals, aims, and values, and who see the other party as potentially interfering with the realization of these goals' (p. 552). Putnam and Poole note that at least one party must perceive the conflict situation as an opposition of goals, and that it is the individuals' perceptions that shape the conflict.

Negotiation involves communication to find a mutually agreeable solution (Putnam and Poole, 1987). The parties are interdependent, which means that both co-operative and conflictual processes are often part of the effort to reach agreement. Sometimes people have completely convergent interests, as when an employer and new employee both want the employee to start work immediately. Sometimes people have completely divergent interests, as when an employer wants to minimize a possible wage increase and employees want it maximized. Most cases of worker–employer conflict are mixed-motive, involving both convergent and divergent interests. This chapter deals with the mixed-motive case and with the determinants of how people behave in such settings.

Research on conflict and negotiation

The literature on conflict and negotiation includes case studies of actual situations (Chamberland and Kuhn, 1965; Kerr, 1954; Peters, 1952, 1955; Walton, 1987), field survey studies (Kochan et al., 1979; Kressel, 1977; Lewin, 1987), and laboratory experiments (Pruitt, 1981; Pruitt and Rubin, 1986). Applied social and organizational psychologists often employ a laboratory methodology to test hypotheses about conditions that affect negotiation process and outcome. Much of the research described in this chapter is based on the laboratory method.

Laboratory research on negotiation has mainly used two types of tasks. The first, labelled 'unidimensional', involves a single issue wherein the parties make demands (e.g. 'The union demands a 15 per cent increase in wages') and make concessions (e.g. 'OK, the union will now demand a 12 per cent increase in wages'). There is a basic dilemma in these situations: parties who make high demands and infrequent concessions are more likely to win, but are more likely to fail to reach agreement (Pruitt, 1981).

The second type of negotiation task, labelled 'multidimensional', involves more than one issue and the parties have different priorities for the issues. In these tasks, the parties can make trade-offs on the issues. Take, for example, a labour negotiation which involves two issues, an employee pension plan and a benefit plan. If the union feels more strongly about the benefit plan than the pension plan, and management feels more strongly about the pension plan than the benefit plan, these different priorities can form the basis of a trade-off: they may agree on the union position for the benefit plan and the management position for the pension plan.

Multidimensional tasks often have 'integrative potential', meaning that there are several possible outcomes and that some outcomes are better for both parties than other outcomes. When there is integrative potential, it is important to distinguish between 'compromise' and 'integrative' agreements. An integrative agreement is one that is mutually beneficial to both parties; these agreements seek to reconcile (i.e. integrate) the parties' divergent interests. Compromise agreements, on the other hand, occur when negotiators concede along an obvious dimension, such as a 50/50 split on each issue, to a middle ground.

The notion of integrative potential first appeared more than 50 years ago in articles by the well known industrial consultant Mary Parker Follett (Follett, 1940). Follett told the story of two sisters who quarrelled over an orange. They reached a compromise, 50/50 agreement to split the orange in half. One sister used her portion of the orange for its peel, that is, for a cake, and threw away the juice. The other sister wanted orange juice to drink. The two sisters did not discuss their interests, their reasons for wanting the orange, and thus failed to see the integrative agreement of giving one all of the juice and the other all of the peel.

Demands and concessions also play a part in multidimensional negotiation tasks. However, it is important that both sides identify and consider the potential for integrative solutions which reflect the parties' different priorities or which satisfy the underlying needs of the parties. This often requires creative problem solving. Parties who make high demands and infrequent concessions often fail to engage in creative problem solving and end either with no agreement or with a sub-optimal compromise agreement (Pruitt, 1981) . High quality, integrative agreements are desirable because they give negotiators more of what they want. Researchers have identified other positive benefits of integrative agreements: they are more stable over time (i.e. they are less likely to break down) and they foster harmonious relationships between groups (Pruitt and Rubin, 1986).

Systems of negotiation

The distinction between unidimensional and multidimensional negotiation has its roots in the influential book, *A behavioral theory of labor negotiations: An analysis of a social interaction system* by Walton and McKersie (1965). Although written almost thirty years ago, the book is highly relevant today. Walton and McKersie identified four systems of activities or sub-processes of negotiation: (a) Distributive bargaining; (b) Integrative bargaining; (c) Attitudinal structuring; and (d) Intra-organizational bargaining.

The function of *distributive bargaining* is to resolve conflicts over issues in which the interests of the parties are in basic conflict with one another. In this type of bargaining, the parties see the outcome as a zero-sum or constant-sum game. That is, the parties bring with them a 'fixed-pie' view of the negotiation, with the negotiation being over who gets the larger piece of the pie. They see a gain for one party as a loss to the other.

To illustrate these points, let us imagine that we are a union negotiator bargaining over a wage increase. One thing that we must know is the amount or percentage increase that our constituents ideally want. This is the 'target point', and defines complete success: if we reach our target point, we shall have achieved the most that we had hoped for. The second thing that we must know is the lowest pay increase that is acceptable to our constituents. This is the 'resistance point'. If both sides make concessions and management's last offer is less than our resistance point, then we would be willing to break off negotiations and risk a strike or other sanctions rather than agree to their offer. The target and resistance points identify the negotiation zone for each side.

A negotiation is not a one-shot event but a process in which both sides make concessions. The area between the union's and the management's resistance points is the settlement range. If the resistance points are compatible (if management's resistance point is higher than the union's resistance point), then the range of settlement is positive. If management is not willing to concede as much as the union wants (if management's resistance point is lower than the union's resistance point), then the settlement range is negative; no outcome is acceptable to both parties.

Integrative bargaining concerns problem solving, which involves finding a solution that meets the needs of both parties at least to some degree. Integrative solutions often involve 'expanding the pie', that is, making trade-offs on issues of differing importance, or satisfying the underlying needs of the parties. An example of expanding the pie, or increasing limited resources, which was described by Mary Parker Follett (1940), concerned two milk companies who quarrelled constantly about which should be first to unload their cans on a loading dock. The quarrel continued until someone came up with the idea of widening the platform so that both groups could use the dock simultaneously. This expansion of resources allowed both parties to satisfy their needs.

The third negotiation sub-process identified by Walton and McKersie is *attitudinal structuring*, which involves attempts by one party to influence the attitudes of the other party. Negotiators attempt to elicit trust, to emphasize the interdependence of their relationship, and to gain respect from their opponent in order to shape the other's opinion positively toward their side. This sometimes reflects a desire to preserve a continuing relationship; sometimes it is trickery. There is evidence that people are helpful to those whom they like, and are especially helpful and co-operative when in a good mood (Carnevale and Isen, 1986). Attitudinal structuring may involve efforts to modify the opponent's expectations of the outcome by emphasizing the costs associated with non-settlement, such as the costs of a strike; this makes it easier for the opponent to make concessions.

The fourth negotiation sub-process identified by Walton and McKersie (1965) is *intra-organizational bargaining*, which refers to the activities that occur within a union or company in order to gain consensus on the positions taken in the negotiation with the other side (see chapter 9 by Morley for a discussion of these activities).

Stephenson (1981b) makes a useful distinction between *interpersonal* bargaining and *intergroup* bargaining. Interpersonal bargaining is direct one-to-one bargaining between two individuals. An example might be informal bargaining between an employee and a foreman. Intergroup bargaining involves group representatives, such as formal negotiations between union and management. Research on negotiation, reviewed below, has shown that interpersonal bargaining, where individuals act on their own behalf, can produce different negotiation processes and outcomes than intergroup bargaining where individuals negotiate as representatives for a group.

Analysing Negotiations: a Review of the Literature

Negotiation processes: strategies and tactics

There have been two traditions, or perspectives, for understanding strategy and its impact on negotiation. The first is the 'effect-defined tradition', which stems from unidimensional negotiation tasks where one can easily classify moves into those which are co-operative (helping the other at one's own expense) and competitive (helping oneself at the other's expense). A concession is co-operative and holding firm is competitive. This perspective views strategy (co-operative, competitive, and various combinations) as having particular short range effects (Deutsch, 1973). For example, a well known strategy is 'tit-for-tat', which involves an initial co-operative move followed by reciprocation of the other's co-operative and competitive moves. This strategy is particularly effective in eliciting co-operation (Axelrod, 1984; Pruitt, 1981).

The co-operative/competitive dichotomy is not as useful for understanding negotiation in multidimensional situations where integrative agreements are possible. In particular, co-operation can have two different strategic meanings: yielding, which is likely to lead to a compromise solution, and problem solving, which is often necessary for finding integrative solutions.

The second tradition for understanding strategy is the 'goal-defined tradition', which assumes that negotiator strategy is determined by the negotiator's goals. Goals elicit 'open-ended scripts', which contain: (a) sets of possible actions for pursuit of the goal; (b) information on the circumstances under which they can be used; and (c) ideas about their probable impact (see Fisk and Taylor, 1984, for a more elaborate discussion of scripts; see also chapter 9 by Morley). These scripts are 'strategies' and the possible actions that they contain are 'tactics'. The goal-defined tradition proposes three strategies – yielding, problem solving, and contending – as scripts (sets of tactics) which serve three kinds of goals:

1   *Yielding,* which comprises tactics for reducing one's aspirations. Yielding is seen in negotiation when people discover that their demands are likely to create a stalemate or to alienate the other party; they then reduce their aspirations to a more workable level. Most people's scripts contain several approaches to yielding. An example of a possible script: 'With one negotiation issue, I can concede slowly or rapidly. If I concede too slowly, this might alienate the other party. If I yield too fast, this might encourage the other party to think that many more concessions are coming.' This example of a yielding script is consistent with research which suggests that conceding very fast lessens the likelihood of agreement by encouraging the other party to expect too much (Pruitt, 1981).

2   *Contending,* which comprises tactics for satisfying one's own aspirations at the other party's expense. This includes all behaviour called 'competitive behaviour', i.e. not making a concession (Deutsch, 1973), and other tactics called 'contentious behaviour' (Pruitt and Rubin, 1986), such as commitments not to make a concession ('This is my last and final offer!') and persuasive communications and threats ('Do this or you will get fired!').

3   *Problem solving,* which comprises tactics for finding an agreement that satisfies the aspirations of both parties. In negotiation, problem solving takes two forms: co-ordination of concessions or seeking new options which advance both parties' interests. A tactic in a problem solving script might be looking for issues that underlie the other party's stated position (Fisher and Ury, 1980). Consider an example of a worker who resists a manager's request to work late one evening in order to complete an important project. The manager may learn, in a problem-solving discussion with the worker, that the worker's reason for not wanting to stay late is that he or she will miss his or her transportation home. To deal with this, the manager might arrange transportation for the worker or compensate the worker for the taxi fare, and thus alleviate the problem.

A central concern in negotiation research is predicting the conditions wherein negotiators are likely to adopt problem solving, contending, or yielding tactics (Morley and Stephenson, 1977; Pruitt, 1981). The research suggests that problem solving and contending tactics are incompatible, although there is evidence that negotiations often proceed in stages from the former to the latter.

The dual-concern model (Pruitt and Rubin, 1986), described below, is a model of the conditions affecting various kinds of behaviour in negotiation, as well as a model of interpersonal conflict style (Van de Vliert, 1990).

Dual-concern model

The dual-concern model deals with the three broad negotiation strategies identified above – yielding, problem solving, and contending – and a fourth strategy, avoidance of the conflict. Avoidance, and the closely related notion of withdrawal from the conflict, are sometimes equivalent to a permanent kind of inaction. At other times, avoidance and withdrawal are forms of contending (e.g. if employed by the party who wants to preserve the status quo) or of yielding (e.g. if employed by the party who wants a change).

According to the dual-concern model, which appears in figure 10.1, bargainers are motivated by two independent concerns: that for their own outcomes (shown on the horizontal axis) and that for the other party's outcomes (shown on the vertical axis). The concerns range from low (indifference) to high (positive concern).

High concern about own outcomes 'means placing importance on one's own interests – one's needs and values – in the realm under dispute' (Pruitt and Rubin, 1986, p. 28). Individuals with a high concern for their own outcomes tend to resist making concessions and tend to maintain high aspirations. Concern about the other's outcomes 'implies placing importance on the other's interests – feeling responsible for the quality of the other's outcomes' (p. 28). Concern for the other may be genuine, motivated by an intrinsic interest in the other's welfare, or it may be instrumental, motivated by self-interest. An example of the latter is an employer who has high concern for the workers' welfare because he or she believes that this will lead workers to be more committed to the organization.

The dual-concern model makes specific predictions about the tactics that individuals use in negotiation. When negotiators have high concern for their own outcomes and low concern for the other party's outcomes, they use contending tactics. These include efforts to maintain aspirations and to persuade the other party to yield, such as threats, persuasive arguments, committing themselves to 'unchangeable' positions, or making excessive demands. Yielding is the strategy that the model predicts when negotiators have high concern for the other party and low concern for their own outcomes. Yielding does not necessarily mean that bargainers will capitulate totally, but they will lower their aspirations and make

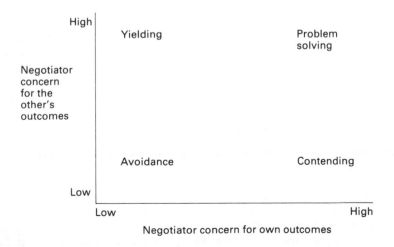

Figure 10.1 The dual-concern model

concessions so that it is possible to find alternatives which previously were not possible.

A high concern for both their own and the other party's outcomes leads to problem solving. Firm aspirations or goals will lead negotiators to resist making concessions while the co-operative goal (concern for the other's outcome) gives an impetus to use a flexible approach to the negotiation. This flexibility may be necessary to find an integrative solution in situations which have integrative potential. Problem solving underlies 'logrolling', where a favourable position on an issue of importance to one side is traded for a favourable position on a different issue of importance to the other side.

When negotiators have low concern for both their own outcomes and those of the other party, the model proposes that negotiators should adopt a wait-and-see atittude. Pruitt and Rubin (1986) call this 'inaction' or 'avoidance', and view it as a temporary move which may allow attempts to resolve the problem in the future.

Much laboratory research supports the propositions of the dual-concern model. In several studies, concern for own outcomes was defined by giving subjects a minimum pay-off that they must meet or exceed (a resistance point) in the negotiation task. In other studies, it involved negotiators acting as group representatives who were accountable to a constituent for their negotiation performance (Ben-Yoav and Pruitt, 1984; Carnevale, 1985). Accountability to a constituent is a feature of intergroup bargaining, which involves group representatives (cf. Stephenson, 1981b).

In several studies, concern for the other negotiator's outcomes was defined by giving subjects explicit instructions to be concerned for the outcomes of the other negotiator (Pruitt and Lewis, 1975). In other studies, it was defined by telling negotiators that they would interact with their opponent in a co-operative task in the future (Ben-Yoav and Pruitt, 1984).

Taken together, the research indicated that firm aspirations (high concern for own outcomes) increases the likelihood of integrative agreements when negotiators adopt a co-operative goal. These studies have also found that having a high resistance point (limit) decreases the likelihood of integrative agreements when bargainers adopt an individualistic goal, and that a co-operative goal in combination with low limits produces compromise agreements (yielding).

Cognition in negotiation

Recent research on conflict and negotiation has taken a distinct cognitive bent, as seen in Bar-Tal et al. (1989), Carnevale and Isen (1986), and Fisher (1990). Perceived conflict is a schema that involves incompatible goals (Bar-Tal et al., 1989). Bar-Tal et al. focus on the events that make a conflict schema salient, and thus make people more likely to take specific actions in a conflict.

Thompson and Hastie (1990) view negotiation as based upon judgements which the participants make about the other party and the task. They argue that negotiators often enter negotiation with the perception that the opponent's interests are in direct opposition to their own, leading them to overlook opportunities for integrative solutions. Thompson and Hastie (1990) measured negotiators' perceptions of the bargaining situation before, during and after a negotiation. They found that bargainers entered the negotiation with the perception that the task was distributive, a win–lose situation. As the negotiations progressed, some bargainers began to realize that their interests were not totally opposed but, after the session, 85 per cent of the negotiators did not realize that the interests of both parties were compatible. They found that negotiators who made more accurate judgements about the negotiation task were more likely to find the mutually beneficial settlements.

Non-verbal communication in negotiation

One interesting area of research is the role of non-verbal communication processes in negotiation and the impact of various forms of communication media. The research indicates that negotiations conducted via telephone differ in important ways from face-to-face negotiation, which can have important practical implications for the resolution of conflicts in organizations.

In several studies, subjects negotiated either face to face or with a partition placed between them (Carnevale and Isen, 1986; Lewis and Fry, 1977). When the negotiators started with a hostile, competitive orientation, the partition placed between them reduced the use of contentious, conflictual tactics (threats, positional commitments, derogatory statements) and enhanced the likelihood of mutually beneficial agreements. The partition had no effect when the negotiators started with a co-operative orientation. Thus, in some circumstances, preventing negotiators from seeing one another enhanced creative problem solving.

The data from these studies indicated that the partition placed between the negotiators interfered with their ability to stare at one another. Apparently, in a hostile, very competitive context, not seeing the other negotiator disrupted the conflict spiral of hostile perceptions, non-verbal gestures, and contentions verbal tactics. It is interesting to note the parallel observation that professional mediators often separate disputing parties to reduce hostilities (Kressel and Pruitt, 1989).

Third parties in negotiation

There are many ways in which conflict can be handled in organizations other than directly in negotiation by the parties themselves. Often third parties are invited to step in when there is impasse in negotiation. Conciliation, mediation and arbitration are the principal forms of intervention. In the past five years, there has been an impressive growth in the study of third party intervention in organizational conflicts, especially of mediation. Much of this work appears in the collection of articles by Kressel and Pruitt (1989).

Mediation

In mediation, a neutral third party helps the negotiators to reach a voluntary agreement. The mediator lacks authority to impose an agreement. Mediation is becoming common in the USA, especially in the public sector. Almost every statute concerning employees of state and local government specifies mediation as the first step of the dispute resolution process.

The ultimate objective of mediation is to help the parties to agree, and this is a key measure of effectiveness. However, other criteria of success can be identified, such as narrowing of the issues (Kochan and Jick, 1978), long term compliance with the agreement (Kressel and Pruitt, 1989), and improvement in the parties' relationship (Lim and Carnevale, 1990).

Practitioners claim that mediation is an art and not a science, that no two mediations are the same. Regardless, recent research has identified some common patterns in mediator behaviour and systematic effects in mediation.

Perhaps the best known taxonomy of mediator tactics is Kressel's (1977), which was recently updated by Kressel and Pruitt (1989). They identified three basic types of tactics: reflexive, substantive, and contextual. Mediators use reflexive tactics to orient themselves to the dispute and to create a foundation for their future activities, for example, establishing their credentials to assure the parties of their trustworthiness. Mediators use substantive tactics when they deal directly with the issues in the dispute, such as making suggestions for specific settlements or telling a negotiator that his or her position is unrealistic. Contextual tactics alter the dispute resolution process so that the parties themselves can discover an acceptable solution, for example, attempting to simplify the negotiation agenda by combining or separating issues.

Lim and Carnevale (1990) recently reported the results of a confirmatory factor analysis that provided empirical support for Kressel and Pruitt's (1989) taxonomy. In addition, their data indicated that the 'substantive' and 'contextual' categories could be further subdivided. Three types of substantive tactics included: (a) forceful, pressure tactics which involved trying to move a party off a position and changing their expectations (e.g. 'Your offer of 18 per cent is completely unrealistic. I can assure you that such an offer will be rejected completely by the other side.'); (b) making suggestions with the expressed purpose of helping the parties to save face with their constituents; and (c) making suggestions for possible settlement which involved creative proposals, such as trade-offs among the issues. The two types of contextual tactics included: (a) attempts to develop trust between the parties; and (b) attempts to affect the agenda of issues, which involved such measures as prioritizing the issues and simplifying the agenda. McLaughlin et al. (1991), using a different sample of professional mediators and different statistical procedures, reported similar dimensions of mediator behaviour.

A central proposition in the mediation literature is that mediation is better suited to some types of conflict problems than others. Kochan and Jick (1978) reported that mediation was highly successful in conflicts which involved a commitment to one fixed position (e.g. when a negotiator states, 'This is our last offer, take it or leave it'). Mediation was least successful when the parties had unrealistic expectations about how well they would do in the final agreement. This supports the proposition that mediation is most successful in cases where there is a positive contract zone, where the bottom-line positions of the parties overlap. One consistent finding is that mediation is less likely to be successful in cases of the most intense conflicts (Kochan and Katz, 1988; Kressel and Pruitt, 1989).

Carnevale and Pegnetter (1985) asked 32 professional labour mediators to rate the extent to which 24 sources of dispute were a problem for a recently mediated case (e.g. the extent to which 'a key issue was at stake'), and the extent to which 37 mediation tactics were used (e.g. 'suggested a settlement'). A correlation analysis revealed that mediators use tactics which are contingent upon the problems that produced or contributed to the dispute. For example, when bargainers were hostile to each other, mediators reported using forceful, pressure tactics, such as trying to change bargainers' expectations and mentioning the costs of continued disagreement; when bargainers brought too many issues to the negotiation, mediators reported using issue-related contextual tactics, such as devising a framework for negotiations and creating issue priorities.

Hiltrop (1985, 1989) conducted two studies of labour mediation in the UK, which examined whether contingent mediator behaviour improves the likelihood of settlement. Hiltrop found that the use of forceful, pressure tactics was positively associated with settlement under high levels of hostility (e.g. when there were strike conditions), but negatively associated with settlement under low hostility. Hiltrop's (1989) second study was largely consistent with the first: the use of forceful, pressure tactics was positively associated with settlement when hostility was high and when the parties' bottom-line positions were far apart. These findings are consistent with Gerhart and Drotning's (1980) observation that 'where disputes are difficult or subject to extended impasse procedures, intense mediator behavior is critical for mediation to be effective' (p. 352). Lim and Carnevale (1990) reported a similar finding for mediators in the USA.

Lim and Carnevale (1990) also reported that the effectiveness of mediator suggestions is contingent upon the dispute conditions. When there were 'internal party problems', such as a lack of negotiation team leadership, mediator suggestions lessened the likelihood of settlement. This suggests that, when one or both sides in a dispute has internal problems, mediator suggestions may add fuel to an already inflamed situation. Consistent with this, Kochan and Katz (1988) provide an example of a teacher–school board dispute which involved extremely hostile intra-organizational negotiations (the school superintendent wanted the board negotiator ousted). The failure to resolve the internal dispute on the management side guaranteed that no progress could be made in the intergroup, union-management negotiation.

Strategic choice model of mediation

The strategic choice model of mediation is based on the assumption that mediator behaviour has goals which guide the use of four basic mediation strategies: integration, pressure, compensation, and inaction (Carnevale, 1986). These strategies are scripts (sets of tactics) that serve distinct goals. The objective of each strategy is to produce an agreement in negotiation; the difference between them is the manner in which the mediator seeks agreement. The four goals include:

1 *Integration*, which involves a goal of finding a creative solution that satisfies both parties' limits or major aspirations. For example, a labour mediator attempted integration when she suggested to the negotiators that they consider a trade-off involving the union's demand for wages, and management's position on a benefit plan.

2 *Pressure*, which involves the goal of reducing one or both parties' limits or aspirations. An example was a labour mediator who tried to persuade the union negotiator to lower the union's demands by threatening to tell the news media that the union position was extreme, with the implication that the union was responsible for the impasse (cf. Lovell, 1952).

3 *Compensation*, which involves the goal of providing a reward or positive benefit in exchange for agreement or compromise. In an analysis of a decade of disputes between the Chicago Board of Education and the Chicago Teachers' Union, Banas (1987) reported that these disputes typically ended when 'some force with power to deliver economic benefits to teachers becomes agitated and acts to end the dispute' (p. 7). One interesting implication of this is that the disputants' hostility was in part designed to lead a third party, the 'force with power', to provide compensation. Harris and Carnevale (1990) present laboratory evidence consistent with this implication.

4 *Inaction*, which involves the goal of letting the disputants handle the conflict by themselves. An example of this was a labour mediator who excused himself from a joint negotiation session involving a school board and a teachers' association. He stayed away for about an hour because he wanted them to try to work things out on their own. The mediator thought that it was better that they should work it out themselves because it might lessen the likelihood of their requiring the services of a mediator in future disputes.

A laboratory experiment by Carnevale and Conlon (1988), using university students as mediators in a simulated dispute, suggests that mediators base their choice of a strategy in part on the interaction of two factors: (a) the value that mediators place on the disputants' achieving their aspirations, and (b) the mediator's assessment of whether a mutually acceptable solution can be found, called 'perceived common ground'. Perceived common ground implies that the parties are being co-operative with one another. The strategic choice model appears in figure 10.2.

The laboratory evidence was consistent with the general proposition of the model that a mediator's decision to pursue a strategic goal derives from a cost benefit analysis of the use of the strategy and a judgement about its likely success. Mediators chose to integrate most when it was important to them that the parties should achieve their aspirations (it was worth the effort to integrate) and there was perceived common ground (an integrative agreement was possible). Mediators chose to press most when it was not important to the mediator that the parties should achieve their aspirations and there was little common ground. Mediators chose to compensate most when it was important to them that the parties should achieve their aspirations and they perceived little common ground.

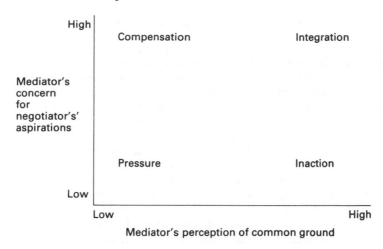

Figure 10.2 The strategic choice model of mediation

The mediators were inactive when it was not important that the parties should achieve their aspirations and there was much common ground (they thought that the negotiators could reach agreement on their own).

Several studies have extended the strategic choice model. Carnevale and Conlon (1988) extended it to the effects of time pressure in mediation, as when mediators faced a deadline. The results indicated that time pressure induced mediators to increase their use of pressing and compensating; this was because of a reduction in the mediator's beliefs about the likelihood of a mutually acceptable agreement (reduced perceived common ground).

Sometimes negotiators attempt to affect a mediator's choice of strategy. This was shown in a laboratory study of how negotiators reacted to mediator compensation and pressure strategies (Harris and Carnevale, 1990). When the mediator could compensate and cared about the negotiators' aspirations, negotiators reduced their concession-making in an apparent effort to obtain the compensation. When the mediator could press and did not care about the negotiators' aspirations, negotiators increased their concession-making in an apparent effort to avoid the pressure. This study suggests that a mediator's ability to compensate can sometimes undermine the effectiveness of mediation, especially if the mediator has an overtly high concern for the negotiators' welfare. Negotiators viewed a mediator who could compensate, and who had high concern, as weak and ineffective. Another conclusion from this study was that a mediator's ability to press can enhance his/her effectiveness. The prospect of a punitive mediator can facilitate concession-making, especially if the negotiators believe that the mediator has low concern for their welfare. This latter effect may be driven by the negotiators' desire to avoid the mediator's punishment.

Arbitration

The most important distinction between mediation and arbitration is the extent of control that the third party has over the outcome: a mediator cannot decide the outcome but an arbitrator can. Arbitration appears in many forms. It can be voluntary, where the parties submit their dispute for a judgement after failing to resolve it on their own, or compulsory, meaning that it occurs in the context of a system of law. In the USA, arbitration is not as common in the private sector as it is in the public sector (while in the UK it is used more in the private sector), but many believe that it should be limited to national emergencies or to where the parties agree to it voluntarily (Kochan and Katz, 1988). These authors present a useful overview of the various types of arbitration.

In conventional arbitration, the arbitrator is free to construct an outcome in any way which he or she wants; often it is half-way betwen the offers of management and union. An interesting, more recent form of arbitration is 'final-offer arbitration' (also called 'pendulum' arbitration), where the arbitrator must select either the management's offer or the union offer, and cannot construct a novel one. This occurs sometimes in a 'package' manner (i.e. all of the issues together) and sometimes issue by issue. There have been only a handful of psychological studies on arbitration. The evidence does support the proposition that final-offer arbitration enhances the parties' motivation to settle (Notz and Starke, 1978; see also Pruitt, 1981).

Design of dispute resolution systems

One exciting area for development in the study of worker–employer conflict is the design of organizational conflict resolution systems. There are many choices available for the design of dispute systems, and there are new third party roles, such as mediation–arbitration (med–arb) and ombudsman, which are gaining in popularity (Kolb, 1989: Ury et al., 1989).

One option is med–arb, where the individual who serves as mediator becomes an arbitrator after the decision that mediation will not succeed. In a field experiment in a community mediation centre, McGillicuddy et al. (1987) provide evidence suggesting that med–arb is better than mediation. Med–arb led to lower negotiator hostility and to an increase in problem solving, presumably because of the additional control that the third party could exercise over the negotiation process.

Many conflicts in organizations in the USA occur within the framework of a grievance system, which is a formal procedure designed for handling complaints by employees about something in their relationship with their employer (Lewin and Peterson, 1988). Often, a grievance pertains to an alleged violation of a labour agreement and it involves written forms that communicate the parties' positions in the dispute, conveyed between the employee, or employee's representative, and management. Grievance systems are very common in union contexts in the USA. They are contractually established and are growing rapidly in the non-union sector.

The literature on grievance systems in organizations is highly qualitative, containing anecdotal and often interesting observations. The few systematic, quantitative studies in the literature tend to emphasize demographic predictors of grievance behaviour, and correlational relationships between grievance activity and post-grievance outcomes such as turnover, performance ratings, and organizational productivity (Ichniowski, 1986; Klaas and DeNisi, 1989; Lewin, 1987; Lewin and Peterson, 1988).

Lewin (1987) and later Lewin and Peterson (1988) reported an important study of non-union appeal systems in three large US companies over a 4-year span (1980–3). The study examined the relationship between the appeal system files and the personnel records. An appeal system may have a series of steps, for example: (a) written appeal filed with a personnel officer, who meets separately with employee and immediate supervisor; (b) written appeal filed with the functional or facility manager, who meets separately with employee and immediate supervisor; (c) written appeal filed with the divisional or corporate vice-president of personnel, who chairs a management committee; and (d) written appeal filed with the chief executive officer who makes a final decision (Lewin, 1987). Lewin examined the impact of the use of appeal systems on post-appeal behaviours, such as voluntary turnover, work attendance, performance ratings and promotion rates.

Lewin's (1987) data supported an organizational-punishment model of involvement in conflicts. The personnel who were directly involved in workplace disputes, including both employees and managers, were more likely to receive punishments (poorer performance ratings) and less likely to receive rewards (raises and promotions) than personnel not involved in conflicts. Klaas and DeNisi (1989) reported similar negative consequences for employees who filed grievances, especially when the grievance focused on a specific supervisor and not organizational policies.

A formal dispute resolution mechanism, such as a grievance system, is one in which explicit, commonly shared rules govern the conduct of behaviour. If the purpose of grievance systems is to further employee interests, the negative consequences of using such systems, mentioned above, may speak against their value. As Klaas and DeNisi (1989) put it, 'A potential implication is that a grievance system might cease to serve as a mechanism through which workers and managers can freely communicate' (p. 714). Lewin (1987) noted that many managers (27%) in the companies that he studied did not use grievance systems, citing 'fear of management reprisal' as the main reason.

Carnevale and Olson (1991) conducted a laboratory study, which simulated an organizational grievance system, to test the grievance and performance evaluation relationship in a controlled context. It was not entirely clear in Klaas and DeNisi's (1989) and Lewin's (1987) studies, which were field correlational studies, whether the grievance–punishment effects resulted from lower real performance of the employees who filed grievances or from another idiosyncratic characteristic of employees who filed grievances, before the grievance was filed, during its filing or just after it was filed.

Carnevale and Olson's (1991) study also investigated the role of informality in the grievance process. One problem with formal grievance systems is that they may inhibit workers and managers from talking informally, and privately, about problems. Filing a formal grievance may reflect either an unwillingness, or an inability, to talk in a friendly manner. Greenhalgh (1987) argues that people who have positive relationships are more likely to deal with conflicts face to face, in an open and friendly manner.

The results of the Carnevale and Olson (1991) study were clear: the laboratory 'managers' showed similar effects to those of their counterparts in natural settings. That is, the subjects who received a formal grievance which their employee then appealed, compared to subjects who received a formal grievance which was not appealed, were more likely to punish the employee with low performance ratings, to give him or her fewer rewards for performance, and to assign to him or her less desirable jobs in the post-grievance period. This was very similar to what happened to people who filed grievances in Lewin's (1987) sample of three large non-union organizations. The results of the Carnevale and Olson study also pointed to the importance of informality in organizational dispute resolution. When subjects received an informal attempt by the subordinate to resolve the dispute, they did not punish the subordinate for appealing the grievance. In other words, the negative consequences of grievance filing, shown in Lewin (1987), were possibly a result of an inability of workers and managers to talk about conflicts informally.

A comment on the positive aspects of conflict

Although conflicts often have disastrous effects on interpersonal and work relationships, it should be emphasized that there are many positive aspects of the conflict. This has received considerable theoretical discussion in the past but much less empirical attention. Coser (1956) has argued that conflicts can balance power relationships. Dahrendorf (1959) has written about the positive impact of conflict on group formation. As noted by Pruitt and Rubin (1986), conflict can mean change, and change can be good.

Although much of the current research assumes that conflict is destructive, there are notable exceptions. Putnam's (1989) analysis of teacher–school board contract negotiations revealed that bargaining served constructive organizational ends. It enabled members to exchange information: bargaining was the primary form of information exchange between the lowest level of the organization and upper management. It clarified misunderstandings about policies and signalled potential problems. Putnam's results showed that exchanging information and reaching common understandings of events accounted for a large portion (29 per cent) of the variance in predicting satisfaction with the contract.

Conclusion

This chapter reviewed some current theoretical and empirical work in the study of worker–employer conflict. Current research on negotiation takes a goal-defined approach and focuses on three negotiation strategies – yielding, problem solving, and contending – as scripts (sets of tactics) which serve distinct goals. A model of negotiator strategy, the dual-concern model, posits that two factors, the relative concern that negotiators have for their own outcomes and the concern that they have for the other party's outcomes, determine negotiator strategy. An implication of this model is that negotiators can predict which strategy an adversary is likely to use in a negotiation, if they can determine where the adversary may be located on the two dimensions of the model. For example, if the adversary is highly accountable to a constituent, and there is little chance of a co-operative future relationship with the adversary, then the negotiators might expect the adversary to use contending competitive tactics in the negotiation.

Much recent work on organizational conflict focuses on the role of third parties, such as mediators, in the resolution of conflict (cf. Kressel and Pruitt, 1989). A good deal of research has focused on understanding the likely strategy that a third party will use in attempting to resolve disputes, and the contingent effectiveness of third party strategies. One area of research on mediation that is likely to receive considerable attention in the future is the application of decision theory models to mediation. In a recent laboratory study, for example, Carnevale and Mead (1990) extended the concept of 'frame' (cf. Kahneman and Tversky, 1984) to mediation and to social perception. Mediators saw a concession by bargainers who had a negative frame (i.e. the bargainers were trying to prevent a loss) as greater and more co-operative than the *equivalent concessions* made by bargainers who had a positive frame (i.e. the bargainers were trying to make a gain). In other words, mediators apparently view negatively framed concessions as greater than positively framed concessions, suggesting that there are interesting context effects in mediator perception which are consistent with predictions of decision models (cf. Kahneman and Tversky, 1984).

An exciting future development in the study of organizational conflict is the design of dispute resolution systems. Many organizations have procedures for handling conflicts between workers and employers, in both union and non-union settings (Lewin and Peterson, 1988), and there is considerable interest in how these systems should be designed (Ury et al., 1989). One promising development in the study of organizational dispute resolution systems is the evident success of the laboratory simulation methodology. Subjects in the laboratory grievance system (Carnevale and Olson, 1991) appear to act in a manner consistent with observations in natural settings in field research (Lewin, 1987). This suggests that the laboratory grievance system, which involves university students acting as workers in a simulated organization, can serve as a test chamber in which to discover grievance procedures and to experiment with alternative forms of organizational dispute resolution systems.

In research described in this chapter, informality was an important component of organizational dispute resolution systems (Carnevale and Olson, 1991). This finding is consistent with the general assumption in dispute resolution that it is better for the parties to reach their own agreement than one determined by formal intervention from an outside force, especially government. This assumption rests on the belief that the parties know their own values and interests best, and that they will be more likely to live up to the terms of an agreement that is voluntary. There is also a general assumption that parties are less effective in resolving their disputes if they come to rely on outsiders (Kochan and Katz, 1988). This is an important issue that needs to be addressed in future research on the design of dispute resolution systems.

References

Axelrod, R. M. (1984) *The Evolution of Cooperation*. New York: Basic Books.

Banas, C. (1987) Signs show movement on schools. *Chicago Tribune*, 16 September, 7.

Bar-Tal, D., Kruglanski, A. W. and Klar, Y. (1989) Conflict termination: An epistemological analysis of international cases. *Political Psychology*, 10, 233–55.

Ben-Yoav, O. and Pruitt, D. G. (1984) Resistance to yielding and the expectation of cooperative future interaction in negotiation. *Journal of Experimental Social Psychology*, 34, 323–35.

Carnevale, P. J. (1985) Accountability of group representatives and intergroup relations. In E. J. Lawler (ed.), *Advances in Group Processes: Theory and Research* (vol. 2), Greenwich, Conn: JAI Press, 227–48.

Carnevale, P. J. (1986) Strategic choice in mediation. *Negotiation Journal*, 2, 41–56.

Carnevale, P. J. and Conlon, D. (1988) Time pressure and strategic choice in mediation. *Organizational Behavior and Human Decision Processes*, 42, 111-33.

Carnevale, P. J. and Isen, A. M. (1986) The influence of positive affect and visual access on the discovery of integrative solutions in bilateral negotiation. *Organizational Behavior and Human Decision Processes*, 37, 1–13.

Carnevale, P. J. and Mead, A. (1990) *Decision frame in the mediation of disputes*. Paper presented at the annual meeting of the Society of Judgment and Decision Making, New Orleans, November.

Carnevale, P. J. and Olson, J. B. (1991) Formality and informality in a laboratory grievance system. Unpublished manuscript. Department of Psychology, University of Illinois at Urbana–Champaign.

Carnevale, P. J. and Pegnetter, R. (1985) The selection of mediation tactics in public-sector disputes: A contingency analysis. *Journal of Social Issues*, 41, 65–81

Chamberland, N. W. and Kuhn, J. W. (1965) *Collective Bargaining*. New York: McGraw-Hill.

Coser, L. (1956) *The Function of Social Conflict*. New York: Free Press.

Dahrendorf, R. (1959) *Class and Class Conflict in Industrial Society*. Stanford, Calif: Stanford University Press.

Deutsch, M. (1973) *The Resolution of Conflict*. New Haven, Conn: Yale University Press.

Fisher, R. and Ury, W. (1980) *Getting to Yes: Negotiating Agreement Without Giving in*. Boston: Houghton Mifflin.

Fisher, R. J. (1990) *The Social Psychology of Intergroup and International Conflict Resolution*. New York, Springer-Verlag.

Fisk, S. T. and Taylor, S. E. (1984) *Social Cognition*. Reading, Mass: Addison-Wesley.

Follett, M. P. (1940) Constructive conflict. In H. C. Metcalf and L. Urwick (eds), *Dynamic Administration: The Collected Papers of Mary Parker Follett*, New York: Harper, 30–49.

Freeman, R. B. and Medoff, J. L. (1984) *What do Unions do?* New York: Basic Books.

Gerhart, P. F. and Drotning, J. E. (1980) Dispute settlement and the intensity of mediation. *Industrial Relations*, 19, 352–9.

Goodman, J. F. B. and Whittingham, T. G. (1969) *Shop Stewards in British Industry*. London: McGraw-Hill.

Greenhalgh, L. (1987) Relationships in negotiations. *Negotiation Journal*, 3, 235–43.

Harris, K. L. and Carnevale, P. J. (1990) Chilling and hastening: The influence of third-party power and interests on negotiation. *Organizational Behavior and Human Decision Processes*, 47, 138–60.

Hiltrop, J. M. (1985) Mediator behavior and the settlement of collective bargaining disputes in Britain. *Journal of Social Issues*, 41, 83–99.

Hiltrop, J. M. (1989) Factors associated with successful labor mediation. In K. Kressel and D. G. Pruitt (eds), *Mediation research: The process and effectiveness of third party intervention*, San Francisco: Jossey-Bass, 241–62.

Ichniowski, C. (1986) The effects of grievance activity on productivity. *Industrial and Labor Relations Review*, 40, 75–80.

Kahneman, D. and Tversky, A. (1984) Choices, values, and frames. *American Psychologist*, 39, 341–50.

Kerr, C. (1954) Industrial conflict and its mediation. *American Journal of Sociology*, 60, 230–45.

Klaas, B. S. and DeNisi, A. S. (1989) Managerial reactions to employee dissent: The impact of grievance activity on performance ratings. *Academy of Management Journal*, 32, 705–17.

Kochan, T. A. and Jick, T. A. (1978) The public sector mediation process. *Journal of Conflict Resolution*, 22, 209–41.

Kochan, T. A. and Katz, H. C. (1988) *Collective Bargaining and Industrial Relations*. Homewood, Ill: Irwin.

Kochan, T. A., Mironi, M., Ehrenberg, R. G., Baderschneider, J. and Jick, T. (1979) *Dispute Resolution under Factfinding and Arbitration: An Empirical Analysis*. New York: American Arbitration Association.

Kolb, D. (1989) Labor mediators, managers and ombudsman: Roles mediators play in different contexts. In K. Kressel and D. G. Pruitt (eds), *Mediation Research: The Process and Effectiveness of Third Party Intervention*, San Francisco: Jossey-Bass, 91–114.

Kressel, K. (1977) Labor mediation: An exploratory survey. In David Lewin, Peter Feuille and Thomas Kochan (eds), *Public Sector Labor Relations*, Glen Ridge, NJ: Horton, 253–73.

Kressel, K. and Pruitt, D. G. (eds) (1989) *Mediation Research: The Process and Effectiveness of Third Party Intervention*. San Francisco: Jossey-Bass.

Lewin, D. (1987) Dispute resolution in the nonunion firm: A theoretical and empirical analysis. *Journal of Conflict Resolution*, 31, 465–502.

Lewin, D. and Peterson, R. B. (1988) *The Modern Grievance Procedure in the United States: A Theoretical and Empirical Analysis*. Westport, Conn: Quorum.

Lewis, S. A. and Fry, W. R. (1977) Effects of visual access and orientation on the discovery of integrative bargaining alternatives. *Organizational Behavior and Human Performance*, 20, 75–92.

Lim, R. and Carnevale, P. J. (1990) Contingencies in the mediation of disputes. *Journal of Personality and Social Psychology*, 58, 259–72.

Lovell, H. (1952) The pressure lever in mediation. *Industrial and Labor Relations Review*, 6, 20–33.

McGillicuddy, N. B., Welton, G. L. and Pruitt, D. G. (1987) Third party intervention: A field experiment comparing three different models. *Journal of Personality and Social Psychology*, 53, 104–12.

McLaughlin, M, Carnevale, P. J. and Lim, R. (1991) Professional mediators' judgments of mediation tactics: MDS and clustering analyses. *Journal of Applied Psychology*, 76, 465–72.

Morley, I. and Stephenson, G. (1977) *The Social Psychology of Bargaining*. London: Allen & Unwin.

Notz, W. W. and Starke, F. A. (1978) Final offer versus conventional arbitration as means of conflict management. *Administrative Science Quarterly*, 23, 189–203.

Peters, E. (1952) *Conciliation in Action*. New London, Conn: National Foremen's Institute.

Peters, E. (1955) Strategy and tactics in labor negotiations. New London, Conn: National Foremen's Institute.

Pruitt, D. G. (1981) *Negotiation Behavior*. New York: Academic Press.

Pruitt, D. G. and Lewis, S. A. (1975) Development of integrative solutions in bilateral negotiation. *Journal of Personality and Social Psychology*, 31, 621–33.

Pruitt, D. G. and Rubin, J. Z. (1986) *Social Conflict: Escalation, Stalemate and Settlement*. New York: Random House.

Putnam, L. L. (1989) *Formal negotiations: The productive side of organizational conflict*. Paper presented at the annual meeting of the Academy of Management, Washington, DC, August.

Putnam, L. L. and Poole, M. S. (1987) Conflict and negotiation. In F. M. Jablin, L. L. Putnam, K. H. Roberts and L. W. Porter (eds), *Handbook of Organizational Communication*, Beverly Hills, Calif: Sage, 549–99.

Stephenson, G. M. (1981a) Negotiation and collective bargaining. In P. B. Warr (ed.), *Psychology at work*. Baltimore: Penguin.

Stephenson, G. M. (1981b) Intergroup bargaining and negotiation. In J. C. Turner and H. Giles (eds), *The Social Psychology of Intergroup Behaviour*, Oxford: Blackwell, 168–98.

Thomas, K. W. and Schmidt, W. H. (1976) A survey of managerial interests with respect to conflict. *Academy of Management Journal*, 19, 315–18.

Thompson, L. and Hastie, R. (1990) Social perception in negotiation. *Organizational Behavior and Human Decision Processes*, 47, 138–60.

Ury, W. L., Brett, J. M. and Goldberg, S. B. (1989) *Getting Disputes Resolved: Designing Systems to Cut the Costs of Conflict*. San Francisco: Jossey-Bass.

van de Vliert, E. (1990) Sternberg's styles of handling conflict: A theory-based reanalysis. *International Journal of Conflict Management*, 1, 62–81.

Walton, R. E. (1987) *Managing Conflict: Interpersonal Dialogue and Third-party Roles*. Reading, Mass: Addison-Wesley.

Walton, R. E. and McKersie, R. B. (1965) *A Behavioral Theory of Labor Negotiations: An Analysis of a Social Interaction System*. New York: McGraw-Hill.

Further Reading

Kochan, T. A. and Katz, H. C. (1988) *Collective Bargaining and Industrial Relations*. Homewood, Ill: Irwin. Presents a broad overview of the history and context of collective bargaining with a particularly informative overview of dispute resolution procedures, including mediation and arbitration.

Kressel K. and Pruitt, D. G. (eds) (1989) *Mediation Research: The Process and Effectiveness of Third Party Intervention*. San Francisco: Jossey-Bass. A state of the art collection of articles on mediation in a variety of contexts, including labor-management and organizational disputes. Other articles are on international, community, and divorce mediation. The concluding chapter is a comprehensive summary of research on mediation.

Lax, D. A. and Sebenius, J. K. (1986) *The Manager as Negotiator*. New York: Free Press. A highly readable overview of negotiation processes in organizations, with an emphasis on rational models of decision making.

Walton, R. E. and McKersie, R. B. (1965) *A Behavioral Theory of Labor Negotiations: An Analysis of a Social Interaction System.* New York: McGraw-Hill. The classic work that defined and focused attention on many of the key issues in the study of negotiation, including integrative bargaining. Written more than 25 years ago, it is highly relevant today.

11

Industrial Action

John Kelly and Caroline Kelly

Introduction

Approaches to industrial action

During the twelve-month British miners' strike of 1984–5, involving up to 150,000 workers, there was an intense and bitter struggle between those miners who were in favour of the strike and those who were not. Miners in Nottinghamshire, one of the largest coalfields in the country, mostly rejected the strike call and stayed at work. After eight months on strike, miners in other coalfields began drifting back to work, precipitating an upsurge of picketing and violence as striking miners fought to maintain the strike. After twelve months, most miners were back at work and the strike was called off.

The strike raised in a particularly acute and intense manner the very questions that psychologists have addressed in looking at this area. Why did some miners support the strike but not others? Why did some participate in strike activities, such as picketing, whilst most stayed at home? Why were some willing to stay out on strike until the bitter end whilst others returned? In other words, the strike brought to the fore questions about individual and group differences which psychologists would seem uniquely equipped to analyse. Miners themselves advanced numerous theories and hypotheses to explain the behaviour of their fellow workers. For the miners, as for any workers on strike, these were not just academic or theoretical issues but immensely practical and important questions affecting the whole of their lives, as they struggled to make sense of, and to influence, what was happening around them.

Whilst the strike is the most visible and dramatic form of workers' collective industrial action, it is not the only one. Workers can ban overtime, go slow, work without enthusiasm, work to rule and deploy a range of other sanctions limited only by their own ingenuity and resources. Some writers have suggested that individual actions, such as absenteeism or quitting, may constitute forms of industrial action on the grounds that they are often motivated by the same types of discontent that generate collective industrial action (Edwards and Scullion, 1982). Whilst absenteeism and quitting may be expressions of work-related frustration or dissatisfaction, they may also reflect many other, quite different

246

factors: the decision to start a family or to move house, or a desire for time off work. Moreover, these individual forms of action are normally attempts to escape from a situation rather than measures designed to change it, as is the case with collective action. This chapter will concentrate on collective action by workers. The majority of studies in this area have concentrated on strikes as the most powerful sanction open to workers. We shall do the same, but readers should bear in mind that there are many other sanctions available.[1]

Three main approaches to industrial action have been developed by psychologists and are based on, first, *individual attributes*, such as biography or attitudes (e.g. job satisfaction), second, *individual decision-making* and, third, *social processes*, such as patterns of identification with groups at work.

Individual Attributes

Demographic attributes

In trying to predict attitudinal and behavioural militancy, a number of individual attributes have been used, including age, gender, personality (e.g. locus of control; Klandermans, 1983), occupation, seniority and wage level. As in the field of trade union joining (see chapter 7), the reasoning behind most of these putative associations is often flimsy and no clear body of theory has emerged. A brief examination of one of these variables is sufficient to illustrate the theoretical problems and limitations of this strand of research. On the one hand, it could be argued that young workers might be *less* militant than older workers because they have weaker attachments to firms and can more easily resolve job dissatisfactions through quitting. On the other hand, it could be hypothesized that they might be *more* militant because the absence of financial commitments and family dependants would reduce the costs of industrial action.

The largely empiricist literature on age and militancy has produced conflicting results and to date there has been no serious attempt to reconcile them. Several studies reported that younger workers were *more* militant than older workers, as measured by their approval of strike action (Alutto and Belasco, 1974, in a study of teachers and nurses), by their reported willingness to strike (Schutt, 1982: social workers), by their actual participation in strike action (Cole, 1969: teachers), or by a mixture of attitudinal and behavioural criteria (Shirom, 1977: white collar union officers). On the other hand, several studies found no relationship; these used measures of actual participation in strikes (Brett and Goldberg, 1979: coal miners; Ward, 1973: police officers; Winterton and Winterton, 1989: coal miners), of willingness to participate (Klandermans, 1986b: factory workers), and of attitudes to strikes (Dolan, 1979: union officials; Fosh, 1981: steelworkers). Finally, one study reported age effects for some strike issues but not others (Martin, 1986: municipal manual workers).

One possible interpretation of this contradictory set of results emerges when we focus on exactly which groups of workers were studied. Reports of negative age – militancy relations have come solely from white collar workers, whilst the opposite findings have come mainly from blue collar workers. The comparatively recent unionization of many white collar workers and the transformation of their erstwhile professional associations into militant trade unions have often been associated with marked inter-generational conflict, as a 'young guard' has challenged the older incumbent leadership (e.g. Nicholson et al., 1981). In these settings, therefore, age and militancy are strongly (and negatively) correlated. However, in blue collar settings, trade union organization is often a long established and deeply rooted part of the workplace and has given rise to a much stronger collectivist culture that overrides age differences amongst workers. Hence, in these settings, age has little or no association with attitudinal or behavioural militancy, although it may be associated with the *forms* of militant action in which workers engage (cf. Hartley et al., 1983; Winterton and Winterton, 1989). The same sorts of mixed results and the same type of interpretation could also apply to other demographic and biographical variables such as wage level.

Worker attitudes

Psychologists have studied two sets of worker attitudes as possible precursors of industrial action: attitudes towards work and attitudes towards 'militancy'. The first of these points to job dissatisfaction as the chief precursor of industrial action. Proponents of job redesign, such as Hackman and Lawler, argue that the deprivations and dissatisfactions of modern industrial work generate a range of behaviours of which strike action is one (see Kelly, 1982 for details). They also point to the strike incidence on car assembly lines as proof that monotonous and repetitive work, devoid of challenge or meaning, results in industrial action, particularly wildcat strikes in which workers storm out of the factory. The apparently awkward fact that these strikes often centre on wage demands, rather than job content, is explained by saying that workers displace their job-related grievances into wage demands because these are more 'legitimate' and more readily understood within traditional systems of collective bargaining (Kornhauser, 1954; Gouldner, 1954). There is little evidence on the strike-proneness of workers following job redesign, although the authors of one study boasted that members of a newly designed 'autonomous work group' were the only car workers to cross the picket line during a plant wide strike (Cummings and Srivastva, 1977, p. 208).

The job dissatisfaction hypothesis sounds plausible to many people: assembly line work *is* boring, and car assembly workers are fairly strike prone. In fact, a deeper examination of the evidence reveals a far more complicated picture. Car companies vary considerably in their strike rates, with BL and Ford (UK) being more strike prone than Vauxhall and Chrysler (Marsden et al., 1985, pp. 132ff.). Traditionally in the UK the most strike prone groups of manual workers have not been semi-skilled assembly line workers in vehicles and electrical engineering but workers enjoying a high degree of skill and/or job autonomy, such as coal miners, construction workers, dockers and printers (Smith et al., 1978). Moreover, the post-war period witnessed a significant increase in strike activity amongst skilled white collar workers, such as teachers, nurses, civil servants and social workers

(Durcan et al., 1983). In any case, workers who experience dissatisfaction with their job have a series of options – to raise an individual grievance, to retrain, to press for promotion, to work harder, to quit – of which collective industrial action is but one. Not surprisingly, therefore, correlations between overall job dissatisfaction and militancy are positive but small (Flanagan et al., 1974; Scott et al., 1963). Dissatisfaction *per se* is not sufficient to induce collective action. Indeed, there may be circumstances where dissatisfaction is not necessary for collective action, such as sympathy strikes.

Attitudes to industrial action itself have been used in a number of studies to try to explain whether or not workers actually will participate. The reasoning goes that dissatisfied workers will take part only if they believe that strikes and other sanctions are legitimate forms of action. Two studies have confirmed this prediction (Brett and Goldberg, 1979; Schutt, 1982), but interestingly two others showed no relationship between *current* 'attitudinal militancy' and *past* militant behaviour (Martin, 1986; Shirom, 1977). One explanation for these mixed results may be that positive attitudes to militancy will translate into behaviour only under specific conditions, such as appropriate union organization and leadership (Cole, 1969). In the presence of such conditions, attitude–behaviour correlations should be good, but in their absence they are likely to be poor.

In fact, the weak relationship often found between attitudes and actual behaviour (frequently in the region of 0.2 to 0.3, expressed as a correlation coefficient) has been the subject of considerable social psychological debate (see Eiser, 1986). The most successful attempts to reduce the discrepancy between attitudes and behaviour have focused on the level of specificity involved in measurement and have argued that one cannot expect an attitude measured at a very *general* level (e.g. attitudes towards industrial action in general) to predict a *specific* behaviour (e.g. the decision to participate oneself in a particular form of action at a particular time and place) (see Ajzen and Fishbein, 1980). Instead, a general measure indicates a predisposition to behave in a particular way which may or may not be realized in a given situation.

Individual Decision-making

Two models predominate in this category of strike theory: the value expectancy approach of Klandermans (1983, 1984, 1986a,b) and the social cognitive approach of Waddington (1986, 1987, 1989).

Klandermans' value expectancy model

It is worth devoting considerable space to Klandermans because his model represents the most rigorous and comprehensive attempt by any psychologist to sharpen our understanding of industrial action. Klandermans' model has two components, a theory of consensus mobilization and a theory of action mobilization (see figure 11.1).

Consensus mobilization is the process by which a union familiarizes its members with the objectives of intended action and tries to win their support for those objectives. This process is necessary but not sufficient for action to occur because rational workers will think not only about the desirability of a given objective but also about the costs and benefits of achieving it. Hence the need for *action mobilization*, in which the union tries to persuade its members that the benefits of action will outweigh the costs and that they should participate. Klandermans describes three motives for participating in action: goal motives, social motives

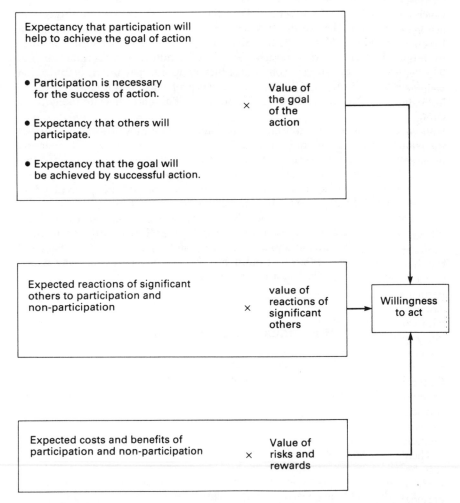

Figure 11.1 Klandermans' theory of action mobilization

and reward motives. In each case workers are said to estimate the respective costs and benefits and to place a value on them. Under the heading of *goal motives*, Klandermans argues that workers must believe the following in order for participation to ensue: that a high level of worker participation is necessary for the success of the proposed action; that other workers will participate (in other words, any costs of participation will be spread over a large number of workers); and that the action will lead to the achievement of their objective. These *expectations*, multiplied by the value of the intended goal, generate the worker's goal motive (and hence the term value expectancy). Likewise, the expected reactions of 'significant others', multiplied by the value assigned to those reactions, determine the strength of the worker's social motive. Significant others could be family, friends, workmates or bosses: the model merely stipulates that they are psychologically significant for the worker in connection with his/her industrial action decision-making. Finally, the worker's assessment of the personal costs and benefits of action (e.g. lost wages, victimization, time at home with a family), multiplied by their value, determines the strength of the worker's reward motive. The worker's willingness to act is a 'weighted sum' of these three motives, weighted because the three motives can take different weights for different individuals and can also compensate for one another. One worker may have strong goal motives and weak social and reward motives, whilst another may have strong social motives but weak goal and reward motives. Taken as a whole, the model is both clear and predictive and it allows for individual differences. Let us now look at the evidence in support before considering some problems.

Evidence on value expectancy and strikes

Klandermans (1984, 1986b) reported on three studies of Dutch trade union campaigns in the late 1970s over work reorganization, manning agreements, and the shorter working week, although most of the data available in English relates to the last of these three. He found that inter-plant variations in willingness to participate in strikes were closely correlated with differences in all three motives. Those who were willing to participate were more optimistic about the numbers who would take part, about the positive reactions of fellow workers, about the likely personal costs and about the probability of the action achieving its objective. Incidentally, Klandermans uncovered an interesting paradox about moderate and militant industrial action (for instance, overtime bans vs. strikes). Conventional wisdom has it that mobilization for militant action is harder than for moderate action. However, Klandermans found that militant action, whilst it was seen as more costly, was seen as more effective and so, paradoxically, it may sometimes be easier to mobilize workers behind a more effective (if costly) militant tactic than behind a less costly but less effective moderate action.

There are several case studies which have shown that some workers do make cost–benefit calculations about industrial action. In Batstone et al.'s (1978) study of vehicle assembly plants, clerical staff were concerned about the personal costs of proposed strike action. White collar workers involved in the occupation of a Scottish tractor plant eventually withdrew when faced with the cost of losing their entitlement to redundancy pay (Woolfson and Foster, 1988). Finally, there is questionnaire evidence from a number of studies underlining the importance of the value expectancy variables. Brett and Goldberg (1979) found a positive correlation between miners' perceptions of the effectiveness of strikes (goal motives) and the incidence of pit level strike activity. Cole (1969) found that strike participation was higher among New York school teachers with pro-strike as compared with anti-strike friends, and that having pro-strike friends led teachers to overcome their fear of the personal costs of strike participation, a finding confirmed by Martin (1986) amongst US municipal employees.

Evaluating the value-expectancy approach

Consensus mobilization may be sufficient A series of well known and widely cited case studies of strikes have provided strong evidence that consensus mobilization alone may be sufficient to generate industrial action. Batstone et al. (1978) reported hardly any discussion amongst manual workers in a vehicle assembly plant about the costs and benefits of strike action or the probability of success. They argued principally about the nature of their bargaining demands, and whether they were right to reject management's proposed new pay system. Lane and Roberts (1971) reported that many manual workers in Pilkingtons walked out because they were incensed at management's refusal to correct pay anomalies. Turnbull et al. (1991) reported that, during a 1989 meeting of port shop stewards to discuss unofficial industrial action, one Liverpool docker declared that if he did *not* strike to protect jobs, he would feel ashamed: 'I wouldn't be able to live with myself, I wouldn't be able to look my kids in the face' (Field notes).

In a study by Beynon (1984), a similar moral defence of strike action was given by the leader of Ford's Swansea car workers on hearing that workers elsewhere had voted against strike action: 'He saw it as a question of principle. The Swansea plant may be out on its own but there was no question in his mind who had behaved correctly. The lads in the other Ford plants . . . had taken a wrong decision' (Beynon, 1984, p. 215; see also Fantasia, 1988; Gouldner, 1954; Woolfson and Foster, 1988).

In all of these cases it appeared, contrary to Klandermans' model, that consensus mobilization *was* sufficient to persuade workers to take strike action, and that action mobilization was superfluous. Whilst some of these cases involved very short stoppages, which arguably entailed too few costs even to think about, others were widely anticipated to be long, set-piece confrontations. Given the obvious costs of such action (e.g. lost wages), why did workers apparently not consider these costs? We say 'apparently' because the data in these case studies may be incomplete. It is possible, for instance, that discussion at large meetings focused on the legitimacy of workers' demands and that discussions about costs and benefits took place in private or informal meetings. It is also possible that debate at 'public' meetings is dominated by activists whose strike participation is less influenced by cost–benefit calculations than that of the rank-and-file union members. The strategic nature of strike action means that we must always be cautious in relying on public statements made by either side during a strike.

Workers may be insensitive to the costs but sensitive to the benefits of action   Case studies of long strikes suggest that once consensus mobilization has succeeded, and workers believe in their demands, they become insensitive to personal costs and simply accept that strike action involves sacrifices. As one worker said during a mass meeting of Scottish strikers, 'I'm here as long as it takes – suppose it be another nine weeks or another nine months, I'll still be here' (Woolfson and Foster, 1988, p. 164; and cf. Olson, 1965). This is not to say that workers are unconcerned about costs: those who voted for strike action were anxious to learn about tax rebates, social security payments, union strike pay and other sources of income (Batstone et al., 1978; Hartley et al., 1983; Winterton and Winterton, 1989). But the costs of strike action appeared to be accepted as simply inevitable and therefore did not enter into workers' calculations.

It is above all in these long strikes, lasting for months or even years, that value expectancy theory and its assumption of individual rationality is tested to the limit. During the twelve-month British miners' strike of 1984–5, many strikers suffered acute financial hardship (Winterton and Winterton, 1989; also Hartley et al., 1983). They were subject to sustained criticism in the media and to incessant propaganda about the impossibility of victory. Hundreds were sacked for strike activities, thousands were arrested and convicted, and scores went to jail (Winterton and Winterton, 1989). Why did miners bear these costs for so long and remain on strike? Value expectancy theory could attempt to explain their behaviour by looking at fresh sources of income to alleviate hardship, or by noting the social support from sections of the trade union movement. But these attempts hardly begin to cope with the scale of costs and suffering that miners endured.

The benefits of strike action are a different matter. Batstone et al. (1978) reported many discussions amongst workers about whether management would concede, and about how vulnerable they were to strike action. Shop stewards, in particular, frequently discussed the company's balance sheet, the state of the order books, and the level of stocks in trying to reach an assessment of the impact of strike action.

Those who objected to strike action, or defected from strikes once they were under way, displayed a different pattern of cognitions, either showing heightened sensitivity to costs, as in the 1984–5 miners' strike (Winterton and Winterton, 1989), or combining cost and benefit calculations, as with the white collar workers at Caterpillar who doubted whether the occupation would succeed and were not prepared to risk losing their large redundancy entitlements (Woolfson and Foster, 1988).

Rationality or rationalization?   The studies described by Klandermans showed impressive correlations between cost–benefit calculations and willingness to participate in strike action, but what is the direction of causation? Klandermans assumes that workers make rational calculations *before* deciding to act but it would be just as plausible, and equally consistent with his data, to suggest that workers first decide to act and *then* proceed to rationalize their decision with *post hoc* justifications. There is indeed evidence of such rationalization from a number of cases. For example, a detailed analysis of strike committee decision-making during the 1980 steel strike showed that the 'rational' sequence of operations was often reversed. Instead of setting goals and then proceeding to list, evaluate and choose between different courses of action, strikers would often decide on actions and *then* justify them by retrospectively criticizing the other options (Hartley et al., 1983, chs 8,11; see also Lane and Roberts, 1971; Turnbull et al., 1991). The important theoretical point is that workers' strike calculations may be rationalizations which are designed to justify their decision, just as much as rational reflections which precede their decision.

Waddington's Social – Cognitive Approach

Waddington's (1987) model sets out to explain both the decision to go on strike and the decision to remain on strike. He argues that strike action requires two preconditions: (a) that a group of workers has a sufficiently strong grievance to make them feel that industrial action is justified; and (b) that they believe that such action is likely to be successful (cf. Klandermans' ideas of consensus mobilization and action mobilization). In the Ansell's brewery dispute, described by Waddington, the strike began following management's suspension of workers for refusing to accept new working practices and ended six months later when the workers' union called it off.

The model proposes that, in thinking about strike action, workers try to infer the meaning and significance of the other side's behaviour by 'recognising their acts as part of a "plan" to achieve a specific goal or objective' (Waddington, 1987, p. 16). Having reached an understanding of management's 'plan', they will then create a 'plan' of their own involving assumptions about their own resources, their union leaders and the actions of other workers. The 1984–5 miners' strike, for instance, was triggered by the closure of a colliery at Cortonwood in South Yorkshire, an action presented by management as merely another component in the well-established policy of old pit closures. Union leaders, however, saw the action as a deliberate provocation, part of a well worked out management 'plan' to test the union's resolve and to confront them in a major strike. *Not* to have struck would therefore have signalled union weakness (Adeney and Lloyd, 1986).

In trying to understand management's *plan*, workers look around for another, similar situation to help them to make sense of management's actions and to predict their likely consequences. In other words, they look for what Waddington calls a *cognitive script*: 'an interlocking series of "event chains" (scenes or vignettes) defining how well-known situations are likely to proceed' (Waddington, 1987, p. 17).

In historical studies, for example, researchers often try to understand contemporary revolutions by comparing them with earlier events, such as the

French or Russian Revolutions: in other words, they use the earlier examples as 'scripts' to try to understand the present. What determines which of the many situations will be used by workers as a 'script' to shape their behaviour? According to Waddington, the use of a particular script is a function of three properties: its *availability*, its *visibility*, and its *representativeness* (or similarity to one's own situation) (see Eiser and van der Pligt, 1988, ch. 4 for more detail). In addition, the use of particular scripts is influenced by the *social context* of industrial relations in a given workplace; that is, by the level of intergroup (union–management) trust, the values of the union membership and the sources of arguments about different scripts (e.g. shop stewards, union officials).

The 'script' that was to dominate the thinking of the Ansell's strikers was the 'BL script'. BL (British Leyland as it was then known) was a state-owned car manufacturing firm with a large plant just a few miles from the Ansell's brewery. In 1978 the company embarked on a widespread programme of factory closures, redundancies and sweeping changes in working practices. Union opposition was countered by dismissal of the chief shop steward and a downgrading of the resources and facilities available to union officers.

When Ansell's managers announced new working practices in January 1981, just two years after the BL events, and responded to worker resistance with suspensions, workers perceived management's plan as an enactment of the 'BL script', as an attack on the union and its organization, and they responded accordingly. The 'BL script' was readily available and visible – one of the main BL plants was nearby; it was representative in so far as both companies were large manufacturing concerns with a history of strong unions and industrial conflict. Acceptance of the BL script by Ansell's workers was also facilitated by the social context of workplace industrial relations: a recent history of disputes and low trust relations was conducive to workers thinking the worst of management's motives.

If reference to the 'BL script' explains the readiness of workers to strike in the first place, how can we explain the persistence of strike action in the face of threats of dismissal and plant closure, and the formal announcement of closure just one month into the strike? The workers' interpretation of these events was mediated through other available and visible scripts. Several times in the past, management had declared that it would dismiss strikers and shut down breweries but on each occasion stiff resistance by workers had shown these to be idle threats. In any case, the company had only recently invested £2 million in the West Midlands brewery and it was seen as inconceivable that they would simply write this off. Essentially, strikers assumed that the past was a reliable guide to the present and immediate future, in much the same way as miners' leader Arthur Scargill may have assumed that the strike tactics that brought victory in 1972 and 1974 could be successfully repeated in 1984–5 (Adeney and Lloyd, 1986).

However, the consequence of using scripts in this way can be a failure to realize how much the present situation differs from the past and to what degree opponents have learned from previous mistakes and changed their behaviour. Information discrepant with the dominant script was ignored, explained away or downplayed, with disastrous consequences: the Ansell's brewery did close and the workers went down to a crushing defeat.

Evaluating the social–cognitive approach

Analytically it is worth separating Waddington's arguments into two components, the general and the particular, because the former seems to possess more validity than the latter. His general argument is that workers' decision-making and information processing before and during strikes is subject to cognitive distortions.

Evidence from other disputes supports this proposition. Hartley et al. (1983) found a series of mechanisms brought into play during the three-month British Steel strike in 1980. Both the official strike newsletter and local strike leaders accentuated the positive, highlighting facts and events consistent with the idea that the strike was having a major effect and was heading towards victory. Strike activists displayed a classical pattern of attribution in explaining the successes and failures of their strike tactics. They claimed the credit for actions which promoted the strike's objectives, such as a successful picket at a steel depot, but blamed others, such as union leaders, parochial union members and the police, for actions which failed. This pattern of attribution was highly functional in promoting the view that success lay within the strikers' own hands. Indeed, in one sense all of these social and cognitive processes have a functional as well as a dysfunctional side in so far as they help to maintain the morale, commitment and participation of strikers and to protect them from hostile communications.

However, Waddington's particular argument is that distortion happens because workers rely on cognitive scripts. To prove this proposition, Waddington chose two settings (the Ansell's brewery dispute and the 1984–5 miners' strike) where powerful scripts were available. What is supposed to happen, however, if workers fail to locate any relevant scripts or have no personal experience of strike action on which to draw? In the vast majority of strikes which are documented in the literature, there is simply no evidence that strikers used cognitive scripts as described by Waddington. Although the idea of scripts may be useful in particular cases, its range of applicability is likely to be rather limited.

Social Processes

All of the approaches which have been discussed so far locate the origins of industrial conflict in the psychology of the individual worker. Thus, these 'individual' explanations focus on the demographic characteristics and attitudes of potential strikers or non-strikers and on the cognitive processes by which discontent at the workplace may be translated into action. These approaches not only underplay the wider social processes affecting industrial conflict but also, by focusing exclusively on workers, fail to consider industrial conflict as an instance of *intergroup relations*. In other words, it is the relationship *between* management and workers which underlies strike action and it is the social psychology of this relationship, rather than of one of the parties involved, which should be the focus of attempts to understand conflict and co-operation in the workplace. The approaches to be considered in this section have in common the attempt to analyse the factors impinging on relations between groups, three of which have been at the forefront of social psychological theorizing on intergroup relations: the degree of contact between the members of different groups; members' feelings of identification with their respective groups; and perceptions of conflicting goals.

The role of contact

Interest in the role of contact between the members of different social groups has a long and rather chequered history in social psychology (see Hewstone and Brown, 1986a; Miller and Brewer, 1984). At its simplest, the contact hypothesis suggests that increasing the amount of contact between the members of different groups has a positive effect on the climate of intergroup relations. Contact provides an opportunity for the discovery of common beliefs and opinions which might lead to the development of friendship across group boundaries and the erosion of negative stereotypes.

The most famous application of these ideas in an industrial sphere is the work of Kerr and Siegel (1954), who argued that strike-proneness in certain industries, such as mining and dock work, results from the social location of the workforce as an 'isolated mass' which, lacking any informal contact with management, develops its own distinctive norms and sub-culture. The role attributed to contact in this situation not only is intuitively appealing but also seems to provide a possible explanation for the well established size effect on strike-proneness; namely, that large organizations appear to be more strike-prone than small organizations, possibly because there is less informal contact between managers and workers in large organizations (see Allen, 1986 for further discussion). Underlying this idea are two assumptions: (a) that intergroup conflict has its origins in ignorance (see Stephan and Stephan, 1984) and so becoming more knowledgeable about the other group (through contact) will reduce the likelihood of overt conflict; and (b) that friendly interpersonal relations generated through contact will spill over to improve intergroup relations.

The first assumption has been questioned in research by Allen and Stephenson (1983, 1985), who examined patterns of conflict and co-operation in organizations of differing size. Managers and workers were asked to respond to a number of questionnaire items concerning industrial relations and results showed significant differences of opinion between them. In addition, each respondent was asked to indicate the likely response of a typical member of the other group for each item. In analysis, these attributed responses could take three forms: (a) they could be a perfectly accurate reflection of the other group's actual responses; (b) they could be inaccurate in a traditional stereotyped direction, i.e. 'group differentiation' (e.g. workers seeing managers as more anti-union than they really are); or (c) they could be inaccurate in the reverse direction, i.e. 'group assimilation' (e.g. workers seeing managers as less anti-union than they really are). Findings showed that large companies tended to be characterized by 'group differentiation' whilst small companies tended to be characterized by 'group assimilation'. Furthermore, these attitudinal patterns were related to various indices of industrial conflict, such that companies showing the greatest 'group differentiation' also showed the highest levels of conflict. This research suggests that the industrial peace which seems more prevalent in small companies may result not from more accurate knowledge of the other side but from the misperception of the other side as being closer in outlook than they really are. Industrial peace of this sort may prove rather fragile if a situation arises in which the opinions of either side are put to the test (e.g. Gouldner, 1954).

With regard to the second assumption, research suggests that even if increased contact between workers and managers does promote friendly interpersonal relations, there is a problem with the generalization of this positive effect to situations and to people beyond the immediate contact situation. In a recent discussion of this issue, Hewstone and Brown (1986b) argue that there is an important distinction between people acting as *individuals* compared with people acting as the *representatives of social groups*. Several accounts of bargaining and negotiations have illustrated the way in which friendly interpersonal relations between an individual manager and an individual worker are subtly transformed when they meet as representatives of their social groups around the bargaining table (Hyman, 1972; Stephenson, 1981). Thus, promoting informal contact between workers and managers may lead to interpersonal liking but may not necessarily 'spill over' to affect the underlying climate of intergroup relations.

The role of social identity

The idea that people sometimes act as representatives of their social groups underlies the second major social psychological approach to intergroup relations. According to this approach, an individual's sense of identity comprises both personal identity (e.g. personality) and social identity (e.g. membership of a political group or trade union). The value attached to any particular social identity is determined by comparisons between an individual's own group and other groups in his/her environment. At certain times, a particular social identity becomes highly salient, with the result that the individual tries to promote group interests (rather than personal interests). It is argued that the successful promotion of group interests will provide the individual with a positive social identity (as a member of a successful group) and thereby boost self-esteem (see Hogg and Abrams, 1988 for a detailed account of social identity theory).

There are two ways in which social identity theory can be used to illuminate strike processes. The first concerns the effects of social identification on workers' propensity to become involved in conflict. For example, in a study of relations between different workgroups in an aircraft factory, Brown (1978) asked shop stewards to imagine a situation in which management announced a 10 per cent redundancy programme across the whole factory. This represented a clear threat which could best be dealt with by a programme of inter-union industrial action across the different workgroups. However, only one-fifth of respondents reacted by suggesting such a joint strategy against management. The majority were more concerned with defending the interests of their own particular department over and above those of other departments. It was concluded that, 'The atmosphere of intense rivalry between some of the departments rendered the possibility of collaborative action difficult' (Brown, 1988, p. 210). In this way, the theory provides some insight into the problem of sectionalism and the *lack* of industrial action in some situations when workers are threatened by managerial decisions. According to the social identity perspective, one route to transforming separate grievances into joint action involves the promotion of a *superordinate identity* as 'a worker at company X' as opposed to 'a member of department Y' (e.g. electrician, toolmaker or production worker).

The second application of social identity theory concerns the ways in which people's identities are transformed in the course of strike action. Once the salience of identity (as a worker or as a manager) is enhanced by industrial action, one might predict both a greater degree of conformity to group norms and a polarization of attitudes; in other words, the attitudes of workers and managers will move further apart or become 'hardened'. Social psychological research has established a positive relationship between the salience of group identity and the expression of more extreme, or polarized, attitudes concerning group-relevant issues (e.g. Wetherell, 1987; but see Reid and Sumiga, 1984). In addition, the individual will tend to see members of both parties in more stereotypical terms ('them' and 'us') when social identity is salient (e.g. Kelly, 1989; Wilder, 1984). These processes map directly on to the research discussed earlier by Allen and Stephenson (1983, 1985) which showed that, in large companies, where one might expect social identity to be more salient than in small companies, the pattern of attitudes attributed to the other side took the form of 'group differentiation' or stereotyping. Indeed, by using a procedural variation to enhance the salience of group identity, Allen and Stephenson (1983) found that attitudes attributed to the other side shifted in the direction of greater stereotyping.

Furthermore, it may be that during the course of a strike identifications with broader social groups become salient. In the miners' strike, several activists defended their participation by invoking a broader social identification with the working class: 'It's a matter of fighting for your industry, fighting for the community, fighting for a *future*' (North Yorkshire miner, 1984); 'Everybody now – every working person in this country – is looking at us and saying, "If these miners go down, it's God help the rest of us" ' (South Yorkshire miner, 1984) (both cited in Waddington, 1989).

Workers occupying the Caterpillar factory in Scotland, in an effort to save jobs, defended the continuation of their costly action by claiming that they were acting in the interests of the unemployed (Woolfson and Foster, 1988; see also Fantasia, 1988). The groups in these cases – miners and engineers – represented sections of the working class which have long traditions of union organization, collective action and solidarity. In other words, strikes are not only instrumental actions designed to achieve particular ends but also expressions of particular social identities.

Finally, a number of studies have been conducted to investigate relations between different workgroups (e.g. Brown and Williams, 1984; Brown et al.,

1986; Oaker and Brown, 1986). Exploring the impact of group identification on these relations, Brown and Williams (1984) argue that it is necessary to examine the ideological *meaning* of identification with different groups at work. In their own study, they suggest that in certain groups (e.g. those with little or no history of trade unionism and a high degree of contact with management) a strong sense of identification with the departmental group was synonymous with a sense of company loyalty which, in turn, did not encourage clear differentiations between company sub-groups. Moreover, each of the different workgroups seemed also to be characterized by a distinct internal structure and ethos, reflecting varying degrees of individualism or collectivism. It seems likely that such differences will have important implications for intergroup behaviour and therefore that studies focusing on the impact of group identity (as worker or manager) should examine not only the *strength* but also the *meaning* of that identity to the individual.

The role of conflicting goals

In the study conducted by Brown et al. (1986), a more powerful predictor of antagonism between workgroups than either the strength of own-group identification or the amount of intergroup contact was the perception of conflicting goals. In other words, the expression of intergroup conflict was at its strongest amongst individuals who felt that the goals of their own group (the ingroup) were at odds with the goals of the other group (the outgroup); that is, the two groups were seen as 'on opposite sides' rather than 'pulling together'. An emphasis on material goal relations underlies the third major social psychological approach to intergroup conflict, namely, realistic conflict theory (see Sherif, 1966). This theory was developed from a number of ingenious field studies in which groups of schoolchildren in summer camps interacted in the pursuit of either conflicting (win–lose) goals or superordinate goals. A superordinate goal is one which both groups wish to attain but which neither group can attain on its own. Analysis of the interactions showed a dramatic deterioration in the climate of intergroup relations when the groups were pitted against each other in competition, a climate that was reversed with the introduction of superordinate goals.

The impact of conflicting and superordinate goals has been replicated in occupational settings (e.g. Blake et al., 1964) and recent theoretical developments have suggested that, in addition to the *existence* of superordinate goals *per se*, attention should be given to the *means* by which such goals are pursued by the groups involved. For example, it seems to be important that each of the interacting groups should be able to retain something of its distinct identity in pursuit of the superordinate goal (e.g. Brown and Wade, 1987). In the context of the 1980 steel strike in the UK, Hartley et al. (1983) described how inter-union co-operation was facilitated by a division of labour on the strike committee, so that each union had a distinctive contribution to make.

Social psychological research which has been conducted within the framework of realistic conflict theory has also paid particular attention to the effect of intergroup conflict on the dynamics within each of the groups concerned. Studies have shown that competition *between groups* causes an increase in group cohesiveness *within groups*, especially in the case of a group which feels that it is in a strong bargaining position (Rabbie et al., 1974). A study of American car workers by Stagner and Eflal (1982) examined a number of changes within a group of strikers at Ford plants (compared with non-strikers at General Motors and Chrysler plants). The strikers showed more militancy towards their employers, higher evaluation of their union leadership, greater participation in the union and a slight increase in group cohesiveness. Although there is no evidence relating to intragroup structure and process in the management side at times of industrial conflict, similar changes would be expected to occur amongst this group as well.

The main problem with realistic conflict theory as an approach to industrial conflict is that of predicting the circumstances under which a particular goal will or will not be perceived as superordinate. For example, a number of managerial initiatives, subsumed under the title of 'new industrial relations' and involving techniques such as quality circles, profit-sharing and share ownership, could be seen as promoting the superordinate goal of company profitability (see Kelly and Kelly, 1991). However, whether or not workers *perceive* profitability as a superordinate goal will depend on a number of factors, the most important of which may concern the strength and meaning of workers' sense of social identity.

Thus, the theories of realistic conflict and social identity may be seen as complementary rather than as alternatives. An individual's identification with various groups (e.g. workgroups, unions) will affect his or her perception of intergroup goal relations, as conflicting or superordinate. In situations in which managers and workers believe that they are 'on opposite sides', the two groups may become locked in conflict in which social identities as 'them' and 'us' are reinforced. The 1984–5 miners' strike with which we began this chapter provides an example of just such a battle.

An Integrative Model

In this chapter, a number of different theoretical approaches to industrial action have been discussed. They were classified into three types: individual attributes, individual decision-making, and social processes. Theories from the last two categories have proved most useful in illuminating the social psychological processes underlying industrial conflict, though the emphasis in the two categories is rather different.

Theories of individual decision-making put forward a model of the striker (or non-striker) as a rational processor of information, weighing up the costs and benefits of various forms of action. Klandermans' value expectancy approach is the best example of this type of theory. Waddington's 'cognitive scripts' approach incorporates certain elements of rational choice, whilst also pointing to the biases which creep into information processing as scripts are drawn upon by the individuals concerned in order to make sense of their own situation. Underlying both theories is an image of the worker acting as an individual – calculating costs and benefits, or drawing on cognitive scripts – rather than as a member of a particular social group. By contrast, the importance of group membership and the social identity that it provides characterizes the social process approaches to industrial action. According to these accounts, the roots of intergroup conflict are to be found primarily in the relationship between management and the workforce and, in particular, in identification with these respective groups and in perceptions of material intergroup conflict. Thus, the norms of behaviour associated with important groups may override any individual cost–benefit calculations.

Faced with a number of models stressing calculative and non-calculative elements in strike decision-making, it is tempting to conclude that there is probably some truth in all of them. Indeed, one solution might be to incorporate into a model of information processing (such as that of Klandermans) factors such as social identity and perceived goal conflict. Thus, for example, the perceived costs of taking strike action could be weighted according to the strength of the striker's identification with the union. The result of such an exercise, however, would be an unwieldy and descriptive model, accumulating *post hoc* elements in an attempt to explain a particular individual's decision to strike or not to strike. The theoretical power of the model would be lost in the search for specific predictors of behaviour.

A more fruitful way forward is to advance hypotheses about the conditions that are conducive to different modes of individual decision-making. In the light of earlier discussion, we can suggest a number of hypotheses based on the importance of two basic dimensions, the first *psychological* and the second *situational*.

Personal vs. social identity   Workers are more likely to engage in cost–benefit calculations where personal rather than social identity is salient. On the other hand, if workers have a strong sense of social identity (as a worker, union member, or member of the working class), then cost–benefit calculations will be less important than group norms. Of course, the *outcome* of the decision will be very different depending on the *meaning* of that social identity. For example, strike action may serve an expressive function for workers with a clear perception of workers and managers as being 'on opposite sides'. In other cases, e.g. for some health service workers such as nurses, a strong sense of group identification may discourage strike action.

Novelty vs. familiarity   Workers are more likely to engage in cost–benefit calculations if they are in a novel situation; for instance, if they are new to industrial action (e.g. some types of white collar workers), if they are promoting a new bargaining issue (e.g. redundancy rather than pay or hours) or if they are using new methods of decision-making (e.g. secret ballots rather than mass meetings). The reasoning is that new situations generate uncertainty and that, faced with uncertainty, people are more likely to refer to sources of relevant information and weigh up the pros and cons more carefully.

Using these dimensions, it is possible to go further and to locate the different theoretical perspectives in a 2 × 2 framework, as shown in figure 11.2. Cell (a) refers to a situation in which workers are most likely to engage in individual cost–benefit calculations. The situation is new and workers are conscious of their

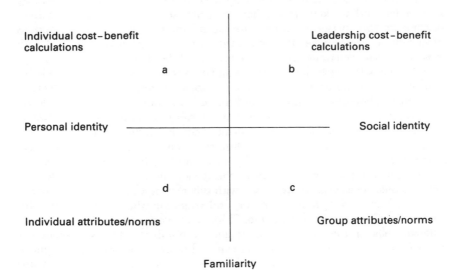

Figure 11.2 A contingency model of psychological and situational determinants of strike action.

personal identities and personal interests. The information processing approach embodied in Klandermans' value expectancy model predominates in this cell. Television clerical workers contemplating strike action for the first time (as in the 1989 BBC dispute) would be a good example.

Cell (b) refers to a situation which is again characterized by novelty but in which workers have a strong sense of social identity. In this situation cost–benefit calculations may still be important but workers, because of their strong sense of group identification, turn to the leaders of their groups for information and decisions. Thus, this cell is characterized by a reliance on people such as trade union leaders for cost–benefit calculations. Because of the high degree of trust in group leaders, workers in this cell may also be susceptible to 'cognitive scripts' which are suggested to them by leaders as appropriate comparison points for understanding their own novel position. Unionized workers facing redundancy or factory closure after many years of secure employment would be a good example. Steelworkers who were called out in 1980, in the first national UK steel strike since 1926, would be an equally good example (Hartley et al., 1983).

Cell (c) refers to a situation in which workers have a strong sense of social identity but the circumstances are familiar to them. In this cell, workers are least likely to engage in individual cost–benefit calculations. Instead, there will be a reliance on prevailing group norms and on perceptions of intergroup goal relations as conflicting or interdependent. Social process theories, such as social identity theory and realistic conflict theory, are most useful in this cell. Print workers at Stockport who struck to defend the closed shop in 1986 and dockers who struck in 1989 to protect jobs and conditions would be good examples.

Cell (d) refers to a situation in which the circumstances of industrial relations are familiar and workers do not have a strong sense of group identification. Because workers' personal identities are salient, the tendency to strike or not to strike will be largely dependent on a variety of individual attributes. Thus, the most important determinants of strike action will be demographic factors (e.g. age), attitudes (e.g. job dissatisfaction) and habits or personality (e.g. locus of control). One would expect the greatest variability of response in this cell, since individual differences will strongly determine behaviour. The 1989 dispute by the Association of University Teachers (AUT) over pay in universities provides a good example of a familiar situation (financial cuts in education) and a workforce with weak union attachment and little history of collective action. The result was action which was strictly adhered to by some and largely ignored by others.

It is important to stress that this contingency model does not imply that different cells are associated *exclusively* with different modes of decision-making. It merely provides a framework for understanding the factors which will predominate in any particular situation. Moreover, workers may move across the different cells of the model as social and economic conditions change. For example, in time of recession (when labour and product markets are changing), workers will move up the situational dimension as conditions change from familiarity to novelty, but whether they move into cell (a) or cell (b) will depend on the strength of social, as opposed to personal, identity. Furthermore, workers may move from one cell to another during the course of a strike as continuing intergroup conflict heightens the salience of social identity. On the other hand, it is possible that a prolonged strike may gradually weaken workers' social identity, which is centred on the union, with the result that individual calculations and attributes gradually become more important in their decision-making. This process was observed among many strikers during the twelve-month British miners' strike of 1984–5.

The contingency model can also be used to map debates within public policy on trade unions. Government legislation compelling unions to adopt secret ballots (preferably postal ballots) before official industrial action can be seen as a way of enhancing personal identity (and therefore individual processes and attributes) at the expense of social identity.

Although much of the argument in this concluding section has been speculative and remains to be tested, we believe that many of our propositions are at least highly plausible in the light of existing evidence and that the attempt to locate different modes of decision-making in different contexts provides a way of moving beyond debates about individual versus social approaches to industrial action.

Notes

1 The social psychology literature has also concentrated on explaining behaviour and attitudes and has neither sought to develop nor assumed any particular theory concerning the respective interests of workers and employers that give rise to conflict

in the first place. A concentration by academics on industrial action can sometimes give the impression that industrial peace is both normal and desirable and therefore does not require any explanation (cf. Hartley, 1984 for criticism of this view). Although this chapter does not explicitly address the issue of industrial peace, we do not assume that peace is either normal or always desirable and that conflict is a deviant form of behaviour.

References

Adeney, M. and Lloyd, J. (1986) *The Miners' Strike 1984–85: Loss without Limit*. London: Routledge & Kegan Paul.

Ajzen, I. and Fishbein, M. (1980) *Understanding Attitudes and Predicting Social Behaviour*, Englewood Cliffs, NJ: Prentice-Hall.

Allen, P. T. (1986) Contact and conflict in industry. In M. Hewstone and R. Brown (eds), *Contact and Conflict in Intergroup Encounters*, Oxford: Blackwell, 137–52.

Allen, P. T. and Stephenson, G. M. (1983) Inter-group understanding and size of organizations. *British Journal of Industrial Relations*, 21, 3, 312–29.

Allen, P. T. and Stephenson, G. M. (1985) The relationship of inter-group understanding and inter-party friction in industry. *British Journal of Industrial Relations*, 23, 2, 203–13.

Alutto, J. A. and Belasco, J. A. (1974) Determinants of attitudinal militancy among nurses and teachers. *Industrial and Labor Relations Review*, 27, 2, 216–27.

Batstone, E., Boraston, I. and Frenkel, S. (1978) *The Social Organization of Strikes*. Oxford: Blackwell.

Beynon, H. (1984) *Working for Ford*. Harmondsworth: Penguin.

Blake, R. R., Shepard, H. A. and Mouton, J. S. (1964) *Managing Intergroup Conflict in Industry*. Texas: Gulf.

Brett, J. M. and Goldberg, S. B. (1979) Wildcat strikes in bituminous coal mining. *Industrial and Labor Relations Review*, 32, 4, 465–83.

Brown, R. (1978) Divided we fall: an analysis of relations between sections of a factory workforce. In H. Tajfel (ed.), *Differentiation Between Social Groups*, London: Academic Press, 395–428.

Brown, R. (1988) *Group Processes: Dynamics within and between Groups*. Oxford: Blackwell.

Brown, R. J. and Wade, G. S. (1987) Superordinate goals and intergroup behaviour: the effects of role ambiguity and status on intergroup attitudes and task performance. *European Journal of Social Psychology*, 17, 131–42.

Brown, R. J. and Williams, J. (1984) Group identification: the same thing to all people? *Human Relations*, 37, 547–64.

Brown, R. J., Condor, S., Mathews, A., Wade, G. and Williams, J. A. (1986) Explaining intergroup differentiation in an industrial organization. *Journal of Occupational Psychology*, 59, 273–86.

Cole, S. (1969) Teachers' strike: a study of the conversion of predisposition into action. *American Journal of Sociology*, 74, 506–20.

Cummings, T. G. and Srivastva, S. (1977) *Management of Work: a Socio-Technical Systems Approach*, Kent State: Kent State University Press.

Dolan, S. (1979) Determinants of officers' militancy: the case of the National Union of Teachers in Israel. *Relations Industrielles — Industrial Relations*, 34, 2, 287–311.

Durcan, J., McCarthy, W. and Redman, G. (1983) *Strikes in Post-War Britain*. London: Allen & Unwin.

Edwards, P. K. and Scullion, H. (1982) *The Social Organization of Industrial Conflict.* Oxford: Blackwell.

Eiser, J. R. (1986) *Social Psychology: Attitudes, Cognition and Social Behaviour.* Cambridge: Cambridge University Press.

Eiser, J. R. and van der Pligt, J. (1988) *Attitudes and Decisions.* London: Routledge.

Fantasia, R. (1988) *Cultures of Solidarity: Consciousness, Action and Contemporary American workers.* Berkeley: University of California Press.

Flanagan, R. J., Strauss, G. and Ulman, L. (1974) Worker discontent and workplace behaviour. *Industrial Relations*, 13, 2, 101–23.

Fosh, P. (1981) *The Active Trade Unionist.* Cambridge: Cambridge University Press.

Gouldner, A. (1954) *Wildcat Strike.* New York: Antioch Press.

Hartley, J. F. (1984) Industrial relations psychology. In M. Gruneberg and T. D. Wall (eds), *Social Psychology and Organizational Behaviour*, Chichester: Wiley.

Hartley, J., Kelly, J. and Nicholson, N. (1983) *Steel Strike.* London: Batsford Academic.

Hewstone, M. and Brown, R. (eds) (1986a) *Contact and Conflict in Intergroup Encounters.* Oxford, Blackwell.

Hewstone, M. and Brown, R. (1986b) Contact is not enough: an intergroup perspective on the 'Contact Hypothesis'. In M. Hewstone and R. Brown (eds), *Contact and Conflict in Intergroup Encounters*, Oxford: Blackwell, pp 1–45.

Hogg, M. A. and Abrams, D. (1988) *Social Identifications: A Social Psychology of Intergroup Relations and Group Processes.* London: Routledge.

Hyman, R. (1972) *Disputes Procedure in Action.* London: Heinemann.

Hyman, R. (1989) *Strikes.* 4th edition. London: Macmillan.

Kelly, C. (1989) Political identity and perceived intragroup homogeneity. *British Journal of Social Psychology*, 28, 239–50.

Kelly, J. (1982) *Scientific Management, Job Redesign and Work Performance.* London: Academic Press.

Kelly, J. and Kelly, C. (1991) 'Them and Us': Social psychology and the 'new industrial relations'. *British Journal of Industrial Relations*, 29, 25–48.

Kerr, C. and Siegel, A. (1954) The inter-industry propensity to strike. In A. Kornhauser, R. Dubin and A. M. Ross (eds), *Industrial Conflict*, New York: McGraw-Hill, 189–211.

Klandermans, B. G. (1983) Rotter's I.E.-scale and socio-political action-taking: the balance of 20 years of research. *European Journal of Social Psychology*, 13, 399–415.

Klandermans, B. (1984) Mobilization and participation in trade union action: a value expectancy approach. *Journal of Occupational Psychology*, 57, 2, 107–20.

Klandermans, B. (1986a) Psychology and trade union participation: Joining, acting, quitting. *Journal of Occupational Psychology*, 59, 2, 189–204.

Klandermans, B. (1986b) Perceived costs and benefits of participation in union action. *Personnel Psychology*, 39, 379–97.

Kornhauser, A. (1954) Human motivations underlying industrial conflict. In A. Kornhauser, et al. (eds), *Industrial Conflict*, New York: McGraw Hill.

Lane, T. and Roberts K. (1971) *Strike at Pilkingtons.* London: Fontana.

Marsden, D. et al (1985) *The Car Industry.* London: Tavistock.

Martin, J. E. (1986) Predictors of individual propensity to strike. *Industrial and Labor Relations Review*, 39, 2, 214–27.

Miller, N. and Brewer, M. B. (eds) (1984) *Groups in Contact: The Psychology of Desegregation.* New York: Academic Press.

Nicholson, N., Ursell, G. and Blyton, P. (1981) *The Dynamics of White Collar Unionism: A Study of Local Union Participation.* London: Academic Press.

Oaker, G. and Brown R. J. (1986) Intergroup relations in a hospital setting: a further test of social identity theory. *Human Relations*, 39, 767–78.

Olson, M. (1965) *The Logic of Collective Action*. Cambridge, Mass: Harvard University Press.

Rabbie, J. M., Benoist, F., Oosterbaan, H. and Visser, L. (1974) Differential power and effects of expected competitive and cooperative intergroup interaction upon intra- and outgroup attitudes. *Journal of Personality and Social Psychology*, 30, 46–56.

Reid, F. J. M. and Sumiga, K. (1984) Attitudinal politics in intergroup behaviour: interpersonal vs. intergroup determinants of attitude change. *British Journal of Social Psychology*, 23, 335–40.

Schutt, R. K. (1982) Models of militancy: support for strikes and work actions among public employees. *Industrial and Labor Relations Review*, 35, 3, 406–22.

Scott, W. H. et al. (1963) *Coal and Conflict*. Liverpool: Liverpool University Press.

Sherif, M. (1966) *Group Conflict and Cooperation*. London: Routledge.

Shirom, A. (1977) Union militancy: structural and personal determinants. *Industrial Relations*, 16, 2, 152–62.

Smith, C. T. B. et al. (1978) *Strikes in Britain*. Manpower Paper 15, Department of Employment. London: HMSO.

Stagner, R. and Eflal, B. (1982) Internal union dynamics during a strike: a quasi-experimental study. *Journal of Applied Psychology*, 67, 37–44.

Stephan, W. G. and Stephan, C. W. (1984) The role of ignorance in intergroup relations. In N. Miller and M. B. Brewer (eds), *Groups in Contact: The Psychology of Desegregation*, New York: Academic Press, 229–58.

Stephenson, G. M. (1981) Intergroup bargaining and negotiation. In J. C. Turner and H. Giles (eds), *Intergroup Behaviour*, Oxford: Blackwell, 168–99.

Turnbull, P. et al. (1991) *Dock Strike*: Conflict and Restructuring in Britain's Ports. Aldershot: Gower.

Waddington, D. (1986) The Ansell's brewery dispute: a social cognitive approach to the study of strikes. *Journal of Occupational Psychology*, 59, 3, 231–46.

Waddington, D. (1987) *Trouble Brewing: A Social Psychological Analysis of the Ansell's Brewery Dispute*. Aldershot: Avebury.

Waddington, D. (1989) Towards a model of strike mobilisation: the case of the 1984–85 British Miners' Strike. Paper for the Fourth West European Congress on the Psychology of Work and Organization, Cambridge, England, April.

Ward, R. H. (1973) The psychology of a police strike: an analysis of New York's 1971 police 'job action'. In J. T. Curran, et al. (eds), *Police and Law Enforcement 1972*, New York: AMS Press.

Wetherell, M. S. (1987) Social identity and group polarization. In J. C. Turner, M. A. Hogg, P. J. Oakes, S. D. Reicher and M. S. Wetherell (eds), *Rediscovering the Social Group: A Self-Categorization Theory*, Oxford: Blackwell, pp 142–71.

Wilder, D. A. (1984) Predictions of belief homogeneity and similarity following social categorization. *British Journal of Social Psychology*, 23, 323–33.

Winterton, J. and Winterton, R. (1989) *Coal, Crisis, and Conflict: The 1984–85 Miners' Strike in Yorkshire*. Manchester: Manchester University Press.

Woolfson, C. and Foster, J. (1988) *Track Record: The Story of the Caterpillar Occupation*. London: Verso.

Further reading

Brown, R. (1988) *Group Processes: Dynamics within and between Groups*. Oxford: Blackwell. Provides a comprehensive coverage of social psychological approaches to group processes, including Realistic Conflict Theory and Social Identity Theory, with plenty of examples from industrial and other contexts.

Hartley, J., Kelly, J. and Nicholson, N. (1983) *Steel Strike*. London: Batsford Academic. A case study by a team of psychologists with material on intergroup relations and decision-making.

Hewstone, M. and Brown, R. (1986) *Contact and Conflict in Intergroup Encounters*. Oxford: Blackwell. An edited collection of studies in which the Contact Hypothesis is applied in many varied situations of intergroup conflict including industry. The theoretical overview provided by the editors in the first chapter is particularly recommended.

Klandermans, B. (1984) Mobilization and participation in trade union action. *Journal of Occupational Psychology*, 57, 2, 107–20. The main theoretical and empirical source for the value expectancy approach.

Waddington, D. (1987) *Trouble Brewing: A social psychological analysis of the Ansell's brewery dispute*. Aldershot: Avebury. An important case study of a protracted dispute.

Part V
The Organizational Context

12

Equal Opportunities: an Attempt to Restructure Employment Relations

Sonia Liff and Marilyn Aitkenhead

Introduction

A major British manufacturing company has been thinking about introducing equal opportunities since the early 1980s.[1] At the end of 1990 some progress has been made but a policy has still not been fully implemented. Part of the reason why it has taken so long to agree an approach has been the contradictory values, perceptions and interests between and within the parties involved.

The first initiative was to declare, in recruitment materials, that the company was an equal opportunity employer. However, the development of a formal written policy detailing the objectives, procedures and criteria for recruitment, career development and so on, was rejected for a number of reasons. These seemed to relate primarily to employee relations managers' anxieties about the anticipated reactions of both other managers and the workforce.

A policy of equal opportunities is often promoted to managers on the grounds that it will lead to better availability and utilization of the human resources within an organization. In the case above, employee relations managers were doubtful about whether the policies and procedures available would actually achieve this in practice. This undermined their ability to overcome the objections of other managers to the changes required. Combined with this was an uncertainty about whether the financial and staff resources needed to implement a policy would be made available. Managers further anticipated that workers would be hostile to equal opportunity monitoring of the current workforce, particularly that of ethnic origin. There was also the fear that equal opportunities policies might draw workers' attention to areas of racial and sexual difference, which might otherwise be overlooked, and which the company might not be able to resolve in the short term.

Since then, the company has made various attempts to develop and implement a policy, once in response to an industrial tribunal case under the Race Relations Act. The situation has also been exacerbated by poor industrial relations in the company. This has been used by management as a reason to put off doing anything 'controversial' unless it was necessary for the new business strategy. Despite this strategy being about better utilization of the workforce, managers responsible for its implementation did not seem to see the connections with equal opportunities.

The unions in this company, when asked for their views on equal opportunities, are positive but they have not chosen to press these concerns as a priority with management. They see equality primarily in male/female terms whereas management concern has focused on the representation of ethnic minorities. Black employees do not appear to have found effective representation within the recognized trade unions and a few have chosen to pursue their concerns via the law rather than through the structures established by either management or unions.

The situation in which this company finds itself is far from unique and it highlights the complexity of equal opportunities as an industrial relations issue. While few managers or trade unionists would nowadays admit to being opposed to equal opportunities, it is rarely top of their list of negotiating issues. The people for whom equal opportunities is likely to be a primary concern – women, ethnic minorities, homosexuals and the disabled – tend to be poorly represented within both management and trade union power structures.

Equal opportunities should improve the benefits available to some sections of the workforce. However, it is not a straightforward 'gain' for the workforce and a 'loss' for management in the way that, say, an agreement to reduce the working week would be. Improved opportunities for some sections of the workforce can mean reduced ones for others. This was certainly the case in the finance sector where the fact that women were rarely promoted increased career opportunities for men by reducing the competition (Boyden and Paddison, 1986). Management face similar contradictions. For example, accepting the consequences for payment schemes of fair job evaluation of the work of men and women can be expensive, but other aspects of equal opportunies, such as reducing the barriers to the recruitment and promotion of women, can help to solve costly skill shortages.

These conflicts of interest can affect not just *whether*, but also *how*, equal opportunity is pursued by different sections of management and workers. For example, for groups already in employment at low grades, such as ethnic minorities employees in the company discussed above, a high priority may well be improved opportunities for internal promotion. Other groups, particularly women, who have traditionally been largely excluded from most types of manual work, might give greater priority to external access to jobs.

The intention of this chapter is to explore and evaluate experiences and conceptions of equal opportunities in organizations. Equal opportunities are taken to be those policies and practices which attempt to change the terms of the employment relation in order to avoid benefits (jobs, wages, promotion opportunities, training, and so on) being differentially available to certain individuals on the basis of their social group membership.

The chapter begins by briefly examining the context within which equal opportunity initiatives are occurring, in order to identify why they became a significant issue for organizations and their members in the 1980s and will continue to be so in the 1990s. It will then examine the dominant approach to achieving equal opportunities in the UK. This has generally involved the adoption of a set of procedures based on the recommendations of the Equal Opportunities Commission (EOC) and the Commission for Racial Equality (CRE). It will be argued that equal opportunity initiatives have failed to live up to the expectations that many had for them. Possible reasons for this limited success will then be explored. The chapter will conclude with a consideration of possible ways forward in the development and implementation of equal opportunity, both in the UK and more generally.

Context for Equal Opportunity

Legislation

The predominant form of industrial relations in the UK has been voluntaristic. Equal opportunities legislation passed in the 1970s and 1980s in part represents a break with that tradition. It provides certain legal rights for workers, allowing them to bring cases against their employers (or potential employers) if they feel that they have been denied employment or employment benefits on the basis of their sex, marital status or ethnic origin. Guides to this legislation have been produced by the Commission for Racial Equality (CRE, 1988) and the Equal Opportunities Commission (EOC, n.d.).

These legislative pressures on organizational practice have been experienced to a greater or lesser extent by many other countries. The USA relies more heavily on legal remedies (Meehan, 1985). In Sweden there is greater reliance on collective bargaining and state provision (Scott, 1982; O'Donnell and Hall, 1988). Developments within the European Community around the Social Charter may lead to a convergence of members states' legislation on equal opportunities.

Labour market trends

The last twenty-five years have seen dramatic changes in the composition of the labour force in the UK. Women now constitute over 46 per cent of the workforce compared with 36 per cent in 1965 (Department of Employment, 1989, pp. 10–14). Most women still spend some time out of the labour market while their children are very young but this period is becoming increasingly short (Martin and Roberts, 1984). The proportion of ethnic minorities in the workforce, while remaining low at around 4.5 per cent in 1988, has also increased over this period (Department of Employment, 1988a; Runnymede Trust and Radical Statistics Group, 1981).

The main change in the 1990s seems likely to be a decline in the number of school-leavers entering the labour force (Department of Employment, 1988b). The 1990s are set to see a shortage of applicants for those jobs traditionally filled by school-leavers and, to a lesser extent, graduates. These labour market changes have had some effect on organizations' interest in equal opportunity. The experience of employing more women has made organizations aware of some of their needs and wants. Extensive skill shortages in high technology occupations have made companies consider ways of attracting a wider range of candidates. Reduced numbers of school-leavers has also led organizations to reflect on recruitment practices and to think about ways of retaining existing employees, particularly women with children (Atkinson, 1989).

Trade unions

Trade unions have found that their traditional membership has declined with the drop in full-time manual jobs. Searching for new members, they have had to reassess their view that certain groups, such as part-timers and women, are 'unorganizable'. For example, the Transport and General Workers' Union commissioned research which showed that young women were not hostile to trade unions but that they found it impossible to raise issues of importance, such as sexual harassment, because of the masculine solidarity among trade union officials and workers (Clement, 1988). The TUC (1989) now stresses that unions need to promote themselves differently to recruit new members and that therefore they should start from the needs, concerns and interests of those whom they are trying to recruit. This process has been helped by pressure from women, ethnic minorities and gay trade union members who are increasingly active within unions.

Implementing Equal Opportunity

In some cases, equal opportunities initiatives have been instigated by management, in others they result from negotiations with trade unions. In either case, most organizations have followed closely, at least in formal terms, the guidelines contained in Codes of Practice issued by the Commission for Racial Equality (CRE, 1983) and the Equal Opportunities Commission (EOC, 1985). These aim to show the ways in which changed personnel practices can ensure legal compliance and promote greater equality of opportunity.

The thinking behind both the legislation and the Codes seems to be that equal opportunity can be achieved by ensuring free competition for resources and by ensuring that benefits are distributed on the basis of appropriate criteria. Thus, the answer to discrimination is to have an organization based on rational and meritocratic procedures which judge individuals on their ability rather than making assumptions based on their social group membership. This is sometimes referred to as making a strong distinction between suitability (i.e. functionally specific criteria of performance) and acceptability (i.e. whether someone will fit into the organization) (Jenkins, 1986).

At a more general level, the Codes concentrate on increasing the amount of formalization of personnel procedures so that there can be increased awareness about the basis on which decisions are being made (see Liff, 1989 for a more developed presentation of this argument). The procedures which are seen as critical by the authors of the Codes are those controlling access, either to the organization or to new positions within it. The guidelines are highly prescriptive about the procedures which should be implemented, whilst giving few insights into ways of overcoming the political and practical difficulties of implementing these procedures.

To what extent is this procedural approach to achieving equal opportunities successful? There are a number of ways of trying to answer this question. Given that the strategy focuses primarily on improving procedures, it could be argued that assessment should be based on the extent to which new procedures have been implemented. For example, a measure might be taken of the proportion of companies who were now monitoring the composition of their workforce. However, this would be to assume that this procedural approach to implementation is an effective route to equal opportunity. A more telling evolution would be to measure directly the outcomes from these changed procedures, by, for example, assessing the changing distribution of men and women within occupational groups. Again, this is not as straightforward as it might appear. For example, a continuing under-representation of women electronic engineers might be the result of unequal opportunities in engineering firms but it might also be, at least in part, the result of a differential distribution of skills, qualifications, experience, or simply interest in this area, between men and women.

There are surveys and studies which explore these different approaches. At the most aggregated level it is clear that more women are entering the workforce but that they still remain highly concentrated within a narrow range of occupations (EOC, 1989a), despite some improvement during the 1970s (Hakim, 1981). The more detailed studies of individual jobs show high levels of segregation (Martin and Roberts, 1984). Studies of ethnic minority employment also show high levels of occupational segregation (Department of Employment, 1988a).

The results of studies of procedural measures are not promising either. One approach has been to submit false applications in response to advertisements to see whether the ethnic origin of the applicant makes any difference to the employer's response. These show continuing high levels of discrimination (Brown and Gay, 1985).

One explanation of such studies could be a failure to implement the recommended procedures and other research has attributed poor recruitment practice to the absence of procedures or to their informal nature (for example, Jenkins, 1986). Yet there have also been studies in highly formalized settings which show the persistence of discriminatory practices (for example, Collinson, 1987a). These suggest that implementation is not as simple as the Codes suggest.

Reasons for Failures

In this chapter we shall concentrate on the possible reasons for the apparently limited success of current approaches to equal opportunities. We posit three broad types of explanation. These are not exclusive and indeed interact in important ways. The first is based on the recognition that equal opportunities policies and practices do not exist in isolation. Rather, they are one element within the fundamental relationship between management and labour, interacting with a range of personnel policies and more broadly with business strategy. Thus, the form in which equal opportunities policies are implemented may reflect the outcome of sometimes conflictual and sometimes reinforcing interactions with contextual, organizational and social factors.

Second, people have a variety of conceptions of the purpose of equal opportunities. These can lead to different levels of commitment to particular aspects of the policy and to different expectations of the consequences of successful implementation (and hence concern with non-achievement of equal opportunities). The third level of explanation is based on the concept of group identity and the way in which groups' distinguishing characteristics are embedded in organizational structures and occupational requirements. This leads to a variety of psychological resistances to the opening up of opportunities to previously excluded groups.

Conflicts with other concerns and priorities

Why should management be interested in pursuing equal opportunities? It has been argued that management gains significant benefits both from the continued existence of disadvantaged segments of the labour market and from maintaining a divided workforce. In particular, it has been claimed that married women can be regarded as a reserve army of labour, being drawn into, and expelled from, the workforce as required (Beechey, 1978). The existence of such a reserve, as well as giving flexibility, is thought to act as a check on the militancy of other workers. On the basis of these arguments it would appear that managers might wish to introduce women into previously male preserves but that their essential interest lies in reducing the rewards for men rather than increasing them for women – a rather different conception of equal opportunities! Historical studies show that, in practice, management have tried relatively rarely to challenge existing patterns of segregation.

There is currently much discussion about the ways in which demographic trends, skill shortages and increased competitiveness are increasing employers' interest in equal opportunities. However, there is often a slippage in the rhetoric of those supporting equal opportunities between acceptance of a specific need to fill particular types of jobs and a general commitment to equal opportunities (see, for example, EOC, 1989b). It is commonly argued, for example, that equal opportunities recruitment and selection practices are in managements' interests because they ensure that the best person fills the job. However, this argument has greater plausibility in the case of software engineers than for, say, copy typists. In the latter case, the added costs of an equal opportunities procedure may not be felt to be worth the benefits.

There are clearly other reasons why management might feel that equal opportunities are in their interests, such as establishing a good public image. As yet there is little research from which to judge the important of these factors.

Individual managers may have rather more specific concerns. The dominant procedural model of equal opportunities involves considerable time, paperwork and expense. Thus, managers may feel sympathetic to the principle of equal opportunities but may not feel that it is sufficiently important to justify giving it the necessary level of priority. Managers may also resent the ways in which elements of equal opportunities policies, such as monitoring reasons for short-listing and for selecting candidates, constrain the extent to which they can exercise discretion and imply that they might act in a discriminatory way (Collinson, 1987b). Indeed, the Institute of Personnel Management (IPM, 1987) recognized as one of the indirect advantages of equal opportunities initiatives that they may well increase the power of personnel managers relative to other management functions!

Is the situation more straightforward for trade unions? At TUC level it would appear so, as witnessed by long-standing support for policy initiatives such as equal pay for women. However, in practice, individual trade unions have been faced with fundamental choices about the best way to represent their members' interests.

One way for trade unions to limit the use of women and other groups to reduce skill and pay levels is to organize widely and to insist that everyone is employed on the same basis. In terms of the balance of power between management and labour, this would represent a gain for labour. Milkman's (1983) study of industries and trade unions in the USA did find some examples of such an inclusive approach. However, it is easier to find examples of unions acting to exclude certain groups from employment. Examples are included in Milkman's study and have also been documented in the UK among printing unions (Cockburn, 1983) and engineering unions during the world wars (Beechey, 1978). More recently, the British National Union of Mineworkers opposed government initiatives to repeal legal prohibitions on women working underground. Humphries (1981), in an historical study of this original legislation, argues, however, that such strategies of exclusion should not be simply dismissed as against women's interest, since they may act to protect them from exploitation from employers.

Currently, in the UK, job segregation linked to the occupational basis of many trade unions has meant that many memberships are predominantly of one sex and from a narrow range of occupations. Thus, many trade unions, in attempting to represent their members while not treading on the toes of other unions, have in practice been more enthusiastic about supporting improved benefits for women, such as better maternity provisions, than they have been about tackling issues of pay differentials or promotion routes. Dickens et al. (1988) discuss the ways in which many collective agreements in these latter areas frequently contain sexually discriminatory clauses.

However, many general manual and white collar trade unions are trying to represent a range of members and this is leading some to promote equal opportunities issues. For example, the white collar union, Manufacturing, Science and Finance, has produced research which suggests that organizations with union representation have gone considerably further than the average in implementing equal opportunities (Ball, 1990). However, in other cases, representing a range of interests may lead to unavoidable conflicts of interest. Wrench (1987) discusses many of the problems that unions have had to overcome in challenging their own racist practices and in developing equal opportunity policies. On a day to day basis, they may also face conflicts about resolving sexual or racial harassment issues *between* their members. In such a case, one member may want the union to support him or her in a disciplinary hearing while another expects the union to press for a strict punishment. The TUC is supporting a moral stand over such issues by drawing up guidelines which encourage unions to expel members found guilty of racism.

In a range of personnel areas, apparently unconnected policies and practices can come into conflict, raising contradictions for both management and workers. For example, internal recruitment has long been recognized as having a number of attractions for management. It is a very cheap way of making appointments, management are in a good position to judge the candidates' strengths and weaknesses, the candidate knows the organization and will not need to spend time moving or adjusting to new surroundings, and it provides a way of rewarding good performance and motivating current staff. For many jobs, such advantages have been felt to outweigh disadvantages, such as possibly not obtaining the 'best' candidate. Trade unions have also tended to favour such approaches, sometimes arguing, in addition, that such promotions should be based on seniority rather than strictly on merit. However, equal opportunity codes (CRE, 1983; EOC, 1985) stress that such recruitment methods, along with 'word of mouth' methods of attracting candidates, have the added disadvantage of tending to reproduce the broad social characteristics of the current workforce and thus perpetuate the exclusion of those who are currently under-represented.

Another area of conflict which has proved even more contentious has been the issue of basing payment systems on job evaluation schemes. The Equal Value amendment to the British Equal Pay Act has made it necessary for firms to be able to justify differences in pay between men and women in terms of a formal evaluation of the jobs that they do. Whereas in the past this could only be done via an existing job evaluation scheme, employees are now entitled to have an independent assessment carried out. This provision sits extremely uncomfortably alongside, on the one hand, pressures to pay the going rate to those with skills in short supply and, on the other, persuading people to 'price themselves back into jobs', both of which are current concerns of management. It may also disrupt union members' cherished differentials.

In the past, those designing job evaluation schemes were often counselled to adjust weighting between factors until the ranking of jobs 'seemed right' or accorded, at least roughly, with current rankings (e.g. Armstrong, 1977). Such attempts are now likely to be judged as discriminatory by independent experts. Tribunal cases and some new organizationally based schemes, such as those introduced by local authorities (Lodge, 1987), show the extent to which conventional relativities between jobs can be changed. The conflicts here have proved so great that the CBI are campaigning for the repeal of the Equal Value Amendment, because they claim that the cost of restructuring payment systems will seriously endanger profitability.

The segments of the workforce for whom equal opportunity policies are being developed are not homogeneous and this in itself could be a source of conflict. Codes of Practice, which form major equal opportunity policy initiative in the

UK, focus, for the most part, on improving the quality of personnel decisions in a general way rather than on addressing the specific needs of particular groups. The implication is that the same developments will be equally beneficial to all groups. But this is not always the case. Cockburn (1989) discusses a retail organization where ethnic minorities, who were severely under-represented in the workforce, placed most emphasis on an open recruitment policy. Women who were over-represented at the bottom of the organization thought that it was more important to develop an internal recruitment policy for more senior positions.

Different groups may also have different specific needs, for example for childcare or for opportunities to take time off during important (non-Christian) religious holidays. These tend to be referred to as desirable elements of positive action programmes. They are seen not as essential elements of an equal opportunity programme but rather as measures which can be introduced to attract or retain specific groups. In a situation where one cannot do everything, deciding between priorities poses dilemmas. In Cockburn's example, those with dependants wanted relevant support services while those without thought that the money could have been better spent on other issues (see also chapter 5). Where management have to make choices between such conflicting priorities, perhaps on the basis of the relative strength of different interest groups or in response to recruitment or retention problems, they may well generate ill will, mistrust or disillusionment among other groups of employees or potential employees.

Different understandings of equal opportunities

At a broader level, people may have very different views on what equal opportunities are trying to achieve and what should be counted as success. One view is that such policies are simply intended to ensure that individuals are considered on their merits in terms of suitability for any particular job. Another is that they are intended to redress current imbalances between members of different social groups in terms of their occupancy of certain jobs. These two approaches have been categorized respectively by Jewson and Mason (1986) as 'liberal' and 'radical' approaches to equal opportunities.

According to the liberal approach, people should be recruited and promoted on the basis of merit (i.e. suitability). Thus, a good equal opportunity policy should remove any barriers to decisions being made on the basis of merit, such as restricted recruitment or irrelevant selection criteria. However, as will be elaborated in the next section, psychological factors can make it difficult to consider suitability in isolation from membership of social groups. In addition, the prior belief in the existence of meritocratic decision-making, inherent in this view, makes it difficult to accept evidence of unequal opportunities. Lack of distributional change may come to be justified in terms of the relative lack of merit of people excluded. We have seen this recently with the British Prime Minister, John Major, who, whilst extolling the virtues of a meritocracy, ended up with no women in his Cabinet! This was justified on the grounds that there were 'no women of sufficient merit' available and that women 'were not ready yet'. Thus, lack of distributional change need not trouble holders of meritocratic views.

In a study designed to assess managers' understandings of equal opportunities, Aitkenhead (1988) carried out telephone interviews with twenty managers of large companies who defined themselves as having some responsibility for equal opportunities. Nearly all had a very limited understanding of organizational processes of inclusion and exclusion (discussed in the next section) and they did not have access to information which would disturb their belief in their organization as meritocratic and hence fair. For example, few engaged in monitoring of any sort. In other words, for the dominant white male management group distributions tend not to be salient. Moreover, attributional mechanisms were identified which tended to foster their belief in the organization as fair, such as defining people who were under-represented as lacking in merit, or not wanting to apply for the jobs. If one holds the view that equal opportunities already prevail, it is easy to see how people who hold a contradictory view could come to be defined as 'troublemakers' or 'malcontents'.

The 'radical' approach, by contrast, has as its main concern changes in outcomes, for example, more women in senior jobs. Holders of this view are thus likely to be highly dissatisfied by equal opportunity policies which do not result in changed distributions. As indicated above, such a view is uncommon among managers. From the perspective of a group of under-represented workers, such as black workers in a white male dominated organisation, matters could look very different indeed. Having a readily available comparison group of workers in similar jobs but of a different ethnic origin (or, less usually, gender, since men and women tend to do different jobs) may foster a feeling among the under-represented members that they are being discriminated against. And, since the under-represented group will tend to exist at the lower end of organizational hierarchies, it becomes easy to see how the liberal–radical split in understandings predominantly follows hierarchical lines, with management being more often liberal in their approach and the under-represented group more often radical.

Such was the case in the Jewson and Mason (1986) study, where the small number of black workers were highly discontented with the lack of organizational change concerning the employment of more black people. This happened *despite* the development of a procedurally based, liberal equal opportunities policy by a joint management/trade union negotiating committee. The different understandings (radical for the black workers, liberal for the managers) led to allegations of tokenism. Indeed, allegations of racial discrimination actually *increased* after the introduction of the equal opportunities policy.

Jewson and Mason (1986) argue that a failure to articulate and resolve these differing perspectives can be highly destructive. However, resolution between these differing positions is not helped by the ambivalent position expressed in the Codes. The EOC Code (1985) suggests that monitoring (a procedure following the radical approach by indicating a concern with outcomes) should be carried out but that an under-representation of members of a particular group, which is revealed through such a process, should not necessarily be interpreted as evidence of discrimination (i.e. a failure of liberal procedures). Instead, it suggests, it is cause for further investigation which may show that there is a perfectly acceptable reason for such discrepancies (see Aitkenhead and Liff, 1990 for a further elaboration of these arguments).

As can be seen from the EOC's position, the division between liberal and radical models, while being analytically appealing, can be difficult to maintain in practice. For example, it seems likely that many people see liberal methods as appropriate ways of achieving radical ends (this certainly seems to be the implication behind the EOC and CRE approaches). Others may be aware of problems with the liberal approach, as outlined above, but may nevertheless feel unhappy with the radical alternative of seeking changes without regard for the methods used. For example, Webb and Liff (1988) argue that 'Women fail not because they are less able to carry out the tasks; they are excluded because of the way that necessary qualifications are defined. . . . What should be asked of employers is not that they accept less qualified, less able women in preference to men but that they rethink what the job requires in ways that do not rule out competent women' (p. 549). A simple example of this approach would be the way in which many management jobs continue to be offered only on a full-time basis. A liberal approach of considering all applicants on their ability to do the job as defined would invariably result in fewer women being appointed. However, the radical approach of simply insisting that a certain proportion of women be appointed may result in selectors having difficulty in finding suitable female candidates. If, however, the unnecessary criterion of working full-time were removed, it is more likely that a decision made on merit would also result in improved distributions. Neither the liberal nor the radical approach is likely to draw attention to this option.

Cockburn (1989) proposes another way out of the dualistic model by suggesting that an incremental strategy is needed:

> At its shortest it involves new measures to minimise bias in procedures such as recruitment and promotion. It is formal and managerial, but nonetheless desirable. At its longest, its most ambitious and most progressive it has to be recognised as being a project of transformation for organisations. As such it brings into view the nature and purpose of institutions and the processes by which the power of some groups over others in institutions is built and renewed.
>
> (Cockburn, 1989, p. 218)

This is an important integration of the spectrum of ideas that is sometimes included under equal opportunities, although going far beyond what most people would consider to be achievable under an equal opportunity policy! It requires a fundamental restructuring of power relationships, and an awareness by people, particularly those in positions of power, that simple rhetoric is not enough. Managers need to be aware that the barriers to equal opportunity cannot be overcome by policies based purely on liberal strategies of meritocracy and on formalization of suitability criteria to ensure fairness. Trade unions need to be aware of how the social psychological processes that are engaged in by their members may undermine attempts to change distributions. And legislative barriers to change also need to be removed.

Processes of inclusion and exclusion

As Salaman (1986) points out, organizations, by virtue of being structured, constrain people's interactions with each other in three important ways. First, the structure largely defines who interacts with whom. Second, because of the organizational position that a person holds, he or she is more likely to meet with some people than with others. Thus, frequency of interactions is also constrained. Third, the nature of the interaction is constrained because people tend to interact on the basis of their role positions; the kind of job that they do dictates their reasons for interacting with others. Such interactional constraints have important psychological effects which, by themselves, may limit the effectiveness of equal opportunity policies in changing distributions. But these interactional constraints, when operating in conjunction with the tremendous gendered occupational segregation which already exists, foster a resistance to change which may be extremely powerful.

One way of understanding these psychological effects is from the perspective of social identity theory (e.g. Tajfel, 1978, 1981). According to this theory, people tend to divide up the world into groups of which they are members (ingroups) and groups of which they are not members (outgroups). Furthermore, our sense of social worth (social identity) becomes entwined with our social group membership. People prefer to have a positive social identity. This implies attaching a more positive value to our ingroups than to our outgroups, and also directing some effort into *maintaining* a positive group identity, necessarily at the expense of other groups. A basic assumption of the theory is that we need to keep a cognitive differentiation between our ingroups and outgroups. One way to do this is to stereotype: to regard members of any group as more similar than they really are, and to increase psychologically the perceived differences between our ingroups and our outgroups.

The theory draws attention to several mechanisms which can be used to foster this positive social identity. One way is for individuals to use what power they have to promote the interests of their ingroups at the expense of outgroups. Several experimental studies (see those in Tajfel, 1978; Turner and Giles, 1981) have shown this to occur even when individuals know only to which group people belong, without knowing who the actual individuals are. Another way is to value the perceived attributes of the ingroup more than those of the outgroup.

The implications of this psychological desire for positive social identity are profoundly important for equal opportunities. In so far as jobs are gendered, and interactions are constrained by organizational structure, there will be many opportunities to relate to other people where social group membership is highly salient, and gender will be one important indicator of social group membership. To maintain positive social identity, both men and women will have a vested interest in maintaining the status quo. This is true of men because of the likelihood that various stereotypical 'manly' attributes will become associated with holders of their particular job position (whatever it is) and be positively valued as a way of maintaining positive social identity in that occupation. Since most organizational positions which are predominantly occupied by men are generally more valued in our society (e.g. the financial rewards are greater), there is little difficulty for men in maintaining their positive social identity when comparing their ingroups with the outgroups occupied by women. But there is obviously a great disincentive for change in terms of either increasing the value placed on women's jobs or welcoming women into the male preserve. Since men hold positions of greater power, their processes of exclusion through social identity mechanisms have the effect of limiting the effectiveness of equal opportunity policies.

Salaman (1986) brilliantly illuminates such mechanisms in his study of the London Fire Brigade. He shows how the intense ingroup pressures, fostered by the high interdependence of team members, led to resistance towards and an undermining of the implementation of equal opportunities. The dominant group simply did not want any member of a perceived outgroup (women, black people) coming in to disturb their 'family' feeling. Moreover, since it is easier to interact with people who are defined as similar, there will even be a desire to reorganize along gendered lines when such divisions have been disrupted. This is one interpretation of the restructuring of occupational gender divisions, following the introduction of new technology, as shown in studies by Game and Pringle (1984) and Cockburn (1985).

Obviously, organizational pressures towards ingroup identity will vary from one organization to another. In many cases, group identities will not be structured along gender lines (see Brown, 1978 for an example of two all-male groups attempting to maintain their primary ingroup values during pay negotiations). But, since organizations currently tend to be run on gender lines, male versus female group identities will be very frequent, very powerful, and very under-mining of positive equal opportunity change.

Why should women also resist change, however? Again, social identity theory might provide us with some clues at the psychological level. Being female may become a positively defined attribute of certain jobs and it is easy to see that male entrants into predominantly female occupations will be resisted by women for the same reasons that men resist women 'intruders'. According to theory, there are also several ways in which people who are members of low status occupational groups cope with their position. One is to place value on the occupation, not along the dimensions where social identity would be negative in relation to other groups but along dimensions where it would be positive. Thus, 'money' would be unlikely to be chosen, but 'helpfulness' or the 'essential nature' of the work done might be. Once the current position is valued, there is less incentive for change. Moreover, organizational hierarchies tend to become accepted as legit-imate and this, too, limits the push for change.

However, the theory predicts that there would be circumstances under which low status groups would attempt to change the status quo; when it becomes perceived as unjust or illegitimate, for example. But within organizations this rarely happens. First, where could the definition of injustice come from? Unions might be one source but the same groups tend to be absent from positions of power in both the occupational and the trade union hierarchies. Individuals might be another, but the personal costs of fighting a system are often too great to be perceived as worthwhile. Second, more and more organizations are adopting the rhetoric of being equal opportunity employers, so women (and others) may feel that their interests are to some extent being promoted. Social identity mechanisms, such as stereotyping of outgroups and valuing the managerial ingroup thinking more highly, would tend to enhance the predominant view that the organization is fair because its procedures are fair, and hence that equal opportunities already exist. Third, to define something as unjust means more than risking the wrath of organizational superiors. It means leaving behind one's colleagues and ingroup members, and one's positive social identity. All of these factors, therefore, are significant disincentives for change by people in less powerful positions.

A further implication of social identity theory for equal opportunity initiatives is that it suggests that the apparently straightforward separation between suitability for a job and the sex of the applicant cannot occur. Group identity features will enter the selection decisions and confound the process of selecting on the basis of suitability. This can be seen clearly in Curran's (1988) research on recruitment practices. As she puts it, 'employers, consciously or unconsciously, may fail to distinguish between a requirement for "a pleasant personality" and one for a pretty girl with a smile, or between "someone with qualities of leadership and self-reliance" and a man. . . . gender is incorporated in the functional specification of jobs and of "ideal candidates" (pp. 344–5).

It is not clear to what extent such an approach can be applied to a consideration of discrimination against ethnic minorities. While views of the different capabilities of men and women are imbued with naturalistic assumptions, it appears to be far less publicly acceptable to hold divergent views of the capabilities of those from different ethnic groups. They may be said to have different personality traits but it is less common for these groups to be seen as particularly suitable for some jobs rather than others. For example, Salaman's (1986) analysis of the attempt to introduce equal opportunities to the London Fire Brigade gives extensive consideration to firemen's views of women's unsuitability. He then says, 'no officer ever maintained that non-whites were less able than whites' (pp. 53–4).

It was not that there was no objection to such entrants but rather that the objection took a different form. Jenkins (1986) has made the most extensive study of recruitment policies in relation to ethnic minorities. He points to the significance of acceptability criteria. Ethnic minorities are seen as not fitting in because of their presumed different habits, customs, and strong social grouping. As such, they are regarded as disruptive to existing workgroups and as (potentially) unacceptable to customers or clients. There are, of course, some cases where such apparent 'unacceptability' may itself result in the candidate being considered 'unsuitable' in job specific ways; for example, for the post of a salesman.

Towards More Effective Equal Opportunities

The chapter so far has outlined the current UK approach to equal opportunities and has highlighted a range of possible reasons for its limited impact. Issues of policy approach, form of implementation, and pressures and barriers to change have been shown to interact in a highly complex way. Is it possible to identify new approaches which could be more effective? The experiences of other countries which have taken a different approach to equal opportunities can provide one source. Another is developments currently occurring in the UK which are trying to break way from the dominant approach.

International policy differences

Given the contradictions faced by trade unions in pressing for and supporting equal opportunities, some have argued that increased legislation provides the best pressure for change. In terms of formal anti-discrimination legislation, the USA has the longest and in many senses the strongest record. Legislation has been in place since 1963 and is important both in allowing 'class actions' (those brought on behalf of a group of women or ethnic minorities) and in insisting that firms who have or want to have federal contracts are obliged to provide information about their workforces and to introduce positive action programmes to rectify imbalances (Meehan, 1985; Dex and Shaw, 1986). These elements are important in the light of the issues identified earlier. Class actions reduce the need for individuals to act in isolation, thus allowing 'outgroups' to assert discrimination collectively. Contract compliance forces dominant groups to confront evidence of unequal distributions as a problem, thereby challenging their current understandings of equal opportunities.

Of course, anti-discrimination laws are not the only form of legislative action which can benefit working women. France, for example, has strong day care provision for children of all ages and generous family allowance (Beechey, 1989; Dex and Walters, 1989). These are both areas of weakness in the UK. As suggested earlier, such developments could increase the effectiveness of 'liberal' equal opportunities measures (or at least expose more clearly some of their inadequacies), since women would be more likely to reach the selection stage rather than disappearing from the process as non-applicants.

In other countries, collective bargaining has been an important source of improvements in equal opportunities. This tradition is strongest in Sweden (Scott, 1982). O'Donnell and Hall (1988) argue that trade unions there have managed to secure improved conditions for all of those in lower grade jobs and have reduced wage differentials. Since such jobs are precisely those where women workers are concentrated, they argue that such approaches can be considered as equal opportunities measures. By reconstructing equal opportunities in this way, this approach may avoid generating defensive 'ingroup' feeling among male trade union members, although perhaps at the cost of failing to challenge important aspects of male advantage.

An assessment of these different approaches is beyond the scope of this chapter. However, they do again highlight the differing understandings of equal opportunities by different interest groups and the various ways in which change can be accomplished.

New directions for equal opportunity policies

Moving into the 1990s, equal opportunity policies are receiving an impetus from demographic and other labour market trends. The limitations of the current British legislative framework are apparent but there is little immediate prospect of change. New initiatives are most likely to come from organizations and their members.

The difficulties arising from the contradictions between different areas of policy identified earlier are exacerbated by the way in which equal opportunity is frequently treated as an isolated issue. Although in principle it touches all areas of personnel policies and collective bargaining, it is rarely dealt with in this way. In part this is because equal opportunities issues have tended to be invisible to dominant groups in management and trade unions for reasons discussed above. Thus, treating it as a separate area is one way of ensuring that it receives some attention. However, the result often is that conflicts and contradictions are either not recognized or not dealt with. It also marginalizes equal opportunities as being 'just about doing something for women and black people' rather than its being seen as an essential element of, say, recruitment practices or pay bargaining. The connections with these areas are lost and sectional resentment can be generated as some groups are seen to be receiving 'special treatment'.

Iles and Auluck (1989) suggest that these difficulties can be overcome by integrating equal opportunities within a strategic human resource management approach, which stresses the overall development of the workforce towards organizational goals. This is in line with current suggestions that non-discriminatory practices are not concessions to certain groups but rather allow management to make most effective use of their existing and potential workforce. As was suggested by the example which opened this chapter and some of the later discussion, management may find it difficult to recognize or to accept these connections and when they do may choose to use them selectively, to solve particular problems of skill shortage, rather than in the thorough-going way outlined above. One means by which trade unions could attempt to promote a more integrated approach would be to negotiate for 'equal opportunity impact statements' to be attached to all policy proposals.

Other writers have suggested ways in which policies can be reformulated so that, instead of its appearing as though women and black people are being made a special case, it becomes clear that one is redressing a past imbalance where white men were prioritized. For example, Jones (1988) suggests that equal opportunity statements are rewritten to read: 'We will not discriminate in favour of white, middle-class males' (p. 45). Practical measures which could be in line with this sentiment, without perhaps generating the antagonism of groups who currently feel that they are being treated fairly rather than preferentially, could include making all jobs potentially open to job sharers and having wheelchair access to all buildings.

The issue of how equal opportunity policies can be developed to overcome the perception of jobs as gendered, and the resistance to certain 'outgroups' entering occupations from which they have previously been absent, is more problematic. In theory, restructuring jobs and working conditions to make them open to all should generate less antagonism than making special allowances for particular groups. However, members of dominant groups are unlikely to accept easily the idea that existing terms represent a specific advantage to them.

Some current developments are based on supporting and building up the confidence of under-represented groups to challenge the resistance and hostility of existing 'ingroups'. For example, there have been a number of courses in the UK to encourage women to enter scientific or technical areas and these have included sampler or pre-entry programmes, women-only teaching groups, different teaching methods, and assertiveness training. Some trade unions have adopted a similar approach in providing special training courses for women members, allowing groups to organize within trade unions and reserving seats for women on executive bodies. Alternative models are very underdeveloped but could perhaps include attempts to restructure jobs, such as clerical work and administration across current 'gender divides'. New models could also promote an audit of those words and phrases that are used in job descriptions and in person specifications, which have been traditionally associated with masculinity or femininity, and could attempt to derive new non-gender related forms.

Underlying all of these moves must be a greater attempt to understand people's hopes and fears for equal opportunities and through this to engage their commitment. Policies need to be supported by senior management and trade union leaders but, if they remain simply top-down initiatives or the concern of only one department or group, they will almost certainly achieve very limited success. Equal opportunities policies are often said to fail because they are not promoted enthusiastically enough or are not implemented in a comprehensive enough manner. An examination of the differing interests and understandings of the groups involved and of the social psychological processes that result from these make it clear that such views are too simple.

Notes

1 This example is based on an unpublished Loughborough University undergraduate project by Jon Sparkes.

References

Aitkenhead, M. (1988) Perceptions of Equal Opportunities. In S. Oliver (ed.), *The Psychology of Women at Work*. Worthing Centre for Psychological Services to Education and Training, 127–46.

Aitkenhead, M. and Liff, S. (1990) The Effectiveness of Equal Opportunity Policies. In J. Firth-Cozens and M. A. West (eds), *Women at Work: Psychological and Organisational Perspectives*, Buckingham: Open University Press, 26–41.

Armstrong, M. (1977) *A Handbook of Personnel Management Practice*. London: Kogan Page.

Atkinson, J. (1989) Four Stages of Adjustment to the Demographic Downturn. *Personnel Management*, August, 20–4.

Ball, C. (1990) *Trade Unions and Equal Opportunities Employers*. London: Manufacturing, Science and Finance Union, London Region.

Beechey, V. (1978) Women and Production: A Critical Analysis of Some Sociological Theories of Women's Work. In A. Kuhn and A. M. Wolpe (eds), *Feminism and Materialism*, London: Routledge & Kegan Paul, 155–97.

Beechey, V. (1989) Women's Employment in France and Britain: Some problems of comparison. *Work Employment and Society*, 3, 3, 369–78.

Boyden, T. and Paddison, L. (1986) Banking on Equal Opportunities. *Personnel Management*, September, 42–6.

Brown, C. and Gay, P (1985) *Racial Discrimination: 17 Years After the Act*. London: Policy Studies Institute.

Brown, R. (1978) Divided We Fall: An Analysis of Relations Between Sections of a Factory Workforce. In H. Tajfel (ed.), *Differentiation Between Social Groups: Studies in the Social Psychology of Intergroup Relations*, London: Academic Press, 395–429.

Clement, B. (1988) Officials of Unions 'Aggressive and Sexist', *Independent*, 18 October.

Cockburn, C (1983) *Brothers: Male Dominance and Technological Change*. London: Pluto Press.

Cockburn, C. (1985) *Machinery of Dominance: Women, Men and Technical Know-How*. London: Pluto Press.

Cockburn, C. (1989) Equal Opportunities: The Long and Short Agenda. *Industrial Relations Journal*, 20, 3, 213–25.

Collinson, D. L. (1987a) Banking on Women: Selection Practices in the Finance Sector. *Personnel Review*, 16, 5, 12–19.

Collinson, D. L. (1987b) Who Controls Selection? *Personnel Management*, May, 32–6.

CRE (1983) *Code of Practice*. London: HMSO.

CRE (1988) *Equal Opportunity in Employment: A guide for Employees*, CRE.

Curran, M. (1988) Gender and Recruitment: People and Places in the Labour Market, *Work Employment and Society*, 2, 3, 335–51.

Department of Employment (1988a) Ethnic Origins and the Labour Market. *Employment Gazette*, Dec., 633–46.

Department of Employment (1988b) New Entrants to the Labour Market in the 1990s. *Employment Gazette*, May, 267–74.

Department of Employment (1989) Employment Statistics: Historical Supplement No. 2. *Employment Gazette*, November.

Dex, S. and Shaw, L. (1986) *British and American Women at Work: Do Equal Opportunity Policies Matter?* Basingstoke: Macmillan.

Dex, S. and Walters, P. (1989) Women's Occupational Status in Britain, France and the USA: Explaining the Difference. *Industrial Relations Journal*, 20, 3, 203–12.

Dickens, L. Townley, B. and Winchester, D. (1988) *Tackling Sex Discrimination Through Collective Bargaining*. Equal Opportunities Commission Research Series. London: HMSO.

EOC (n.d.) *Equal Opportunities: A Guide for Employers*. London: EOC.

EOC (1985) *Code of Practice*. London: HMSO.

EOC (1989a) *Women and Men in Britain 1989*. London: HMSO.

EOC (1989b) *From Policy to Practice: A Strategy for the 1990s*. London: EOC.

Game, A. and Pringle, R. (1984) *Gender at Work*. London: Pluto Press.

Hakim, C. (1981) Job Segregation: trends in the 1970s. *Employment Gazette*, December, 521–9.

Humphries, J. (1981) Protective Legislation, the Capitalist State and Working Class Men: The Case of the 1842 Mines Regulation Act. *Feminist Reviw*, 7, 1–34.

Iles, P. and Auluck, R. (1989) From Racism Awareness Training to Strategic Human

Resource Management in Implementing Equal Opportunity. *Personnel Review*, 18, 4, 24–32.

Institute of Personnel Management (1987) *Contract Compliance: The UK Experience*, IPM/IDS report, London: Income Data Services.

Jenkins, R. (1986) *Racism and Recruitment: Managers, Organisations and Equal Opportunity in the Labour Markets*. Cambridge: Cambridge University Press.

Jewson, N. and Mason, D. (1986) The Theory and Practice of Equal Opportunities Policies: Liberal and Radical Approaches. *The Sociological Review*, 34, 2, 307–34.

Jones, P. (1988) Policy and Praxis: Local government, a Case for Treatment? In A. Coyle and J. Skinner (eds), *Women and Work: Positive Action for Change*, London: Macmillan, 37–57.

Liff, S. (1989) Assessing Equal Opportunities Policies. *Personnel Review*, 18, 1, 27–34.

Lodge, D. (1987) Working Equality into Manual Job Evaluation. *Personnel Management*, September 27–31.

Martin, J. and Roberts, C. (1984) *Women and Employment: A Lifetime Perspective*. London: HMSO.

Meehan, E. M. (1985) *Women's Rights at Work: Campaigns and Policy in Britain and the United States*. London: Macmillan.

Milkman, R. (1983) Female Factory Labour and Industrial Structure: Control and Conflict over 'Women's Place' in Auto and Electrical Manufacturing. *Politics and Society*, 12, 2, 159–203.

O'Donnell, C. and Hall, P. (1988) *Getting Equal*. North Sydney: Allen & Unwin.

Runnymede Trust and Radical Statistics Group (1981) A Profile of Black Employment. In P. Braham, E. Rhodes and M. Pearn (eds), *Discrimination and Disadvantage in Employment*, London: Harper & Row, 96–108.

Salaman, G. (1986) *Working*. Tavistock: Ellis Horwood.

Scott, H. (1982) *Sweden's Right to Be Human*. London: Allison & Bushby.

Tajfel, H. (ed.) (1978) *Differentiation Between Social Groups: Studies in the Social Psychology of Intergroup Relations*. London: Academic Press.

Tajfel, H. (1981) Social Stereotypes and Social Groups. In J. Turner and H. Giles (eds) *Intergroup Behaviour*, Oxford, Blackwell, 144–67.

TUC (1989) *Organising for the 1990s*. London: TUC.

Turner, J and H. Giles (eds) (1981) *Intergroup Behaviour*. Oxford: Blackwell.

Webb, J. and Liff, S. (1988) Play the White Man: The Social Construction of Fairness and Competition in Equal Opportunity Policies. *Sociological Review*, 36, 3, 543–51.

Wrench, J. (1987) Unequal Comrades: trade unions, equal opportunity and racism. In R. Jenkins and J. Solomos (eds), *Racism and Equal Opportunity Policies in the 1980s*, Cambridge: Cambridge University Press, 160–86.

Further reading

Cockburn, C. (1985) *Machinery of Dominance: Men, Women and Technical Know How*. London: Pluto. Provides important insights into the ways in which jobs came to be seen as appropriate for men and women.

Coyle, A. and Skinner, J. (eds) (1988) *Women and Work: Positive Action for Change*. Basingstoke: Macmillan. Provides thoughtful accounts of attempts to improve women's positions in a range of British organizations.

Dex, S. and Shaw, L. (1986) *British and American Women at Work: Do Equal Opportunities Policies Matter?* Basingstoke: Macmillan. An interesting attempt to contrast two differing approaches to equal opportunities.

Jenkins, R. (1986) *Racism and Recruitment Management, Organisations and Equal Opportunity in the Labour Markets*. Cambridge: Cambridge University Press. Explores the ways in which managements' conceptions of job requirements and the people capable of filling them discriminates against ethnic minorities.

Salaman, G. (1986) *Working*. London: Tavistock. Shows the complexity of organizational processes, individual and group actions with respect to equal opportunity policies.

13

Workers' Participation in Management

George Strauss

Workers' participation in management (WPM) has been prescribed worldwide as a solution for social and organizational problems ranging from low productivity and poor quality to alienation, social inequality and destructive labour–management relations. Why do organizations adopt WPM? What forms does it take? How successful has it been? What factors affect its success or failure? These are among the issues this chapter considers.

Why Participation is Introduced

Two arguments support WPM: the first is that WPM will redistribute social power, protect workers' interests, strengthen unions and extend the benefits of political democracy to the workplace. The second is that it will promote workers' satisfaction and organizational efficiency (Dachler and Wilpert, 1978). For those who make the first or 'structural' argument, power equalization is an end in itself; for those who take the second 'functional approach', it is a means toward an end (Lammers, 1974).

Power equalization arguments were plentiful in the 1970s and earlier (in Britain, for example, in the Bullock (1977) Report). More recently the discussion has focused on WPM's organizational impacts (Lammers and Szell, 1989). There are three explanations for this shift toward more modest goals: (a) experience with real participation in numerous contexts has demonstrated that, while WPM has other advantages, it is unlikely to transform society; (b) the lengthy European economic recession has required greater attention to productivity than to social justice; and concomitantly (c) the political pendulum has swung to the right, especially in eastern Europe. Unions have lost power in most countries.

Support by the Institute of Industrial Relations, University of California is gratefully acknowledged as are useful criticisms and suggestions provided by Peter Auer, Jack Barbash, Stephen Frenkel, Jennifer Halpern, Frank Heller, Richard Long, Michael Poole and Eli Rosenstein. For an outmoded but more lengthy discussion of the issues covered here see Strauss (1982). WPM in the United States is discussed more intensively in Strauss and Hammer (1992).

291

Organizational explanations of the positive psychological impacts of WPM also abound (e.g. Lowin, 1968; Locke and Schweiger, 1979). Below I outline these arguments and indicate some of WPM's drawbacks. The basic argument here is that WPM may change (a) how workers do their jobs, (b) how they perceive these jobs, and (c) how they and their unions relate to their employer.

1   WPM may result in better decisions. Workers often have information that higher management lacks. Further, WPM permits a variety of different views to be aired. *On the other hand*, workers may be less informed than managers and the premises upon which they make their decisions may be different. Further, if decisions are made by groups, reaction to changing environments may be slow.

2   People are more likely to implement decisions they helped make themselves. Not only do they know better what is expected of them, but helping make a decision commits one to it. *On the other hand*, once committed to a decision, employees may be reluctant to change it even when a changing environment mandates flexibility.

3   The mere process of WPM may satisfy workers' non-pecuniary needs including creativity, achievement and social approval. *On the other hand*, many people do not feel these needs, or they satisfy them sufficiently off the job (see also chapter 2).

4   WPM may improve communications and co-operation: workers may co-ordinate each other rather than requiring all communications to flow through management, thus saving management time. Further, participative workers supervise themselves, thus making management's life easier. *On the other hand*, WPM is itself time consuming.

5   WPM enhances participants' sense of power and dignity and so reduces their need to show their power through fighting management and restricting production. *On the other hand*, once people are given power, they want to keep it. Once management establishes WPM, workers will fight withdrawal of their 'right' to participate.

6   WPM increases loyalty to and identification with the organization, particularly if the group's suggestions are implemented – and especially if WPM includes ownership. *On the other hand*, cohesive, participative groups may unite against management, restrict production and prevent change (see also chapter 6).

7   WPM frequently results in the setting of goals. There is considerable evidence that goal setting is an effective motivational technique. *On the other hand*, workers may set lower goals than management likes.

8   WPM teachers workers new skills and helps identify and train leaders. (This is particularly an advantage in underdeveloped countries where management skills are scarce.) *On the other hand*, retraining workers and managers can be expensive. Technology may have to be redesigned so that workers can control it more easily.

9   When union and management leaders jointly participate to solve problems on a non-adversarial basis, the improved relationship may also improve union-management relations generally. *On the other hand*, joint decision making may degenerate into a power struggle.

There are numerous other reasons for WPM. For example, according to Hartmann (1970) co-determination was introduced in West Germany after the war because of the fortunate juxtaposition of numerous interests: the British occupying forces sought to curb industrialists' power, managers hoped WPM would protect their plants from Allied dismantling, while Catholic liberals found it consistent with papal encyclicals, and Social Democrats perceived support for WPM as means of preserving their credentials as socialists while abandoning the class struggle.

In Britain, in the mid-1970s, the Labour government offered unions 'industrial democracy' in part in return for acquiescence (through the Social Contract) in an incomes policy. Similarly, through much of Europe, WPM was viewed as a key element in 'corporatism'. In the US, it was often a key part of a programme through which companies obtained union co-operation in reducing production costs in the face of serious competitive pressures. Non-union firms often offer it as a substitute for union representation.

Given the variety of reasons for which WPM has been introduced, it is understandable that the parties have a variety of expectations as to how it should work and what it should accomplish. Nevertheless the reasons for which WPM is introduced may have little to do with how it works in practice. Despite the possibly cynical reasons for introducing WPM in Germany, in actuality it has had considerable impact. By contrast many elaborate WPM structures, introduced for the best reasons, have never taken off. Indeed the reasons why WPM is introduced may have little to do with its success.

Forms of Participation

The various forms can be classified under four headings as table 13.1 illustrates. Under each head forms of participation are ranged in a continuum, from weak workers' power to strong. Let us examine each classification in turn.

A Organizational level The most important distinction is between *direct* and *representative* (indirect) WPM. Direct participation involves individual workers and includes such schemes as quality circles and work teams. Representative participation involves representatives of workers, often selected by their union. Typically this form of WPM is concerned with plant- or higher-level problems. Direct WPM is more frequently initiated by management, while representative WPM tends to be initiated by unions.

B Degree of control Consultation means that management listens to workers' suggestions and may even seek their ideas; nevertheless management retains the right to make the final decision. Joint decision making requires consent from both sides. In theory, with self-management, workers give orders to management, rather than vice versa.

Table 13.1 Forms of workers' participation in management

Classification	Example
A *Organizational level*	
Individual	Job enrichment
Small group	Autonomous work team
Department	Quality circle
Plant	German works council
Company	Worker directors
B *Degree of control*	
Joint consultation	French works councils
Joint decision-making	Co-determination in the German iron and steel industry
Self-management	Yugoslavia (until recently); producers' co-operatives
C *Range of issues*	
Wages	Collective bargaining in most countries
Personnel issues (e.g. redundancy and training)	Collective bargaining in the US; works councils in Germany
Welfare benefits	French works council regarding medical service
Production methods	Quality circles, autonomous work groups
Selecting managers	Yugoslav workers councils
Major investment decisions	Supervisory board under German co-determination
D *Ownership*	
No worker ownership	Typical company
Some worker ownership	Employee stock ownership plans
Complete worker ownership	Producers' co-operative

C Range of issues Participation regarding production methods typically occurs at lower levels, while investment decisions are discussed higher up. In any case, the greater the range of issues discussed, the broader the participation.

D Ownership is sometimes called 'Economic Participation'. Worker-owned companies are not necessarily democratic, and high levels of worker input can be achieved in conventionally owned companies.

Rather than consider each form in detail, the discussion below deals with only three types; direct participation, representative participation and worker ownership. To save space, it will be only concerned with *formal* schemes and thus ignore informal boss-worker relations and also collective bargaining, even though this may be the most important form of all.

Direct participation

Among the most common forms of direct WPM are quality circles and work teams (also called autonomous work groups). Work teams can implement decisions on their own, within specified limits, while quality circles can only make recommendations to management. (Other forms of participation, such as job enrichment, which provide autonomy for individuals, will not be discussed here.) Together these work reforms, often called Quality of Worklife programmes (or 'work humanism' in Germany), represent an attempt to empower workers. They constitute a reaction against Taylorism and the tendency to deskill workers. Their popularity derives also from their frequent association with Japanese management.

Quality circles (sometimes called job involvement programmes) typically consist of small groups of employees from the same work area who meet together voluntarily on a regular basis. Their chair may be their supervisor, a staff 'facilitator' or even another employee. Frequently members of the group receive special training in such subjects as group dynamics and statistical analysis.

Despite their name, quality circles typically deal with other subjects in addition to quality, for example work flow, productivity, safety and employees' welfare generally. Often such committees start with individual employees' complaints, move on to quality and working conditions, and later, as members gain confidence in working with each other and trust in management's receptivity to their suggestions, they progress to questions relating to safety and eventually productivity.

Though the concept was originally developed in the US, quality circles were first widely adopted in Japan. In recent years they have spread throughout the world. According to the limited figures available, quality circles are more common in Japan than in the US and much more common in both countries than they are in Britain. Interestingly, quality circles are more prevalent in unionized plants in Britain than they are in non-union plants, while the reverse is true in the US (Marginson et al., 1988; Lincoln, 1989; Cooke, 1990).

In some circumstances quality-circle meetings may be little more than managerial pep talks, with little opportunity for employee input. Under these circumstances employees conclude that participation is a meaningless 'Mickey Mouse' exercise. Sometimes, however, quality circles evolve into work teams.

In *work teams* employees are given wide discretion to organize their own work and operate with very little supervision. The concept of work teams developed out of research conducted on 'socio-technical systems' in Norway (with union and management support) and by the Tavistock Institute in Britain. Work teams have spread more slowly than quality circles, in part because they require a substantial transfer of power from supervisors to the work force. Work teams have been given responsibility for developing relations with suppliers, determining which operations are handled individually and which by the group as a whole, setting work pace, repairing their own equipment and training new employees. In the US such groups often meet weekly. Sometimes work team members serve in roles normally reserved for staff personnel or supervisors: chairing the plant safety committee, redesigning work equipment or trouble-shooting customers' problems. At times, the job of supervisor is rotated among members of the group.

One of the more successful recent turnabouts in American industry occurred at NUMMI, the joint GM-Toyota venture located at GM's former drugs-absenteeism-poor-labour-relations plagued Fremont, California plant. Using almost the same technology and workers as the old plant, NUMMI has now zoomed close to the top in productivity and the lowest in absenteeism. Here 'work teams' are responsible for planning job rotation, balancing work assignments to equalize work loads, and engaging in 'kaizen' (continuous job improvement). Team leaders, who remain union members, are selected on the basis of recommendations of a joint union–management committee (Brown and Reich, 1989).

At NUMMI the basic assembly technology, with its short job cycle, is retained. In some Scandinavian experiments (for example, in some Volvo shops) the technology itself has been changed: each individual worker performs a major portion of the total assembly process and the continuous assembly line has been eliminated. With Scandinavian-style groups, substantial changes are required in technology, workflow and work layout. The goal of the Scandinavian approach has been to adapt technology to the workers' needs, rather than to require workers to adapt to technology. Often workers are involved from the beginning in designing new work systems.

For work teams to succeed, extensive cross-training is frequently required. At times, to reduce resistance to switching jobs, the number of job classifications has been greatly reduced (a process often called 'broad banding' or 'multiskilling'; see also chapter 14). Thus, at NUMMI the 85 job classifications existing under previous GM management were cut to four. And with 'pay for knowledge', compensation is based on the number of skills a worker has mastered and is willing to practise – rather than (as is traditional) the workers' primary job assignment.

The introduction of work teams is often accompanied by flexitime and the elimination of important managerial status symbols. All 'team members' at NUMMI, managers and workers alike, wear the same uniform and share common dining rooms and car parks, in sharp contrast to the practice under the old GM management. Similar changes have been made in other US factories.

Despite their current popularity, quality circles and work teams often fail to live up to their promise. Management may give groups too little discretion. Multiskilling may merely give management greater flexibility to move workers arbitrarily. Lengthening the job cycle doesn't necessarily mean more participation if workers have little discretion in determining the sequence and methods by which various portions of the cycle are done (Lawler, 1986). Further, quality circles often have short lives.

Representative participation

Representative participation, in which committees of workers' representatives meet with management, take many forms. Participation may occur at the plant, divisional or company levels; there may even be representation on the company board of directors. It may deal with narrow topics, such as safety, or broad ones such as overall organizational policy. Workers may be merely able to make recommendations or they may have the right to block company action until agreement has been reached. Representatives may be appointed by the workers or appointed by their unions. Here we consider three types of representative participation: consultative committees, works councils and worker representation on boards of directors.

Perhaps most common in English-speaking countries are joint *consultative committees* (given a variety of names in practice). These meet periodically with management for discussion, but have no power to make decisions. Consultative committees exist in about half the large UK companies (and a quarter of all companies). Half these committees include union representatives, yet only a third of the committees meet as frequently as monthly (Millward and Stevens, 1986). Among the topics discussed most frequently at these meetings are production, pay and employment. Similar committees exist in the US. In Wisconsin (a typical state), 28 per cent of the unionized manufacturing firms had joint union-management committees which discussed *general* problems (other than collective-bargaining issues), while 43 per cent had committees to deal with *specialized* topics, such as safety (Voos, 1987, p. 199; for comparative Canadian and Australian data, see Long, 1989, and Frenkel, 1989).

Such committees have varying degrees of success. One reason for their frequent failure is that the parties fail to agree on their mission and to give much priority to their activities. Management seeks to confine the discussion to safety, housekeeping and similar problems, and occasionally production, whereas the workers want to deal with grievances and labour relations. Because neither side pays enough attention to the other, not much gets done. Workers suggestions are too often ignored and often the committees' scope is restricted to trivial matters of little importance to either side. Consequently in Britain such committees have sometimes been called 'tea and toilet' committees. Since committees lack the power to block management's actions, their influence may depend on management's faith and good will. According to a British study, 'the consultative machinery was of prime importance [only] where union organizations were weak and management was human-relations oriented' (Clarke et al., 1972, p. 80). On the other hand, when management is truly interested in collaboration such committees can be quite successful. 'Lifeboat democracy' of this sort appears most common in time of financial difficulty (Cressey, Eldridge and MacInnes, 1985).

Union-management joint consultative committees are common in Japan as well. In some companies these committees engage in traditional collective bargaining. In other companies the bargaining and consultative functions are kept separate. Quite often management shares confidential information with these committees, including details of major new investments and changes in policy. Further, management normally revises its plans when faced with strong union objections (Morishima, 1991).

Recent US auto contracts have spawned a maze of consultative committees. Special plant committees have been charged to review job design, new plant layout, changes in manufacturing equipment, and major new processes, all with the purpose of reducing stress and increasing efficiency. Plant-level committees permit exchange of information and the discussion of investment and other issues which might affect employment or workers' welfare.

Works councils are required by law in most continental Western European countries for middle and large size companies. The councils are elected directly by employees, sometimes after a considerable electoral battle, often between rival unions. By contrast with the consultative committees, works councils are expected to negotiate with management.

In France these councils function mainly in the health, safety and welfare areas. In other countries, management is required to consult with these councils on a broader set of issues. In some cases management cannot move ahead without the council's approval. In Sweden, for example, management is required to 'negotiate' with its works council with regards to 'any important change in working conditions', including the introduction of new technology.

West German works council members are elected by blue- and white-collar workers in separate elections. The basic law carefully distinguishes among subjects which the works council has the right to 'co-determine' (and so block action) from those about which it has merely the right of consultation or obtaining information. However, the matters subject to co-determination are quite broad, including working hours, piece rates, discipline and even the design of workplaces. Further, by threatening to exercise its rights in an area over which co-determination is required, councils may extend their rights in other areas.

West German works councils, along with worker representatives on company boards of directors (see below), have had a considerable impact. As Streeck (1984, pp. 414, 416) puts it, 'Management under co-determination is essentially comanagement, especially but not exclusively in the manpower area. It is based on a close, symbiotic relationship between the personnel department and an increasingly 'managerial' works council . . . [which] not only shares in what used to be managerial prerogatives, but also accepts responsibility for the implementation and enforcement of decisions made under its participation.' Thus German works councils have made it considerably more difficult for management to lay-off workers, thus forcing management to pay more attention to planning, training and internal mobility.

Works councils are somewhat like grievance and bargaining committees in Canada and the US and to a lesser extent like stewards committees in the UK and Australia, a major difference being that German and Swedish works councils have a significantly broader scope than their Anglo-Saxon counterparts. Another difference is that the rights of German works councils and US grievance committees are carefully defined by law (in Germany) or by the union contract (in the US). By contrast in Britain, 'the shop stewards' committee thrives in the open country of "custom and practice"' (Kahn-Freud, 1979, p. 12).

Union and/or worker representation on boards of directors of most large companies is legally required. Similarly there are union/worker directors in a small number of British and US companies, in the latter country often as a quid pro quo for union wage concessions, and also in Australian publicly owned firms.

In the German steel and coal industries, workers and management have equal membership (with a neutral selected to cast tie-breaking votes). Similarly, labour and management had equal representation on the British Post Office board in the late 1970s (an experiment halted by the Thatcher Government) (Batstone, Ferner and Terry, 1983). Before the system broke down, all the members of Yugoslav Workers Councils (the equivalent of boards of directors) were elected. Elsewhere worker representatives are in the minority. Yet they have considerable influence in many (but not all) cases, even with regard to major investment plans (such as Volkswagen's ill-fated venture into building an assembly plant in the US).

A basic dilemma faced by all union representatives – whether works councillor or worker director – is that many of the problems faced by participative bodies require technical skills which workers rarely have. Worker directors, in particular, lack the experience to deal with the legal, accounting, marketing and general strategy issues that take up much board time. Further, since management controls the agenda and the relevant information, normally it also controls the results. (If necessary, management representatives can caucus earlier and so transform the official board meeting into a formality.) In any case, worker directors frequently defer to management's expertise with regards to most matters (but so do other outside directors).

Over time, worker representatives may become more knowledgeable. But knowledge comes at a price. The more familiar representatives become with management problems and the more involved they are in dealing with them, the less sensitive they may be to their constituents' needs and the more dependent they become on the management which provides their information. As Wilpert (1975, p. 61) explains, the 'professionalization of the representative functions could easily create an estrangement from the constituency. Representatives may now appear part of "them", the upper management.' Eventually union representatives may see themselves as co-managers, and put the long-term interests of the organization as a whole above the immediate interests of their constituents. When this happens workers may either vote their representatives out of office or become alienated from the entire participative process.

This problem may perhaps be avoided if representatives successfully educate their constituents as to the organization's real needs. However, communication between representatives and their constituents is usually quite poor, in part because (as we shall see) formal union leaders may feel threatened by the WPM representative's independent role.

Worker Ownership

The most common forms of worker ownership in the Western world can be divided into three categories: (a) stock (or share) ownership, (b) worker 'buy-outs' of financially troubled facilities that might otherwise be closed, and (c) producers' co-operatives established with the *purpose* of being democratic and highly participative. In practice these three forms overlap, differing mainly in the extent of worker ownership and the purposes for which it is established.

Employee share (or stock) ownership[1] plans have spread widely in both the UK and the US. In 1984 such plans existed in almost a quarter of British firms, although only 35 per cent of these plans covered all workers and only 15 per cent of the workers in these firms took advantage of their opportunities (Millward and Stevens, 1986, pp. 259–60). As of 1989 almost 10 million US employees worked in firms with Employee Stock Ownership Plans (ESOPs). Of these, 1.5 million worked in firms in which employees owned a majority of the shares. By contrast with Britain, in the US most employees in ESOP firms own some stock.

A major reason for stock ownership's spread has been the substantial tax subsidies provided in the UK and especially in the US. But stock ownership plans have been established for other reasons as well: to motivate workers through giving them a sense of ownership and identification with their company; to inhibit takeovers by corporate raiders; and to permit the transfer of corporate control from one generation of top managers to another without requiring the sale of company shares to pay death duties. In Britain, stock ownership plans and profit sharing are offered more frequently by firms that espouse and practise consultation and participation (Poole, 1988).

Though the impact of stock ownership has been extensively studied in the US, the findings are somewhat mixed, particularly as to whether stock ownership *alone* affects profitability, productivity or union–management relations (for a review, see Strauss and Hammer, in press). There is only weak evidence that it raises satisfaction or commitment. On the other hand, there is stronger evidence that stock ownership, *when combined with participation*, does increase productivity. Put another way, stock ownership and participation tend to reinforce each other.

Buy-outs have occurred in the UK, US, France, Canada, Sweden and the Netherlands when workers (and managers) take over financially troubled facilities that might otherwise have been closed. The most famous British buy-outs – at Scottish Daily News, Meriden Motorcycles and Kirkby Manufacturing – were organized in the mid-1970s. More recently, in the UK, the National Freight Corporation was sold to its workers as part of the Thatcher government's drive for privatization. To date it has been very successful.

Typically buy-outs are financed by a combination of worker–equity contributions, bank loans, government loans and grants, and wage cuts. Changes in ownership, however, rarely mean that workers take control, even though individual workers are occasionally elected to boards of directors. In fact, 'buy-out' arrangements are often put together so hastily that little thought is given to how the firms are to be run. Workers' prime motivation is to save (not change) their jobs and radical new ideas might scare off financial support.

In the US, buy-outs often appear successful at first: profits improve, productivity climbs and apparently hopeless plants are restored to seeming prosperity. At least three factors seem to be at work: (a) wages and manpower have been cut, thus increasing profits, (b) the newly purchased plants are freed from the requirement to contribute toward corporate overhead, and finally, (c) once the often formidable barriers to workers' ownership have been overcome, workers feel a sense of triumph; in turn this leads to an immediate burst of enthusiastic co-operation as the parties enjoy the hope that, by pulling together, their previously threatened jobs can actually be saved.

Often, after a year or so of worker ownership, disillusionment sets in. Workers move 'from euphoria to alienation' (Whyte et al., 1983). Once fear of job loss subsides, worker ownership, by itself, seems to have little impact on either productivity or satisfaction. For the average worker, the job and the boss are unchanged. As one observer put it, 'People are happy their jobs were saved and the company is doing well . . . On the other hand, insiders say, many workers do have a vague if unarticulated demand for greater involvement in participation – and they feel frustrated that they've been denied it' (Zwerdling, 1979, p. 78). In several prominent cases frustrated expectations contributed to a dramatic increase in labour-management and internal union conflict (Hammer and Stern, 1986).

Producers' co-operatives are worker owned and in most cases have been designed from the beginning to allow high degrees of employee participation (see also chapter 4). There have been producer co-operatives in the UK and US since the early 1800s and today they are found throughout the world, including in underdeveloped and communist countries. The Israeli kibbutz, in which members live as well as work communally, may be the logical extension of this kind of organization, but small worker-owned and democratically controlled firms are common in many parts of Europe. An estimated 500,000 people are employed by producer co-operatives in Western Europe, especially in France and Italy (Estrin, Jones and Svejnar, 1987).

Perhaps the best known producer co-operative is Mondragon, located in the Basque section of Spain. With 21,000 worker–owners and £1.3 billion in annual sales, Mondragon is a complex of linked organizations, including manufacturing companies, a large savings bank (which generates money to invest in the manufacturing firms and also provides new firms with technical assistance) and technical schools. The governing boards of all the manufacturing firms are elected by their member-owners.

In their purest form, producer co-operatives meet the following conditions: (a) all workers are owners, (b) only workers are owners, and (c) every worker–owner has an equal say in making major decisions. In practice, these principles are often relaxed. For example, in two of the better-known British worker-owned firms,

John Lewis and Scott Bader, the original owners still retain significant rights of control.

Proponents of producer co-operatives cite many potential advantages of this kind of organization, including increased productivity, satisfaction and commitment. On the other hand, a substantial literature predicts that even when successful at first, co-operatives will degenerate over time. Potential problems include: members lack needed managerial skills; they are unwilling to take orders; factionalism develops and members are unwilling to make hard decisions or to discipline their colleagues. In other words, workers will be incapable of managing themselves (see chapter 5).

There are predictions of long-term financial and growth problems as well. The initial members will bring in too little capital. Once started, owners may pay themselves high wages rather than investing for the future. Consequently, because of inadequate capital, co-operatives may 'self-strangulate' (Jones, 1980). Even if the firm is successful, present owners may hesitate to share their good fortune with newcomers. Instead, as the firm expands, newcomers are denied ownership rights, the original owners become bosses, and so the organization loses its unique characteristics as a co-operative. And, if this does not happen, as members approach retirement age they may be unable to find replacements able to buy out their investment. Instead they may sell out to a capitalist organization – or simply shut down. In short, theory suggests that co-operatives will be short-lived.

Fortunately these problems may be exaggerated. Increasing evidence suggests that co-operatives can survive as long as do conventional firms (the mortality of small firms generally is high). At first they are at least as productive as their capitalist counterparts, and sometimes more so, especially 'in firms with the most co-operative features' (Jones, 1984, p. 52); unfortunately, this advantage may decline over time (Estrin et al, 1987). Producer co-operatives may survive best in certain niches, for example in craft work, which requires little capital. In any case they are a viable form of organization. And some, such as Mondragon, have been very successful.

Assessing WPM's Impact

Efforts to measure WPM's success are beset by methodological problems.

1	It is assumed that (a) the introduction of a formal WPM scheme leads to changes in actual behaviour, and that (b) this behaviour change has a positive impact on some important output variable, such as productivity. If a study shows negative results, it is important to know whether this is because of a failure of (a), of (b) or of both.
2	Most research is cross-sectional, examining a number of organizations at a single periods of time. But short-term measurements may be misleading, particularly since a participation scheme may seem successful for a few years and then peter out. Thus comparisons over time (longitudinal studies) may be necessary (cf. Macy, Peterson and Norton, 1989).

3 Cause and effect problems need to be untangled. For example, US companies with stock ownership plans tend to be more successful than those without. But do companies adopt these plans because they already enjoy profits? Or do they become more profitable because they adopt ESOPs? Again, longitudinal studies may help to answer this question.

4 Even with a longitudinal study, it is never clear whether an observed improvement in performance is due to WPM or to other things happening at the same time. Ideally we should take two matched samples of identical organizations which have identical experiences over a considerable period of time, with the single exception that participation is introduced into one set of organizations and not the other. Such perfect experimental conditions are rarely possible.

With these reservations in mind, there is little we can safely conclude regarding *all* forms of WPM in *all* countries of the world. The numerous studies of direct participation in the US, for example, show that more often than not it leads to at least short-term improvement in *one* or more of the following variables: satisfaction, commitment, quality, productivity, turnover or absenteeism (Strauss and Hammer, in press). In some cases, one factor is improved, in others, a different factor. The most we can say is that WPM *can* work (but with a variety of measures of 'work'). Certainly it does not always work; neither, when it works, does it always work in the same way.

Generalizing very broadly, the research (IDE, 1981; Strauss, 1982; Strauss and Hammer, in press) suggests:

1 Direct participation often increases *job satisfaction*. So does *substantial* employee stock ownership. Not all studies find this, however, and it is possible that frustration with the failure of a WPM scheme may lead to less satisfaction. Direct WPM may also reduce turnover and absenteeism and improve quality. By contrast, representative WPM has little impact on satisfaction variables.

2 The evidence as to *productivity* is more uneven, though there is a fair amount of research. Taken as a whole it suggests that the impact of WPM on productivity is less than it is on satisfaction. Increases in productivity occur only under special circumstances. Work teams may increase productivity, for example, but only when workers themselves make significant inputs into how the work is done (Katz, Kochan and Keefe, 1987). Producers' co-operatives, as we have seen, are often more productive than capitalist firms, in part because they combine participation with pecuniary rewards.

3 For some of its proponents, WPM's major objective is to *equalize power*. Representative WPM has increased German union power at the plant and company levels. Direct WPM in the US may be accompanied by some status equalization. In Europe the extent of formal participation correlates with workers' actual sense of involvement (IDE, 1981). The impact of WPM on management is less clear. If we view the amount of power in a system as fixed, as some socialists do, then management's relative power may be reduced when WPM is introduced. Whether management's actual power – ability to get things done – increases or decreases is more debatable (Lammers, 1967;

IDE, 1981). Overall, 'the degree of democratization of decision-making processes [caused by WPM] within work organizations appears to be fairly low' (Bean, 1985, p. 179).

4 Though WPM competes with the union in some cases, it also extends *union power*. In US terms, it broadens 'the scope of bargaining', increasing the number of subjects about which the parties bargain. In continental Europe it has somewhat increased union power at the plant level. WPM may also make labour relations less adversarial. Differences have not been obliterated, but conflict has been brought out in the open and its mode of expression has become less ritualistic. On the other hand, union leaders tend to be more comfortable with adversarial than co-operative relationships. Thus they can be easily frustrated when co-operation fails to provide immediate pay-offs. Both sides seem to assume that once they have made the 'sacrifice' that co-operation requires, the other side will behave 'reasonably' and there will be no further conflict. Of course this is unrealistic. As a consequence labour relations tend to behave in an erratic 'yo-yo' fashion (Hammer and Stern, 1986).

5 Finally, WPM has trouble surviving and growing. Some WPM efforts are still-born: management goes through the motions of consultation but ignores all but the most the trivial of suggestions. Alternatively WPM may flourish for a while, enjoy a 'honeymoon' and then, as the agenda of easily solvable problems grows smaller, interest begins to wane, meetings become less frequent and eventually cease altogether (MacInnes, 1985).

Initially, direct WPM raises expectations of opportunities for steadily increased participation, yet after workers have successfully coped with the problems of redesigning their jobs and found solutions to production problems and work quality difficulties, a period of let-down ('burnout' or 'plateauing') is almost inevitable. Workers' decision-making skills have increased but the unresolved problems that management lets them handle have decreased (Walton, 1980). US studies conclude that three out of four quality circles atrophy within four years (Strauss and Hammer, in press; see also Long 1989).

Representative participation schemes may last longer, especially if they are established through union-management agreement. Nevertheless, even joint committees tend to meet less frequently over time and to deal with increasingly trivial problems.

Problems

Whether WPM survives may depend on how well the following problems are solved.

Worker support

Not all workers want the added responsibilities of enriched jobs; some would rather not change their secure routines (Fenwick and Olson, 1986; Leitko et al., 1985). Most workers want more participation than they presently enjoy, but not much more (IDE, 1981). When workers in a twelve-country study were asked how much participation they wanted, on a six-point scale, . . . ranging from 1 ('not involved') to 6 ('decide on my own') . . . the average response was 3.0 (informed beforehand and can give opinion). As might be expected, desire to participate personally is greatest regarding such subjects as holidays and personal equipment and least with regards to investments and hiring procedures (IDE, 1981; Wall and Lisheron, 1977).

It is rare for more than a quarter of the workers in any plant to participate in quality circles or similar activities (e.g. Griffin, 1988). (Japan is the major exception here: according to Lincoln (1989) in those plants that had quality circles, 94 per cent participated, though often not voluntarily.) Further, according to one poll (IDE, 1981, pp. 189, 230), only in Yugoslavia were as many as 20 per cent of the workers willing to be candidates for positions on the representative participative body. Willingness to participate differs not just by countries, but by education, occupation and personality. For example, professionals and skilled trades workers seem to have greater than average interest in participation.

There is some evidence that participation is addictive, that is the more people have, the more they want. On the other hand, participation may also be frustrating and actual experience with it may reduce one's desire for more (Obradovitch, 1970).

Job security

US employees often fear that WPM may threaten their job security. This is not an unreasonable fear since management's main purpose in introducing WPM is often to increase efficiency and cut labour costs. Limited evidence suggests that direct WPM works best when it is combined with job security. In practice the two tend to be associated (Levine, 1990). Unions commonly ask for increased job security in return for the introduction of co-operative schemes. Greater job security has been one of the main objectives and accomplishments of representative WPM in continental Europe. Maintenance of job security has been a major problem at Mondragon (Whyte and Whyte, 1988).

Managerial resistance

WPM is resisted and sometimes sabotaged by middle- and lower-level managers and especially by supervisors (Klein, 1984; Bradley and Hill, 1983; Walton, 1980). Whereas for workers one of the main advantages of direct WPM is greater freedom to make decisions on their own (rather than having managers hover over them), this same freedom may threaten managers. Among the problems are the following:

1   WPM threatens the supervisor's authority and status (loss of separate parking lots, as occurs in some US plants, is symbolic of wider losses). Workers are encouraged to make decisions on their own. Discussions in quality circles may reveal managers' mistakes. In representative WPM, workers' representatives

may bypass supervisors and contact higher management directly. German works councillors, for example, are more likely to communicate directly with higher management than with lower management (Furstenberg, 1978).

2   In some cases, supervisors' very jobs are threatened. The introduction of direct WPM may lead to one or more levels of management being eliminated. Supervisory unions in the Netherlands and Australia have objected vigorously to the spread of direct WPM.

3   Managers are forced to learn wholly new techniques of supervision, such as soliciting workers' ideas or 'encouraging self-goal setting' (Manz and Sims, 1987). Often these techniques are completely at variance with what tradition has taught them is right. As a US executive put it, introducing shopfloor WPM in his company involved changing 'an old-line hierarchical organization into a more participative company from the executive suite to the shop-floor' (Hoerr, 1988, p. 465). In fact, though firm evidence is lacking, there is reason to believe that if formal WPM schemes are to enjoy long term success they must be complemented by informal participative managerial styles (see also chapters 4 and 6).

4   Lower level managers feel discriminated against. Though forced to share power with subordinates, they do not see their bosses sharing theirs. Although supervisors and middle managers have an understandably greater desire to participate in key decisions than do rank-and-file workers, often they are left out of the formal representative participation machinery altogether. They are forced into a system that typically they had no part designing.

5   While direct WPM is especially threatening to supervisors, representative WPM threatens top management. There is weak evidence that WPM reduces top management's absolute influence and stronger evidence that it does so relatively (Strauss, 1982). On the other hand, with proper 'handling', WPM can increase management's effectiveness through improving communications, reducing interpersonal conflicts, and legitimating management decisions. The managers of worker owned firms, especially producers' co-operatives, are in a particularly difficult position. Yugoslav and kibbutz top managers were less satisfied (and had more ulcers) than their counterparts in conventional US firms (Tannenbaum et al., 1974).

Union ambivalence

Union attitudes toward WPM differ. Some unions are only interested in WPM ideologically as a means of wresting control for the working classes; for them *sharing* control is small potatoes. Other unions, including some quite conservative ones, fear that WPM will co-opt both workers and union leadership. In the US, union attitudes toward WPM are closely related to attitudes toward concession bargaining. Unionists who are willing to make wage and other concessions to management (in return, hopefully, for greater job security) are also more likely to support WPM as a legitimate union goal. Their opponents are likely to view WPM as a sell-out to management.

Unions in Scandinavia, Germany and Austria have invested considerable effort in strengthening representative WPM. In these countries, collective bargaining was traditionally conducted at the industry rather than the plant or company level and dealt primarily with wages and hours. Here representative WPM is a means of extending the scope of bargaining to subjects other than wages and of strengthening the union at the plant level.

By contrast with the situation on the European continent, Anglo-Saxon countries have enjoyed relatively decentralized collective bargaining. The thrust of US and Canadian collective bargaining has been to rigidify and codify personnel practices. In the typical unionized plant, decisions as to promotions, job assignments and the allocation of work are made on the basis of collectively bargained seniority and job demarcation 'work rules'. Similar though less formal 'customs and practices' exist in the UK and Australia, typically negotiated by shop stewards. Workers in these countries believe strongly that these rules give them quasi-property rights, rights that WPM may threaten.

Self-managing work teams, for example, tend to erase the sharp line between workers and managers, a distinction which American unions have long sought to maintain. Combining jobs disturbs established promotional ladders. In plants with the most advanced new forms of participation, decisions as to the allocation of work and even pay and discipline are made by the work teams on a flexible ad hoc basis. In short, traditional Anglo-Saxon collective bargaining leads to what the Webbs (1920) called the 'common rule'; by contrast, the whole participation movement promotes experimentation and diversity. For direct participation to work, workers and their unions must learn to give up their fixed rules and management must agree to make joint decisions regarding a variety of subjects that were previously within its sole prerogative. Neither change comes easily.

Union attitudes toward direct participation on the continent are somewhat mixed. Only in Scandinavia is it an important union goal and even here it is frequently articulated as a means of protecting workers' health from excess pressures and unsafe conditions, rather than as a means of improving productivity. For example, despite some rhetoric, Swedish schemes rarely interfere with management's prerogatives to divide how work is to be done, provided it is done safely and without undue strain.

Regardless of the country, direct WPM threatens the role of union leadership to the extent that decisions once made at the leadership level are now made by ordinary workers. (No wonder members of German works councils have been reported as objecting to 'giving all this power to Turks'.) If workers resolve their problems, there will be fewer grievances, thus giving shop stewards less to do.

Representative WPM presents still other problems for the union. In the UK there is considerable overlap between union functions and those of consultative committees (Millward and Stevens, 1986, pp. 141–7). Indeed the representative participation machinery represents a 'parallel' organization rivalling the traditional union hierarchy. Since works councillors in most European countries are directly elected by employees and need not be union members, unions typically go to considerable lengths to ensure that good trade unionists are elected – and once elected, appropriately indoctrinated in union-sponsored training programmes. Nevertheless, elected representatives have an independent source of power. Some US participative schemes provide for union-selected, but company-paid 'facilitators'. These may develop interests and approaches which are often quite different from those of the old-time, adversary-relationship-oriented stewards. Serious political strains often occur.

Complicating matters further, the national union represents workers in the industry as a whole, while participative representatives are concerned with the welfare of a given plant or company. From the national union's point of view, participative bodies frequently engage in 'plant egotism', putting the interests of their own plant above those of the union movement generally. Often, for instance, the national union wants to preserve uniformity and to prevent erosion of national conditions while local workers seek to preserve their jobs. This creates tension. In Germany the national unions have sought to broaden apprenticeship training while many works councils sought to restrict apprenticeship openings to relatives of present employees.

In most countries direct participation has been initiated by management. Union attitudes toward it reflect the overall state of labour-management relations. Representative WPM, by contrast, has been union sponsored. Its impact is largely a function of union clout.

The Importance of Infrastructure

Most organizations are non-participative, so participation exists in a hostile environment. Producers' co-operatives in particular are strange beasts, 'isolated islands in a capitalist sea' (Clarke et al., 1972). Evidence suggests that participation of any kind is more likely to survive if it is sustained by what Blasi, Mehrling and Whyte (1984) call an 'infrastructure'. Elements of this infrastructure are discussed below.

Ideology and value systems

The most successful examples of worker ownership – the kibbutz and Mondragon, in particular – have been supported by an ideology. In the kibbutz it was one of socialism and nationalism (building a Jewish state in a hostile environment). Mondragon was founded by a Catholic priest. Its leaders were motivated by Basque nationalism and hostility to Franco.

According to psychological tests (Hofstede, 1980), Sweden, Norway and Israel are countries which are high in collectivism and low in power distance; these are all countries in which WPM is high. Industrial relations tend to be less adversarial in Norway than in the UK; this may explain the greater prevalence and success of Norwegian WPM. Japanese culture has much to do with the success of Japanese quality circles. Japanese transplants in the US, such as NUMMI, have induced strong corporate cultures. Indeed, participation has been most successful in US plants that have tried to introduce new organizational cultures with metaphors stressing 'team work' and 'organizational learning'.

Legal support

You can lead a horse to water, it is said, but you can't make it drink. Yet the evidence (IDE, 1981) suggests that legal arrangements that require organizations to introduce WPM do in fact increase workers' influence (both self-reported and as reported by informed observers). The law legitimates participation. Also it gives the workers clout to insist that participation take place.

Training

Participation requires a heavy investment in training and skill development generally. Both workers and managers require retraining. If workers are to make important technical and other decisions, they must learn technical, human-relations and decision-making skills. This is required for both direct and representative participation. Some US firms, for example, provide extensive schooling for members of quality circles and autonomous work teams. Mondragon was a training programme before it started manufacturing. Today it supports (and is assisted by) an elaborate educational network. German and Swedish unions believe it to be essential that they train worker directors.

Advice

Organizations implementing WPM schemes need technical advice; and the successful diffusion of WPM through an economy seems to require the services of trusted organizations capable of providing this. JUS, a decentralized mass-membership quality circle society in Japan, provides opportunities for workers and managers from different companies to exchange experiences and to spread the quality circle movement among the uninitiated. National employer and union-management bodies in Sweden serve somewhat the same function, but on a more centralized basis (Cole, 1989). Caja, the co-operative bank, provides a variety of important planning and technical services for Mondragon members.

Financial support

Employee-owned firms require financial as well as technical support. Banks typically are unwilling to lend money to worker-owned industries. Kibbutz organizations support each other (and currently are in financial difficulty for doing so). Mondragon's Caja has generated the capital required for Mondragon's expansion. Without such support, producers' co-operatives may 'self-strangulate'.

Conclusions

There is growing interest in participation as a principle, though the principle is applied differently in various countries. In the post-war period and the 1970s

European unions pushed for representative participation, especially co-determination and work councils. Their objective was to increase union power. More recently management has promoted direct participation. Today there is a growing constituency for shop-level quality of working life (QWL) type participation. Better educated workers want more variety and discretion in their work, and management is increasingly convinced that participation pays off in terms of a more committed and responsible workforce and greater flexibility in deploying manpower.

Formal structures of representative participation are in place in much of continental Europe. They serve as the locus for plant- and firm-level bargaining in these countries, much as stewards and bargaining structures serve in English-speaking countries. Though producers' co-operatives exist in many countries, as yet they play only minor roles.

Much research makes several points clear. First, having a formal structure facilitates changes in actual behaviour (IDE, 1981) but does not guarantee it. Formally prescribed and actual participation are far from perfectly correlated. Informal participation can occur at the workplace, and unions and management may co-operate at high levels, both without formal participative structures. On the other hand, many formal structures atrophy quickly. For formal participative schemes to have any lasting effect they must receive strong support from top management and, in unionized plants, from top union officials.

Recent research (e.g. Long, 1990) suggests that one form of participation, if introduced alone, may have little effect, especially if it is incongruent with other managerial and union policies (Lawler, 1986). Formal participation must be reinforced by genuine informal participation at the workplace, not 'psuedo-participation' (Heller, 1971). Specific formal programmes work best when combined with other policies designed to develop a 'high commitment' culture, such as pay for knowledge, profit-sharing and matrix organization (see also chapter 6).

Further, US experience suggests that WPM is most likely to be successful if direct and representative participation occur simultaneously. Without co-operative relations at the higher levels, co-operation at lower levels will never win support (Kochan, Katz and McKersie, 1986). Representative participation can survive without direct participation, but its full benefits are unlikely to be obtained. Worker ownership alone has few significant payoffs. On the other hand, through providing tangible rewards for participative activities it can reinforce those which are intangible.

Finally, participation may lead only to stalemate and frustration unless overall labour–management relations are reasonably good. Leaders on all levels and both sides must develop new attitudes and skills. This is far from easy. Perhaps most difficult of all, since conflicts of interest are unlikely to disappear, all parties must learn to tolerate the tensions which arise when adversarial and co-operative relations coexist.

WPM has both advantages and costs. To the extent that technology becomes more complex and the environment more turbulent, management may become increasingly dependent on workers' knowledge, commitment and ability to exercise discretion. Only then will WPM's relative advantages become apparent and WPM become more widespread.

Note

1 Stock ownership should not be confused with profit sharing, although the two forms of benefit are granted for much the same reasons and have somewhat similar impacts.

Bibliography

Batstone, E., Ferner, A. and Terry M. (1983) *Unions on the Board*. Oxford: Blackwell.

Bean, R. (1985) *Comparative Industrial Relations*. London: Croom Helm.

Blasi, J., Mehrling, P. and Whyte, W. F. (1984) Environmental influences in the growth of worker ownership and control. *International Yearbook of Organizational Democracy*, 2, 289–313.

Bradley, K. and Hill, S. (1983) 'After Japan': The quality circle transplant and productive efficiency. *British Journal of Industrial Relations*, 21, 291–311.

Brown, C. and Reich, M. (1989): When does cooperation work? A look at NUMMI and GM-Van Nuys. *California Management Review*, 31(4), 26–37.

Bullock, Lord Alan (1977) *Report of the Committee of Inquiry on Industrial Democracy*. London: HMSO.

Clarke, R. O., Fatchett, D. J. and Roberts, B. (1972) *Workers' Participation in Management in Britain*. London: Heinemann.

Cole, Robert (1989) *Strategies for Learning: Small Group Activities in American, Japanese, and Swedish Industry*. Berkeley: University of California Press.

Cooke, W. (1990) *Labor–Management Cooperation: New Partnerships or Going in Circles*. Kalamazoo, MI: Upjohn.

Cressey, P., Eldridge, J. and MacInnes, J. (1985) *Just Managing: Authority and Democracy in Industry*. Milton Keynes: Open University Press.

Dachler, H. P. and Wilpert, B. (1978) Conceptual dimensions and boundaries of participation in organizations. *Administrative Science Quarterly*, 23, 1–39.

Estrin, S. Jones, D. and Svejnar, J. (1987) Productive effects of worker participation: evidence for producer cooperatives. *Journal of Comparative Economic Systems*, 11, 40–61.

Fenwick, R. and Olson, J. (1986) Support for worker participation: attitudes among union and non-union workers. *American Sociological Review*, 51, 505–22.

Frenkel, S. (1989) Explaining the incidence of worker participation in management: evidence from the Australian metal industry. *Australian Journal of Management*, 14, 127–50.

Furstenberg, F. (1978) *Workers' Participation in Management in the Federal Republic of Germany*. Geneva: International Institute of Labor Studies, Research Series No. 32.

Griffin, R. (1988) Consequences of quality circles in an industrial setting: a longitudinal assessment. *Academy of Management Journal*, 31, 338–58.

Gurdon, M. (1985) Equity participation by employees: the growing debate in West Germany. *Industrial Relations*, 24, 113–29.

Hammer, T. and Stern, R. (1986) A yo-yo model of cooperation in management at the Rath Packing Company. *Industrial and Labor Relations Review*, 39, 337–49.

Hartmann, H. (1970) Codetermination in West Germany. *Industrial Relations*, 9, 137–47.

Heller, F. (1971) *Managerial Decision Making*. London: Tavistock.

Hoerr, J. (1988) *And the Wolf Finally Came: the Decline of the American Steel Industry*. Pittsburgh: University of Pittsburgh Press.

Hofstede, G. H. (1980) *Culture's Consequences: International Differences in Work-Related Values*. Beverly Hills: Sage.

IDE (1981) *Industrial Democracy in Europe*. Oxford: Clarendon Press.

Jones, D. (1980) Producer cooperatives in industrialized western economies. *British Journal of Industrial Relations*, 18, 141–54.

Jones, D. (1984) American producers' cooperatives and employee-owned firms. In R. Jackall and H. M. Levin (eds), *Worker Cooperatives in America*. Berkeley: University of California Press.

Kahn-Freud, O. (1979) *Labor Relations: Heritage and Adjustment*. Oxford: Oxford University Press.

Katz, H., Kochan, T. and Keefe, J. (1987) Industrial relations and productivity in the US auto industry. *Brookings Papers on Economic Activity*, 3, 685–726.

Kochan, T. Katz, H. and McKersie, R. (1986) *The Transformation of American Industrial Relations*. New York: Basic Books.

Klein, J. (1984) Why supervisors resist employee involvement. *Harvard Business Review*, 63(4), 87–95.

Lammers, C. (1967) Power and participation in decision-making in formal organizations. *American Journal of Sociology*, 73, 201–16.

Lammers, C. (1974) Self-management and participation: two conceptions of democratization in organizations. *Organization and Administrative Sciences*, 5, 17–33.

Lammers, C. and Szell, G. (1989) Organizational Democracy: Taking Stock. *Handbook of Organizational Participation*, 1, 315–30.

Lawler, E. (1986) *High-involvement Management*. San Francisco: Jossey-Bass.

Leitko. T. A., Greil, A. L. and Patterson, S. A. (1985) Lessons at the bottom: worker nonparticipation in labor-management committees as situational adjustments. *Work and Occupations*, 12, 285–306.

Levine, D. (in press) 'Demand variability and work organization', in Samuel Bowles, Herbert Gintis and B. Gustason, (eds) *Democracy and Markets*. Cambridge: Cambridge University Press.

Lincoln, J. (1989) Employee work attitudes and management practices in the U.S. and Japan. *California Management Review*, 32, 89–106.

Locke, E. and Schweiger D. M. (1978) Participation in decision-making: one more look, in B. Staw and L. L. Cummings (eds), *Research in Organizational Behavior*, 1.

Long, R. (1989) Patterns of workplace innovation in Canada. *Relations Industrielles*, 44, 4 805–26.

Long, R. (1990) The effects of various workplace innovations on productivity: a quasi-experimental study. Paper presented at the 1990 Conference of the Administrative Sciences Association of Canada.

Lowin, A. (1968) Participative decision-making: a model, literature critique, and prescriptions for research. *Organizational Behavior and Human research*, 3, 68–106.

MacInnis, J. (1985) Conjuring up consultation: the role and extent of joint consultation in post-war private manufacturing industry. *British Journal of Industrial Relations*, 23, 93–114.

Macy, B., Peterson, M. and Norton, L. (1989) A test of participation theory in a work re-design field setting. *Human Relations*, 42, 1095–165.

Manz, C. and Sims, H. P. (1987) Leading workers to lead themselves: the external leadership of self-management work teams. *Administrative Science Quarterly*, 31, 106–21.

Marginson, P., Edwards, P. K., Martin, R., Purcell, J. and Sisson, K. (1988) *Beyond the Workplace: Managing Industrial Relations in the Multi-Establishment Enterprise*. Oxford: Blackwell.

Millward, N. and Stevens, M. (1986) *British Workplace Industrial Relations, 1980–84*, Aldershot: Gower.

Morishima, M. (1991) information and firm performance in Japan, *Industrial Relations*, 30, 37–61.

Obradovitch, J. (1970) Participation and work attitudes in Yugoslavia. *Industrial Relations*, 9, 161–9.

Poole, M. (1988) Factors affecting employee financial participation. *British Journal of Industrial Relations*, 26, 1, 21–36.

Strauss, G. (1982) Workers' participation in management: an international comparison. In B. Staw and L. L. Cummings (eds), *Research in Organizational Behavior*, 4, 173–265.

Strauss, G. and Hammer, T. (in press) Workers' participation in the United States. *Workers' Participation: Some Significant National Experiences*. Geneva: International Labour Office.

Streeck, W. (1984) Codetermination: the fourth decade. *International Yearbook of Organizational Democracy*, 2, 391–422.

Tannenbaum, A., Kavcic, B., Rosner, M., Vianello, M. and Wiser, G. (1974) *Hierarchy in Organizations*. San Francisco: Jossey-Bass.

Voos, P. (1987) Managerial perceptions of the economic impact of labor relations programs. *Industrial and Labor Relations Review*, 40, 195–208.

Wall, T. and Lisheron, J. (1977) *Workers' Participation: a Critique of the Literature and Some Fresh Evidence*. London: McGraw-Hill.

Walton, R. (1980) Establishing and maintaining high commitment work systems. In J. R. Kimberly and R. H. Miles (eds), *The Organizational Work Cycle*. San Francisco: Jossey-Bass.

Webb, S. and Webb, B. (1920) *A Constitution for the Socialist Commonwealth of Great Britain*. London: Longman.

Whyte, W. F., Hammer, T., Meek, C., Nelson, R. and Stern, R. (1983) *Worker Participation and Ownership*. Ithaca, New York: ILR Press.

Whyte, W. F. and Whyte, K. (1988) *Making Mondragon: the growth and dynamics of the worker cooperative complex*. Ithaca, New York: ILR Press.

Wilpert, B. (1975) Research on industrial democracy: the German case. *Industrial Relations Journal*, 6, 65–72.

Zwerdling, D. (1978) Employee ownership: how well is it working? *Working Papers for a New Society*, 7, 15–27.

Further reading

IDE (1981) *Industrial Democracy in Europe*. Oxford: Clarendon Press.

Lawler, E. (1986) *High-involvement Management*. San Francisco: Jossey-Bass. *International Yearbook of Organizational Democracy*. 1983–86: 1–3.

Poole, M. (1986) *Toward a New Industrial Democracy: Workers Participation in Industry*. London: Routledge Kegan Paul.

14

Flexible Working and New Technology

Wally S. Mueller

Introduction

The framework of change

During the past two decades, organizations in industrialized countries have had to respond to rapid technological change, worldwide recession in the early 1980s, increasingly uncertain and competitive global markets, and changing worker expectations (Kanawaty et al., 1989). One strategy has been to remove rigidities in the labour market, such as restrictive work and managerial practices, fixed working hours, outdated demarcations and inadequate education and training. Governments in most of the developed countries have provided national infrastructure support for labour flexibility by pursuing deregulation policies of various kinds. Organizations which have adapted best to the changing circumstances are those which have, among other strategic measures, adopted new technology and implemented more flexible working and management practices (Curtain, 1988; Newton, 1989; Yamashita, 1989). Changes in technology and working practices have also been accompanied by radical organizational restructuring, resulting in leaner, flatter structures. The move towards responsive organizational structures sets the pace for constant change, now a reality of organizational life for the 1990s.

Changes in labour market strategies and in technology have also placed another major stakeholder group, the unions, under increasing pressure. Union membership is declining rapidly, mainly because of stagnant employment growth in the blue collar section (e.g. manufacturing and mining), which was their traditional area of strength, and because of the inability of unions to attract new members in the growing information/service sector (see also chapter 7). Furthermore, the unions have been struggling to provide adequate representation for the labour market segment that is experiencing the greatest rate of employment increase, namely, part-time or temporary work, which attracts predominantly females, young job-seekers or minority groups. After adopting a reactive stance to proposed changes in technology and to flexible working strategies, an increasing number of unions are now accepting the 'new reality' (Horstman, 1988) that such changes are essential for long term competitiveness and ultimately for employment growth (Sarfati and Kobrin, 1988). Their latest policies go beyond the immediate concerns of their members and focus on wider issues which traditionally have been the concern of management, for example productivity, efficiency, and investment in new technology (Kanawaty et al., 1989; Mansfield, 1988; Swedish Metal Workers' Union (SWMU), 1987; ACTU/TDC, 1987).

At the level of organizations, the flexibility debate is about competitiveness and responsiveness. This has not translated in a simple way to the level of individuals. If the employment relationship is defined in terms of power distribution, both vertically and horizontally, within an organization, then labour flexibility has to be defined within the same framework. To an employee, flexibility may mean the freedom to decide how a particular set of tasks is performed, by whom and at what time. To a fellow worker from a different union, this decision may be regarded as an imposition on his or her autonomy. To a manager or supervisor, worker autonomy may be perceived as a threat to authority or a loss of direct control over operational decision-making. Conversely, flexibility to a manager may mean the freedom to move employees around at will.

The concept of flexibility can only be fully understood in the context of working relationships between organizational stakeholders. Of particular importance is the relationship between managers, unions and workers. Flexibility is a key component of managerial control. The adoption of different forms of flexibility provide additional oportunities to redefine, overtly and covertly, the power relationship between stakeholders within organizations. This chapter explores the changing nature of employment relationships in organizations adopting flexible working strategies and/or new technology.

Figure 14.1 provides a framework for examining the circumstances surrounding the adoption of flexible working strategies, the role of new technology as a

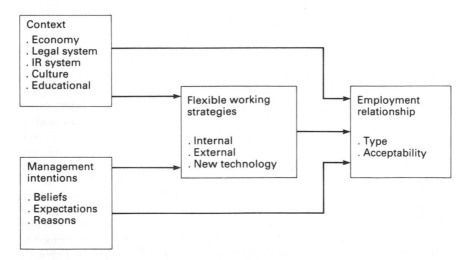

Figure 14.1 Flexible working strategies, new technology and employment relationship.

flexibility option, and the implications for the type and acceptability of employment relationship, with particular emphasis on autonomy within this relationship. In order fully to understand the effect of flexible working schemes or new technology on the employment relationship, it is important to examine the reasons for their introduction into an organization (Kossek, 1989; Mueller et al., 1986). The translation of managerial intentions into actions is guided in part by the beliefs or expectations that are held about the expected outcomes. Furthermore, the 'success' of the outcomes cannot be readily understood without knowledge of what was expected.

In any organizational change process, stakeholders such as workers, mid-managers, union officials and technical specialists influence the translation of managerial intentions into actions. They have to interpret the intentions, often inarticulate or driven by hidden agendas, and select appropriate implementation tactics. This process can easily muddy the links between intentions, strategies, implementation processes and acceptability of employment relations (Clegg and Kemp, 1986).

Decisions about the adoption of new technology and flexible working strategies are made within the context of broad external factors such as legal, financial, political, educational, industrial relations and wages systems, culture, the economy, demographic structure, trade relations with other countries, and government control (Sarfati and Kobrin, 1988; Mueller, 1989). There is insufficient scope in this chapter to examine contextual factors separately, but some are considered in the discussion of the flexibility choices that are available to organizations. As shown in figure 14.1, context also influences the degree of acceptability of the employment relationship that is experienced by organizational stakeholders.

External Labour Market Flexibility

Impact on employment relations

Managers who pursue external labour flexibility strategies manipulate the staff levels that are required to handle variations in throughput of work by varying the number of workers who have only a peripheral relationship to the organization (McCune et al., 1989). Such an employment relationship allows the organization to shed staff with obsolete skills and to hire those with skills required to handle particular tasks. Examples of this type of flexible working include: self-employment, consultancy, subcontracting, secondments, relief work, seasonal work, part-time contract work (temporary, alternating work/rest), fixed-term contracts, government-sponsored schemes for the unemployed, voluntary work, multiple job holders, clandestine work (moonlighting, undeclared work, family work, foreigners without valid permits), contract teleworking (especially electronic cottage work) and outwork (e.g. textiles). Where circumstances make it difficult to retain usual staffing levels, organizations have sought to reduce numbers by natural attrition, non-replacement of retired employees, reducing wage and salary levels during periods of economic difficulty, or retrenchment as a last resort.

The past two decades has witnessed a significant increase in the use of subcontractors and temporary workers by organizations. These forms of labour market flexibility allow managers to deal with market uncertainties and rapidly changing skill requirements in the marketplace without incurring long term costs. Through the use of temporary workers, managers are able to cover for temporary peaks in activity or demand. Temporary workers represent the most common form of part-time work. Employment growth has been greatest for females, minority races and younger members of the workforce, mainly in clerical work, industrial, recreational and service industries. The transitory nature of the employment relationship suits the needs of those who require only part-time work. Such employees can tolerate low levels of autonomy in the workplace in the knowledge that they can choose when to terminate the relationship. To the extent that an employee becomes dependent on such work as the primary source of income, the employment relationship is characterized by deep insecurity for the worker. Managers have almost total direct control over who works, when and how. Union coverage of temporary workers is extremely low.

The growth of temporary work and subcontracting has been at the expense of the permanent, tenured workforce. Characteristic of modern organizations is the trend towards a diminishing core of well paid, tenured staff and an expanding peripheral workforce (Atkinson, 1984; Wood, 1989). Managers use the latter to protect the job security of the former. There are fewer core staff, but they are very well treated by their organization. This issue is treated more extensively later in the chapter.

Where subcontacting is heavily used, Curtain (1988) argues that the main disincentive for organizations to train their own staff in the required skills is the fear of poaching by other firms (cf. Child, 1985). Under these circumstances, managers fear loss of control over their investment in human resources, preferring to treat expertise as a commodity. Other writers argue that the main reasons why organizations subcontract work include: concentration of resources on core business activities, reduced need to add permanent staff, and ability to employ extras to meet deadlines (Evans and Walker, 1986). In the case of the last two reasons cited, unions have often taken a strong stand against the use of subcontracting because increased workload is normally an opportune time to press for an increase in the workforce. Instead, subscontracting increases management's control over the labour process and allows them to resist union pressures to increase the numbers of unionized workers.

Internal Labour Market Flexibility

Managers who pursue internal labour flexibility strategies can implement alternative work schedules or in-house skill acquisition programmes (usually accompanied by organization and job redesign). These strategies involve existing employees as the primary source for handling variations in workload distribution, a wider variety of tasks and new tasks based on advances in technology.

Alternative work schedules

Variations in the standard working week include: overtime, flexitime, staggered hours, annual hours, compressed working week, extended schedules, variation in days per week, choice of specific days worked, rostering systems, shift systems, part-time (permanent tenured), compressed part-time, job sharing, teleworking, sabbaticals, extended leave, unpaid leave, and career breaks.

The nature and acceptability of the employment relationship depends not only on the structure of the work schedule but also on the divergent needs of different workers. Only those work schedules which seem to have the most important implications for the employment relationship are discussed here.

Flexitime   This refers to a regular work day which can commence at any time within a particular range. The daily number of work hours are constant. This is the one form of alternative work schedule where the balance of control is clearly in the employee's favour. Managers who offer flexitime cite among the advantages: better coverage of the workplace, improved productivity, reduced tardiness, easier recruiting, and fewer commuting problems (Levine, 1987). Many supervisors, however, resent the reduced lack of control over workflow during the early morning and late afternoon periods of the regular work day.

Flexible hours   This refers to work schedules which coincide with actual demand for goods and services. The flexibility can be in the form of daily, weekly or annual hours. Within each of these, the hours are constant overall, but there is a tight fit between output requirements and hours worked. This gives employers considerable power over workers as to when they work and for how long, particularly in industries subject to seasonal demand for products or services. The productivity gains that employers can achieve with this form of employment are one of its major attractions to management. This is one strategy which has led to heated management–union clashes in the 1980s, since it represents to the unions a relinquishing of control over a fundamental work condition issue which they fought for decades to secure. In cultures where work centrality is not high, the control by managers over when employees report to work can cause severe disruption to family life. This form of employment relationship therefore includes direct management control over the employee and indirect control over other family members.

Compressed working weeks   These are defined as standard weekly hours squeezed into less than five days. Employees cite greater control over leisure time and an ability to schedule commitments outside working hours as reasons for preferring this type of work schedule. Supervisors, however, feel greater stress with this work schedule because of co-ordination difficulties with supplies and maintenance (Levine, 1987).

Job sharing   This involves two or more people who share the responsibilities of a full-time position. It differs from part-time work in that the entitlements enjoyed by permanent staff are shared by the job sharers. This form of work became popular during the 1980s recession. At other times, it has been offered as a way of attracting married women to the workforce. Most of the jobs are clerical, but many professional jobs are structured in this way (Evans and Bell,

1986). Other reasons for job sharing include decreased turnover and accommodation of working parents. Managers and supervisors lose some control in this type of employment relationship owing to the communication difficulties often experienced between the job sharers. Apart from occasional errors of omission in communicating technical or procedural information to a job-share partner, much of the political context within which work is carried out is difficult to pass on or is forgotten. The tacit knowledge possessed by a single job incumbent has to be made more explicit when the position is shared, resulting in more fragmented working relationships with fellow workers and supervisors.

Remote work and telework A significant development in the past decade has been the growth of remote work. In the 1985 USA Household Survey, over 8 million people worked for more than 8 hours per week at home. The majority were full-time workers who do a small amount at home (Horvath, 1986). Similarly, some 7 per cent of the UK workforce work from home (Evans and Bell, 1986). Some of this growth has resulted from work done by professionals and clerical staff on personal computers at home, which are linked to head office computers (telework).

Predictions of massive increases in computer-based home employment have not been realized, but numbers are steadily rising. For professionals, teleworking bridges the career gap for women with children, accommodates locational preferences, permits people to combine work with other interests, is ideal for single parents with family pressure, allows childcare at home for dual career families, and integrates work and non-work activities. For management, tele-working facilitates recruitment and retention of people with scarce skills, allows the organization to call on people who otherwise might not be available to them (e.g. retired or disabled people), provides perhaps the optimal way of dealing with peripheral staff, facilitates any moves towards decentralization, is a way of providing extra space, and reduces fixed capital costs (Bailyn, 1988; Evans and Bell, 1986; Olson, 1988).

Employees do experience some loss of control in this type of employment relationship. The intrusion of work-related issues into the home is the most serious implication. The boundary between home and work life is difficult to manage and generates stress for the worker and partner. Furthermore, it is difficult for clerical teleworkers to organize or gain control over their work. There are also concerns that teleworkers who carry out mainly clerical or data processing work are exploited, especially when the work is performed overseas or by minority groups (Chamot, 1988). In general, the degree of auto-nomy that is experienced with telework is a function of the type of work performed. Where there is a high degree of fragmentation of the work pro-cess and payment is based on piece rates, autonomy is low. This form of indirect management control over labour may be less preferable for these tasks than the collective control exercised by a group of workers and supervisors at the workplace. On the other hand, professionals seem to prefer the absence of external control that is offered by telework and indeed are attracted to this work primarily because of the autonomy it provides (Huws et al., 1990).

Multiskilling

Multiskilling (variously called polyvalence, functional flexibility, craft flexibility, skills extension or additional skills training) is defined as a process for increasing a worker's range of skills so that a greater range of tasks can be performed, often across previously different occupational specializations. Horizontal multiskilling refers to additional competencies which are acquired at approximately the same level of intellectual, technical or interpersonal skill. Vertical multiskilling includes higher levels of skill and responsibility within a particular skill category; for example, the addition of quality control in the repertoire of a production operator or the training of peers new to an area of competency.

Typically, enterprise-based multiskilling programmes contain a number of interdependent features (Cordery, 1989):

1 Few occupational categories.
2 Job rotation, to facilitate skill acquisition and use.
3 Formal training and assessment programmes – points are awarded for each successfully completed module of the programme.
4 A skill-based (rather than performance-based) pay system (Luthans and Fox, 1989; Gupta et al., 1986).
5 Site-based (rather than industry-based) industrial agreements.

Management reasons for pursuing multiskilling as a flexibility strategy include: reduction in staffing levels of core staff, securing employee commitment, a more docile industrial relations climate, ability to cover absences without extra staff, required skills not available externally, cutting across old occupational demarcations, more stable workforce and greater employee responsibility and accountability.

Workers in many cases are attracted to multiskilling because of promises of job challenge through greater control over their work, an opportunity to learn a wide range of skills and greater protection against changing skill requirements on the job market (cf. Child, 1984). Unions, however, have often expressed suspicion at management motives for multiskilling, primarily the de-manning strategy. In the union's view, multiskilling means job intensification. At green-field sites, however, unions have in recent years been competing against each other for coverage of new job designs that span traditional boundaries. Therefore, since some unions secure benefits (at the expense of others), the degree of resistance to multiskilling programmes has been only temporary. Where craft unions lose tasks to unions covering semi-skilled workers, resistance is maintained for lengthy periods. The resistance is ultimately dysfunctional because the semi-skilled workers not only gain the necessary skills required to perform tasks competently but are also paid for the skills acquired. At the top levels, their pay matches that of skilled labour covered by the craft unions.

Nevertheless, even those unions who accept multiskilling as superior to traditional job designs believe that multiskilling is another management tool for subtle social control, because it is not integrated sufficiently into the mainstream fabric of the organizational structure (SMWU, 1987). In the early phases of a multiskilling programme, there is an expectation among workers that acquisition of skills across many areas, recognized by increases in pay, will lead to greater decision-making responsibility about when and how work is performed. If the multiskilling programme occurs within the context of self-regulating teams, as it often does, the group is also able to decide who performs the work (Cordery et al., 1991). The employment relationship in this situation is characterized by teams of workers who control the work process, supported by first-line supervisory staff whose function is to co-ordinate the interface between the team and the rest of the organization.

The acceptability of the employment relationship in a team-based multi-skilled environment is a function of worker expectations about the degree of team decision-making responsibility that is desired. These expectations are shaped in large part by management promises made at inductions for recruits to the organization. These promises linger in the minds of workers for a number of years, placing considerable pressures on managers to deliver the promised support services and supervisory behaviour styles which are appropri-ate for effective team decision-making (Mueller and Cordery, 1991). In particular, the most appropriate managerial and supervisory styles under these circumstances require the replacement of direct control by control that is more indirect and supportive. Directive management control gives way to strategic management control or management by commitment (Walton, 1985; see also chapters 4 and 5).

In reality, strategic management control is rarely maintained in a uniform way by different managers and supervisors. Some are capable only of directive management control. Even when managers do not explicitly state that control is an objective, their decision-making behaviour can betray such an intention. Managers may espouse bilateral control strategies but they may not be aware that their actual behaviour is more consistent with a unilateral control strategy (Argyris, 1985).

To workers who were led to believe that their autonomy would be greater than in a traditional job design, the restriction placed on their scope for decision-making by directive managers and supervisors leads to widespread dissatisfaction, lack of commitment to the organization's goals and lack of trust in management (Mueller and Cordery, 1991). Conversely, where first line supervisors in particular relinquish most of their control over the work process to the team of multiskilled workers, the latter's satisfaction, commitment and trust in management are higher. Under these circumstances, management maintain their control via 'responsible autonomy' of the employees (Friedman, 1977; see also chapter 4). One can argue that their control over labour is greater because high quality work is produced in the absence of close supervision. This leaves intact the basic organizational and decision-making structures above first-line supervision, suggesting that innovations such as multiskilling and semi-autonomous work groups are cocooned from the mainstream of organizational decision-making processes (Jenkins, 1986; Mansell, 1987; Mueller and Cordery, 1991; Newton, 1989; SWMU, 1987).

Child (1985) also believes that managers' control over employees increases in multiskilled environments but for different reasons; that is, the internal training programmes are enterprise-based and therefore not readily recognized by other organizations. For example, workers in multiskilling programmes in the Australian iron ore mining industry are concerned that their competencies are not transferable to, say, the gold mining industry. From their point of view, as more on-the-job training occurs, assessment and accreditation will need to be centralized outside the organization to ensure that workers have mobility in the workplace. This would normally provide managers with a great deal of control over workers' career development.

In practice, however, multiskilled employees in the mining industry have found themselves in great demand by organizations who value employees with a demonstrated capacity to thrive in a learning environment. In organizations undergoing rapid change, such readily trainable employees are more likely to adapt to changing skill and work organization requirements. Furthermore, employees who have mastered the full multiskilling programme at a horizontal level can bargain for an extension to the programme by introducing vertical multiskilling opportunities. Employers are under pressure to provide such vertical programmes in order to retain their core multiskilled staff. Thus, the verdict on who is in control in a multiskilled environment is not at all clear. Very few systematic longitudinal studies have been conducted. The employment relationship in a multiskilled environment is very complicated and dynamic, partly because of the inherent unpredictability of a situation that is not an integral part of the main organizational decision-making structure and processes. This reinforces the point that Keenoy makes about the contradictions inherent in the employment relationship (chapter 4).

Flexibility and New Technology

Much of the debate about the influence of new technology on the employment relationship has been couched in terms of technological determinism versus organizational choice. During the 1970s, many commentators predicted that widespread de-skilling would accompany the march of advanced technologies in the workplace, most notably Braverman (1974). Whilst there have been a number of instances of de-skilling (e.g. Shaiken et al., 1986; Burnes, 1988), the bulk of the evidence generally supports the view that automation is most often accompanied by the upgrading of skills (Buchanan and Boddy, 1983; Adler, 1987; Davis, 1988). The critical point is that the increasing flexibility of new technology provides decision-makers with choices in both organization and work design (Blackler, 1988; Buchanan and Boddy, 1983; Clegg and Kemp, 1986; Mueller, 1990), although the choices available to management and other stakeholders appear to be constrained by the technology to varying degrees (Mueller, 1985; Wall, 1987).

Unfortunately, the choices exercised by management can include both skills upgrading and de-skilling on the shopfloor in these instances (Buchanan and

Boddy, 1983). One study did find that skills upgrading was associated with the most advanced form of flexible manufacturing system, whilst de-skilled jobs were designed around tasks that the new technology could not at that stage handle (Wall et al., 1987). In other words, two contrasting types of employment relationship existed within neighbouring areas of the same shopfloor.

Several authors (e.g. Curtain, 1988; Gustavsen, 1986; Warner, 1986; Graham and Rosenthal, 1986) argue that the increasing number of options made possible by new technology require more flexible skill formation strategies if enterprises intend to become more competitive (cf. Shaiken et al., 1986). Gustavsen (1986) offers three reasons why flexible working practices are needed to take advantage of the options made possible by new technology. First, different forms of technology are often to be found in the one production area. A single way of organizing work would be inappropriate.

Second, Gustavsen argues that any one person may experience different organizational patterns depending on the tasks being performed, particularly in the case of employees working in more than one project team. Third, as the technology continues to evolve, new patterns of work constantly emerge. A history of flexible work organization would place an enterprise in a more responsive, capable position to deal with the changes necessary.

In Child's (1985) view, managerial policies about internal and external labour market strategies cannot be divorced from new technology strategies. He argues that four such policies have been facilitated by new technology: the desire to eliminate direct labour, an increase in contract labour, the removal of job demarcations, and the de-skilling of jobs. Although managerial control strategies appeals as a straightforward explanation for many case study findings, there are difficulties in accepting it as a sufficient explanation of how work is organized in new technology environments.

New technology and control over work

When managers contemplate and plan for the introduction of new technology, they do so for reasons that appear publicly to be rational and well articulated. On the surface, they also seem to hold a unitary set of beliefs about the effects of new technology. The reality at the individual level, however, reveals a different picture: managers do not seem to be altogether conscious of the range of possibilities that the technology offers, the reasons for adoption are vaguely explained and driven by technical considerations, the technology is introduced in incremental fashion into the organization, and beliefs about the effects of the new technology and how jobs should be designed around it vary widely amongst managers (Clegg and Kemp, 1986; Mueller et al., 1986).

Since new technology is often introduced in a relatively unplanned way, there are various opportunities, during the implementation process, for other stake-holders to influence the amount of control that workers eventually attain over work around the new technology. Wilkinson (1983) provides several examples of workers gaining control over key features of new technology, and Child (1985) cites a case of supervisors altering work practices whilst accommodating to the unreliable aspects of technology functioning. There are also cases where the loss of control by skilled trades people as a result of new technology triggered successful attempts to regain a measure of control whenever the technology provided an opportunity to do so (Thompson, 1983). In general, the reclaiming of control may always be possible because of the non-determinant nature of new technology. Whilst the software component often constrains choices in intended, predictable ways, it always allows unpredictable possibilities that can be exploited by alert operators. The informal practices resulting from this process eventually consolidate into a *de facto* strategy, which does not usually reflect original managerial intentions but which can sometimes result in managers themselves attempting to reassert control on the next occasion that new technology is introduced. Under these circumstances, management typically set up the hardware at a location out of sight of the main shopfloor in order to establish the possibilities of the technology and of laying down control procedures before introducing it to the shopfloor (Wilkinson, 1983).

Child (1985) argues that, when a flexible working strategy is adopted for new technology, indirect forms of managerial control in this situation are more effective than direct forms of control:

> responsible autonomy, which tends to complement polyvalence [i.e. multiskilling], is a control strategy with its focus typically on output measurement. For instance, the allocation of responsibility to a worker or work group for a more 'complete' set of tasks can make it easier for management to identify accountability for sub-standard performance. The application of new microelectronic monitoring devices and information transmission systems facilitates performance measurement, and may thereby make a transition from direct personal supervision of the labour process to a responsible autonomy format that is much more acceptable to management. In effect, new technology can substitute supervision at a distance for supervision in the workplace.
>
> (Child, 1985, p. 127)

New technology can therefore provide the best of both worlds for managers: strategic control and unobserved monitoring of work performance. Such is the flexibility of new technology, however, that it can provide astute workers with the means to bypass constraining authority structures in organizations and thereby transform employment relationships (Mueller, 1990). The next section develops this theme in more detail.

New technology and transparency of work behaviour

There are now several published examples of new technology being used to increase the visibility or transparency of employee behaviour in both blue collar (Dawson, 1987) and white collar sector jobs (Buchanan and McCalman, 1988), with far reaching implications for the employment relationship. Howard (1987) argues that information systems in an environment where work is highly interdependent allows individual work performance to become more transparent to others. With the increase in organizational knowledge, Kling and Iacono (1984) argue that peer surveillance becomes the new institutional form of control over work.

Where new technology has been used at the managerial level, increased visibility of individual performance in hotel management via a computer-based information system led to reduction of conflict and empire building with no increase in stress (Buchanan and McCalman, 1988). This has consequences for management styles: managers unable to adjust to a more participative form of decision-making find themselves unable to utilize the new technology effectively (Kanawaty et al., 1989).

At the level of workers, it is possible for new technology not only to reduce autonomy through its monitoring capability but also to provide employees with the means to increase the amount of control over their work (Dawson, 1987). This can be done in two ways: by direct control over tasks performed by the technology (Corbett, 1987), or by indirect control through an understanding of how the system as a whole functions (Frese, 1987). In short, new technology can provide the opportunity to see the 'big picture', and can therefore aid the understanding of how other processes impinge on a particular area, or are influenced by it. This should allow operators to respond to one part of the system in a way that reflects their understanding of wider aspects (much as management understanding of the total system is reflected in their decision-making). The concept of transparency in this instance is not whether the individual's behaviour becomes visible to others via new technology but whether the system or organization becomes more transparent to the individual by means of the same technology.

There are some claims that Japanese workers in the major manufacturing corporations have, through interaction with their integrated computerized information systems, a relatively advanced understanding of how their organizations function. It is difficult to evaluate such claims for four reasons at least. First, most workers in the larger organizations have experienced an extensive job rotation system, which is likely to provide knowledge not only about each job but also about how the tasks within and between jobs are linked. Second, Japanese managers are less hesitant to sit down with their workers and to provide them with company information that is both directly and indirectly relevant to their jobs. Third, the union officials tend to work closely with management and therefore obtain more relevant and timely information to disseminate to their members. Fourth, since integrated information systems can never cover all work interdependencies and contingencies, workers have to negotiate the application of general rules to align with the complexities of the production process. This implies a need for flexible working practices to cope with variances in the system. It is more likely, therefore, that it is the internal flexible working strategies, and not the new technology *per se*, that has given the Japanese workers a seemingly wider understanding of how their organization functions.

On a final note, Crozier (1983) argues that, when new technology uncovers previously hidden layers of an organization, the increased transparency may reduce flexibility in an organization's functioning. For example, the rostering of nursing staff on shifts by a new computerized patient care system may cut across previous practices based on mutual adjustment. In many cases, it is middle management that is adversely affected by an increasingly transparent organization, particularly if their subordinates are computer competent and communicate laterally and vertically via computer/communications technology (Kanawaty et al., 1989; Mueller, 1990). Clearly, the flexibility of new technology can increase transparency of both individual work behaviour and organizational practices and, in the process can shift the balance of power in the employment relationship.

Conclusion

New technology and flexible working strategies are transforming employment relationships in the workplace. Together, they are seen as the linchpins for marketplace competitiveness and long term employment creation. This is the 'new reality' of the late 1980s, increasingly accepted by trade unions. It is the key to understanding their willingness to negotiate major organizational and work design changes. This is a major factor in the increasing pace of workplace change and in the growing pressure to remove the barriers to change. Governments have sought to dismantle a number of institutional barriers in order to foster enterprise competitiveness in the global marketplace.

The growth in the peripheral workforce during the 1980s underlines a shift in the balance of power between employers and unions. The latter are struggling to address the needs of the peripheral labour market. Their membership is declining rapidly, but they still represent a major force in the change process and have an opportunity to provide organized cover for a growing but precarious segment of the workforce. In some countries, the unions have taken a proactive role in pursuing flexible internal labour market strategies which are based on tripartite negotiations with employers and governments.

The proliferation of new technology and flexible working strategies in the organizations of industrialized countries is accompanied by the emergence of different forms of social control over labour. Traditional forms of direct management control, still the most common model in most countries, appear to be inappropriate for handling internal flexible working strategies. Indeed, the attempt by management to maintain, regain or increase direct control over the way in which work is organized interferes with the effective implementation of new technology and initiatives in internal labour market flexibility strategies such as multiskilling.

Granting employees wider responsibilities to use their broader range of skills requires management to relinquish a good deal of direct control but leaves strategic control in their hands. The locus of control over labour shifts from procedures to outputs. Correspondingly, managers require more sophisticated interpersonal skills to coordinate the work of such employees within and across functions.

First-line supervisors facilitate rather than direct and act as a resource to those directly involved in the production of goods and services.

Flexible organizational structures provide the framework within which internal flexible working strategies can be accommodated. This involves: dismantling both horizontal and vertical boundaries of occupational categories, forming broad-band categories containing a range of skills within each band, allowing easy access to career paths through extensive training programmes and opportunity to exercise skills acquired, and implementing a pay-for-skills wages and salary structure. Increasingly, these opportunities are available only to a comparatively diminishing group of permanent, full-time core staff of an organization. This intensifies the imbalance in job security and working conditions between the core employees (the 'haves') and peripheral labour (the 'have-nots'). The Japanese model of life-long job security for core employees of major corporations and an external labour flexibility strategy for subcontractors, part-time workers and other peripheral forms of labour is being rapidly approached by a number of enterprises in Western industrialized countries.

New technology has provided management with additional forms of control over labour. Two direct forms of control include the de-skilling of jobs and the monitoring of individuals' work through information systems that make the work of employees transparent not only to management but also in some cases to their peers (leading to claims of a new form of institutional control, i.e. peer control). Two forms of indirect control include the removal of artificial barriers between occupational boundaries and the design of jobs that require skill upgrading, responsible autonomy and therefore greater commitment to management objectives.

Managers do not often use technology to achieve direct control over labour. They are not always aware of the potential for control and implementation is haphazard and incremental. Thus, opportunities exist for unions and workers to re-assert or increase their level of local control over work designed around the technology. In white collar private industry and public service jobs, the combination of communications and decentralized computer capabilities allows employees at lower levels of the organization to bypass the formal lines of authority in the interests of effectiveness and efficiency. This places both middle and some upper levels of management under considerable pressure because new technology is accelerating the process of shifting the emphasis of authority from a seniority-based to a competency-based system. The net result is a reduction of levels of management in modern organizational structures.

Although predictions about the growth in telework as a technology-driven form of flexible working strategy have proved to be overly optimistic, there is considerable scope for systematic longitudinal studies of the impact of such jobs on: (a) individual outcome measures, such as productivity, quality and job satisfaction; (b) the quality of employer–employee and peer relationships for teleworkers who differ in tenure, type of occupation (e.g. professional vs. clerical), and degree of electronic monitoring experienced; (c) degree of coverage by unions; and (d) exploitation of clerical workers who are from disadvantaged groups or located in another country.

A wealth of case study material and surveys of several organizations has provided the basis of arguments presented in this chapter. Whilst it has been possible to highlight converging lines of evidence on some issues, it is premature to draw general conclusions about the effect of different flexible working and new technology strategies on the type and acceptability of the employment relationship. Too little is known about how management intentions and a wide range of contextual factors determine the choice of strategies. Managerial intentions and context are likely to influence the acceptability of different forms of employment relationship. More powerful research designs, utilizing both qualitative and quantitative types of data, are required to evaluate the effect of flexible working and new technology on the acceptability of the employment relationship, particularly the impact on autonomy. Given the rapid pace of organizational change, however, it is equally important to evaluate models of implementation of new technology and flexible working strategies. Findings from these implementation evaluations are of considerable importance to those charged with the responsibility of facilitating the change process.

References

Adler, P. S. (1987) Automation and skills: New directions. *International Journal of Technology Management*, 2, 5/6, 761–72.

Argyris, C. (1985) *Strategy, Change and Defensive Routines*. Boston: Pitman.

Atkinson, J. (1984) Manpower strategies for flexible organisations. *Personnel Management*, August, 28–31.

Australian Council of Trade Unions (ACTU)/Trade Development Council (TDC) (1987) *Australia Reconstructed* Canberra: Australian Government Publishing Service.

Bailyn, L. (1988) Freeing work from the constraints of location and time. *New Technology, Work and Employment*, 3, 2, 143–52.

Blackler, F. (1988) Information technologies and organizations: Lessons from the 1980s and issues for the 1990s. *Journal of Occupational Psychology*, 61, 113–27.

Braverman, H. (1974) *Labor and Monopoly Capital: The Degradation of Work in the Twentieth Century*. New York: Monthly Review Press.

Buchanan, D. A. and Boddy, D. (1983) *Organisations in the Computer Age: Technological Imperatives and Strategic Choice*. Aldershot: Gower.

Buchanan, D. A. and McCalman, J. (1988) Confidence, visibility and pressure: the effects of shared information in computer-aided hotel management. *New Technology, Work and Employment*, 3, 1, 38–46.

Burnes, B. (1988) New technology and job design: the case of CNC. *New Technology, Work and Employment*, 3, 2, 100–11.

Chamot, D. (1988) Blue-collar, white-collar: homeworker problems. In K. E. Christiansen (ed.), *The New Era of Home-Based Work*, Boulder, Colo: Westview Press, 168–76.

Child, J. (1984) New technology and developments in management organization. *Omega* 12, 3, 211–23.

Child J. (1985) Managerial strategies, new technology and the labour process. In D. Knights, H. Willmott and D. Collinson (eds), *Job Redesign: Critical Perspectives on the Labour Process*, Aldershot: Gower, 108–41.

Clegg, C. and Kemp, N. (1986) Information technology: Personnel, where are you? *Personnel Review*, 15, 1, 8–15.

Corbett, M. (1987) Computer-aided manufacturing and the design of shopfloor jobs: Towards a new research perspective in occupational psychology. In M. Frese, E. Ulich and W. Dzida (eds), *Psychological Issues of Human–Computer Interaction in the Workplace*, Amsterdam: North Holland, 23–40.

Cordery, J. L. (1989) Multi-skilling: a discussion of proposed benefits of new approaches to labour flexibility within enterprises. *Personnel Review*, 18, 3, 13–22.

Cordery, J. L., Mueller, W. S. and Smith, L. M. (1991) Attitudinal and behavioral outcomes of autonomous group working: A longitudinal field study. *Academy of Management Journal*, (in press).

Crozier, M. (1983) Implications for the organization. In H. J. Otway and M. Peltu (eds), *New Office Technology: Human and Organizational Aspects*, London: Frances Pinter, 86–101.

Curtain, R. (1988) Skill formation in manufacturing: Obstacles and opportunities. *Human Resource Management Australia*, November, 7–21.

Davis, D. J. (1988) Technology and deskilling: the case of five principal trade areas in New South Wales. *New Technology, Work and Employment*, 2, 1, 47–60.

Dawson, P. (1987) Computer technology and the job of the first-line supervisor. *New Technology, Work and Employment*, 2, 1, 47–60.

Evans, A. and Bell, J. (1986) Emerging themes in flexible work patterns. In C. Curson (ed.), *Flexible Patterns of Work*, London: Institute of Personnel Management, 2–25.

Evans, A. and Walker, L. (1986) Subcontracting. In C. Curson (ed.), *Flexible Patterns of Work*, London: Institute of Personnel Management, 143–65.

Frese, M. (1987) A theory of control and complexity: Implications for software design and integration of computer systems into the workplace. In M. Frese, E. Ulich and W. Dzida (eds), *Psychological Issues of Human–Computer Interaction in the Workplace*, Amsterdam: North Holland, 313–37.

Friedman, A. (1977) *Industry and Labour*. London: Macmillan.

Graham, M. and Rosenthal, S. (1986) Flexible manufacturing systems require flexible people. *Human Systems Management*, 6, 3, 211–22.

Gupta, N., Jenkins, G. D., Jun. and Carrington, W. P. (1986) Paying for knowledge: Myths and realities. *National Productivity Review*, Spring, 107–23.

Gustavsen, B. (1986) Evolving patterns of enterprise organization: The move towards greater flexibility. *International Labour Review*, 125, 367–82.

Horstman, R. (1988) Labour flexibility strategies and management style. *Journal of Industrial Relations*, September, 412–31.

Horvath, F. W. (1986) Work at home: new findings from the Current Population Survey. *Monthly Labor Review*, 109, 11, 31–5.

Howard, R. (1987) Systems design and social responsibility: the political implications of 'computer-supported cooperative work'. *Office: Technology and People*, 3, 175–87.

Huws, U., Korte, W. B. and Robinson, S. (1990) *Telework: Towards the Elusive Office*. Chichester: Wiley.

Jenkins, C. (1986) Anticipating the 1990 workforce. *Journal of the Operational Research Society*, 37, 10, 933–6.

Kanawaty, G., Gladstone, A., Prokopenko, J. and Rodgers, G. (1989) Adjustment at the micro level. *International Labour Review*, 128, 3, 269–96.

Kling, R. and Iacono, S. (1984) Computing as an occasion for social control. *Journal of Social Issues*, 40, 3, 77–96.

Kossek, E. E. (1989) The acceptance of human resource innovation by multiple constituencies. Personnel Psychology, 42, 263–81.

Levine, H. Z. (1987) Alternative work schedules: Do they meet workforce needs? Parts 1, 2. *Personnel*, February, 57–63; April, 66–71.

Luthans, F. and Fox, M. L. (1989) Update on skill-based pay. *Personnel*, March, 26–31.
McCune, J. T., Beatty, R. W. and Montagno, R. V. (1989) Downsizing: Practices in manufacturing firms. *Human Resource Management*, 26, 1, 145–61.
Mansell, J. (1987) *Workplace Innovation in Canada*. Ottawa: Economic Council of Canada.
Mansfield, W. (1988) Industrial democracy's role in industry restructuring. *Work and People*, 13, 1–2, 22–6.
Mueller, W. S. (1985) Computerized office systems: to centralize or decentralize? *Human Resource Management Australia*, 23, 3, 45–51.
Mueller, W. S. (1989) Cultural factors in technology transfer. In B. Fallon, P. Pfister, and J. Brebner (eds), *Advances in Industrial and Organizational Psychology*, Amsterdam: North Holland, 153–63.
Mueller, W. S. (1990) Information technology and organizational structure. In C. Clegg, N. Kemp and K. Legge (eds), *Case Studies in Information Technology*, London: Harper and Row, (in press).
Mueller, W. S. and Cordery, J. L. (1991) Management of internal labour flexibility strategies. In N. Anderson and D. Hosking (eds). *Organizing Changes and Innovations*, London: Routledge (in press).
Mueller, W. S., Clegg, C. W., Wall, T. D., Kemp, N. J. and Davies, R. T. (1986) Pluralist beliefs about new technology within a manufacturing organization. *New Technology, Work and Employment*, 1, 2, 127–39.
Newton, K. (1989) Technological and organizational change in Canada. *New Technology, Work and Employment*, 4, 1, 42–7.
Olson, M. H. (1988) Corporate culture and the homeworker. In K. E. Christiansen (ed.), *The New Era of Home-Based Work*, Boulder, Colo: Westview Press, 126–34.
Sarfati, H. and Kobrin, C. (1988) *Labour Market Flexibility*. Aldershot: Gower.
Shaiken, H., Herzenberg, S. and Kuhn, S. (1986) The work process under more flexible production. *Industrial Relations*, 25, 2, 167–83.
Swedish Metal Workers' Union (1987) *Rewarding Work*. Stockholm: Swedish Work Environment Fund.
Thompson, P. (1983) *The Nature of Work*. London: Macmillan.
Wall, T. D. (1987) New technology and job design. In P. B. Warr (ed.), *Psychology At Work*, Harmondsworth: Penguin, 270–90.
Wall, T. D., Clegg, C. W., Davies, R., Kemp, N. J. and Mueller, W. S. (1987) Advanced manufacturing technology and work simplification: an empirical study. *Journal of Occupational Psychology*, 8, 233–50.
Walton, R. E. (1985) From control to commitment in the workplace. *Harvard Business Review*, March/April, 77–84.
Warner, M. (1986) Human resources implications of new technology. *Human Systems Management*, 6, 3, 279–87.
Wilkinson, B. (1983) *The Shopfloor Politics of New Technology*. London: Heinemann.
Wood, S. (ed.) (1989) *The Transformation of Work?* London: Unwin Hyman.
Yamashita, T. (1989) Training and development in Japan. *Asia Pacific Human Resource Management*, February, 40–7.

Further reading

Flexible working and new technology are both topics which are explored in a number of disciplines, including psychology, human resource management, economics, sociology and industrial relations. Each discipline provides a different perspective on what the key issues are, on what is the appropriate level of conceptual analysis and on what data are relevant for empirical analysis.

Curson, C. (1986) *Flexible Patterns of Work*. London: Institute of Personnel Management. A useful introduction to the variety of internal and external labour market flexibility strategies.

Siefert, M., Gerbner, G. and Fisher, J. (1989) *The Information Gap: How Computers and Other New Communications Technologies Affect the Social Distribution of Power*. Oxford: Oxford University Press. Addresses the political dimension of new information technology utilization.

Wilkinson, B. (1983) *The Shopfloor Politics of New Technology*. London: Heinemann. Provides a fascinating series of case studies which explore the strategies pursued by different stakeholders in their attempt to secure control over the way in which work is designed around new technology in manufacturing environments.

Wood, S. (ed.) (1989) *The Transformation of Work?* London: Unwin Hyman. Contains some excellent critical analyses of core issues.

Empirical and conceptual analyses of the effects of flexible working and new technology on employment relations are regularly reported in *International Labour Review* and *New Technology, Work and Employment*.

Author Index

Subject Index

Indexes complied by Mary Madden